BEYOND ESTABLISHMENT

Also by Jackson W. Carroll

As One with Authority:
Reflective Leadership in Ministry

Carriers of Faith:
Lessons from Congregational Studies
(edited with Carl S. Dudley
and James P. Wind)

BEYOND ESTABLISHMENT

Protestant Identity in a Post-Protestant Age

Jackson W. Carroll
and
Wade Clark Roof,
Editors

Westminster/John Knox Press
Louisville, Kentucky

Scripture quotations are from the New Revised Standard Version of the Bible, copyright © 1989 by the Division of Christian Education of the National Council of the Churches of Christ in the U.S.A., and are used by permission.

The definition of *style* on p. 101 is from Stanley Sadie, ed., *The New Grove Dictionary of Music and Musicians,* vol. 18 (London: Macmillan Publishers Ltd., 1980). Reprinted by permission of Grove's Dictionaries of Music, Inc.

Book design by Gene Harris

First edition

Published by Westminster/John Knox Press
Louisville, Kentucky

This book is printed on recycled acid-free paper that meets the American National Standards Institute Z39.48 standard. ∞

PRINTED IN THE UNITED STATES OF AMERICA

9   8   7   6   5   4   3   2   1

Library of Congress Cataloging-in-Publication Data

Beyond establishment : Protestant identity in a post-Protestant
    age / Jackson W. Carroll and Wade Clark Roof, editors.
        p.   cm.
    Includes bibliographical references.
    ISBN 0-664-25396-2 (pbk. : alk. paper)

    1. Protestant churches—United States—History—20th century.
2. United States—Church history—20th century.   I. Carroll,
Jackson W.   II. Roof, Wade Clark.
BR526.B48 1993
280'.4' 097309045—dc20   92-30370

Contents

Acknowledgments

This book was made possible by a grant to Hartford Seminary from the Lilly Endowment as part of several research probes into the future of mainline Protestantism. In acknowledging the Endowment's support, we would especially express our gratitude to Robert Wood Lynn, retired senior vice president for religion, during whose tenure the grant was made. Through his stewardship and leadership at the Lilly Endowment, Bob Lynn has made a significant, lasting impact on American religious life, including mainline Protestantism. For his support and encouragement we are deeply grateful. Dorothy Bass, who has served as coordinator for Lilly's emphasis on mainline Protestantism, also has given important assistance as well as writing one of the chapters of this volume.

We wish to express appreciation to all those authors whose contributions have made this volume possible. During the course of the project, they met twice to propose and present their chapters for discussion and critique. Also joining our meetings were colleagues William McKinney and David A. Roozen and a group of denominational leaders who were participants in a Hartford Seminary-sponsored leadership education program.

For her assistance in preparing the book for publication, we are especially indebted to Mary Jane Ross, administrative assistant of Hartford Seminary's Center for Social and Religious Research.

Contributors

DOROTHY C. BASS is director of the Valparaiso University Project on the Education and Formation of People in Faith. She is also associate professor of church history at Chicago Theological Seminary.

JACKSON W. CARROLL is the William Douglas Mackenzie Distinguished Professor of Religion and Society at Hartford Seminary. A sociologist and ordained United Methodist minister, he is the author and coauthor of a number of books and articles on American religious life, congregational studies, and ministry. His latest book is *As One with Authority: Reflective Leadership in Ministry*. He will join the faculty of the Divinity School of Duke University in mid-1993.

LINDA J. CLARK is assistant professor in sacred music at Boston University School of Theology and has been involved in a project studying the relationship between music and faith in local congregations. She holds an S.M.D. from Union Theological Seminary in New York and is director of the Master of Sacred Music Program at Boston University.

W. CLARK GILPIN is dean of the University of Chicago Divinity School and a historian of Christianity in America.

J. FREDERICK HOLPER is associate professor of liturgics and homiletics at Union Theological Seminary in Richmond, Virginia. He has written and lectured widely on matters related to the theology and practice of ordination, particularly in American Presbyterianism.

LAWRENCE N. JONES is dean emeritus of the Howard University School of Divinity and professor (retired) of African-American church history.

CREIGHTON LACY was a third-generation Methodist missionary in

China and has served other appointments in India, Japan, Taiwan, and Zimbabwe. From 1953 until his retirement in 1988, he was professor of World Christianity at the Divinity School of Duke University.

DONALD A. LUIDENS teaches at Hope College. He is currently involved in studies of baby-boom Presbyterians and the membership and clergy of the Reformed Church.

ALLEN J. MOORE is dean and the E. Stanley Jones Professor of Education and Mission at the School of Theology at Claremont, California. Dr. Moore has degrees in sociology and theology with a major interest in the social significance of religious development. He has served as a local church pastor, a denominational executive, and a consultant to religious and social institutions. His most recent book is *Religious Education as Social Transformation.*

MARY ELIZABETH MOORE is professor of theology and Christian education at the School of Theology at Claremont and the Claremont Graduate School. She is author of *Education for Continuity and Change* and several essays and chapters. She holds degrees in psychology (B.A. and M.A.) and in theology and education (M.A. and Ph. D.). She has worked in the mental health community, served a local church in educational ministry, and given leadership in ecumenical and interfaith organizations. She is now engaged in teaching and in an extensive series of congregational studies.

GWEN KENNEDY NEVILLE is professor of sociology and holder of the Elizabeth Root Paden Chair in Sociology at Southwestern University, Georgetown, Texas. She holds a degree in English from Mary Baldwin College and M.A. and Ph.D. degrees in anthropology from the University of Florida. Her most recent book is *Kinship and Pilgrimage: Rituals of Reunion in American Protestant Culture.*

WILLIAM M. NEWMAN is a member of the sociology faculty at the University of Connecticut and is a past editor of the Society for the Scientific Study of Religion Monograph Series. He is coauthor with geographer Peter L. Halvorson of the 1952–1971 and 1971–1980 editions of the *Atlas of Religious Change in America.*

DANIEL V. A. OLSON is assistant professor of sociology, Indiana University, South Bend. He is completing a book, with William McKinney, on Protestant denominational leaders.

RUSSELL E. RICHEY is associate dean for academic programs and professor of church history at Duke Divinity School. Related publications include *Early American Methodism,* "Institutional Forms of Religion," *Encyclopedia of Religion in America,* vol. 1, and *Denominationalism.*

KEITH A. ROBERTS is professor of sociology at Hanover College, Hanover, Indiana. He is author of *Religion in Sociological Perspective.*

WADE CLARK ROOF is J. F. Rowney Professor of Religion and Society at the University of California at Santa Barbara, California. He is coauthor of *American Mainline Religion* and is presently involved in research on the baby-boom generation and religious change in America. His book reporting on this research, *A Generation of Seekers,* will appear in 1993.

THE REVEREND ALLISON STOKES has served as acting associate university chaplain at Yale University and Vassar College chaplain. She is pastor of the Congregational Church in West Stockbridge, Massachusetts.

LOUIS B. WEEKS is professor of church history and dean of the Louisville Presbyterian Seminary. He is a member of the Board of Directors of the Louisville Institute for the Study of Protestantism and American Culture.

BARBARA BROWN ZIKMUND is a church historian with special interest in the contributions of women. She is also a historian of her own denomination, the United Church of Christ. Since July 1990 she has been the president of Hartford Seminary.

Introduction

The denomination, says Martin E. Marty, is a "betwixt and between institution" in the late twentieth century. A structure born in an earlier era to give expression to free and voluntary religion in a country without an established church, the denomination often appears out of kilter, if not hopelessly obsolete, in an America where religion has become more pluralist and privatized. The religious climate that nourished its growth throughout the nineteenth century and well into the twentieth has drastically changed, and the momentum that once made it into a strong, viable institution has waned. Now that which is left of the old structure strikes many as belonging to a past era, something back there as Marty says with "fossils, Studebaker wagons, blacksmiths and the Grange" (Foreword to Scherer, 1980).

For none of America's several hundred religious denominations is this sense of being betwixt and between more real than for mainline Protestants. The term "mainline" (or "mainstream") is imprecise and difficult to define, some preferring to speak of "old-line" or "established," yet the label is helpful if used in a descriptive, not a normative, sense. We use the term for identifying a set of Protestant institutions now sharing a similar niche in the American religious economy.[1] What these institutions share are some common theological understandings about the role of the church in society, memberships with somewhat similar socioeconomic characteristics, a sense of historic religious status, and also, increasingly, an awareness that their cultural and religious authority has declined, that as religious bodies they no longer wield the power and influence they once did.

By "mainline" denominations, we refer essentially to those groups—Episcopalians, Presbyterians, Congregationalists (now United Church of Christ), United Methodists, Disciples of Christ, American Baptists, Lutherans, and the Reformed Church in America—that have functioned as an unofficial religious and cultural

11

establishment within America and within American Protestantism. The first three were the established colonial religions; the others are later additions. We would also include as mainline several of the historic African American denominations that grew out of the Baptist and Methodist traditions.

Both religious and social factors are involved in the making of this particular establishment: a historic religious concern arising out of the Magisterial Reformation for the well-being of the common good, an emphasis on public as well as private faith, and more recently in the American experience, the social location of these groups among the more socioeconomically privileged classes. While the first encouraged Christians to assume a responsibility for the world at large, the second assured them of the social, economic, and political resources to do so. It is also the case that these denominations were on the scene early in American history, and thus, as Charles R. Strain (1989) points out, have had an advantage over latecomers in ascending to positions of power and influence.

Whatever the difficulties in defining a religious "mainline," common experiences and destinies have united these groups in the American context. Throughout much of this century, these institutions exerted considerable influence on core American values. They regarded themselves, and were regarded by others, as the public Protestant presence in the nation. They exerted an influence on the culture in greater proportion than any other religious constituency—partly a reflection simply of a continuing strong majority status. Though their influence had begun to wane beginning in the 1920s, when forced to confront a growing religious diversity and the realities of a modern, secular society, still they sought to maintain a Protestant hold on America and relinquished it only as they had to (see Handy, 1984). Influence rested not simply on religious vision and the persuasive force of rhetoric, both of which were in decline during these years, but also, and perhaps more importantly, on the familial, social, and old-school-tie relationships that bound many members from these groups together. The more privileged sectors of the white Protestant community (WASPs) were brought together by means of marriage, friendship patterns, and clique and organizational ties. Protestantism continued to have force as a cultural and group presence. As historian William R. Hutchison says, the Protestant establishment had power because of a "personal network as well as a congeries of institutions" (1989, 6).

Since the 1960s, however, we can no longer speak of a Protestant establishment in the same way. All the mainline Protestant denominations have lost members in the period since that watershed decade. The losses in some instances are staggering—by as much as 10 percent or more per decade (for a statistical summary and interpretation, see Carroll, Johnson, and Marty 1979, 12–17; Roof and McKinney 1987, 18–22). Boundaries separating the denominations, once meaningful to believers, have blurred, with a resulting loss of clarity about doctrinal identity and distinctiveness. Religious and cultural change in the 1960s and 1970s, brought on by the rise of the youth counterculture, the Vietnam War, and a large postwar baby-boom generation, weakened denominational loyalties as well as the church's hold on the culture and its public influence. The older mainline Protestant churches now find themselves eclipsed by a more aggressive, accommodating evangelicalism speaking as the Protestant voice and are characterized by malaise and demoralization, or as Benton Johnson (1985, 50) says, "tired blood." The period witnessed as well additional strains between religious liberals and religious conservatives in all the major denominations, as one after another social or lifestyle issue has polarized church constituencies. And the social infrastructures so important to sustaining a Protestant establishment in years past have all diminished significantly, raising questions about the future of denominations in the contemporary world.

Why Study Denominations?

With all this said, why then another study of Protestant denominations? And why look at the shrinking mainline denominations especially? Rather than dismiss them, we prefer to think of them as institutions undergoing a major transition, a shift as Hutchison (1989, vii) says "from Protestant America to pluralist America." Because of the shifts now occurring in the Protestant landscape, and the changing religious ethos in the country as a whole, we think the timing is right for looking at how churches and denominations seek to maintain a sense of identity and to transmit their own distinctive religious cultures in an age of religious disestablishment. Our concern is not to advance a neo-denominational position,* or to hold out for their intrinsic goodness as institutions. To the contrary, we see a much changed religious climate for these institutions and want to explore the basic question: how has the changing context of American religious life affected the way in which denominations survive as religious communities? What is their future as institutions in an era "beyond establishment"?

A denomination, as Americans understand the term, is a voluntary association, which in its larger expression is both an *organization* and a *community*. Precisely because denominations take shape in modern

---

*By "neo-denominationalism," we mean a turn to a heightened emphasis on one's own denominational identity and programs, typically using strategies whose aim is self-preservation.

America in these two basic ways, they are significant in ways that often get overlooked. As *organizational* realities, denominations remain as the arenas in which most of the business of American religion is conducted: within these institutions funds are raised, mission boards and other agencies operate, educational programs are devised and administered, millions of people worship in ways that are liturgically familiar and comfortable, religious and spiritual activities are coordinated. Unlike many European countries where organized religion is no longer strong and institutionally alive, in the United States the denomination remains the dominant religious form.

While liberal versus conservative tensions exist in all the major mainline Protestant denominations, it is easy to exaggerate a "great divide" within them (see Wuthnow 1988, 133–172). There has been a considerable growth in "para-church" organizations and special purpose groups over the past several decades, yet it is a mistake to assume that this proliferation of groups and activities has undermined denominations as organizational realities or necessarily diminished loyalty to denominational heritages. One recent study of churches in a Chicago community finds that very few of the conflicts in them can be understood as being between liberals and conservatives within the church, or along liberal versus conservative lines when the church was struggling with some external issue. Nor were the more liberal, mainline churches more conflict-ridden than conservative churches (Becker et al. 1990). As stodgy and bland as denominational structures can be, still they contain and give expression to a wide spectrum of religious opinion and outlook.

Denominations are more than organizations, they are socioreligious *communities.* For all that is said about the decline of denominationalism, the vast majority of Americans who claim some religious identity still use denominational labels to characterize themselves. Among Protestants, 85 percent name a denomination when asked in national polls and surveys about their religious affiliations. Liberals and conservatives, liberationists and antiliberationists, pro-choice and pro-life constituencies, all within the same church, continue to think of themselves as Methodists, Presbyterians, Lutherans, or whatever, despite enormous differences among them. Americans want for themselves, and grant to others, a wide latitude in matters of faith. It makes for denominational identities that are deeply rooted and flexible, and gives them a remarkable staying power—they persist as frames of reference socially and psychologically, especially in a pluralist society such as the United States.

The nation's ethnic and religious pluralism, its heritage of religious freedom, and its separation of church and state have all fostered, as

Andrew Greeley (1972) says, a "denominational society." In the American case, this has meant norms of tolerance for religious diversity while at the same time encouraging quasi-*Gemeinschaft* religious groups to flourish. Denominational loyalties persist, in large part because religion provides for Americans not merely "meaning" but also a sense of "belonging." The fact that church life is experienced largely as local community involvement is itself a factor. "Denominations fit people into the local community," writes William Swatos (1981, 223), "while providing reference to the larger society." Religion is thus deeply enmeshed in the social fabric, hardly separate or distinct from it. Perhaps in no other modern nation has this belonging and status-conferring role for religion developed to the extent it has in the United States.

Mainline Protestant denominations, in particular, have played a variety of social roles that enmesh them in the community. They have served not only as a bridge between the local community and the larger society but also in helping individuals deal with personal issues and concerns of public life. In *Habits of the Heart,* Robert Bellah and his associates (1985, 237) expressed this as follows:

> [Mainline Protestant churches] have tried to relate biblical faith and practice to the whole of contemporary life—cultural, social, political, economic—not just to personal and family morality. They have tried to steer a middle course between mystical fusion with the world and sectarian withdrawal from it.

These institutions have taken a more "churchly" form—the third of Ernst Troeltsch's important types (Troeltsch 1931). American-style denominations are more accepting of the world as it is, yet always in some tension with it. Compared either to mysticism or sectarianism, denominations embody more of an organic conception of life: the individual lives in society, neither in isolation nor in a sectarian enclave. Religion relates to life as a whole or it lacks meaning to any single part of life.

Trying to steer a middle course, neither withdrawing from the world nor becoming fully absorbed in it, denominations occupy a precarious position. They both benefit and suffer from their relationship to the larger society. To identify them as historically mainline is to point to a close association with core American values, which has given them access to power and influence and gained them much respectability and status. The values and lifestyles found within the mainline churches have a close affinity with those of middle-class America. But it is also to acknowledge their vulnerability to that culture. The temptation always for the more established churches is to compromise their religious and ethical vision and to become captive to worldly powers. For this reason, transmitting this vision as embodied in the traditions of the church is a critical issue.

Denominational Cultures

We take a cultural approach to studying denominations by focusing upon a group's distinctive moral and religious vision and how it is passed on over time.[2] By a denomination's culture, we mean that persistent set of beliefs, values, norms, symbols, stories and style that makes a group distinctive. The distinctiveness of a group is what is meant by its identity. Put another way, a denomination's culture, following Clifford Geertz (1973), is the "web of meanings" by which a group interprets its life to itself and to others. (This includes elements from the broader Christian tradition as well as the more distinctive, denominationally derived aspects.) For Geertz, culture includes two fundamental components: worldview and ethos. Worldview is a people's picture of the way things are, their notions of nature, of self, of society. Ethos, on the other hand, is a people's "tone, character, and quality of their life, its moral and aesthetic style and mood."

Geertz's perspective avoids the temptation to restrict a denomination's identity only to its beliefs and values, especially its "official" doctrines. This is important because denominational cultures are complex and extend into the far reaches of an institution's life. A denomination's worldview and ethos are stored in its beliefs, values, symbols, rites, and hymns; in the founders and other heroes; in the stories it remembers, tells and retells; in the titles it uses for leaders; in the names it uses to describe its sacred space; in the norms by which it governs itself and by which it prescribes a member's style of living; and in organizational patterns embodying its own life. In these and other ways that extend beyond official beliefs, denominational cultures are expressed, and insofar as they distinguish one denomination from another, we can speak of a denomination's identity.

We can say that denominations are "communities of memory" (Bellah et al. 1985)—that is, they are communities that affirm, preserve, and transmit a distinctive sense of who they are. This identity is rooted in a cultural narrative, or set of meanings, shaped by historical and social experience. Memory draws upon values, symbols, and traditions that reach far into the past, but always it is the memory of a particular group as it understands its own history and experience in the present moment. Cultural narratives are influenced in content and style, especially in a voluntary religious order, by a variety of inputs, some distinctly religious in the sense of doctrine or theology, others peculiar to group experience—as related to social class, race, ethnicity, nationalism, regionalism, or the like. Richard H. White describes the situation well:

> Any given religious group has a history of its own—a history that is affected by the cultural location of its members, by their relative economic positions, and a host of other "so-called" ethnic factors. The point to be made is that insofar as religious groups are characterized by group-specific norms, these norms constitute the "religious factor" regardless of whether they have been logically derived from theology or picked up somewhere on the Italian countryside (1970, 19).

As a socioreligious entity, the denomination is also always in a state of flux. Even its narratives—the fundamental stories told about life—undergo change. The stories as expressed in common worship, in public witness, in everyday lives, all change as leaders and participants adapt to new challenges and circumstances. The rate of adaptation varies with the denomination. Unlike Roman Catholics (at least until Vatican II) and evangelical Protestants, who have attempted to resist cultural change, mainline Protestant denominations have been more accommodating to the modern world.[3] Again, theological heritage and social location have helped to fashion such a stance historically. Mainline Protestantism has confronted modernity, as Peter Berger (1979) observes, more massively and for a longer period than any other Western religious tradition. Protestantism has of course a special relationship to modernity: it helped give rise to the modern, secular world, and ever since the Reformation has sought to adjust to that world. If by modernity, as it affects religion, one means the pervasive realities of religious pluralism and religious privatism, then the history of Protestantism has been, and continues to be, an ongoing struggle to shape a meaningful narrative about life in the modern Western world.

This ongoing effort is in one sense a source of Protestant strength as leaders have sought to preserve the core of their tradition while resymbolizing the tradition to address new circumstances. Many of mainline Protestantism's difficulties institutionally follow from this willingness to deal head on with the culture of which it is a part. The cutting edge of this theological agenda is creative but also very threatening. Much of the struggle within contemporary mainline Protestantism revolves around this basic problem: how can religion adapt to the culture without losing itself in that culture? Too much adaptation easily results in a loss of religious identity or distinctiveness. That was often a charge leveled at the mainline churches in the 1960s: the churches were so identified with the culture that when the culture fell into travail, so did the churches. Concerns about too much adaptation lead to internal conflicts and sometimes schism, with charges by various internal reform groups that religious leaders have gone too far and given up too much, that the denomination's culture needs repristinating. This perspective lies behind many neo-denominational efforts. Others have argued just the opposite, that because of the heritage of liberal Protestant theology it must ever engage itself in its surrounding culture. Most mainline denominations are still experiencing such tensions, whether they always express them in these terms or not.

Compared with Roman Catholics and evangelical Protestants, the problem of a distinctive religious culture for mainline Protestants currently is quite different. Catholics have practiced a more inclusive, churchlike mode of incorporating members despite considerable ethnic variation; while American Catholics have come to know greater flexibility in the post-Vatican II period, there is still considerable unity of Catholic liturgy and experience from parish to parish. To be Catholic is to have a distinct identity, something which, as Greeley (1990) points out, is deeply rooted in religious images and symbols that Catholics share in their families and communities, even if they are not highly involved in the church. Evangelical Protestants have traditionally held to a more sectarian, "gathered church" ideal: membership should be only for well-qualified, tested members. This places more emphasis on conversion and conformity to the denominational culture and less emphasis on adapting one's culture to attract and hold new members—on what Dean Kelley (1972) describes as "strictness" as a mark of effectiveness in growing churches. Boundaries with the outside world are critical to maintaining their own sense of identity.

In contrast, mainline Protestants have neither a strong unifying religious consciousness nor a sectarian model of institutional membership. They cannot at present point as easily to a singular sustaining vision which gives them a religious identity nor to a set of institutional norms that define who they are in relation to a hostile world. Instead, having affirmed in a more radical way what Sidney Mead (1954) once called "the voluntary principle," they hold that religious participation is fundamentally a matter of personal choice. If there is one thing that Protestants agree on, it is that individuals should believe and practice religion in keeping with their conscience—and thus they tend to see religion as something deeply individual, prior to organizational involvement. As a result of the need to attract and to retain the loyalty of members, we might say a "market sensitivity" principle is widely incorporated into the cultures of mainline Protestants. Knowing that they must offer something to get and hold new members, these churches are sensitive to what people are looking for in religious participation and tend to cater to those interests. It is a vulnerability all churches face in an open, pluralist context, but probably more so for more liberal, mainline Protestant churches.

Transmitting the Culture

This leads to the question we are most concerned with in this volume: How are denominational cultures transmitted? The question is an important one for mainline Protestant churches and denominations occupying a niche in the contemporary American scene.

In our view, the works of Peter Berger (1967, 1969) and Berger and Luckmann (1967) offer a helpful perspective on this question. Symbolic worlds ("culture" as we have used the term) are socially constructed. Once a symbolic world is constructed, it must not only be legitimated as objectively real but also become (and remain) subjectively real in the consciousness of the individuals who constitute the group or society in question. The process by which the external becomes internal is known generally as socialization, or enculturation, either of a primary or secondary sort. The transmission of a denomination's culture, while probably more accurately a form of secondary socialization, has primary elements as well. Indeed, much of religious socialization in the United States occurs in the family at an early age as one internalizes the "world" of one's parents and of significant others. The beliefs, values, and fundamental identities one learns in this setting take on, as Berger says, a "taken-for-granted" character. This type of learning is largely involuntary, often more implicitly rather than explicitly religious, passed on to an individual in the course of everyday life. Obviously, more formal and explicit religious socialization occurs later in life as well, especially in the case of one who "joins" a particular denomination, an act which is more deliberate and voluntary.

In either case, for the person brought up in a religious tradition or the adult joiner, internalizing a religious culture is not a onetime occurrence. It is a continuing process in which the individual renews his or her understanding and commitment to a particular belief, value, or identity in a myriad of ways: in conversation with others who share the culture, in relationships with those of the same tradition, in learning its lore, in participating in its rites and symbols, and in other programs and processes which maintain definitions of reality and negate threatening experiences or the appeal of alternative interpretations. Berger refers to these various mechanisms for transmitting and sustaining the culture as "plausibility structures." That is, the social infrastructures affirm the beliefs, values, and identities, and thus render the culture believable. By reinforcing the shared elements of a worldview, such activities and exchanges make that world seem real to the participants. Depending on their strength and effectiveness, the plausibility of a religious culture for the individual will range from "unquestioned certitude through firm probability to mere opinion" (Berger 1969, 45). Indeed, the strength and effectiveness of these denominational plausibility structures in a time of massive social and religious change is what we are examining in this book.

The dilemma of mainline Protestantism, in one sense, is that of weak plausibility structures. Traditional religious beliefs and affirmations have lost much of their plausibility, or as Berger says, "unquestioned certitude" has been reduced to "mere opinion." Fundamentally, this is a social-interactional problem: the social processes which serve to confirm and reconfirm the reality of a religious world have eroded, and consequently, so has the religious reality itself.

A brief foray into autobiography helps to make the point: both of us were reared as Methodists in the South in the postdepression era through the 1950s. We grew up in different small towns, but both towns were predominately white and almost exclusively Protestant. The vast majority were Southern Baptist, Methodist, Presbyterian, Lutheran, and Episcopalian; there were some Holiness and Pentecostal groups, who lived literally and figuratively on the "fringes" of the town. We understood pluralism to mean a choice among white Protestant churches—and mostly among the mainline churches! Youth activities, including baseball and basketball, were organized largely along religious group lines. Protestantism was taken for granted: the public schools reinforced a Protestant culture by daily prayers, occasional visits of Protestant clergy to school assemblies, and baccalaureate addresses at commencement given on an annual rotating basis by clergy from the largest Protestant churches. During Holy Week every year, the mainline churches held interdenominational services with each denomination providing the preacher for one of the services. What seems strange about this from today's perspective, but quite natural at the time, is that public schools and many of the businesses in the town closed to allow students and townspeople to take part in the services. In other words, not only the churches, but also the public schools, sports teams, and the town itself functioned as a kind of plausibility structure for religion. The reality of a Protestant world, or at least a Dixie version of it, was unquestioned.

However typical, or atypical, our experiences of what went on in small towns in the rest of the United States at the time,[4] we know that this is not the way it is today except in some remote, isolated places. To grasp just how much the religious situation has changed, let us look briefly at the ways in which the social fabric supporting a religious culture has been altered.

One obvious change is the extent of pluralism: the growth of new religions in the period since the 1960s has drastically revised the religious map of America. We refer not just to the many religious and spiritual movements but also to the increasing numbers of Muslims and Buddhists that have migrated to the United States in the past several decades, all of which have helped to undermine the old "Protestant-Catholic-Jewish" canopy of religious identities. J. Gordon Melton's *Encyclopedia of American Religions* (1978), which attempts to count religious bodies, currently carries over twelve hundred entries, and the revised edition will reportedly carry a much larger number.

Pluralism drastically changes the normative context. It opens up contacts with people who believe and practice their faiths differently, and hence increases the possibilities of religion-switching and greater interfaith marriage. According to a 1980 Gallup survey, fewer than half of U.S. adults (43 percent) say they have always been a member of their present denomination. Switching for Protestants is quite high, more so than for Catholics or Jews. Interfaith (and interdenominational) marriages have increased during the twentieth century, especially among mainline Protestants, but also for Catholics and Jews (McCutcheon 1988). Only conservative Protestants appear to have avoided the trend. The trends for both religion-switching and interfaith marriage work against a strong plausibility structure for religious groups, and for mainline Protestants in particular. The fact that mainline Protestants generally are of higher socioeconomic status means they are more likely to be socially and geographically mobile, thereby weakening institutional attachments and making them even more vulnerable to confrontations with pluralism.

Pluralism also "relativizes" religion in the sense that one becomes aware there are alternative worlds, or competing definitions of reality. This relates to a second major trend—increased religious privatization or religious individualism. An indicator is the growth of the so-called religious nones—that is, those claiming no religious preference when asked by pollsters. The figure is currently at 9 percent, not large in light of the 91 percent who give some religious preference, but seven times greater than at mid-century. While there are defections to "none" from all religious groups, mainline Protestants, along with Catholics and Jews, have suffered the greatest losses (Roof and McKinney 1987, 170ff.). Part of the problem for the more liberal, mainline Protestants, who have been so closely identified with the culture, is the lack of any boundaries: those who drop out often have no sense of having "left" anything, they just quit attending church. The majority of those switching into the ranks of the unaffiliated come from the highly educated, younger-age cohort—a large and crucially important constituency that is setting religious trends in the country today.

These persons are not necessarily without any religious faith; rather, they do not identify with any of the traditional faith communities and often define their religion in highly individualistic terms. An example is the young nurse, Sheila Larson, described in *Habits of the Heart* (Bellah et al. 1985, 221), who defined her private religion as "Sheilaism": "I believe in God. I'm not a religious fanatic. I can't remember the last time I went to church. My faith has carried me a long way. It's Sheilaism. Just my own little voice."

In addition to the "nones," there is a considerably larger number of persons who express a religious preference but do not actively belong to a church. While this is nothing new, and while it reveals that people still identify with denominations, it is hardly an indicator of strong denominational identity. A recent study of unchurched Americans suggests that mainline Protestants in this category have especially weak denominational identities. Those who were estranged from evangelical Protestant groups were more likely to hold traditional Christian beliefs and continue to affirm the importance of religion in their lives. They believe without belonging. In contrast, their counterparts who express a mainline Protestant preference were significantly more likely to be indifferent to religion, less certain of their beliefs, and less likely to acknowledge a commitment to Christ (Perry et al. 1980). The researchers suggest that people dropping out of mainline Protestant congregations do so less from anger, hurt, or conflict than from indifference, a sense that religious involvement is unimportant in their lives.

Greater religious privatism, or individualism, affects the people in the pew as well. Regular churchgoers in the more liberal, mainline Protestant traditions especially, hold to highly privatized religious beliefs and commitments, often having little or no relation to "official" denominational culture, while continuing to belong and to participate actively in the church. Traditional beliefs are privately reinterpreted or simply ignored to reduce dissonance with other experiences. Roof and McKinney (1987) speak of the "new voluntarism," referring to a greater choice factor in religious life. Bibby (1987) speaks of "fragmented gods" in his Canadian study, showing that religious consumers in that country—as in the United States—pick and choose what they will believe or how they will practice their faith. This is not surprising in light of an American survey some years ago in which 76 percent of active church members believed that "one should arrive at his or her own religious beliefs independent of a church or synagogue" (Gallup 1978). Even when church members hold to traditional beliefs, they frequently hold them in company with astrology, beliefs in reincarnation, or more recently, various "New Age" spiritualities.

Trends more broadly in American life have helped to push mainline Protestantism away from the center of the culture, and more toward the margins. Religious and secular changes have undermined the hegemony for denominations that once enjoyed considerable influence and status as "custodians of the culture." A revitalized evangelical Protestantism, a more public Roman Catholicism, and a larger secular constituency are all developments in the post-1960s period that have led to a repositioning of players on the religious scene. A major consequence is that the old Protestant churches can no longer expect the culture to prop them up as it once did. Many of the plausibility structures outside the churches, such as those we described in our hometowns, no longer provide mainline Protestantism with the kind of external social support that it once enjoyed. Denominations no longer can assume a Protestant world view and ethos. Presently, whether or not one becomes a member of a particular denomination, active or inactive, is much more a matter of personal choice than it was earlier in this century.

For Americans generally, levels of education have increased significantly in the post-World War II era. All religious groups have been affected, but mainline Protestants have been especially vulnerable to the corrosive influences of higher education. As institutions they have been, and continue to be, deeply divided along educational lines. The proportions of Protestants with college educations have increased significantly during this time, resulting as Wuthnow (1988, 161) says, in an "education gap": splits between those believing in literal versus symbolic interpretations of the Bible, cleavages between those supporting and those opposing clergy involvement in social issues, and reduced levels of regular church attendance and institutional loyalty generally. For decades, higher levels of education were associated with greater religious involvement, but since the 1960s patterns have reversed. The relation of religion and social class appears to be undergoing a profound realignment in our time. The implications for religion are not all fully apparent, but the restructuring bears directly on the class-based constituencies that have long supported the mainline denominations.

At the level of moral beliefs and attitudes, the evidence is mixed with respect to how well the denominations are holding up currently. Roof and McKinney (1987) examine attitudes on a number of moral issues (for example, civil liberties, racial justice, women's rights, and new morality). On the one hand, they find evidence of considerable diversity, strain, and conflict within denominations and denominational families on the various issues, especially for the moderate Protestants

(Methodists, Lutherans, Baptists) and Catholics, both of whom occupy a middle position between liberal and conservative positions on the issues. On the other hand, when they compare denominational families with one another, the families emerge as relatively distinct moral communities. Differences among many mainline denominations have declined, but families of denominations (liberal, moderate, conservative) share a great deal. To quote Roof and McKinney:

> Generally the results point to the important role of religious traditions as subcultures. The churches are carriers of distinctive values and norms, the content of which depends in part on the social locations of their members. Even among those whose level of churchgoing is low and whose group attachments are weak, the traditions persist and sustain their own particular constellations of moral and cultural views (1987, 220).

In short, in at least the area of morality—ethos in Geertz's definition of culture—mainline Protestants seem to be having some influence on the attitudes of their members, in spite of internal tensions and conflicts. That they look somewhat like moral communities is, of course, also a reflection of the social and economic similarities of these religious clusters, factors probably more important than the religious influence in a narrow sense.

These, then, are some of the major considerations that feed into the question of "how well are mainline Protestant denominations transmitting their cultures today?" In a time when many of the older plausibility structures have eroded, we must examine anew how churches pass on their heritages from one generation to the next. This is a matter that takes us into institutional terrains largely uncharted, for we know far more about Protestant institutions under conditions of expansion than of contraction. There are extensive literatures on sects becoming churches but far less about churches undergoing waning influence and having to adjust to a loss of turf. Yet we know religious institutions are resilient, capable of adjusting to new circumstances. They take on new shape as times and conditions change. They accommodate to their environments in search of a niche. In America especially, religious institutions have long been known to have these qualities.

The essays that follow attempt to tell us about how mainline Protestant denominations are adjusting to new conditions. The chapters are organized into three parts. Part One looks at local congregations and how activities and support structures within them help to foster religious identity. Part Two looks at activities and structures that extend beyond the local congregation and the role they play in sustaining denominational cultures. Part Three looks at several denominational case studies, exploring how mergers and other recent developments have altered ways in which these bodies understand and affirm who they are.

NOTES

1. William R. Hutchison uses the term "establishment" in his recent book on Protestants with power and influence in America in the years between 1900 and 1960 (1989). Leonard Sweet (1986) is one among many historians who prefers the term "old-line" in describing the same denominational cluster.

2. We take a broad approach to denominations as essentially social and cultural institutions. For a collection of essays that present historical perspectives on denominations, see Richey (1977). For sociological perspectives on denominational organizations, see Scherer (1980).

3. It would be a mistake to claim that evangelical Protestants have not adapted to modernity, in spite of their protests against modernity. As James Davidson Hunter (1983) has shown, evangelicals have made significant adaptations to the modern world both in style and in the technology they use to evangelize.

4. The southern setting obviously made for a different religious context in its Protestant ethos and the way in which religion dominated the culture; however, Vidich and Bensman (1958) in their study of Springdale, a small community in upstate New York, find remarkably similar social and religious patterns. See also Warner and Lunt's (1941) study of Newburyport, Massachusetts, a setting more Catholic but not that different in the way religion and community interaction overlapped.

REFERENCES

Becker, Penny E., Stephen J. Ellingson, Richard W. Flory, Wendy Griswold, Fred Kniss, and Timothy Nelson
  1990   "Straining at the Ties that Bind: Church Conflict in the 1980s," unpublished manuscript.
Bellah, Robert N., Richard Madsen, William M. Sullivan, Ann Swidler, and Steven M. Tipton
  1985   *Habits of the Heart.* Berkeley, Calif.: University of California Press.
Berger, Peter
  1967   *The Sacred Canopy.* Garden City, N.Y.: Doubleday & Co.

1969   *A Rumor of Angels*. Garden City, N.Y.: Doubleday & Co.
1979   *The Heretical Imperative*. Garden City, N.Y.: Doubleday & Co.
Berger, Peter, and Thomas Luckmann
1967   *The Social Construction of Social Reality*. Garden City,
       N.Y.: Doubleday & Co.
Bibby, Reginald W.
1987   *Fragmented Gods*. Toronto: Irwin Publishing.
Carroll, Jackson W., Douglas W. Johnson, and Martin E. Marty
1979   *Religion in America: 1950 to the Present*. New York:
       Harper & Row.
Gallup Organization
1978   *The Unchurched American*. Princeton, N.J.: Princeton Reli-
       gion Research Center.
Geertz, Clifford
1973   *The Interpretation of Cultures*. New York: Basic Books.
Greeley, Andrew M.
1972   *The Denominational Society*. Glenview, Ill.: Scott, Fores-
       man, & Co.
1990   *The Catholic Myth: The Behavior and Beliefs of American
       Catholics*. New York: Charles Scribner's Sons.
Handy, Robert T.
1984   *A Christian America: Protestant Hopes and Historical Re-
       alities*. New York: Oxford University Press.
Hunter, James Davidson
1983   *American Evangelicalism*. New Brunswick, N.J.: Rutgers
       University Press.
Hutchison, William R.
1989   *Between the Times: The Travail of the Protestant Establish-
       ment in America, 1900–1960*. New York: Cambridge Uni-
       versity Press.
Johnson, Benton
1985   "Liberal Protestantism: End of the Road?" *Annals of the
       American Academy of Political and Social Science* 480
       (July): 39–52.
Kelley, Dean M.
1972   *Why Conservative Churches Are Growing*. San Francisco:
       Harper & Row.
McCutcheon, Alan L.
1988   "Denominations and Religious Intermarriage: Trends
       Among White Americans in the Twentieth Century." *Re-
       view of Religious Research* 29 (March): 213–227.
Mead, Sidney E.
1954   "Denominationalism: The Shape of Protestantism in Amer-
       ica." *Church History* 23: 291–320.

Melton, J. Gordon
  1978   *Encyclopedia of American Religions.* Two vols. Wilmington, N.C.: McGrath.
Perry, Everett L., James H. Davis, Ruth T. Doyle, and John E. Dyble
  1980   "Toward a Typology of Unchurched Protestants." *Review of Religious Research* 21 (4): 388–404.
Richey, Russell E. (ed.)
  1977   *Denominationalism.* Nashville: Abingdon Press.
Roof, Wade Clark, and William McKinney
  1987   *American Mainline Religion: Its Changing Shape and Future.* New Brunswick, N.J.: Rutgers University Press.
Scherer, Ross P. (ed.)
  1980   *American Denominational Organization.* Pasadena, Calif.: William Carey Press.
Strain, Charles R.
  1989   *Prophetic Visions and Economic Realities.* Grand Rapids: Wm. B. Eerdmans Publishing Co.
Swatos, William
  1981   "Beyond Denominationalism?: Community and Culture in American Religion." *Journal for the Scientific Study of Religion* 20 (September): 217–227.
Sweet, Leonard
  1986   "Can a Mainstream Change Its Course?" In *Liberal Protestantism,* edited by Robert S. Michaelsen and Wade Clark Roof, 235–262. New York: Pilgrim Press.
Troeltsch, Ernst
  1931   *The Social Teachings of the Christian Church.* 2 vols. Translated by Olive Wyon. New York: Macmillan Co.
Vidich, Arthur J., and Joseph Bensman
  1958   *Small Town in Mass Society.* Garden City, N.Y.: Anchor Books/Doubleday.
Warner, W. Lloyd, and Paul S. Lunt
  1941   *The Social Life of a Modern Community.* New Haven, Conn.: Yale University Press.
White, Richard H.
  1970   "Toward a Theory of Religious Influence." In *American Mosaic: Social Patterns of Religion in the United States,* edited by Phillip E. Hammond and Benton Johnson, 14–23. New York: Random House.
Wuthnow, Robert
  1988   *The Restructuring of American Religion.* Princeton, N.J.: Princeton University Press.

BEYOND ESTABLISHMENT

PART ONE

Denominations
as Local Institutions

The first, and perhaps only, contact most people have with religious institutions is at the local level. People join local congregations. Here they participate in worship and religious activities, attend church school classes, develop and maintain friendships, make financial contributions, and relate to others of a similar faith.

The five essays in this section look at activities at the local level and how they contribute to religious identity. Daniel V. A. Olson's chapter provides a theoretical perspective on religion in modern society that builds on and augments that provided in the Introduction, as he examines the importance of congregational fellowship ties. Social interaction among those sharing common beliefs, as sociologists have long pointed out, reinforces religious commitment and identity. But as Olson observes, fellowship ties among mainliners tend to be less dense: people in these churches do not limit their friendships within their own groups as much as do those in conservative churches. Thus the fellowship groups and the congregations have a less distinctive identity. As he sees it, mainline churches have two options: one, to accept a priestly role as custodians of a less distinctive religious identity, or two, to redefine prophetically mainline identity to make it more distinctive.

Historically, church schools have helped to shape Protestant denominational identity. Mary Elizabeth and Allen J. Moore briefly trace the history of the church school and then report on an ethnographic study of a United Church of Christ congregation and its church school. In this particular setting, they observed little emphasis on indoctrination of beliefs, but did find insistence upon values of inclusiveness, diversity, self-acceptance, and caring for others. Although its role within the church is ambiguous, the church school, the authors suggest, reinforces the values of the congregation and is in keeping with the denomination's heritage.

For a large number of Americans, the primary involvement in religion is through corporate worship. Over 40 percent of the population of the United States attends worship on an average Sunday. In spite of declines in mainline Protestant church membership since the mid-1960s, worship attendance figures have remained relatively constant. Thus, corporate worship—its rituals and its music—is a crucial point of encounter with both universal Christian symbols and the cultures of particular denominations. Signaling the importance that worshipers attach to ritual patterns and hymns are the heated controversies that develop when there are moves to change liturgical language or ritual practice, or to omit favorite hymns from the hymnal. Two chapters explore the role of ritual and hymns in the transmission of culture, both of Christian symbols and of particular denominations.

Focusing on ritual, Keith A. Roberts shows how the corporate ritual celebrations of congregational worship are enactments that regularly lift up and make sacred the church's central values and myths. He reminds the reader that the patterning of Sunday worship is not random but is a rehearsal of a particular covenantal view of life that is central to most of Protestantism but takes on different nuances according to denominational traditions. He also considers ways in which a denomination transmits its distinctive polity through norms governing ritual performance and spatial arrangements. Subtle and not-so-subtle understandings of authority, power, statuses, and roles are conveyed through these norms and practices. Roberts also explores ways in which denominations differ in how the senses are involved in ritual practices and the kinds of sensory experiences that are deemed appropriate. Sensory experiences in worship both reflect denominational culture and contribute to its transmission. Finally, he considers how conflicts arise over efforts to incorporate ideologies and values from the broader culture into the church's worship. The use of the American flag in the church's sacred space is a case in point.

Music is also an important means of transmitting a denomination's particular angle of vision on the Christian tradition. The hymns sung within a congregation convey meanings and experiences that are dear to its denomination's heritage and its own past and present. Like rituals, hymns express core values, reflect a group's mythos at a fundamental level of experience and identity, and help to maintain the plausibility of the group's culture. Linda J. Clark argues that it is not simply the text or the music, or even the two together, that enables a person to experience a particular set of meanings. Rather, it is the alchemy of text, music, and the feelings and experiences—past and present—of the singers that shapes the meanings which the hymns convey. She demonstrates this perspective as she reports on her research on the use of hymns in congregational life. In a sample of United Methodist and Episcopal congregations, she asked members about their favorite hymns. Focusing on the hymn "Amazing Grace," which was near the top of the list for both traditions, she links meanings attributed to the hymn (and to hymns generally) to experiences of the worshipers whom she interviewed. She also explores how the same hymn text and tune can carry different meanings, depending upon the denominational heritage and the congregational setting.

Women's organizations have long been recognized, though not always fully appreciated, for their important role within Protestant denominations. Barbara Brown Zikmund traces the rise of these organizations in American Protestant churches and the many types of women's organizations, including separate orders, mission boards, Ladies' Aid Societies, and prayer and support groups. As her title suggests, these organizations have often functioned in a dual way. Women's organizations have not only been responsible for fostering understanding of and loyalty to core values of their denominations but also have led the way in promoting inclusiveness and denominational unity. This dual focus is an important legacy and continuing contribution of these organizations. Zikmund concludes her historical analysis of women's religious organizations in the broader context of the changing roles of women and the feminist movement. She speculates about the future of these organizations and their roles for women and for the church as a whole.

1

Fellowship Ties
and the Transmission
of Religious Identity

Daniel V. A. Olson

One of the oldest generalizations in the sociology of religion is that religious identity, belief, and commitment depend for their vitality upon the frequency and character of social interaction among persons sharing a common belief. Without regular contact with others who share one's beliefs, a person slowly forgets the vitality of his or her religious experience, religious identity begins to blur, and beliefs lose much of their plausibility and relevance for life (Durkheim 1915; Berger 1967). In this chapter, I argue that modernization and religious pluralism are transforming the nature and frequency of interactions among fellow believers and thus the nature of religious identity and its transmission.[1] These changes tend to favor the development of religious groups with distinctive identities in contrast to those, like mainline Protestantism, with less distinctive identities.

First, I explore how modernization transforms taken-for-granted cultural religious identity to chosen subcultural religious identities. Second, I explore why social ties are stronger and more numerous in some religious subcultures compared to others. Third, I examine the nature of relatively dense fellowship ties within a conservative denomination. Fourth, I suggest reasons why mainline fellowship ties tend to be less dense and why they may also differ in content from ties among conservatives.

Identity and Modernization

By identity I mean the answers one gives to the questions "Who am I?" and "Who are we?" Sociologists stress that one's identity is largely shaped by one's social relationships, the social roles one plays, and the groups in which one participates. Peter Berger (1967) suggests that we sustain our belief in our own identity through others' recognition and affirmation of our identity. To a large extent, we are what others say we are. This does not mean one is unable to change one's identity. We can manipulate our "presentation of self" (Goffman 1959) and convince others to accept a new definition of our identity. Or, we can change the persons with whom we associate, choosing those who affirm an identity we prefer.

The classical sociological theorists of the nineteenth century (such as Marx, Weber, Durkheim, Tonnies, and Simmel2) argue that in preindustrial societies religion, kinship, and community form the central bases of individual identity, interaction, and solidarity among persons. Moreover, the three spheres are coextensive and indistinguishable; one's neighbors are one's kin and one's fellow believers. One's religious identity is virtually indistinguishable from one's total identity. It is taken for granted by others and by one's self in the same way one's identity as a member of the community is taken for granted. The entire community, its values, institutions, and individual members act to transmit and reinforce religious identity.

These same theorists contend that modernization changes the nature of social relationships and, therefore, the nature of personal and group identities. Industrialization and urbanization increase mobility and improve communication, thereby increasing exposure to nonkin, strangers, and people of differing beliefs—people with differing identities. The division of labor and the rise of specialization increase differences among persons in their experiences, values, outlooks, and identities. In general, modernization greatly increases the variety of identities within society and the potential for contact among persons of differing identities.

Such conditions can create problems for the transmission and reinforcement of religious identity. Berger (1967) and Luckmann (1967) argue that modern societies accommodate religious pluralism and the potential for religious conflict by removing religion from the *public sectors* of society and culture, the polity, economy, the legal system, and all areas of life in which all persons must participate in order to live as members of society. Religious diversity is allowed, but it is limited to the *private sectors* of life, the family, the congregation, voluntary interpersonal ties, and, generally, those areas of life that need not be shared publicly with others. Berger calls this the privatization of religion.

Privatization means that one's beliefs and religious identity are no longer reinforced by the public culture and the public institutions of society. No longer is religious identity taken for granted as an indistinguishable aspect of one's identity as a member of society. One's personal contacts outside the private sphere, especially in the workplace, may not share or reinforce one's religious identity. In fact, discussion of religious identity or specific beliefs may be considered inappropriate.

Berger claims that as religion and religious identity lose their public taken-for-granted quality they become matters of personal preference. Faced with a diversity of religions, each making absolutistic truth claims, people either ignore religious belief systems or construct their own out of bits and pieces borrowed from various religious and cultural traditions. The resulting heterogeneity of preferences diminishes the potential for interpersonal social support and reinforcement of beliefs. This is especially critical when facing life crises such as divorce, illness, and death. When one is unable to discuss personal crises with others who affirm a religious interpretation and response to these experiences, religious beliefs and identity begin to lose their relevance for life. Berger suggests that without institutions and social networks acting to reaffirm and sustain one's religious beliefs and identity (what he calls plausibility structures) religion may fade from the private sector just as it has from the public sector.

But is religion fading from the private sector? Stark and Bainbridge (1985) and Finke and Stark (1988) propose an alternative model of the modern religious situation, the religious economies model. While this model and the data supporting it do not directly challenge the reality of privatization and secularization of the public sphere, it argues that religious pluralism actually functions to increase *individual* religious commitment and behavior in the private sphere because a variety of religious "products" can provide a greater range of options to meet the needs of a heterogeneous religious "market." Moreover, competition motivates each religious group to make the best use of resources to attract adherents and engender commitment. In contrast, state church "monopolies" become "lazy."

Finke and Stark (1986; 1988) and Stark and Finke (1988) use historical statistics for the United States to show that religious participation has been increasing, along with religious pluralism, since the colonial period. Moreover, participation increases most where religious pluralism is greatest (for example, in cities). They contend that rates of individual religious participation are actually quite low in historic societies with only one religion. Iannaccone (1988b) extends their analysis cross-culturally and finds that, in general, levels of religious participation in industrialized countries have a strong positive correlation with the religious heterogeneity of each country.

The religious economies model suggests that as religion was pushed out of the public sector ("de-monopolized") its presence in the private sector increased. If true, what are the plausibility structures that sustain religion in the private sector? Given the religious pluralism of modern societies, how do people maintain contact with persons and institutions that reaffirm and support their religious identity? The religious economies model does not explain how individuals can confront a diversity of beliefs and yet maintain the plausibility of their own beliefs.

A third model of the contemporary religious situation, the subcultural model, suggests that the growth of religious subcultures facilitates interaction among persons who share a religious identity and shields many from significant exposure to religious pluralism. I derive the subcultural model primarily from Fischer's (1982) analysis of rural versus urban personal networks (the persons with whom a single person has important interaction). Elements of the model, however, are present in other works (such as Herberg 1955; Lenski 1961; Greeley 1972). Fischer argues that urbanization and, by implication, modernization need not lead to heterogeneous social ties among individuals. Rather modernization's major impact is to increase people's *choice* of associates and affiliations. People use this choice to develop relationships with others who share important aspects of their identity.

One's associates are determined by a combination of constraint and choice. Geographic and social location drastically restrict potential contacts (Verbrugge 1977; Feld 1981), but within a particular setting one may exercise some selectivity in the formation of one's social ties. In preindustrial societies one has little choice, one cannot easily escape the associates one encounters in the local community. Modernization increases choice because it increases the range of one's contacts. Better transportation and communication increase the potential geographic range of contacts. Urbanization (because it brings large groups of diverse persons together in close proximity) increases the potential social range of contacts (Wirth 1938). Abundant research[3] shows that when given a choice, people tend to select others like themselves. The more choice they have, the more homogeneous their personal networks become (Fischer 1977). Thus while modern societies exhibit great pluralism and heterogeneity, the actual social contacts of many persons may exhibit comparatively little pluralism or diversity. The religious heterogeneity of one's associates is increasingly a matter of choice.

Fischer feels the freedom to choose associates resembling one's self leads naturally to the creation of subcultures, "communities" whose members share a common identity more than a particular location. Subcultures develop when people believe they have a minority, or at least a distinctive, identity compared to mainstream culture or other groups in society. When a sufficient number of persons sharing such an identity come together in close proximity (such as in cities) they may preferentially choose one another as associates, thus creating subcultures. Subcultures can arise out of a variety of identity bases, for example, ethnicity (Italian), occupation (truck driver), age (youth culture), sexual preference (the gay community), leisure activity (ham radio operator), or religion.

The subcultural model is important because it suggests that the very forces of modernization that disrupt the homogeneity of the preindustrial community simultaneously give moderns greater control over the construction of their personal networks, control that can be used to rebuild networks of shared identity. The difference between contemporary subcultures and the preindustrial community lies in the greater freedom of moderns to choose which elements of their identity they will emphasize in the construction of their personal networks and the degree of their involvement in subcultures based on those identities. Moderns are freer to shape their personal networks and thus their own identity.

Unlike the preindustrial community where religious identity is taken for granted and affirmed by both the public and private sectors, religious identity is increasingly a matter of choice. It is dependent upon the social ties and institutions of religious subcultures based in the private sector for its continued transmission and reaffirmation. With the decline of the public sector as a religious plausibility structure, religious subcultures increasingly play this role.

The Strength of Religious Subcultures

Rather than providing rigid guidelines for defining when a subculture exists and when it does not, where it begins and where it ends, who is a member and who is not, a more realistic perspective suggests that the strength of subcultures varies with the extent that persons sharing an identity preferentially choose one another as associates.

One belongs to a subculture to the extent that one's personal contacts share an important aspect of one's identity. However, as Fischer points out, subcultures are not simply interpersonal phenomena. As they develop, they usually create institutional structures (such as clubs, magazines, events, and regular meeting places) that facilitate subcultural interaction and help to maintain, shape, and transmit the shared identity. Thus subcultures vary in strength according to their levels of within-group ties and levels of institutionalization.

What determines the strength of subcultures? Fischer's (1982) analysis suggests that the number of within-group ties depends on the relative proximity and availability of others sharing the subcultural identity (subcultures are more common in cities) and the strength of subcultural institutions that facilitate interaction. More importantly, within-group ties and levels of institutionalization both vary with the extent of perceived difference between the shared subcultural identity and the identity of others in society. The greater this difference, the more rewarding subcultural participants find interaction with partici- pants relative to nonparticipants (Homans 1961). For example, sect adherents may have difficulty finding acceptance among nonmembers because their identity, beliefs, and values are so different. The result- ing discomfort discourages interaction with nonmembers and encour- ages interaction with members.

Similarly, subcultures with more distinctive identities tend to have institutions that receive stronger support from subcultural participants. Such institutions provide access to a scarce commodity (others who share the distinctive identity) and may be the only institutions promot- ing the values and interests of subcultural participants. In contrast, participants in subcultures based on less distinctive identities find that many of their value concerns and interests are represented by public institutions or other voluntary organizations. Thus they feel less need to create and support separate subcultural institutions.

While the subcultural model affirms that modernization, pluralism, and privatization need not lead to the demise of religion, neither does it suggest that all subcultural plausibility structures will be equally strong or that all persons will be equally involved. Levels of involve- ment will vary from person to person depending on the emphasis they place on the religious elements of their personal identity. The ability of religious subcultures to transmit and maintain a religious identity will vary with the depth and number of fellowship ties among subcul- tural participants and the number and strength of subcultural institu- tions.[4] Both within-group ties and institutional strength will vary with the distinctiveness of the religious identity.

The data in table 1–1 is evidence of these patterns. It provides the findings from the *General Social Survey,* a recent national survey of the American adult population (Davis and Smith 1988). Respondents were asked to indicate their religious affiliation if they had one. The results for Protestants are divided into three groups according to the denominations with which respondents are affiliated. The three divisions (see notes to table 1–1) are based on numerous other classifications of Protestant denominations in the social science literature and (as the data in this table suggests) the categories correlate well with many other indicators of religious participation. The primary distinction among the groupings is the relative theological conservatism of the denominations in each group. This is apparent in table 1–1 from the row showing percentages that believe "the Bible is the actual word of God and is to be taken literally, word for word" (an item that other studies [for example, Stark and Glock 1968] find to be highly correlated with many other measures of theological conservatism).

Unfortunately, the *General Social Survey* contains no items that directly measure distinctiveness of religious identity. Religious groups distinguish themselves from the rest of society and from other religious groups in a variety of ways, including distinctive behavioral practices (orthopraxy), distinctive ethnicity, distinctive worship styles and liturgy, and distinctive church governance. However, among Protestant groups, beliefs and values (orthodoxy) are especially important for defining religious identity. Thus I view a conservative response to the item measuring views of the Bible as an indirect indicator (for Protestants) of distinctive religious identity. I interpret orthodox beliefs as distinctive, since they include supernatural beliefs that run counter to the beliefs of mainstream culture (if not the majority of American adults).

The numbers shown in the first row of table 1–1 are the average proportion of friends considered to belong to a "similar" denomination (see note b in the table). While it is not an ideal indicator, this proportion roughly reflects the degree to which persons in each denominational category prefer associates who share their religious identity, for example, the number of within-group ties in each group. The results from the first two rows are in accord with the predictions of the subcultural model. Conservative Protestants, having more distinctive beliefs, also have more within-group associations.

TABLE 1–1

**Density of Within-Group Ties, Conservative Theology,
Church Commitment, and Private Religiosity
by Type of Religious Group**

	Conservative Protestants	Moderate Protestants	Liberal Protestants	Total[a] Protestants
Number of Respondents (Maximum)	505	105	222	832
Average proportion of "good friends"[b] who belong to a denomination similar to respondent's denomination	.478	.337	.348	.425
Percentage believing "the Bible is the actual word of God and is to be taken literally, word for word."	55.8	28.8	26.9	44.7
Percent indicating faith is "free of doubt"[c]	74.7	54.8	52.7	66.3
Percent "strong" members[d]	51.4	42.0	29.4	44.3
Percent attending nearly every week or more	41.1	37.1	22.5	35.6
Average percent of income given to "your religion"	3.8	2.3	2.3	3.2
Average annual family income (thousands in 1987)	23.7	26.7	31.6	26.2
Percentage praying several times a week or more	81.8	73.0	66.2	76.6
Percentage reading the Bible several times a week or more	38.9	33.3	18.0	32.6

SOURCE: Davis and Smith, *General Social Survey* (1988)

a. Divisions among Protestants based on respondent's denomination as classified by the *General Social Survey* for the variable FUND. (See *GSS* Methodological Report number 43.) Major conservative denominations include (among others) Southern Baptist Convention, National Baptist Convention, USA, Inc., Lutheran Church Missouri Synod, Assemblies of God, Mormons, and Church of the Nazarene. Moderate denominations include (among others) United Methodist, American Lutheran Church

The subcultural model suggests that within-group ties may help serve as plausibility structures for belief. The findings from the third row support this prediction. Conservative Protestants are more likely to say their faith is free of doubt. The subcultural model also suggests that persons with distinctive identities are more likely to provide stronger support to subcultural organizations and institutions. Findings in the fourth through the seventh rows support this conclusion. Conservative Protestants are more likely to indicate a strong affiliation with their denomination, attend religious services more frequently, and give a higher percentage of their income to "their religion" despite their lower family incomes. Likewise they are more regular in private religious practices. They pray more frequently and read the Bible more frequently. Other analyses, not shown here, indicate that the same relationships hold true when individuals (rather than groups) are compared on the items shown in table 1–1.

While these patterns are especially apparent from the data in this table, they are not unique to this study. Stark and Glock (1968) and Roof and McKinney (1987) report similar results from national samples, and Roof (1978) reports similar results within a single denomination (those with distinctive beliefs and many church friends pray more, attend more, and are more likely to say their religion is important in their life).[5]

(now ELCA), Lutheran Church in America (now ELCA), African Methodist Episcopal. Liberal denominations include (among others) Episcopal, United Presbyterian Church in USA, Unitarian Universalist, United Church of Christ. Protestants who did not list a denomination or who said their church was nondenominational have been excluded.

b. Respondents were asked "Many people have some good friends they feel close to. Who are your good friends (other than your spouse)? Just tell me their first names." The first three names were recorded. For each of these friends, respondents were asked if the friend was a member of the respondent's congregation. If they were not a member of the respondent's denomination, the respondent was asked to indicate the friend's denominational affiliation. If the friend was a member of the respondent's congregation or if the friend belonged to a denomination that is similar to the respondent's (in the conservative, moderate, liberal classification above) the friend was considered to belong to a "similar" denomination. The proportions refer to the proportion of friends named (some listed less than three) who met the criteria for this item.

c. Respondents were asked to describe the degree of doubt they have in their faith using a scale from 1 to 7 where 1 indicates "my faith is completely free of doubt" and 7 indicates "my faith is mixed with doubt." The percentages reported here indicate those answering 1 through 3.

d. Respondents were asked "Would you call yourself a strong (denomination listed earlier) or a not very strong (denomination listed earlier)."

Fellowship Ties in a Conservative Denomination

Findings such as those referred to above suggest that fellowship ties may play an important role in the transmission of religious identity and the promotion of commitment to religious organizations. But important questions remain. Do conservative churchgoers have more church friends simply because they attend more frequently, or do their church friendships independently promote religious commitment and identity? Do they choose their ties on the basis of a shared conservative religious identity (as the subcultural model suggests) and if so, what is the nature of these ties? Can voluntarily chosen ties be deep ties that involve all aspects of churchgoers' lives, the kind of ties that can potentially reinforce religious belief and commitment?

To explore these issues, I examined the number and nature of ties among church attenders of five congregations, all located in Minneapolis-St. Paul suburbs and all belonging to the Baptist General Conference (BGC), an evangelical denomination with a stable membership of approximately 130,000 persons. Questionnaire results suggest that in comparison with results from other denominations in terms of number of church friendships, levels of church attendance, giving, praying, and the like, the BGC respondents fall between the levels reported for American Baptists and those reported for the Southern Baptists (Stark and Glock 1968). In this respect they resemble many other evangelicals, a large and growing segment of the American population. The BGC's location at the moderately involved end of the church friendship spectrum makes it a good setting in which to analyze the potential impact of fellowship ties. If church ties lack depth in settings where they are numerous, they are unlikely to be important in settings where they are sparse.

Despite high levels of religious involvement, the BGC respondents were not economically or educationally deprived, as some theories suggest. Their median income in 1985 was between thirty thousand and forty thousand dollars; 90 percent had high school diplomas; 42 percent had college degrees; and among working respondents 33 percent were in professional or semi-professional occupations.

The research involved several components, a questionnaire distributed to all members and regular attenders of the five churches (762 out of 1,155 returned) and in-depth (two-hour) interviews with a total of twenty attenders selected (on the basis of questionnaire results) to reflect the age, sex, attendance tenure, and church friendship involvement distributions of the five churches. The interviews included a structured section asking respondents to name the persons with whom they have important interactions.[6] After constructing this list, respondents were asked additional questions about the persons on their list, including whether or not they attend the same church and/or have similar beliefs.

Elsewhere (Olson 1987) I report results from quantitative analyses of the structured portion of the interviews. These analyses not only show that the BGC respondents have many church-based ties but also that, when compared to their ties based in most other settings (coworkers, neighbors, relatives, comembers of other voluntary organizations, and persons with similar spare time activities), fellow attenders are more likely to be named as friends, persons with whom respondents socialize, share personal matters, and persons whose opinions respondents value. Analysis shows this pattern arises partly because fellow attenders live nearby and respondents see them frequently but also because fellow attenders share a religious identity. For example, respondents live close to neighbors and see coworkers frequently but claim that few share their religious beliefs. Respondents have few close ties with neighbors or coworkers.

The interviews also included a less structured portion in which I asked respondents about the meaning of their church friendships for their lives. These more qualitative findings, reported here, add depth and credibility to the quantitative results. For example, I asked respondents to compare the depth of their religiously based ties with their ties in other settings. Most felt it was easier to develop close ties with persons who shared their beliefs. One woman in her twenties indicated she could have a close relationship with someone who disagreed with her beliefs, but felt it could not be "as close."

> Because to me, my religious beliefs are a very important part of me. And if I can't share that with someone then there is a big part of me that I am not sharing.

One outspoken thirty-five-year-old man put it more forcefully and more negatively.

> I will not choose a close friend who has a difference of religious belief. Period. Why waste my time. You don't get as much out of a relationship where you have to get on common ground together first. That doesn't mean that I care any less about non-Christian people, because I do. But I am just not going to be close to them.

One woman, a full-time homemaker, said she occasionally shared personal concerns with her neighbors, most of whom did not share her beliefs, but she tended to discount their advice because they "just don't understand." Another respondent said it was hard to share personal matters with "non-Christians" because they were more likely to be critical of her. In accordance with the subcultural model, respondents appeared to favor ties with others who shared their religious identity because they found those ties more rewarding than ties to persons with differing beliefs.

While such religiously based ties may seem exclusive to outsiders, they can be rich and rewarding to insiders. They satisfy many needs, including a need for friendship and socializing. Many respondents stated that one of the reasons they attended church was to see their friends. One retired respondent, an usher in his church for many years, said that when he missed church he missed the people.

> Just visiting with them in the narthex before or after, you miss people you know. You go to church and you find that you don't see certain people. You maybe go home and call them up and see what happened. See, you just miss people.

For some of the respondents most of the people they socialized with were at their church. During an interview with a homemaker who was very active in her church we were interrupted four or five times by phone calls. Out of curiosity I asked her how many of the callers were from her church. She replied that all were fellow attenders. One married respondent told me that she and her husband socialized with only one couple outside their church.

One interpretation of these findings is that the respondents are social isolates that flock to churches out of a hunger for social interaction. There is no question that the respondents satisfy many, and in some cases most, of their social needs through church associates, but they are not generally an isolated group. Using methods of measurement identical to those of Fischer (1982),[7] I found that the BGC respondents have, on average, more associates in their personal networks than those in Fischer's more general sample of northern California residents. As Fischer points out, membership in voluntary organizations, especially religious organizations, tends to increase the number of one's associates without significantly lowering the number of persons one knows in other settings.

Though ties to fellow attenders satisfied social needs, respondents claimed they also involved "fellowship." Because many respondents used this term, I pressed them to define what it meant. Though one respondent said it meant "socializing," the remainder felt it was something deeper. Most said fellowship only applied to relationships among persons with common beliefs. One respondent, a man in his thirties, put it this way.

Fellowship, for me, assumes a spiritual unity. A spiritual bond. And for those of my neighbors who are non-Christians, I don't have any fellowship with them. I can enjoy their friendship, but I don't fellowship with them.

Another respondent felt that it was possible to have "fellowship" with people who don't share your beliefs.

It is a different kind of fellowship. [At work] its strictly job related. . . . With the people that I know in the church they are interested in my job, but they are also interested in my family and my life in general. And also you have the common bond of Christianity.

Many said they specifically sought out a church where they could find close "fellowship." One respondent stated:

We need to be going to a church [where] we feel a sense of belonging and a sense of responsibility to . . . a group of people where if you thought you had a need you could go to them and they would be prepared to help you and support you in whatever it was you needed.

Interestingly, several respondents suggested that it was not necessary to know someone really well to have fellowship with them. One woman, speaking of a church friend with whom she had limited contact, stated:

Mary and I, our relationship is kind of narrow. It bothers me a little bit. . . . I think most of the thing is that Jesus just said to do that, to be with your other brethren. You can learn a lot of things from them. I don't really think I'm being phony by not thinking them [her church friends] my best friends because I think it is something Jesus tells us to do. . . . And they are important to Jesus, so they would be important to me. Sometimes, I can uplift them which makes me feel good, and sometimes they can uplift me.

Even though she did not know her church friends well, she felt closer to them than work associates whom she saw forty hours a week.

[Church people would] care for you if you let them. [They are] people who could care for you even if you don't let them. If you go to work, you see the people eight hours and they leave. If you were not at work for a week and were sick, rarely would they come and contact you or get a hold of you or anything like that. But you know those people at church, you may not say "Hi" to them for a month, but you know if you wanted to and you had to, you could call them up and they would help you.

Their ties to fellow attenders also involved a spiritual dimension. Several respondents claimed they maintained such ties in order to be supported and challenged in their Christian life. One woman, who had few close associates outside her church who shared her beliefs, says she attended church primarily "to be fed spiritually." This occurred for her in the women's Sunday school class. She felt that one needed to "be together with other believers. If you don't go to church, you are not [spiritually] accountable to anybody." Through "listening to other people in their situations" and praying together, the women in her Sunday school class helped her "understand God's will." She felt that the contact with other Christians encouraged her and helped her "get more of a rounded view."

One respondent, after making a similar point, justified her position, adding:

> I think Christ emphasizes that we need to be a body. Over and over in scripture I think it mentions the importance of socialization and being with people who support you in tough times and challenge you in your [spiritual] growth.

In response to a question concerning his motivation for developing fellowship ties, one articulate respondent said that he saw

> a Christian community and Christian fellowship [as] an absolutely essential part of being a Christian. You are not an island, and you can't grow without other people. . . . If you only attend a church, but don't get involved with the people, you are a spectator at that church. You can get something from the sermon, but I think the sermon is a very small part of the church. . . . The members are the body of Christ.

The evidence presented here cannot be used to assess how well respondents' religiously based ties actually reinforce beliefs and commitment, but the nature of these ties seems well suited to the task. Respondents talk with fellow attenders frequently, name them as friends, value their opinions, and share intimate concerns. They seek them out for spiritual advice and prayer when faced with problems and decisions. They claim to exchange physical, social, emotional, and spiritual support. Such sharing would seem to enhance the relevance of religion in their lives and favor the construction of strong plausibility structures.

Fellowship Ties in Mainline Churches

Although I have no comparable interview data on the quality of ties among attenders of mainline churches, the results shown in table 1–1 suggest that even if mainline attenders have numerous ties with fellow attenders, they infrequently name them as close friends. Fellowship ties among mainliners tend to be less *dense*. The subcultural model suggests this is a direct result of the lesser distinctiveness of mainline identity.

Johnson (1963) and Stark and Bainbridge (1985) define sects as religious groups that are in greater tension with the general culture. The greater this tension, the more sectlike the religious group (by definition). Thus defined, sectarianism can be viewed as a religious manifestation of the more general phenomenon of distinctive subcultures. In the church-sect sense, most mainline Protestant denominations in America are "churches." Compared to more sectlike conservative denominations, they are in relatively little tension with mainstream culture and historically have been important in shaping and affirming the public sectors of society.[8] To the extent that it is even appropriate to use the term "subculture," the religious subculture of mainline denominations is based on a shared identity that is only marginally distinct from mainstream culture.

This is not to deny that mainline churches, especially their seminary-trained leaders, embody values that sometimes call them to stand in prophetic opposition to widely held public values. However, these prophetic values are held in common with many who share a liberal political viewpoint but who hold no specific religious beliefs. More significantly, joining a mainline church seldom requires an identity "conversion," a repentance and denial of past identity, or an acceptance of a new, distinctive identity. Such identity conversions, common in more distinctive religious groups, make little sense in mainline settings because identity expectations are relatively indistinct from those of most citizens.

The less distinctive character of mainline identity leads to less dense fellowship ties. Mainline attenders have less dependence upon within-group ties; their less distinctive religious identity makes it easier for them to associate with others like themselves outside of church settings. They meet such persons everyday, in the workplace, in their neighborhoods, and through their interactions in public-sector institutions. If they participate in subcultures at all, they are more likely to participate in subcultures based on other, nonreligious, aspects of their identity. Similarly, they are less likely to support religious institutions since many of their value concerns and interests are served by other secular institutions. Why support the denomination's political action agency when other, specifically political, organizations may be addressing the same issues?

The lower density of mainline fellowship ties is probably not a phenomenon limited to modern times. Finke and Stark (1988) argue that in premodern societies having only one religion individual levels of behavioral religious commitment are quite low even though the public-sector authority of religion may be high. In such societies one need not attend a church to find others who share and affirm one's religious identity, since all share the same taken-for-granted religious identity. Likewise, commitments to religious institutions, beyond those required by law, are unnecessary for the maintenance of these institutions. The public sectors of society and all of one's personal contacts reinforce one's religious identity. When one's church is one's society, one can be "religious" simply by being a citizen.

In contrast sectarian minorities in premodern societies must, as Finke and Stark point out, struggle against the monopolistic power of the majority religion. In this struggle, the survival of their distinctive religious institutions depends on high levels of personal commitment from their members. The resounding denial of their religious identity coming from both the public and private sectors makes their within-group ties especially important for the affirmation of their identity. These ties may be very dense, but poor transportation and communication and the scarcity of persons sharing an alternative religious identity makes the establishment and maintenance of such groups difficult.   Although church-sect differences in the density of fellowship ties probably have existed for a long time, modernization may actually be widening these differences. Modernization facilitates social ties within distinctive groups, while it lessens the dependence on such ties among members of less distinctive groups.

Though I know of no studies comparing fellowship ties in premodern versus modern religious groups, Fischer (1982) compared the personal networks of urban versus rural religious group members. While contemporary rural-urban differences are not the same as premodern-modern differences, both changes increase the freedom to choose one's associates (the key independent variable in this explanation).

Fischer (1982) found that among all persons who belong to religious organizations, rural dwellers have, on average, more friends (than do urban dwellers) who are comembers in the same religious organizations. However, when he looked only at religious organization members who say their religion is the most important area of their life (persons who are likely to have a distinctive religious identity), urban dwellers have more friends in religious organizations than do rural dwellers.

He suggests that urbanism increases the potential of persons with less distinctive identities to associate with others like themselves outside of church settings. In the rural environment the church may be one of only a few settings where one can develop associations with similar others. However, the urban environment provides many such settings. Urbanism therefore decreases dependence on church settings among persons with less distinctive religious identities. But for persons with more distinctive religious identities, urbanism provides the critical mass for the creation of church settings where such persons can associate. There may not be enough Jews in a small town to establish a synagogue, but in a large city this is less of a problem.

Thus, both urbanization and modernization may be giving a selective advantage to more distinctive religious groups. They simplify the construction of interpersonal plausibility structures in distinctive groups, while they lower the dependence upon, and the density of, such ties in less distinctive groups (like the mainline). If true, modernization may be lessening even further the density of mainline fellowship ties and thereby lessening their identity transmitting and reinforcing capacity.

In addition to being less dense, fellowship ties among mainline attenders may also differ in their religious *content*. Though I know of no studies investigating this issue, my personal experience suggests that religious conservatives more frequently discuss their personal life concerns using specifically religious language, for example, "I felt the Lord was telling me to take this job." In contrast, mainline attenders less frequently use such language to interpret their experience when discussing personal issues.

Just as church-sect differences in density of fellowship ties have probably existed for a long time, the same is probably also true of differences in the religious content of these ties. Nevertheless, the privatization of religion may act in at least two ways to widen these differences. By definition, churches (in contrast to sects) affirm much of the dominant cultural identity and values of the general culture. In the past, this identity was religious and was supported by public sector institutions as well as the church. Not only does privatization remove the public sector affirmation of church identity, but it also means that churches now affirm an identity from which much of the specific religious content has been removed. Fellowship ties based on such an identity are less likely to be religious in their content.

Privatization also acts to decrease the acceptability of specifically religious language in public sector settings. Thus, mainline churchgoers who closely identify with the privatized public culture may find, even within the walls of the church, that they carry with them strong taboos against religious talk, especially when it deals with personal matters. Disinclined to interpret their life experiences publicly in religious terms, they choose instead the more acceptable concepts and terminology of modern psychology. Such privatization, when carried within the walls of the church, robs religiously based ties of their religious content and greatly limits their ability to transmit religious identity and reinforce the relevance of religion for the personal and private areas of life.

One final, and somewhat ironic, barrier to strong mainline fellowship ties results from the mainline affirmation of religious tolerance and diversity. Religious tolerance in the public sector allows modern societies to function despite high levels of religious pluralism. While many religious groups affirm religious tolerance when applied to the public sector, many reject it within the walls of the church. Partly because of close ties to the public sector and public-sector values, and partly because of theological conviction, many in mainline denominations actively seek to incorporate the diversity of society within the church. This diversity includes differences of ethnicity, language, class, sexual preference, *and belief.* The irony arises because, in the search to create "community," the resulting diversity makes it difficult to define a common identity upon which strong community ties can be based.

The emphasis on diversity, while laudable in its obedience to mainline interpretations of Christian teachings, creates problems for the transmission and maintenance of mainline identity. These problems, and the response to these problems, reflect, in microcosmic form, the experience of modern societies faced with an increasing heterogeneity of identities. Just as Fischer argues that subcultures naturally arise out of the diversity of modern life, so one response to mainline diversity may be the formation of caucuses representing particular social and theological divisions within the church. Just as Berger argues that the public sectors of society become religiously neutral as religious diversity increases, so the denominational structures of mainline denominations may respond to internal theological diversity by choosing not to take specific theological positions, leaving such matters to the more private spheres of the local congregation and individual conscience. This severely limits the ability of denominational structures to transmit and reaffirm a religious as well as a denominational identity. Similarly, the diversity of beliefs among mainline attenders undercuts their ability to find a common language to communicate interpersonally the meaning of their faith for their lives.

Conclusion

If, as Berger suggests, we are, to a great extent, what others say we are, religious identity maintenance depends on interaction with others who share our identity and confirm the reality and plausibility of our beliefs. The arguments above suggest that fellowship ties are a major avenue of religious identity transmission and affirmation.

These arguments also suggest that modernization favors the growth of religious groups with distinctive identities. As public sector support for religion disappears, the plausibility structures of modern religion are increasingly based in religious subcultures. Religious groups having more distinctive identities are likely to have stronger fellowship ties and tend to receive stronger institutional support from their members. In the past any competitive advantages such groups gained by having stronger subcultures were outweighed by the advantages less distinctive religious groups gained through public sector endorsement and support. Cultural support is always stronger than subcultural support. Today, however, the withdrawal of public-sector support for religion favors distinctive groups with strong religious subcultures.

Mainline church leaders have at least two options.[9] One is to accept a priestly role as custodians of a less distinctive religious identity with which many can identify but to which few are greatly committed. Another is to redefine prophetically mainline identity to make it more distinctive, that is, make it take even stronger stands for mainline values that differ from those of the public culture. Since the public culture no longer supports the mainline, the mainline need not fear opposing public cultural values. However, this strategy leads to ironic contradictions. Any move to make mainline identity more distinctive threatens to exclude many and thereby violates core mainline values stressing inclusiveness, tolerance, and diversity.

It appears that many of the seminary-trained leaders of the mainline find the second, more prophetic, option more appealing (even if it excludes some), while the mass of the laity and lay leaders prefer the first option. If true, the future shape of the mainline may well be determined by its leaders' ability, or lack of ability, to find a religious vision and vocabulary that energize a diverse laity to follow their leaders in prophetic new directions.

NOTES

1. I am indebted to the Hartford Seminary Center for Social and Religious Research for their support during the writing of this essay while I was a postdoctoral research fellow at the Center.

2. Of course, the arguments of specific theorists are much more detailed and refined than the general characterization I provide here.

3. See McPherson and Smith-Lovin's (1987) footnote 1 for a very extensive listing of this literature.

4. A variety of religious institutions transmit subcultural identity, for example, congregational and denominational organizations, summer camps, religious publications, religious broadcasting, and the special purpose/interest groups described by Wuthnow (1988) not connected with denominations but serving specialized interests of particular religious identities. These institutional structures are the topics of other papers in this collection.

5. Iannaccone (1988a) presents a very interesting parallel, though somewhat different, interpretation of these regularities using a formal economic model.

6. The name-eliciting questions are the same as those used by Fischer (1982). See Fischer (1982) or Olson (1987) for further methodological details.

7. Fischer defines a personal network as the set of persons with whom an individual has important interactions. He operationalizes personal networks by asking ten name eliciting questions such as: "Who are your fellow household members?", "Who would care for your house, plants, mail, etc. when you are out of town?", "Who have you socialized with in the past three months?", and "Whose advice would you seek out when faced with an important decision?" The number of persons named is free to vary from person to person. See Fischer (1982) for a full list of questions and exact wording.

8. The concept of distinctive religious identities closely parallels, though it is not identical with, the notion of "tension." For example, ethnic religious subcultures are based on a distinctive identity even though they may be in little "tension" with the general culture.

9. I recognize, at this point, that the following speculations are merely speculations, speculations by someone with but one foot in the mainline, the other being in evangelical Protestantism.

REFERENCES

Berger, Peter L.
1967 *The Sacred Canopy.* Garden City, N. Y.: Doubleday & Co.
Davis, James Allan, and Tom W. Smith
1988 *General Social Survey* [machine readable data file]. Principal Investigator, James A. Davis; Director and Co-Principal Investigator, Tom W. Smith. NORC ed. Chicago: National Opinion Research Center, producer; Storrs, Conn.: The Roper Center for Public Opinion Research, University of Connecticut, distributor.

Durkheim, Emile
   1915   *The Elementary Forms of the Religious Life.* Translated by
          Joseph Ward Swain. New York: Free Press.
Feld, Scott L.
   1981   "The Focused Organization of Social Ties." *American Jour-
          nal of Sociology* 86:1015–1035.
Finke, Roger, and Rodney Stark
   1986   "Turning Pews into People: Estimating 19th Century
          Church Membership." *Journal for the Scientific Study of
          Religion* 25:189–192.
   1988   "Religious Economies and Sacred Canopies: Religious Mo-
          bilization in American Cities, 1906." *American Sociologi-
          cal Review* 53:41–49.
Fischer, Claude S.
   1977   *Networks and Places: Social Relations in the Urban Set-
          ting.* New York: Free Press.
   1982   *To Dwell Among Friends: Personal Networks in Town and
          City.* Chicago: University of Chicago Press.
Goffman, Erving
   1959   *The Presentation of Self in Everyday Life.* New York: Dou-
          bleday & Co.
Greeley, Andrew M.
   1972   *The Denominational Society: A Sociological Approach to
          Religion in America.* Glenview, Ill.: Scott, Foresman & Co.
Herberg, Will
   1955   *Protestant, Catholic, Jew: An Essay in American Religious
          Sociology.* Garden City, N.Y.: Doubleday & Co.
Homans, George C.
   1961   *Social Behavior: Its Elementary Forms.* New York: Har-
          court Brace & World
Iannaccone, Laurence C.
   1988a "A Formal Model of Church and Sect." *American Journal
          of Sociology* 94:S241–68.
   1988b "Religious Economies and Sacred Canopies: Cross-cultural
          Confirmation." Paper read at the annual meeting of the As-
          sociation for Sociology of Religion, Atlanta, Ga., August
          1988.
Johnson, Benton
   1963   "On Church and Sect." *American Journal of Sociology*
          28:539–549.
Lenski, Gerhard
   1961   *The Religious Factor.* New York: Doubleday & Co.

Luckmann, Thomas
  1967   *The Invisible Religion.* New York: Macmillan & Co.
McPherson, J. Miller, and Lynn Smith-Lovin
  1987   "Homophily in Voluntary Organizations." *American Sociological Review* 52:370–379.
Olson, Daniel V. A.
  1987   "Networks of Religious Belonging in Five Baptist Congregations." Ph.D. diss., University of Chicago.
Roof, Wade Clark
  1978   *Community and Commitment: Religious Plausibility in a Liberal Protestant Church.* New York: Pilgrim Press.
Roof, Wade Clark, and William McKinney
  1987 *American Mainline Religion: Its Changing Shape and Future.* New Brunswick, N.J.: Rutgers University Press.
Stark, Rodney, and William Sims Bainbridge
  1985   *The Future of Religion: Secularization, Revival, and Cult Formation.* Berkeley, Calif.: University of California Press.
Stark, Rodney, and Roger Finke
  1988   "American Religion in 1776: A Statistical Portrait." *Sociological Analysis* 49:39–51.
Stark, Rodney, and Charles Glock
  1968   *American Piety.* Berkeley, Calif.: University of California Press.
Verbrugge, Lois M.
  1977   "The Structure of Adult Friendship Choices." *Social Forces* 56:576–597.
Wirth, Louis
  1938   "Urbanism as a Way of Life." *American Sociological Review* 44:1–24.
Wuthnow, Robert
  1988   *The Restructuring of American Religion: Society and Faith Since World War II.* Princeton, N.J.: Princeton University Press.

2

Denominational Identity and the Church School— Teasing Out a Relationship

Mary Elizabeth Moore and Allen J. Moore

In this congregation, the church school is an odd place to look for identity formation.

You will find that we have no identity here.

Being pluralistic is our identity.

Three church leaders raise clearly the issues that pervade this study. What is the role of the church school in transmitting denominational identity or culture? What can one say about denominational identity at all in an "old-line" denomination that attempts to be inclusive across race, gender, class, and belief? Is denominational identity diffuse or nonexistent, or does the identity itself embrace pluralism?

The purpose of this chapter is to explore how the church school in mainline Protestant churches contributes to denominational identity as well as to a broad Christian or Protestant identity. Many today argue that mainline Protestantism is in decline. A factor in the decline seems to be a loss of interest and participation in the church school and youth movements, which have been a major force historically in shaping religious identity.

Although denominations use terms in various ways, the term "Christian education" here is used to refer to the entire educative life of a congregation or denomination, that is, all aspects of the life of the community that foster the formation and transformation of faith. The term "church school" refers to all of the educational settings and groups that are designed intentionally to sponsor persons on their journeys of faith. The Sunday school (the name inherited from the eighteenth- and nineteenth-century movement) is the formal class structure, usually taking place on Sunday, in which persons gather for concentrated study of the Christian faith.

The focus of this chapter is on the church school. This can only be studied, however, in relation to Christian education more broadly conceived and the Sunday school more specifically designated, especially since popular understandings of Christian education often make no distinctions among the three. In fact, to the exasperated groans of educators, many local churches collapse all of Christian education into the Sunday school. We want to avoid such a collapse with vigor, but we want also to acknowledge the interplay among the various elements of educational ministry.

In this study we explore denominational identity in two ways. The first is a brief historical overview of Christian education in Protestant society with particular attention to the Sunday school movement. Several significant histories are already available, and our effort here is simply to provide a brief historical context. Second, we offer a case study of a mainline local church as a way to explore the social role that the church school has in the life of that congregation. We will draw conclusions regarding the church school in modern Protestantism.

A Historical Glance at the Church School

The Jewish and Christian movements have always practiced education in some form. To teach and form disciples is critical to the very mission of the Christian church. Throughout history, Christian education has included both formal and informal structures of teaching. The church has taught both by what it does (socialization) and by what it says (instruction). The weight that Christian movements have given to each of these has varied greatly across time and place (Grimes 1972, 19). For example, the church in the Middle Ages depended largely upon the sacraments, the liturgy, and the visual arts for teaching.

Martin Luther is often credited with establishing the formal day school as the major thrust of Christian education. For him, schooling was not only essential for developing Christian identity but also for preparing persons for civic and church leadership. John Calvin insisted that the duty of the congregation was to teach its members the scriptures and to instruct them in matters of doctrine. Within the Moravian, Pietist, and Methodist movements, schooling structures included day schools, Sunday schools and colleges. In addition, these movements depended heavily on a variety of fellowship groups, such as class meetings. The fellowship groups were designed for mutual support in the life of salvation.

Current streams of Christian education are undoubtedly influenced by these several Christian traditions. Even more dominant has been the influence of the Sunday school movement, which is perpetuated either intentionally or unintentionally in many programs of Christian education within mainline Protestant denominations today.

Although the Sunday school movement had its origins in the late eighteenth century in England, its genius was realized in nineteenth-century Protestantism in the United States. The movement in this country was shaped largely by a particular historical context, sometimes called Protestant Zionism (Lynn 1976, 8). The Sunday school was integral to the ecology of religious and social forces (Lynn 1976, 9–10).

A leading factor in the success of the Sunday school in the nineteenth century was that the vision of the country was integrally linked to the expansion of Protestantism. What we now call the mainline Protestant churches were becoming the established churches of the nation. Kenneth Scott Latourette describes this as a great century in the expansion of Protestant Christianity (Latourette 1953:1226ff.). The motivations for expansion were born out of revivals and the rise of voluntary associations, along with the desire on the part of many private individuals to reform society and to realize a better life in the United States. The Sunday school in this era was a volunteer lay movement, interdenominational in character.

Two forces led to the decline of the Sunday school as a volunteer association independent of denominational control. The first of these was the rise of denominational identity in the late nineteenth century. As Martin Marty has written, persons had religious freedom to make choices in a land where religion was separated from the state, and the growing complexity of the land led to an increased need for a unique group identity. These factors together fed a growing competition among the denominations (Marty 1976, 5–8). Denominations attempted to define their uniqueness more clearly and to compete with one another in gaining members.

The second force leading to the shift was closely related to the first. The competition among denominations led to more interest in controlling the Sunday school. The domestication of the Sunday school was initiated by the denominations in the late nineteenth century and was completed by the 1920s. The Sunday school shifted from an extra-church agency to a denominational program concerned with the evangelization of children and youth and the formation of denominational identity (Seymour 1982).

The power of the Sunday school is attested by Sydney Ahlstrom when he writes: "Although they necessarily mirrored the country's values, the Sunday schools did produce a pious and knowledgeable laity on a scale unequal anywhere in Christendom" (Ahlstrom 1972, 742). On the other hand, the reformers of the Sunday school in the second half of the twentieth century have often not recognized that the social and religious environment that made possible the Sunday school movement was altered, and new forms of Christian education would be needed for a different historical situation. The Sunday school was so grounded in a popular culture that the shift of Protestant denominations to the margins of that culture would naturally affect the schools of those denominations. The problems facing the church schools were cultural, not educational.

As Lynn suggests, the ecology that made possible a strong Sunday school still exists in churches "which have adhered to the spirit and form of nineteenth-century evangelical Protestantism" (Lynn 1976, 13). For the majority of mainline Protestant churches, however, questions regarding the church school and denominational identity remain.

A Local Church Tells Its Story

To explore particularities in the relationship between the modern church school and denominational identity, an ethnographic study was conducted in one congregation in the southwestern United States.[1] The methodology of the research included observations, interviews, and an examination of written materials.[2] Let us hear the story of one mainline Protestant congregation, a congregation that generously agreed to take part with us in this study.

On First Meeting

Walking onto the grounds of this Protestant church, one meets the grandeur of a large sanctuary building; the quiet of the gardens; a building with offices, library, classrooms, and parlor; and the chapel nestled into one corner of the church's block. The church of more than one thousand members is affiliated with the United Church of Christ (UCC). It is located in a large metropolitan area, but its home is a college town of thirty-three thousand inhabitants—a town whose earlier settlers were largely Congregationalists from New England. The church was once the community church for the town; today it is the only church located in the central village area.

The point of entrance for most newcomers to this church is the sanctuary, where Sunday morning worship takes place. On either side of the main sanctuary doors, worshipers see two large wood carvings, the one on the right depicting the parable of the sower sowing seeds on different soils, and the one on the left, the story of Moses and the burning bush. When one proceeds through the entrance, one is greeted at one of the inner doors by one or two persons with a smile and a Sunday bulletin. The cover of the weekly bulletin always includes three symbols—the logo of the United Church of Christ, a drawing of Moses before the burning bush, and a drawing of the sower spreading seed.

As one comes to know this congregation better, one meets these symbols again and again. The weekly newsletter is named *Fire-Seed,* and alongside the title are the same pictures of Moses and the sower. Beneath the title is an explanation: "Moses and the burning bush and the Sower who went forth to sow, the carvings on our sanctuary doors, symbolize the new life alight and growing in our congregation."

Inside Worship

This is a congregation where a large percentage of the congregation gathers on Sundays for worship. When ushers are welcoming persons into the sanctuary, they search for the children so that they can give each child a children's bulletin. These bulletins are filled with activities, such as drawing, coloring, matching, and memorizing. Almost every week the children see the words "Jesus" and "love," and very frequently, "care" and "home."

Sitting in the sanctuary, one is surrounded by space—a high ceiling, large side aisles, and a raised altar area in the front. The focus of the altar is a large cross, under which is the table and Bible. Glancing around the sanctuary on any Sunday, one sees town leaders from the city government, school board, and civic organizations. One sees residents of the local retirement communities, university professors and staff and students, local school teachers, children, youth, nuclear families and single persons. The congregation is mostly Euro-American, but other ethnic groups and nationalities are also represented and active.

Worship is the place where music flows through the vaulted sanctuary with full tones—where the tones of bell choirs, an adult choir, a youth choir, a pipe organ, or a brass ensemble may be heard. Worship is the place where children present a special musical production every year.

Worship is the place where the preaching reminds the people of the love of God, the foibles of human beings, the meaning of being a "resurrection people," the mission of the church in the world, and the cost of discipleship, even "risking your life." The preaching follows the seasons of the church year, and the seasons are commemorated in the design of the whole service. Stories of the people are often woven into the sermon or other parts of the worship. On confirmation Sunday, the sermon included excerpts of the confirmands' statements of faith.

Worship is the place where certain liturgical acts take place every Sunday—where the flow of the liturgy always begins with praise, followed by confession and the proclamation of God's redemptive acts, followed by the responding in faith and the scattering of the people to serve.

Inside the Classes

Every Sunday at 9 A.M. three adult classes meet in this church while the children attend choir or play or go to the nursery. Classes for children and youth meet about 10:15, when the young people leave early from the worship service. All of these groups meet in the building adjoining the sanctuary. What happens in these classes? What kind of identity formation takes place?

These questions receive various answers, depending on whom you ask. One member of the church council said, "In this congregation, the church school is an odd place to look for identity formation." The assistant pastor said that he thought the identity was "dependent on the Sunday morning worship service, for which there was no substitute." He went on to say that all of the rest become "separate things."

On the other hand, one second grader said that the most important thing about the church for her was the church school, and her favorite place in the church was the church school room. Many young people, in fact, named a teacher as a significant person in their faith journey. One older child, when asked about significant persons, said, "Mostly my Sunday school teacher—she takes time to explain; she is not mean and she does not make you do things." The same child said, "We always do fun things in Sunday school and go places with the church; it's fun and that makes me like the church more." Other children and youth also named significant teachers and youth leaders as well as pastors and former pastors. One adult also attested that more relationality existed in the church school than in worship, and more identity formation took place there as well. In fact, class discussions sometimes "just keep going through worship." In short, many voices spoke to the role of the church school; no easy answers were given to our questions.

Adult Classes

Many different activities take place in the church school classes. The three Sunday adult classes have three different foci. The Adult Forum involves many of the retired members and is coordinated by an active lay member or one of the pastors. It is often led by visitors on various theological and social topics, and the number of participants varies from topic to topic. For example, the topic of homosexuality attracted a larger group than usual. On one Sunday the group was smaller (12–15), but the topic of prison reform evoked such interest that people began to ask what they could do to respond. One woman in the class was involved in the prison system, and people lingered after class to discuss the action issues further with her.

The People's Class, led by the senior pastor, is generally a theological or biblical series that extends for a few weeks. In that class, as in the others, different perspectives are freely voiced, sometimes with the pastor submitting an opinion that is clearly different from someone else's.

The third Sunday morning adult class is a small group led by a seminary graduate and called "What Can I Believe?" This class deals with such existential questions as the experience of the absence of God and the despair involved in seeing our country's involvement in tragic events, such as the bombing of Hiroshima or the major oil spill in Alaska.

In addition, other classes meet for special series, like the parenting class and Lenten groups. These various classes were described by the senior pastor as people "aggregating into groups of common concern." Sometimes people in one group are aware of other groups, and sometimes they are not. In fact, the Christian education board, which is not solely responsible for adult education, does not have a full picture of the various groups that gather.

Classes for Children and Youth

With all of this activity among adults, what is going on with children and youth? Most Sundays, they meet in classes about 40–45 minutes. The length of time seems short to the teachers and to the Christian education board; in fact, the education board has been seeking ways to strengthen the education of parents so that they can do more at home to supplement the classes.

The Sunday classes gather children across grades: preschool, kindergarten to second grade, third and fourth grades, fifth and sixth grades, junior high and senior high. The staffing and tending of all of these classes is the responsibility of the Christian education board and the associate pastor. In fact, all of these people know the teachers, children, and youth by name, and they also know when problems arise like a cancelled choir practice or a missing teacher. They discuss such problems in their monthly meetings and follow up with a plan of resolution.

The board seeks inclusiveness by encouraging men as well as women to teach the children and lead youth groups. Men are involved across the ages, and two men co-chair the board. In another aspect of inclusiveness, however, one parent questions whether inclusive language is used as carefully in children's classes as in worship.

Another question that has received considerable discussion has been the question of content. The classes for children usually use "Discipleship Alive" curriculum during the school year, and the Christian education board and associate pastor create special studies for the summers. The study this summer will be "The Community of Faith," and topics include Buddhists, Jews, Catholics, retired persons, refugees, the mayor, and handicapped persons.

The "Discipleship Alive" curriculum is jointly published by seven denominations, including the United Church of Christ. The thematic content accents Jesus Christ and the relationship between God and humanity. An insert includes information about the denomination and suggestions for activities and resources that can be used to supplement the curriculum or to provide resources for special events.

Some teachers follow the curriculum closely, and some modify it or create their own lesson plans. In all cases, teachers ask many questions, and the older children and youth ask questions and express opinions as well. When the fifth and sixth graders were studying Christ in art, they readily identified the pictures of Christ they liked and those they did not. Their favorite was the black madonna.

A glimpse into two classes will give a sense of the interactions. The kindergarten to second grade class is taught by one of the fathers of a child in the class. He greets each child by name as the children line up to check their names on the attendance chart. The children engage in many activities on any Sunday morning. On one Sunday they began by passing an offering can and recalling the Bible story from the week before. The teacher read the children a story about Francis of Assisi and led a discussion about begging and giving up things. The children then worked with a picture chart on what people need to live, and the teacher gave the children pumpkin seeds. They ended the morning by making puppets or drawing pictures of flowers that grow from seeds. The teacher praised the children for their "very clever" work, remarking that they were geniuses. When some of the boys made GI Joe dolls with their puppets, he reminded them that "they could be peaceful and not shoot other people." At the end of the session, the teacher knelt at eye level and brought the children into a circle holding hands or touching elbows, whichever they preferred. He thanked God for bringing them together and for the very nice puppets and pictures they had created. The teacher reflected later that he wants the kids to feel comfortable and happy here and, also, to be socially aware. In the third and fourth grade class on Palm Sunday, a young teacher led the children through the events of Holy Week. She asked the children many questions in outlining the events of the week. She asked what parables are and why Jesus was angry at the money changers in the temple. As the session went on, the children themselves asked more questions, such as why the crowd shouted "Crucify him!" As the class drew to a close, the teacher explained that Jesus asked why God had forsaken him. The teacher challenged the children to think about what this meant. She first suggested that they ask their parents, and then she said, "No, I hope you will think about it." The second teacher supplemented the discussion from time to time, and the two teachers discussed the class briefly at the end of the session. One said she wanted the children "to know how much they need to know;" the other said the most important thing to communicate is "that God loves them."

In addition to regular Sunday classes, one other formal class must be mentioned; children, youth, and adults regularly report how much they value confirmation. A youth who had already been confirmed reported that "confirmation class made a big difference, and that was when I considered myself as having faith." The senior and associate pastors generally lead the twelve-week confirmation series.

Inside Other Significant Groups

In addition to classes, the church has ongoing youth groups, camps and all-church fellowship events that are sponsored by the Christian education board. Other groups also meet with self-conscious educational goals, even if not with a sense of being a formal part of the educational program.

Christian Education Communities

Inside the youth groups, one finds leaders who have worked with the youth over a period of time. The associate pastor normally leads the senior high group, and she arranged for substitutes while she was on parental leave. The adult leaders bring plans to youth meetings, but the youth sometimes add new suggestions as the evening goes on, and they sometimes initiate a new activity.

The activities are varied, and the youth may do several different things in one gathering. On one evening the junior high youth took a taste test, eating foods without seeing them and trying to guess what they were. On this particular evening, the youth leader ended the session a couple of games later by saying, "Remember the taste test, and know that things are not always as they seem." On another evening, the senior high group began with volleyball, which became a big game when the junior high group appeared and challenged them. The senior high group then went inside for a serious discussion of the events of their week and a sharing by the youth leader of some artifacts from ancient Israel.

The sharing in the youth groups can be playful or serious. The senior high youth always begin by sharing what has happened to them during the previous week. They share about how busy they have been with homework and school activities, or how much fun they have when they go to the beach. On one Sunday night, a boy told about helping to lead a walkout at his school when the temperature was very hot. The students decided to take their protest to the school board.

The youth also attend camps, and they often name these camps as important to their faith journeys. The church sometimes sponsors one of its youth to participate in a UCC-sponsored tour, such as a tour to Honduras or an upcoming youth trip to a Just Peace church gathering in Germany. The youth bell choir also travels to a different region of the United States every year.

The Christian education board oversees all of these youth groups and activities, and they also take responsibility for intergenerational fellowship events in the church. For example, they sponsored a potluck dinner, featuring a program of music with a young musician who grew up in the church. Every year they sponsor and plan the family camp for the whole church.

Other Educational Communities

In addition to the officially sponsored education events, many groups meet in the church with educational purposes in mind. One person said that some of the most important adult education happens in the boards of the church, particularly the Board of Deacons. The boards engage in searching discussions of their mission and of issues. For example, when the Christian education board described their mission, they moved quickly into raising unanswered questions, saying finally that they wanted to talk about these matters further.

The congregation as a whole is also seen as a community where big questions are pondered and decisions are made. For example, the congregation will discuss and vote upon the proposed church covenant. People frequently mention in conversation that the final authority for them lies in the congregation and that major decisions are made by the congregation as a whole. They also point with appreciation to the fact that the Sunday bulletin begins the list of ministers with "each church member."

Emerging Themes in the Congregation

Several themes emerge with prominence both in the church school and in the rest of the church's life, and some are accented in one arena more than another. We will explore the range.

Common Themes Throughout

The most frequently mentioned theme throughout the church is diversity and inclusiveness. These words are spoken in almost every setting and by almost every person interviewed. One junior high youth said, "The most important thing about our religion is that we don't exclude people." The same young person added, "Religion is what you believe yourself, not what others make you believe." This sentiment was echoed in the faith statements of the confirmands and by many adults and children.

The diversity and inclusiveness was sometimes expressed in statements of what we are not, such as "we are not evangelical," "we are not totalitarian," or "we are not doctrinal." Other times it was expressed in terms of what we are, such as "we are liberal and inclusive" or "this congregation stresses personal faith rather than group denominational belief." The testimonies stress diversity and inclusiveness rather than UCC identity, but one youth said that to be UCC "means to respect other people and what they say and believe."

A second and related theme is freedom. The value of freedom is also expressed in personal testimonies, sometimes drawing an association with the Puritan heritage of the UCC. Freedom is described as persons' being free to speak their own voices or to think freely. You find this freedom reinforced in the church school when teachers give the children choices among activities, and you find it reinforced in the youth groups when youth are left free to suggest alternative activities. In church boards and other settings, people are quick to point out that authority is spread out in this congregation.

A third very common theme is Jesus Christ. The sanctuary, with its cross, wounded lamb, and stained glass windows, calls attention to the Christ, as do the liturgy and preaching. In the liturgy, people stand for the gospel lesson, and in the preaching, people are reminded that Jesus was involved in social situations and that "the resurrection defines us." The curriculum resources used in the children's classes focus on Jesus one quarter of every year, as well as during Advent, Christmas, Lent, and Easter. One fifth grader described the faith of the congregation in terms of "Jesus and the different things that he did."

Another theme is transcendence, or God. Just as the curriculum resources focus strongly on the relationship between God and humanity, church leaders and teachers named that relationship as a central value. A junior high youth expressed that the most important belief of the congregation was "belief in God and what he had done." The liturgy also focuses on praise of God, God's redemptive acts, and responding to God in faith.

The theme of action appears in all aspects of congregational life, including the church school. The curriculum resources and teaching styles encourage much action in the classroom, and they point to action options in the community. The UCC curriculum insert is particularly filled with action suggestions, including such ideas as writing to other UCC churches and participating in the One Great Hour of Sharing offering (taken in churches of many denominations for world relief).

Although action in general is valued, a specific kind of action receives considerable attention in this congregation, namely the action that is directed to needs in the community and political structures. Adult classes concentrate particularly on such issues. Action projects sometimes grow from these discussions. Also, the church facilities are used extensively by community groups, and announcements of political and social events are part of every worship service.

Yet another common theme in this congregation is ecumenism. People frequently recall the history of the church as a community church, and also recall that their pastors have often come from other Protestant denominations. In fact, the congregation includes people from a variety of traditions. The plans for the youth and children's summer classes will focus on ecumenical and interfaith studies.

The last three themes to be named here emerge naturally from the others, but they are sufficiently distinctive to warrant separate mention. One is intellectual searching. Such searching takes place in classes, youth groups, and preaching. You find teachers, youth, youth leaders, and board persons asking open-ended questions and searching for answers. The Christian education board said that to be a member of this congregation means "you have not memorized something, but that you faithfully search the scripture." In fact, children, youth, and adults often describe their classes and groups as places to search and discover.

The second emerging theme is consciousness of being a congregation. This theme is much discussed in the Church Council and the several church boards. It is frequently associated with being UCC. One young person said that to be UCC was to be congregational, and others described the denomination as one where the final authority rests in the congregation.

In addition to a sense of congregational authority, people often volunteer stories of the history of this particular congregation. As the community church of the town, the church historically engaged in much community service, and this history is much remembered. The church rented space to the Jewish community until they built their temple; then, the people of the temple bought their Torah with the rent money that the church refunded to them. Also, the church helped found two retirement communities and a rehabilitation hospital, and they launched some prophetic ministries in the 1960s and early 1970s, leading to some large internal controversies.

The third theme that appears in many different centers of church life is participation. Many children and youth express that being Christian means to go to church and participate in church school. Participation is encouraged by public invitations to persons to be part of groups and activities, and also, by personal invitations from teachers, leaders, and other participants.

A Theme More Common Outside the Church School

Only one theme emerged as common in the church's life that did not also appear in the church school itself. This was the theme of consciousness of the denomination. Children and youth often paused when asked what being a UCC member meant to them, or they responded initially with an answer such as "I do not know" or "I have not thought about that." Adults would sometimes reminisce in conversations about the Congregational Church in New England. The only other context in which such consciousness was apparent was in the Church Council meeting when people joked about changes in church practices that had come about by the influence of other denominations. Though many of the themes described on these pages can be said to be common themes in the United Church of Christ, the specific references to the denomination were few, especially in the church school.

Themes More Common Inside the Church School

Some themes actually appeared more frequently and self-consciously inside church school contexts than in other contexts. The most frequently expressed were self-acceptance and care for others. One youth said that being a member of this congregation meant "feeling good about yourself and really caring about others." The Christian education board frequently expressed their purposes in terms of these concerns. Teachers often emphasized self-acceptance and caring for others in their classes, and in the four-week parenting class, this was the central theme.

Also appearing frequently in the church school was the theme of family. Leaders in the church school often spoke of the church as an extended family, and one young person described the congregation as "part of God's family." The Christian education board sought to enhance the educational ministry through families, and the theme also appeared at times in worship. When the associate pastor took time from her parental leave to be present for confirmation, she thanked the congregation for their many ways of supporting her and her family, including the parental leave itself and the Sunday morning radio message which was broadcast following the birth of their baby. The message had touched her deeply and telling of it brought tears to her eyes.

One last theme that can be found in various contexts, but is especially emphasized in the church school, is the theme of community. The senior pastor emphasized the importance of small communities in a large congregation such as this one. He explained the need for many diverse groups where people with common interests can gather. This was underscored again by the assistant pastor, who described the congregation as a "created community" in a society where natural communities are less available. On the whole, the church school is the primary place where such groups are formed and relationships are fostered. In addition, the Christian education board spends the majority of its budget on intergenerational fellowship events such as a Halloween carnival, fellowship dinners, and family camps.

What Does This Congregation Tell Us?

Reflecting on this congregation, what do we learn about identity formation in mainline Protestant Christianity? One is aware, of course, that no congregation can be taken alone as a representative of the mainline Protestant church school. Thus, when we ask what this congregation has to teach us, the most obvious answer is that it will not tell us everything we need to know. On the other hand, it may point to some very important clues about the mainline Protestant church school and about the relation between the church school and denominational identity.

Clues About Mainline Protestant Schools

The first clue is that the role of the church school is ambiguous. Quite early in the congregational study we were offered a warning: "In this congregation, the church school is an odd place to look for identity formation." In fact, the Christian education board has a proportionally small program budget, and the Sunday classes for children and youth are fairly short (forty to forty-five minutes). Families have to decide whether the children will remain in worship or attend a class. On the other hand, much pastoral and lay leadership time is devoted to the church school.

Another ambiguity emerges because the board oversees all of Christian education, but they only have primary responsibility for groups relating to children and youth. Also, adult classes meet before worship, so adults with children often choose not to participate in these groups. The board discusses ways to coordinate educational groups more actively, but the resolution of these structural issues is not simple.

Another ambiguity lies in the language of the Christian education board itself. They describe their responsibilities as both education and fellowship, explaining them as different roles. "Education" apparently has more of a schooling connotation and "fellowship" more of a recreational connotation.

A second clue from this congregation is that no emphasis is placed on indoctrination or forming persons in particular communal beliefs. An emphasis repeated again and again in the church school is the need to encourage personal belief or personal faith and to encourage inclusiveness and respect for differences. Individual teachers or youth leaders sometimes express strong positions they want to convey to others, but they name these as their own positions and not the position of the whole church. Certainly, class discussions within all age groups frequently surface differences.

A third clue emerges in this congregation where many children and youth and a few adults are deeply involved in the church school, and other active church leaders are not at all involved. The church school seems to be important to a small number of the congregation, but it is very important to them. In fact, for some children, youth, and adults the church school settings are named as more meaningful to them than worship.

Closely related, the church school fosters community and affirmation in small groups as well as a sense of relationship with the congregation. Many people describe their relationship with the congregation in terms of their relationship with their small group.

Yet another clue about the mainline Protestant church school is that it prepares persons for membership. The Christian education board in this church is self-conscious about this role, and most people in the church look to confirmation as the key preparation time for church membership. One children's teacher described the Sunday classes as a time to study things that children will learn more about during confirmation. Young people and adults who have been confirmed often look back on their own confirmation as a time of growing commitment and responsibility.

Another clue that one can draw from this congregation is that the church school provides a context for intellectual searching. Adult studies are designed to search large questions, be they theological, biblical, or sociopolitical. Likewise, children are encouraged to ask questions; in fact, pastors, youth leaders, and Sunday school teachers often interact with people of all ages by asking questions and encouraging them to do the same.

One final clue regarding the mainline Protestant church school is that the content offered in the church school is ambiguous. Most of the Sunday morning classes for children and youth are guided by the curriculum resources, but teachers and Christian education board people often express a wish that the young people of the church were more biblically literate. Also, the church provides inserts with supplemental resources on the UCC denomination, but the conscious awareness of the UCC traditions are minimal among the young people. In another vein, the value of transcendence is lifted up by many in the congregation, but the practice of prayer or meditation is modest in the church school settings. The discussions of God and God's relationship with the world are more pronounced than the practice of the presence of God. The Christian education board is conscious of the ambiguous content, as are some teachers who have expressed themselves on this subject. Some board members long for more enculturation with specific content, such as the Lord's Prayer and biblical stories. But they also say they do not want to teach these things at the expense of the children's understanding and their sense of support and relationship.

We began and ended this list of clues with issues of ambiguity, and this issue may point to the dilemma in mainline Protestant church schools where diversity, inclusiveness, self-acceptance, and caring for others are especially valued. The emphasis is on a community where everyone is encouraged to think freely and to grow in personal faith.

Clues about Denominational Identity Formation

To say that one cannot learn much about denominational identity from a congregation that is diverse and inclusive would be a hasty and inadequate conclusion. One member of this congregation said of her community, "Being pluralistic is our identity." So how does the church school relate to denominational identity formation in such a congregation?

One obvious clue is that the church school reinforces the values of the congregation. This is evidenced most vividly in the description above, as we compared the themes found in the church school with those found in other contexts of the church's life. The overlap in dominant themes is striking, and the formation that takes place in one setting seems to reinforce the formation in others. Even those themes that do appear more in one context are not completely lacking in others. A second clue is that the church school supplements congregational life by creating small communities for affirmation and caring. We noted above that only a portion of the congregation participates in these church school communities, but those who do participate express great appreciation.

A third clue emerges from the organization of the church. Structural compartmentalization complicates the coordination of congregational life and Christian formation. The church is structurally organized to focus the church school on service within the congregation, while service outside the congregation is designated formally to other boards. Such structural separations are accentuated by other separations, such as that between adult studies and programs for children and youth.

The last clue regarding the church school and the formation of denominational identity is probably the most important. The formation of conscious denominational identity is probably what the church school does the least, but the church school probably does a great deal to foster denominational beliefs and values. The beliefs and values that seem particularly important to this congregation are Christ-centeredness, transcendence, diversity and inclusiveness, action in the church and world, and a sense of relationship and participation in the congregation. The kind of ethnographic, descriptive research that we have done here does not lend itself to drawing cause-and-effect conclusions, but one can surmise that the life of the church school reinforces and supplements the identity of this church. However unconscious the denominational identity may be, many common UCC beliefs, practices, and values are commonly shared in this community, even in the midst of its genuine diversity and inclusiveness. The correspondence is striking between themes in this local church, for example, and those identified in the UCC denomination in William Newman's chapter in this volume (ch. 14).

Conclusions

Such a study as this one raises as many questions as it answers. It does, however, shed some interesting light on the basic questions of the relationship between the church school and denominational identity in mainline Protestant churches. Three broad conclusions are offered here, but they are intended more as invitations for further thinking than as final and complete conclusions.

The first conclusion is that the church school reinforces denominational culture in much the same way that the earlier Sunday school movement reinforced the broader Protestant culture of the United States. The church school is no more independent of the church's life today than the nineteenth-century Sunday school movement was independent of the frontier culture in the United States. They exist together in an ecology of cultural transmission and learning. The culture has changed, however, and the culture transmitted in a mainline Protestant church school is more like the culture of the denomination as a whole (or 1980s United States Protestantism) than like the culture transmitted by the Sunday school movement of an earlier era.

A second conclusion is that information goals and formation goals are often seen in tension, especially in denominations where information is not defined as the center of formation. Many mainline denominations understand themselves to be nondoctrinal or nonliteralistic, viewing creedal or biblical information as important to formation but not as the center of formation. For such denominations, teaching the church's traditions and developing biblical literacy are considered important, but neither is equated with forming Christians.

Denominational identity is clearly formed in the church school if one understands identity in terms of shared beliefs, values, and practices; identity is not formed in the church school if it is understood in terms of learning certain core information and affirming certain orthodox beliefs. The congregation studied here is homogeneous in some interesting ways; it is particularly homogeneous in its celebration of heterogeneity. One does not have to praise heterogeneity in order to join the church, and a few people expressed the wish for the church to be more clear on what it believed and taught. On the other hand, the culture of the church is one in which the heterogeneity is celebrated and supported. People of all ages point with pride to their diversity and inclusiveness, and they openly discuss their differences in classes, board meetings, and sidewalk conversations.

If identity formation implies the formation of identical beliefs, values, and practices, the church school in mainline Protestant churches probably contributes little to that enterprise. If, however, identity formation is a process of incorporating persons into a community of shared beliefs, values, and practices where diversity and inclusiveness are honored, the church school may well play a major part.

NOTES

1. Special thanks go to Kathi Breazeale Finnell and Randy Litchfield who conducted most of the data-gathering and participated helpfully in the analysis.

2. The method is more specifically described in Mary Elizabeth Moore, "Teach Us to Teach," unpublished paper, 1986. The method has been influenced by the ethnographic work of Victor Turner and Clifford Geertz, the ethogenic research of Rom Harre, and the congregational studies of Jackson Carroll, Carl Dudley, William McKinney, and James Hopewell. The method has been used and tested in two major series of research studies, both of which are still in process.

REFERENCES

Ahlstrom, Sydney E.
    1972   *A Religious History of the American People.* New Haven, Conn.: Yale University Press.
Foster, Charles R.
    1978   "Looking from the Past into the Future of Christian Education." Paper presented at the Decision Point: Church School conference sponsored by the General Board of Discipleship, United Methodist Church.
Grimes, L. Howard
    1972   "Church Education: A Historical Survey and a Look to the Future." *Perkins School of Theology Journal* 25 (Spring):19–38.
Latourette, Kenneth Scott
    1953   *A History of Christianity.* New York: Harper & Brothers.

Lynn, Robert W.
  1976 "A Historical Perspective on the Future of American Religious Education." In *Foundations for Christian Education in an Era of Change,* edited by Marvin J. Taylor, 7–19. Nashville: Abingdon Press.
Lynn, Robert W., and Elliott Wright
  1980 *The Big Little School,* 2nd edition. Nashville: Abingdon Press.
Marty, Martin E.
  1976 *A Nation of Behavers.* Chicago: University of Chicago Press.
Moore, Mary Elizabeth
  1986 "Teach Us to Teach: Ethnic Congregations' Teaching through Their Stories." Paper presented in convocation, School of Theology at Claremont, Calif.
Schmidt, Stephen A.
  1983 *A History of the Religious Education Association.* Birmingham, Ala.: Religious Education Press.
Seymour, Jack L.
  1982 *From Sunday School to Church School.* Washington, D.C.: University Press of America.

3

Ritual and the Transmission of a Cultural Tradition: An Ethnographic Perspective

Keith A. Roberts

Corporate celebration of ritual lies at the heart of any culture, for it is there that the central values and the myths by which a society understands itself are lifted up and sacralized. The word "worship" is itself derived from "worth-ship," which means "the state or condition of worth." According to theologian H. Richard Niebuhr (1960), in the act of worship one is recentering one's life around core values which, in one's more reflective moments, one recognizes as supreme. In this view, worship sacralizes central values and places those values back in the center of the life of the worshipers.

Anthropologists confirm what theologians assert: myths[1] are set forth in ritual, and those myths shape the way people conceive of their social and natural environment and the way they relate to that larger world. Indeed, ritual enactments are central because they sacralize (make sacred) the myths and make the faith real and compelling in the lives of participants. As Clifford Geertz (1966, 4) puts it, they "clothe conceptions [of reality] with such an aura of factuality that [they] seem uniquely realistic."

Any understanding of subcultures is enhanced by focusing explicitly on the group's rituals; indeed, some family scholars believe that a family unit cannot be fully understood without an understanding of the family's myths and rituals (Pillari 1986; Satir 1988). Ritual is obviously much more central in religious groups, but its familiarity may also obscure our ability to recognize latent functions and subtle differences in rules about religious rituals.

74

When a society is changing, the unchangeability of rituals may be a source of comfort to those who care to share them. Indeed, the unchanging nature of rituals may contribute to their role as plausibility structures (Ducey 1977). However, the role of ritual in structural change is equally interesting; Ducey reports, in an ethnographic study of a Chicago church, that changes in the organizational structure of the congregation were made possible because of changes in the liturgy. Liturgical reform was a necessary precursor. Thus ritual patterns can help to entrench a group's values and make them less pervious to change, but they may also legitimate and even sacralize change.

The question for us in this context is how ritual becomes an important element in transmitting culture within a denomination, and how norms about the performance of rituals limit the capacity of ritual to play its appointed role. In this chapter I will set forth parameters for understanding liturgy as culture. Rather than focusing on one denomination, I will take a more general overview, attempting to set forth elements in an ethnographic analysis of Protestant Christian ritual in the United States. Some attempt will be made at contrasting denominational traditions.[2] It is important to keep in mind that mainline denominations are open systems which influence and are influenced by elements of the larger culture. Not only do denominations influence each other and become similar in certain respects, but also other ideologies and values in the society may infiltrate the culture of an open system—as will be discussed in the final section of this chapter.

Organizationally, I will examine five issues. The first will be the way the sequencing of the liturgy may enact and reinforce a core theological notion in Christianity. Secondly, we will see that the order and the style of worship may also reflect cultural presuppositions about statuses, roles, authority, and power within the denomination. Churches in which the clergy have great power (notably in churches with a more episcopal polity or others which place the minister on a pedestal of power and prestige) often have an order of worship slightly different from that in which the church is "owned" by the laity. Liturgy not only reflects myths but also transmits assumptions about status and authority in the church. Third, we will look at cultural rules within denominations regarding which senses should be employed to elicit a sense of the holy—and which senses ought not be stimulated in worship. Cultural rules which place a taboo on the utilization of certain senses may well banish a potentially powerful plausibility mechanism. These rules also are part of the tradition which is passed on through denominations. Fourth, we will investigate other subcultural rules about the conduct of worship—those regarding space and use of language—that may reflect either important theological themes or status and prestige emphases within the church. We will conclude with a brief look at an interesting cultural conflict over ritual that is occurring in some churches in the United States: a conflict over pledging allegiance to the American flag as part of a Christian worship service.

Mythology and the Structure of the Liturgy

Religious ritual usually involves affirmation of the groups' myths and gives emotional impulse to the belief system. Ritual may either prescribe the enactment of a story or myth, as is the case when Christians reenact Jesus's footwashing, or it may symbolically remind one of the mythology of the faith by moving participants through a series of moods. In either case, the sacred story is made to seem uniquely realistic and powerful for the celebrants. The worldview of the group is instilled more deeply into the consciousness of members. The interaction and interdependence of ritual and myth are evident in the liturgy of many Protestant denominations.[3]

Protestant theologies build substantially on the biblical notion that God established a covenant with a chosen people. If the faithful obey the commandments and work to establish a kingdom of justice and righteousness, then God will protect and provide for them. The scriptures maintain that the Hebrew people got into trouble whenever they broke the covenant, forgot the demands of justice, and ignored the sovereignty of God. In these circumstances, the prophets called the people back to the covenant, assuring them that if they would repent and renew their covenant, Yahweh would forgive them. Confession restores the violated relationship with God, as long as the people once again heed the word of God and rededicate themselves to the covenant. The New Testament renews this theme, with Jesus calling the wayward to repent and promising God's forgiveness. The most important sacrament in the Christian church is Communion. In instituting this practice, Jesus is quoted in the New Testament as inaugurating a new covenant. Covenantal theology, then, is a core Christian mythology or belief system.[4]

Many Protestant Christians are not consciously aware that the liturgy in which they participate systematically reinforces this theology. Let us look, however, at a consistent pattern that prevails in many American Protestant liturgies. Most liturgies are based on a logical pattern that moves worshipers through successive movements or moods. While there is some variation in the order of Protestant worship services, the majority of mainline American churches tend to follow, in rough outline, the themes spelled out below. In some churches, the logical sequencing of the service is made explicit through subheadings in the bulletin distributed to the congregation. Let us examine the relationship between this liturgical pattern and the mythology of the divine covenant. The myth is expressed in the form of four distinctive moods or movements which occur in the liturgy.

At the outset of the service, the liturgy is designed to create a mood of awe and praise. The architecture of the church may also enhance this sense. Many church bulletins request that worshipers sit in silence and focus their attention on a rose window or some other symbol, or on "the presence of God." The prelude is usually intended to be a powerful and inspiring piece of music that will enhance one's sense of awe. The congregation then joins together in a hymn of praise, which is frequently a joyful, uplifting song of adoration. This section we might call the Service of Praise.

Shortly after the worshipers acknowledge that they are in the presence of God, the mood shifts. The liturgy attempts to make the worshipers aware of the fact that they have not always lived in a way consistent with Christian values. They are reminded that in the push and pull of daily living, they have said an unkind word or failed to do a loving deed (sins of commission and sins of omission). The values they professed on Sunday they may have betrayed by Wednesday (if not by Sunday afternoon). Worshipers become conscious of the fact that they have violated the covenant. Hence, the second mood or theme of the liturgy is a Service of Confession, or An Act of Honesty.

This liturgical movement, however, does not end on a note of guilt. Corporate and/or silent individual confession is followed by "words of assurance," "assurance of pardon," or "word of new possibility." At this point, the congregation is assured by the minister (often through quotation of a biblical passage) that persons "who sincerely confess their sins and who renew their commitment to God are forgiven." The covenantal theme of repentance prior to renewal of the covenant is enacted. The relationship with God is restored.

The liturgy then moves to a third phase, an Affirmation of Faith, or Service of Proclamation, or Encounter with the Word. This phase is frequently the major part of Protestant services. The congregation may repeat a creed or covenant, listen to an anthem or other special music, sing a hymn of proclamation, listen to scripture, and hear a message (sermon) delivered by the clergyperson. In this phase of the ritual, the emphasis is on celebrating God's love, remembering and rehearing the Word of God, and remembering the demands of the covenant. Infant baptisms are usually a part of this movement, although churches that practice only adult baptism and view it as an act of commitment may include it as part of the final movement.

The final movement of most Protestant liturgies is a Service of Dedication. This part of worship calls for a response to God's word by the congregation. The movement is characterized by a monetary offering (a symbolic act of commitment of self and of resources), concerns of the church or announcements from the pulpit, a hymn of dedication, a charge to the congregation, a benediction, and in the more evangelical churches, an altar call. (In one liberal Methodist church that I attended, the service ended with the minister telling the congregation that God did not need them up in front of the church; God needed them out on the streets and in businesses and in the halls of justice. Therefore those who were committed to God's covenant were directed to signify their commitment by going out the door!) In short, the climax of the service is the response of the people to God's word. The people renew their resolve to live in covenant with God and to follow the moral requirements of that covenant.

In some churches, the third and fourth phases of the liturgy (proclamation and dedication) may be merged into one. In this case, some acts of dedication and commitment (such as the offering) may actually precede the sermon, and the minister essentially has the final word. (This will be discussed in the next section in more detail.) However, even in this case a hymn of dedication and a charge to the congregation usually follow the sermon.

The sequence spelled out here is clearly not universal. Indeed, in some periods of history, Christian liturgy emphasized an entirely different model of worship. Huldrych Zwingli, for example, felt that the climax of the service should be confession. Those who adopted this conception of worship believed the major portion of the service should be designed to build a sense of guilt in the worshipers. This influence can be seen in Puritan liturgies of colonial America. Some contemporary sects and evangelical groups continue to be influenced by the Zwinglian tradition in their liturgical formats. It should also be acknowledged that some Pentecostal churches and Christian sects do not have a consistent pattern of worship. The rationale for the order of worship appears to be less important than the experience of the Holy Spirit. Although emotion and experience are key elements, Pentecostal worship also reinforces a core belief system: God is alive, present, and active in believers' lives and experiences through the work of the Holy Spirit (Neitz 1987, 27).

While much of contemporary Protestant worship emphasizes proclamation and commitment, the Catholic Mass seems to place more stress on praise, with a focus on awe and majesty and wonder. This reflects a fundamental difference in Protestant and Catholic views of worship (Pratt 1964), though the distinctions are less pronounced now than they were before Vatican II. The Roman Catholic Church has historically taken an "objective" approach to the Mass. The emphasis was on glorification of God, and the liturgy was designed with that in mind. It was

[handwritten margin note: Perhaps the R.C. church believes that they]

best to have a congregation present at the celebration of Mass, but if no one came, the Mass would go on. On the other hand, a Protestant minister would scarcely think of conducting a full service of worship if no congregation gathered. The more "subjective" emphasis of the Protestant denominations tends to pay more attention to the effect of worship on the worshipers themselves. Hence, the beliefs about worship itself significantly affect the order of a liturgy and the themes it includes. The greater time commitment on "praise" versus "response of the congregation" is consistent with this subtle variation in theological emphasis.

The description provided here of the four moods of Protestant worship illustrates the relationship between myth and ritual: a covenantal mythology is enacted in the ritual by moving the congregation deliberately through four moods: praise and awe in the presence of God, humility and confession of failure to uphold one's part in the covenant, rehearing of the covenantal agreement, and rededication to that covenant. In short, ritual and belief are often closely intertwined and tend to be mutually reinforcing; they provide an interrelated system. It is noteworthy that numerous sample surveys have consistently found a high correlation between regular attendance at rituals and a high level of acceptance of the belief system of the denomination.

The image presented here of highly integrated ritual and myth needs a word of caution. Many lay people are unaware of the logical progression of the worship liturgy and of the theological basis for its order. Hence, the liturgy is viewed as just so many hymns, prayers, and scripture readings in random order. If members of the congregation are not aware of the rationale for the mood sequencing—that the service is based on a theological model—the ritual may have less power as a plausibility structure. Clearly if a participant interprets a ritual and myth as mutually supportive, the ritual and myth are likely to be mutually supportive for that person (Batson and Ventis 1982). What we do not know is how effective such a liturgical sequencing is in implicitly instilling a covenantal theology in attendees. One might argue that the order of the liturgy transmits a worldview in a way that is somewhat subliminal to the participants, though this is a thesis in need of empirical testing.

Variations on the Theme: Roles of Clergy and Laity in Responding to the Covenant

While many Protestant denominations share a basic theological framework and a similar liturgical model, there are important variations. To some extent the culture of different denominations may perpetuate different cultural assumptions about the sequencing of the liturgy. My thesis here is that liturgical style and sequence may reflect and transmit differences in conceptions of roles, power, and authority. These differences, in turn, often underlie differences in denominational polity, and almost certainly legitimate and transmit attitudes about the local organizational structure.

Before exploring this issue it is important to acknowledge that each congregation is itself a subculture with its own style and its own traditions. The diffusion of liturgical styles is no doubt enhanced by the pattern of switching denominations in the United States. Further, many seminaries have large numbers of students from other denominations (exposing those persons to the rationale for other traditions of worship), and it is not uncommon for search committees in churches with a congregational or even presbyterian polity to hire clergy who were ordained in other denominations. This is all part and parcel of mainline denominations' character as relatively open social systems.

These caveats regarding the consistency of denominational cultures notwithstanding, we can identify certain tendencies toward what Ducey (1977) calls "interaction rituals" or "mass rituals." In interaction rituals, the emphasis is more on involvement of the participants—the people in the pews. The laity are key players in the unfolding drama. Lay members may have substantial input and even control of the format of the liturgy, and the presentation may even be modified as it unfolds by spontaneous action by worshipers. The style is somewhat less formal, and the focus is on the implications of the faith for the lives of the worshipers. Churches with interaction rituals, Ducey suggests, place responsibility for all aspects of church life and mission squarely on the laity, with members of the congregation expected to share in responsibility for articulating the theological perspective of the church.

The historic Protestant doctrine of the "priesthood of all believers" is more operative in the worshiping community when the ritual is interactional. Leadership roles of clergy and laity may be interchangeable in interaction rituals; either the minister or a member of the congregation may read scripture, say the "word of assurance," pronounce the benediction, or deliver the message. Nor is the clergy differentiated as completely by distinguishing attire. Interaction rituals are common where the laity "own" the church.

Mass rituals are often found in traditions referred to as "high church," with control of the service in the hands of the formally trained clergy. The authority figure is in charge of organizing the service and is in control of its execution. Congregational response is less emphasized, and a sense of awe, dignity, and reverence is cultivated throughout the service. Because of the "mystification" of the authority structure (Berger 1969; Berger and Luckmann 1967) and the apparently unchanging nature of the liturgy, mass rituals, Ducey suggests, may create strong plausibility structures.

Also in mass rituals, according to Ducey, the service of the word and the service of dedication phases of worship are more likely to be collapsed, and in fact the emphasis is more on proclamation of the word. The sermon may come toward the end of the worship service, followed only by a closing hymn and the benediction. Ducey suggests that this pattern usually occurs in churches in which the clergy are more remote from the congregation and are set aside as "special" and "holy." Indeed, when the minister has finished preaching, the ritual is essentially over. The positioning of the sermon is so dominant that it competes with scripture in importance (Ducey 1977, 157). One might even go further and say that in such a service the scripture is viewed by many attendees as simply preparatory for the sermon. The real meaning and substance of the worship service is believed to reside in the preacher's message. One notes how some Protestants seem to feel that they have not really been to worship unless there is a homily by the pastor. The final hymn and benediction are viewed primarily as "closure" for the service.

Mass rituals are also described as ones in which rules are more clearly delineated about what clergy can do and what lay persons can do. In mass rituals, the clergy role is more sacralized, and such sacred roles as reading of scripture (or perhaps just the reading of the gospels) is limited to the clergy. Likewise, the sermon, the benediction, word of pardon, and other special parts in the drama may be reserved for ordained clergy. The clergy are also set apart by clothing styles. In a variety of ways, lay people are symbolically reminded that theirs is a secondary role—both in the liturgy and in the power structures of the church.

Churches practicing mass rituals may also prefer written prayers which have been formulated by a denominational commission (preferably in a previous century) rather than extemporaneous prayers which are created on the spot by worship leaders. In mass ritual, "the authority of [the prayer] seems to be proportional to its distance from the worshiper" (Ducey 1977, 106).

One might also argue that mass rituals emphasize the otherness of God—the transcendence and difference. The hierarchical structure may likewise communicate the ultimate insignificance of the layperson. Thus, mass rituals may stress transcendence of God and a greater emphasis on objective style of worship. On the other hand, interactional ritual is more concerned with subjective experience of worship by the worshiper and on the immanence of God. Role specialization and liturgical format may be correlated both to theological themes (immanence vs. transcendence of God) and to cultural norms about who has power and authority in the church.

Perhaps instead of a typology, it would be more helpful to think of these as two ends of a continuum, with various denominational styles being closer to one end or the other. Regardless, Ducey's thesis is that mass rituals are correlated to hierarchical authority structures. The ordained leaders are most important; they have the final word on almost everything. Interaction rituals are stressed in more egalitarian churches, which emphasize the "priesthood of all believers" in organizational matters as well as in written word. Frequently, the laity have the final word—in liturgy and in local church policy. My observation, based on a small sample of several dozen churches, suggests that this pattern of the sermon as the climax of worship is more common in churches which are very hierarchical and/or in which the clergyperson has elevated status and authority. Placement of the offering, announcements of mission opportunities, Communion, and other acts of dedication after the sermon appear more common in churches that stress a sense of community, shared responsibility for the theology and mission of the church, and congregational polity. My observation has been that United Church of Christ and Presbyterian congregations are very likely to have such a liturgical format.

Baptist churches utilize congregational polity, of course, but each local church varies in how much authority is ascribed to the pastor. In some Baptist congregations the minister has almost total control of the church, while in others the ordained minister may have authority only in limited areas of church policy. If Ducey's thesis is correct, and I believe it may have merit, one might expect to find the sermon located at the conclusion of the service in those Baptist churches where the pastor has more complete authority and control, and located more at the middle of the service where responsibility and authority is shared more widely. Likewise, other elements of local congregational participation in formulating and shaping the theology of the church would be evidenced.

In Episcopal and Methodist churches, which officially practice an episcopal polity, placement of the sermon at the conclusion of the service seems more common. However, in some local Methodist congregations the subordinate status of the laity is downplayed and the historic Protestant theme of the "priesthood of all believers" is stressed. In these congregations, the climax of the ritual is frequently the congregational response. I would emphasize, however, that my own sample is very small, and I have seen no systematic studies of this hypothesis.[5] The correlation does suggest an issue that any ethnography of worship in a specific denomination would need to explore.

While many denominations may share the myth structure of "covenantal theology," in the culture of some denominations and some local churches the implicit meaning is that the clergy are the nearly indispensable conduits to God, and it is they who will lead the faithful to honor that sacred covenant. In other groups, covenantal theology means that all members share equally in responsibility for understanding and implementing the divine covenant. The central issue is this: the structure of the liturgy (both the order of worship and the fulfillment of key roles) often reflects deeper structural assumptions about authority, roles of clergy, and roles of laypersons within the church and the denomination. The liturgy reflects those assumptions, but it also perpetuates (transmits) those assumptions by highlighting either the role of the clergy or the response of the laity as the climax of worship. The structure of the liturgy communicates something about who is really important in the church—who has the final word. Ritual transmits not only cultural values and myths but also reinforces assumptions underlying stratification and organization of the church.[6]

Ducey (1977) is convinced that modification of the liturgy was a critical precursor to structural reorganization of the Church of the Three Crosses in Chicago. As lay people gained more control over the format and presentation of the liturgy and as mobilization of the congregation came to be seen as the climax of worship, the congregation came to be more egalitarian, more involved in articulating the theological position of the church, and more active in shaping the mission and ministry of the congregation.

Cultural Rules About Stimulating the Sense of Sacredness

Cultures always generate their own ideas about how the sacred or the holy will be experienced. Among many Native American groups in North and South America, for example, hallucinogenic drugs are considered normal during worship and are believed to facilitate communion with the supernatural world. Likewise, Christian groups have their own set of assumptions about how holiness is experienced. More specifically, each group has rules, unwritten but nonetheless strongly enforced, about which of the five senses are appropriate to stimulate as part of worship. Since sacralization of values and a worldview are central functions of ritual, the issue here is which senses are employed to elicit sacred moods and motivations.

Some Protestant groups seem to border on sensory deprivation in worship, believing the auditory sense to be the only one that should be stimulated, at least on a regular basis, during worship. Other groups, such as the Episcopal Church, are rich in the variety of senses

utilized. Part of the aversion to the use of certain types of visual stimulation and of the olfactory sense in worship stems from an intense
countercultural rejection by early Protestants of Roman Catholicism.
Since the Roman Catholic Church used incense and had rich visual
imagery in the form of statues, many Protestant groups defined such
worship aids as sinister. A kind of simplistic reaction formation set in.
Because so few senses are utilized, many Protestant churches may
have a plausibility structure that is less compelling than it would otherwise be. Some mechanisms for effectively and forcefully transmitting the culture are forfeited.

Let me cite some examples from visits to churches as I prepared
this chapter. As I sat in the sanctuary of a small-town Presbyterian
church, I sensed the mustiness of the room and the faded paint on the
walls. The mood was calm and quiet. Compared to the evangelical
church down the road, I was struck with the contrast of stillness vs.
energy. I reflected that many visitors would interpret the stillness of
this church as deadness. The congregation was not actively involved,
but sat passively and listened. Even laughter appeared not to be appropriate in this formal setting. There was no direct contact with others, and the walls had no visual images or symbols. I was aware how
few of my senses were involved. While the musty smell assaulted my
nose, I wondered whether these people associated mustiness with
worship. I was certain my evangelical friends (who feel that worship
should be expressed with vigor and energy) would think this entire
service was musty.

A week later I sat in another Presbyterian church in a nearby town.
The color scheme, the decor, and the ornate lighting fixtures all communicated elegance. The church was truly beautiful in its spacious
formality. While the sanctuary was a delight to the eye, I was aware of
the near total lack of symbols. Windows had stained glass, but they
formed no design; a central cross hung alone on the wall behind the
pulpit. Everything was tastefully done, but the climate was very different from that of the Roman Catholic and Episcopal churches in
town. The environment communicated affluence and elegance, but little else.

Each congregation's ritual excites certain senses, while other
senses may be left dormant. What norms determine these variations?
Any ethnographic study of denominations as cultures needs to take
seriously the rules that exist regarding which senses evoke sacredness
and which do not, and which ought not be associated with holiness.
While the cultural norms of each denomination cannot be investigated
thoroughly here, I shall briefly overview some of the tendencies regarding the senses.

The Olfactory Sense

The sense of smell is an extremely powerful one. When it comes to romance, young men and women are deliberate about picking that special fragrance before the big date. Persons selling their homes are advised, when potential buyers come through, to bake bread or rolls to create a warm cozy feeling about the house. Many people find that an intense affective response comes rushing upon them when they smell stale cigar smoke, or burning juniper in the fireplace, or some other odor which they associate with a grandparent or other loved one. Our sense of smell can stimulate powerful memories and emotional reactions. Yet many Protestant churches pay no attention to this sense in worship. In fact, the worship committee in one Presbyterian church in Ohio was presented with the suggestion that they burn incense during worship on "Ecumenical Sunday." The response was so violently negative that it was clear that utilization of the olfactory sense for worship was virtually taboo. Only a pervasive smell of lilies—and only then on Easter Sunday—was acceptable!

Insofar as the olfactory sense can help create an ethos and can stimulate powerful emotions, the aversion many Protestants have to using this sense may represent a serious loss of a possible plausibility mechanism. While the culture of the Episcopal Church approves such stimulation as an avenue to experience the holy, many other denominations have implicit norms against it.

The Visual Sense

Congregational, Presbyterian, and Baptist churches often seem almost austere in terms of visual imagery and symbols. Visual stimulation may be limited to a cross, a candelabra, a stained glass window with an image embedded in it, and an altar or Communion table with flowers and a Bible. Some churches do not even have the stained glass. Since the 1960s, some churches have added banners, which are changed from time to time as the season dictates. But when one enters a small-town Catholic church in Costa Rica or an Orthodox church in Greece, one is flooded with visual stimulation in a variety of forms: ornate architecture, statues, paintings, stained glass windows, gargoyles, relief works on pillars, and so forth.

Of course, most mainline Protestant churches are not devoid of visual imagery, and many Protestants find the plethora of visual images in Catholic churches distracting. In short, each denominational tradition and each local church evolves its own cultural rules regarding how much visual imagery and what types are acceptable. The obvious appeal of statues to Catholics (in homes, cars, front yards, and in places of work) make clear that three dimensional visual images can evoke important feelings and ideas for those who have not banished them.

Wade Clark Roof has pointed out in personal correspondence that the visual issue is especially interesting as it relates to televangelism. The Crystal Cathedral is equipped with a huge screen so that attenders can view the service from different angles. Roof points out that in a society which is shifting from print media to an image media, the evangelical churches have often been receptive to a diversity of visual media. These churches would seem to be well positioned to exploit this shift in the orientation of the society. It is interesting as well that New Age spirituality plays heavily on "mental journeys" and seems to focus more explicitly on images than words. If the mainline churches are captive to the verbal media, that orientation may have implications for recruitment, especially with a younger generation so accustomed to visual media.

The Auditory Sense

The sense organ most frequently employed in Protestant churches is the ear. The most obvious use of the sense of hearing is through listening to the words. Indeed, words from the Bible and the sermon may be referred to in the bulletin as "The Word," with capitalizations essential. It is not a coincidence that in nonrational religious experiences, Protestants are prone to hearing a still small voice rather than seeing an image of Jesus or of the Virgin Mary. But spoken words are not the only way the auditory sense is utilized in experiencing the holy.

Music is extremely important in evoking powerful moods and motivations in people. In chapter 4, Linda Clark speaks eloquently to this issue. I will point out here only that each denomination has its own set of favorite hymns and anthems, and each also has (usually unwritten) rules about what styles of music are appropriate in calling forth the sense of sacredness. Country and western style or heavy metal, for example, would be most unacceptable in some congregations, regardless of the message communicated in the lyrics. In some churches only the music of the great composers is "religious;" in others, contemporary music styles are acceptable if the words are appropriate.

The Tactile Sense

Skin contact, especially interpersonal touching, is important to human beings; it carries powerful symbolic meanings within families and in other meaningful relationships. Rules about touch vary a great deal between denominations. While it does not represent interpersonal contact, the pressure on the knees of kneeling to pray in an Episcopal church has no counterpart in most other Protestant churches. Yet kneeling is an act that is seldom repeated in other everyday situations, and for some Episcopalians, it comes to be associated very distinctly and uniquely with worship.

There are also rules governing the touching of others. One act of touching that happens in some churches is placing hands on the heads of laypersons. This is especially true in Presbyterian churches with the ordination of elders—local church leaders who are laity rather than clergy. In some Presbyterian congregations, all of the ordained elders gather at the front of the church and place their hands on the heads or shoulders of the ordainees. Since few Americans ever have anyone other than their barber, hairdresser, or doctor touch their heads, the touching and even the sheer weight of the hands can be a unique and emotionally moving experience for the new elders. There is something humbling about that kind of contact. Placement of the hand on the head occurs in some other churches for adult baptism or for confirmation into membership, both considered important rites of passage.

Likewise, few people have anyone other than a family member touch their unshod feet. But during holy week, some churches have worship ceremonies in which they wash one another's feet. This tactile interaction is also described by many participants as an emotionally moving experience. One might argue that it is just the reenactment of a sacred story that evokes emotions, but I strongly suspect it also has to do with stimulation of the skin in a way that elicits feelings of closeness and intimacy. When the idea of footwashing was broached in one affluent Episcopalian church in the Midwest, the response of many members was revulsion. Clearly such contact during worship was taboo in that congregation.

Many churches, in an effort to create a warmer and more friendly environment, have adopted the "Passing of the Peace" or the "Greeting in Christ." While this involves touch, it is commonly limited to the ritualized and emotionally distant act of shaking hands. Even this contact results in controversy and strong opposition in some congregations. But visits to some of the rapidly growing evangelical churches in my own community indicate that their norms endorse hugging and kissing, placing arms around neighbors during hymns, and providing other types of supportive physical contact when someone is either weeping or emotionally ecstatic.

Touch is not taboo in most denominations, but it is usually carefully limited in terms of where, when, and how one touches others. For churches which aspire to be surrogate extended families and emotional support units, norms which prohibit or circumscribe touch may work against this stated objective. In supportive families, touch is normal and communicates ties that bind them together. An ethnographic study of the culture of any particular denomination or congregation would need to explore how rules of physical contact function to enhance closeness, support, and interdependence. Certain types of touch during worship—as in placing hands on someone's head—may come to be associated with sacredness. But for the most part, touch in mainline Protestant churches is limited to a formal handshake.

The Sense of Taste

The sense of taste also is capable of eliciting powerful memories and feelings. Perhaps the best illustration of its utilization for religious purposes is the eating of the bitter herb during the Seder ceremony in the Jewish tradition. (The herb quite literally brings tears to the eyes as the ritual leader explains the bitterness and pain of slavery in Egypt.) Christians have no real counterpart of the Seder meal as a familial ritual. Of course, the taste of bread and wine or grape juice can become central symbols that call forth powerful emotions. While the sense of taste is seldom utilized in Christian worship, it is tied to one of the most essential symbols when it is stimulated.

The important point here is that the symbols and the emotional ethos of each denominational tradition are "stored" in certain sensory experiences. Implicit norms dictate that some senses may be stimulated in worship and others ought not to be aroused. Those senses that are employed are usually stimulated in certain prescribed ways. Insofar as each of the senses is capable of evoking powerful, deeply felt moods and motivations, the limitation on the use of some senses may involve a voluntary forfeiture of a mechanism that could enhance plausibility. Some traditions transmit the culture through the olfactory and tactile senses as well as the visual and auditory ones. Any ethnographic analysis of ritual in a specific denominational culture would need to pay attention to which senses are employed to transmit the culture and to sacralize it. While denominations are not monoliths, they do tend to have shared norms about which senses can carry symbols and/or "store" those special moods and motivations.

Cultural Rules About the Conduct of the Ritual

Denominations tend to display other cultural patterns that seem so common that they might be called rules about the conduct of worship. Let me mention here just two such norms about worship: rules about space and rules about language.

Space

In some churches, certain spatial areas are sacred and are treated differently from other areas (which are somehow more profane). The sanctuary itself is a sacred place in the culture of some denominations; in others it is just an auditorium that has multiple uses, and it becomes semisacred only on certain occasions. Even within the sanctuary, some areas may be more sacred than others. The front pew may be strategically placed fifteen feet or more from the chancel area, which can be entered only by appropriately garbed clergy. The altar or Communion table is especially revered and is centrally located. Such sacralization of certain space creates a sense of mystery and awe, but it also reinforces differences of status of members who are permitted access to these areas. Churches that are more egalitarian in structure appear to have fewer proscriptions regarding access to the sacred areas.

The center of the chancel area is the most sacred area in most churches, and the altar is usually appropriately located there. But other places may also have special meaning and may only be entered by certain people. Melvin Williams (1974) reports that in some African American Pentecostal churches, the pulpit is sacred and must never be defiled by a woman entering it. Denominational norms regarding gender roles and the exalted status of men are thereby sacralized and transmitted to members of the congregation. Likewise, the more centrally located seats in the sanctuary are "reserved" for leaders of the congregation. Marginal members are expected to sit toward the sides and the back. They dare not occupy the more "holy" areas (Williams 1974). While I am not aware of any similar spatial analysis of mainline Protestant denominations, I suspect there are similar implicit norms in many churches about the pulpit and even about seating arrangements.

One interesting spatial issue is highlighted by Ducey. Some churches place the pulpit at the very center of the chancel, either above and behind the altar or in place of an altar. In fact, the pulpit may occupy the most prominent (and sacred) place in the church. Ducey (1977) suggests that this may reflect the centrality of the sermon and of the ordained clergy in such churches. Clearly we must be cautious in jumping to conclusions; the location of the pulpit may be dictated by certain decisions by the architect or it may reflect norms operative at the time the building was constructed. The question of whether the placement of the pulpit in a church is linked to norms about the authority, prestige, and power of the clergy is, however, an interesting one.

Even when the pulpit is not centered, it is often spatially emphasized by being elevated above the lectern—where an open Bible rests and from which scripture is read. Visibility is obviously not the issue in making the pulpit higher, since worshipers presumably can see the liturgist standing at the lectern. Indeed, the pulpit is not only higher, but it is typically much larger than the lectern. Notably, the delivery of the sermon, the pastor's interpretation of the Word of God, is in many churches the only activity which occurs from the pulpit. In some churches the pulpit is so elevated that it is accessible only by a stairway, and it is entered only by the ordained clergy. Laypersons can read the scripture from a lectern, but they dare not stand where the sermon is delivered. I do not have enough data to state that central placement and/or elevation of the pulpit are entirely denominationally linked. Certainly churches in the Reformed tradition have typically given prominence to the preached Word. The region of the country may also play a role. Whatever the reason for pulpit placement, clearly sacred status is not accidental.

I have observed that in churches which emphasize interactional ritual, the minister often preaches from a location other than the pulpit. Ducey may be correct that the location of the pulpit is one way churches communicate the authority of the clergy, but central placement need not be the only way to emphasize the centrality of the minister's word. Certainly, when an especially sacred space is reserved only for the sermon, and when that message is itself located in the liturgy so that it represents the culmination and climax of worship, a powerful message regarding status and authority is being communicated. This message may be irrespective of the content of the sermon and may even contradict verbal affirmations of the priesthood of all believers. Cultural norms about the hierarchical structure of the church are nonverbally affirmed.

Language

Denominations also have rules about language. In some churches, archaic language (manifest in use of such words as "thee" and "thou" or in utilization of an older poetic syntax) is preferred. Such usage tends to set the worship hour apart from everyday life, much as sacred space and sacralized roles set it apart. This separation of worship from the profane world may risk the possibility that worship comes to be seen as a separate reality with little relevance for everyday life. On the other hand, archaic language may create a mystery and specialness that serves as a plausibility mechanism. Everyday experiences do not seem capable of disproving that which is so separate and different. It does appear that the use of archaic language is more common in churches that stress the transcendence of God, an important element in the culture of a denomination.

Other denominations place more stress on the immanence of God, on the involvement of the holy in everyday life situations. These traditions de-emphasize archaic language in favor of that which is contemporary. In its most extreme form, some churches include, along with the scripture reading, a reading of "The Contemporary Word." This may be a work of poetry, or a passage from a twentieth century martyr (Dietrich Bonhoeffer, or Martin Luther King, Jr., or Gandhi), or even a section of a popular psychology book or a popular song. The placement of this reading may put it on a par with the scriptural passage, stressing that God continues to speak to the secular world. This strategy emphasizes relevance of faith to the everyday world, but in submitting the faith to profane standards and to personal choices as to what is God's word for today, the church risks losing plausibility. The absoluteness of the proclamations seems to be compromised. The idea that the Bible is to be read interactively with the experiences of everyday life and that secular readings are to be read with an eye to possible ultimate meaning may create an unsettling feeling of relativism for many Christians.

One can see illustrations of this language conflict in the intense controversy over revisions of the prayer book in the Anglican tradition. Language is powerful for people, and change from archaic to contemporary language may seem like a domestication of the sacred and a loss of awesomeness. Some have argued that the language of the traditional prayer book and the King James Version of the Bible are central influences on English culture as a whole, and that changing them threatens the entire culture. The intensity of the debate demonstrates the fact that it is an important issue.

Strategies which set aside sacred words or "The Sacred Word" may implicitly transmit the culture of a transcendent theology. Other denominations, in placing emphasis on contemporary language and even contemporary readings, transmit a different theological thrust. In the latter case we see the struggle currently within denominations which have modified the language of hymns to be inclusive of both genders. The idea that we contemporary mortals can change the language of a song that has sacred meaning somehow seems to relativize the meaning itself. Within those denominations in which hymns are being modified, some people feel that the denominational culture is being transformed rather than preserved and transmitted, and some of the members feel angry, alienated, and betrayed. They are not necessarily comforted by the response that theirs is a "reforming" tradition that must keep on reforming. Others, women for example, may feel included for the first time.

One other point about language might be highlighted. As indicated earlier in the discussion of the special roles of clergy, some parts of the service, such as assurance of pardon or the sermon, may only be done by ordained leaders. Likewise, some churches make clear that only certain persons may utter certain words during the liturgy. Only the clergy, for example, may be permitted to articulate the words of institution while distributing the Communion elements. More important here is the fact that in some churches only men are allowed to read from the Gospels (women being allowed to read other, less sacred, sections of the Bible). When women are prohibited from such roles, gender role assumptions within the church are again reinforced and sacralized. Denominational values and beliefs may in this way be transmitted through the ritual enactment. Such symbolic actions speak loudly to children about matters of gender roles.

There is clearly not a complete consensus on emphases within any one denomination as to whether the core denominational culture emphasizes immanence or transcendence. Part of this lack of consensus may be because of denominational mergers which blend two traditions or cultures. Mainline denominations have been more active in the ecumenical movement and have experienced more such mergers in the twentieth century, so they are likely to have more of the internal "cultural wobble" that occurs in such blending. Some of the cultural diversity within each denomination may also be due to the amount of denominational switching that is occurring in modern America. Switchers bring with them another tradition, and if they enter leadership positions in their new church, they may enhance diffusion of the religious culture of their childhood church. Finally, diffusion of denominational traditions may occur through candidates for ministry studying in seminaries which are sponsored by other denominations, or even by the denominational diversity of faculty within any one seminary. Seminary students are not always indoctrinated in their own denomination's traditions regarding ritual.

Diffusion can occur in ritual not only from other denominations. It may be introduced from loyalties to other groups. While each denomination may have its own subculture, and while ritual may be a conduit for celebrating and transmitting that culture, it is also true that each local congregation has its own culture. It draws upon the national denominational culture, but the local cultural rules regarding ritual are modified and adapted by local events and loyalties as well. Given the geographical mobility of the population, such local cultural rules sometimes mean that persons who move to a new region and affiliate with a church of the same denomination as their previous membership may still have to adjust to a modified denominational culture.

Conflicts and Tensions: The Pledge of Allegiance to the American Flag During Christian Worship

Another issue over performance of ritual is particularly interesting in Protestant middle America. In the 1980s and 1990s, the United States saw a renewed emphasis on patriotism. Indeed, during the Persian Gulf War patriotic fervor reached a fevered pitch in parts of middle America. During certain holidays (Memorial Day, the Fourth of July, and Veterans Day) some congregations have returned to a 1950s practice of including a pledge of allegiance to the American flag during worship. This pattern is not exclusive to any one denomination, nor is it endorsed officially by any denominational culture. It has resulted, however, in rather intense conflict in several churches. Also noteworthy is another, slightly different, issue—some congregations have chosen to hang an American flag from the back center wall of the chancel or from the ceiling directly over the altar. Its centrality as a symbol is overwhelming when one enters the church.[7] Blending of commitment to Christianity and loyalty to the nation has clearly become part of the folk culture of some local churches.

In two Ohio churches with which I am intimately familiar, one Methodist and one Presbyterian, the issue of the role of the American flag in worship resulted in intense conflict. These congregations are not alone in experiencing such conflict. Some members in each church argued that worship was a time to rise above all petty commitments and loyalties. A pledge of allegiance to a lesser loyalty represented a kind of idolatry, for worship was a time to recenter one's life on exclusive loyalty to God and to Christ. Christianity is universal, they also reasoned. Pledging loyalty to one's nation was as potentially alienating to foreign visitors as was requiring everyone to pledge loyalty to the region's professional football team would be to visitors from another town or fans of another team. Such a pledge was viewed as inappropriate and even theologically offensive. A common commitment as children of God should remain the sole source of personal identification.

Those arguing in favor of a pledge to the flag pointed out that the pledge says the United States is "one nation under God." Since the pledge mentions God, it is entirely appropriate. But the overall reaction in both churches by proponents of fealty to the flag was emotional in nature. The flag elicited many of the same emotions of awe and respect that worship evoked; the flag is the sacralized symbol of something larger than self. The idea that the flag was not to be honored in the church evoked a visceral reaction by some members. Those who objected to its role in worship were attacked as un-American. Some even claimed that they could not possibly worship God if there was not a pledge to the flag. (The latter argument was interesting, since the pledge to the flag had not been said during worship for many years, and no one had complained.)

For some members, the church should lend its sacralizing powers to sacralization of the nation. This was part of the local cultural climate regarding Christian ritual. In these two churches, these cultural assumptions resulted in conflict. Norms and expectations about worship clearly differed and people on both sides felt that this was an issue so central to the life of the church that compromise was unacceptable. Interestingly, in some churches the pledge to the flag is so integral to worship on national holidays that no conflict arises. Its use is normative. This is despite the fact that the denominational officials of most of these churches would be skeptical, if not appalled, by this innovation. In one United Church of Christ congregation in Louisville, Kentucky, the congregation not only said a pledge to the flag, but the entire congregation rose to their feet in respect when an armed color guard presented the colors. In this instance an associate pastor resigned her position in protest against this "idolatry." On the other hand, many members of the congregation could not fathom why this honor to the flag during worship was even an issue.

Conclusion

The central thesis of this paper is that ritual serves not merely to transmit a culture but also to sacralize central values and core myths or beliefs. Rituals help to "clothe conceptions [of reality] with such an aura of factuality that [they] seem uniquely realistic" (Geertz 1966). These rituals may operate in several ways, and each denomination develops its own style and its own rules about the operation of religious ritual.

The sequencing of the liturgy—the order of the worship service—may enact and reinforce a core theological notion, as in the case of covenantal theology and the four major moods of Protestant liturgy. But ideas about status, roles, and power within the denomination may cause a shifting in the order of worship itself, so that those who have the "final word" in church policy are also those who have the final word or most important role in the culmination of the ritual. Beyond this important issue of the relationship of ritual to ideology and social structure, denominations also develop rules which govern the performance of ritual. These rules may determine which senses can be used to "store" powerful moods and motivations, or the rules may reflect theological ideas (such as notions about the transcendence or immanence of God) or reinforce status differentials (such as the authority of the clergyperson). These cultural rules about ritual may even prohibit the use of mechanisms which might help to make the values and ideas seem more plausible, more compelling, more sacred.

Each church has its own culture and its own structure, and an ethnographic analysis makes it clear that the rituals which comprise Sunday morning worship are not a collection of hymns, prayers, and readings thrown together in random order. There is a deeper meaning to liturgy, even if many lay people and even some clergy are not aware of it. Conceptions about the components of worship, the order of worship, and even the rules about the senses to be used all have implications for the transmission of that denominational culture. That not all Methodist churches and not all Baptist churches share the same ritual may be due in part to the variations in congregations within a denomination and in part to cultural diffusion that is occurring as ideas are passed from one denomination to another. While no one pattern of liturgy is universal within any denomination, certain tendencies or "typical patterns" can be observed. Denominations can still be seen as subcultures which attempt to pass along their culture.

Diffusion among denominations is not the only source of change or innovation. Other competing "faiths" or "invisible religions" (Luckmann 1967; Roberts 1990) may also mean that people want to use Christian ritual to sacralize these other values and ideas. Such is the case with the introduction of the pledge to the flag in Christian worship. James Wood (1981) has pointed out that one danger of an open social system, such as any of the mainline denominations (which do not intensively screen their members), is that outside ideologies can infiltrate. He notes that racism as an ideology can come in the back door of a church, even though this attitude is contrary to official doctrine. Likewise, as open systems, mainline denominations may find that other loyalties make their way into the church—loyalties which elicit a sense of intense commitment and which the members want to have sacralized in ritual. Keeping a clear focus on the core values and the central ideology around which the ritual should "re-center" its members is not a simple task for an open social system.

What then can be concluded about the transmission of denominational cultures from these reflections on ritual? Has so much diffusion occurred that denominational affiliations do not matter? I believe they do still matter, even if denominations are open systems. Denominations are not monoliths, but they do still have traditions and norms that continue. Differences in polity, in theological emphases, in use of language, and in styles of worship are significant enough that many people who switch denominations will do so with an eye to joining a certain limited range of denominations. Any of three or four denominations may seem like possibilities, but certain others are viewed as beyond the range of acceptability. Denominational affiliation of a congregation remains a consideration for many switchers.

There is another reason denominational loyalty and identification are still relevant. Anyone who has done much ethnographic work in a local church where changes are proposed has probably heard a statement something like this: "But that is just plain un-presbyterian!" One may substitute other denominational names in that last sentence; still, unacceptable innovations in the ritual or in the theology of a church are often discredited with such a self-evident and damning proclamation. Denominational tradition remains extremely important to many people and sets their congregation aside from others in the community. Sometimes new patterns of worship are rejected precisely because they are too much akin to practices of other denominations. To understand the relationship between ritual and culture of a local congregation, then, one must not expect denominational affiliation to determine all aspects of the relationship, but an ethnographer would ignore denominational ties at great peril.

Finally, the correlations identified and the theories set forth in this chapter are based on research using qualitative methodologies. The intent is to suggest areas of investigation for further ethnographic research on the role of ritual in a denominational culture. The research in this area is in the nascent stage and much more data is needed. Ethnographic analysis of ritual, however, has promise of rich insights into the overall functioning of mainline religious culture in America.

NOTES

1. For sociologists and anthropologists, myths are not "untrue stories." Indeed, a myth is powerful precisely because it carries important values. Myths are stories which transmit core values and an outlook on life. They may be either factual or fantastic, but they carry "truth" for members irrespective of literal veracity. To call a belief a myth, therefore, is to show profound respect for the importance of that belief for the faithful.

2. Most examples will compare and contrast Presbyterian, Methodist, Episcopal, and Baptist liturgies.

3. This description of Protestant liturgy and its relationship to covenantal theology was earlier presented in my book *Religion in Sociological Perspective,* 2nd ed. (Belmont, Calif.: Wadsworth, 1991).

4. There are variations of emphasis on this covenantal idea, with Baptists and Presbyterians, for example, differing in their interpretations.

5. Roman Catholic liturgy seems to run counter to the thesis here. The message is toward the middle of the service and such commitment actions as the offering follow it—even though the denomination's polity is episcopal. The real climax of the service, however, is the Mass, which is celebrated as God's act of grace. The culmination is action by God.

6. Placement of the sermon in the liturgy is not the sole indicator and it is not in itself a reliable indicator of a more authoritarian, status-conscious church structure, but Ducey (1977) believes the correlation is high—too high to be mere coincidence. While my work is still in progress, it tends to support this thesis.

7. Some churches have taken the opposite stance that the flag does not belong anywhere in the sanctuary, but making this decision has itself been one that has created tensions and discord.

REFERENCES

Batson, C. Daniel, and W. Larry Ventis
    1982 *The Religious Experience: A Social-Psychological Perspective.* New York: Oxford University Press.
Berger, Peter
    1969 *The Sacred Canopy.* Garden City, N.Y.: Doubleday & Co.
Berger, Peter, and Thomas Luckmann
    1967 *The Social Construction of Reality.* Garden City, N.Y.: Doubleday & Co.
Ducey, Michael H.
    1977 *Sunday Morning: Aspect of Urban Ritual.* New York: Free Press.
Geertz, Clifford
    1966 "Religion as Cultural System" In *Anthropological Approaches to the Study of Religion,* edited by Michael Banton, 1–46. London: Tavistock.
Luckmann, Thomas
    1967 *The Invisible Religion.* New York: Macmillan Co.
Neitz, Mary Jo
    1987 *Charisma and Community.* New Brunswick, N.J.: Transaction Books.
Niebuhr, H. Richard
    1960 *Radical Monotheism and Western Culture, with Supplementary Essays.* New York: Harper & Row.
Pillari, Vimala
    1986 *Pathways to Family Myths.* New York: Brunner/Mazel.

Pratt, James Bissett
  1964   "Objective and Subjective Worship." In *Religion, Culture, and Society,* edited by Louis Schneider, 143–156. New York: John Wiley & Sons.
Roberts, Keith A.
  1990   *Religion in Sociological Perspective.* Belmont, Calif.: Wadsworth.
Satir, Virginia
  1988   *The New Peoplemaking.* Mountain View, Calif.: Science and Behavior Books.
Williams, Melvin
  1974   *Community in a Black Pentecostal Church.* Prospect Heights, Ill.: Waveland Press
Wood, James R.
  1981   *Leadership in Voluntary Organizations: The Controversy Over Social Action in Protestant Churches.* New Brunswick, N.J.: Rutgers University Press.

4

"Songs My Mother Taught Me": Hymns as Transmitters of Faith

Linda J. Clark

The religious traditions of a particular group, be it a local congregation or a denomination, are transmitted in highly variegated and multiformed ways—some of them explicit and direct, others more subtle and indirect. Using "Amazing Grace" as an illustration, I will explore how the activity of hymn-singing contributes to this transmittal of communal religious identity: how the process itself works in aesthetic forms like hymns and what actually is transmitted. I might add that patterns and practices of worship can also provide the means to study the maintenance, recreation, and modification, generation after generation, of the religious traditions of a denomination.

There are many ways to describe religious traditions. For the purposes of this chapter I want to describe a religious tradition as an uninterrupted string of moments or events connected through the telling of stories. These stories, told by people as a way of making sense out of their lives, are learned or written down, to be told or read aloud in the midst of others who, like themselves, are searching for meaning. In turn, the children of these people stand to tell the stories their parents taught them, and in that way, religious traditions are passed from generation to generation. One form these stories take is the hymn.

According to the theologian Bernard Meland, expressive forms, like stories, hymns, and other imaginative constructs, grow out of or reflect a community's *mythos*.

By mythos I mean something more than a particular mode of reflec-
tiveness or poetry. The mythos encompasses these responses, but it includes them along with other more visceral and imaginative assertions
of the psychical thrust of a people. . . . [It] shap[es] the sensibilities,
apprehensions, expectations, intentions, and valuations of a people. . . .
[T]he notion of mythos partakes of the stream of experience as well as
of the stream of thought. And it gathers in as well inert, though symbolically significant, precedents and practices which body forth. . . the
intentionality of a people (1976, 113).

"Mythos" encompasses and fashions the expressive forms which
tell the identity of a community and of its faith. These forms are
myths and stories, images and symbols, hymns and rituals. Meland is
speaking here of a level of experience, often subconscious, that pre-
cedes and supports what we would recognize as ordinary experience—the sensibilities that declare what is of value, what is
cherished, what is intended of a community.

When I use the term "transmittal," I do not want to convey that the
meaning of these expressive forms is simply handed down unmodi-
fied from one generation of singers to another. The process of transmittal is much more dynamic; a hymn's meaning is reappropriated by
each generation on its own terms. Moreover, the context in which the
hymn is sung can result in a shift in its meaning. Yet as the illustration
will show, something of the original intent of the hymn endures despite the changes.

Hymns and Faith

When asked why a particular hymn was her favorite, a woman responded, "It sounds the way following Christ is like." A connection
between hymns and faith is implicit in this woman's response. Her favorite hymn evokes the path of her faith through its sounds. When
those sounds recur, she remembers what following Christ is like.

Hymns provide the means through which the singer and the congregation of which she or he is a member express their faith, and as
that faith is expressed the singer and the community are changed. A
hymn rehearses or expresses a community's faith because it is a symbol constructed of verbal and musical images held together by an
overarching aural image which is the hymn in its entirety. Avery
Dulles in *Models of the Church* speaks of the way images "mean" in
the religious sphere:

In the religious sphere, images function as symbols. That is to say, they
speak to man existentially and find an echo in the inarticulate depths of

his psyche. Such images communicate through their evocative power. They convey a latent meaning that is apprehended in a nonconceptual, even a subliminal, way. Symbols transform the horizons of man's life, integrate his perception of reality, alter his scale of values, reorient his loyalties, attachments, and aspirations in a manner far exceeding the powers of conceptual thought (1974, 18).

How do hymns possess this capacity to carry meaning? Hymns are not sets of words on a page but events. They have no existence until they are sung. Then they become bodies of sound that exist in time, beginning at one moment, traveling toward a point, and then drawing to a close and stopping at another moment. This movement toward a climax shapes time, and it is this shaping of time that brings out the meaning of texts. The philosopher Susanne Langer explains why. In describing how music has meaning, she states that "what music can actually reflect is . . . the morphology of feeling. . . . [It] conveys general forms of feeling" (1957, 238). In other words, music is an aural image of the *shape* of feeling alive. "It is not self-expression, but formulation and representation of emotions, moods, mental tensions and resolutions—a 'logical picture' of sentient, responsive life." (1957, 222).

Because a hymn is an art form, it allows for, indeed requires that, something in the singer's own experience rise to meet it. In this process the feeling-time, "sentient, responsive life," of the hymn and the feeling-time of the singer are conjoined; the hymn's meaning becomes the singer's meaning *and vice versa.* This process of mixing explains why hymns can carry a variety of meanings and why the context in which the hymn is sung can influence how the hymn is appropriated by the singer. However, the images of the hymn do limit the range of meanings that can be ascribed to it.

Hymns carry meaning through the content of their verbal and musical images, but because they are events they also carry meaning through the style of their performance. What is style? In general usage, the word refers to the form or manner of a thing as opposed to its content or subject matter. One might say of a speech: "She gave that speech in a concise style," meaning that the form in which she delivered her ideas was clear and to the point. Yet in the discussion of style in *The New Grove Dictionary of Music and Musicians,* the distinctions between form or manner and content are not so neatly drawn. *Grove* defines style as "manner, mode of expression, type of presentation. . ." and then says, "[T]o treat of the style of an epoch or culture, one is treating of import, a substantive communication from a society, which is a significant embodiment of the aspirations and inner life of its people." The manner of presentation of an idea can communicate something of substance. According to A. L. Kroeber in *Style and Civilizations,* the ingredients of style in art consist in (1) the subject matter chosen, (2) the "'concept' of the subject, along with its emotional aura," and (3) the specific, technical form given in execution of the work (1957, 30). What is of interest to a particular composer or painter, how she or he conceives of the subject and how its emotional valence is projected, and finally the means or medium of that projection all communicate the inner life of the artist.

In a hymn, style is an important aspect of its meaning. Think for a minute of the contrast between a congregation in a predominantly white suburb and a congregation in a predominantly African American urban neighborhood singing the spiritual "Let My People Go." Ostensibly the subject matter is the same in both instances, yet the style of singing so changes what is sung that the two would have divergent meanings. The contrast in style comes mainly from two interrelated factors: (1) the difference in the relationship between the text and the inner lives of the singers; and (2) the singing traditions of the two communities.

In the case of the former, the experience that African Americans bring to the singing of the hymn is different from that of people of the dominant culture. Oppression is a pervasive reality to African Americans; the *event* which is the singing of that spiritual is a rallying cry that comes deep from within their souls. Whites in a suburb might empathize with their sisters and brothers in the African American neighborhood and might understand how in some ways they, too, are oppressed, but they will not sing the song with the same immediacy and conviction. For African Americans, the immediacy of the cry "Let my people go" is reinforced by slavery's legacy as well as by an ancestry that lived in the slave quarters where the spirituals were born.

That past, handed down in the improvisational quality of the singing in which the drum is heard in its rhythms and melodic complexity, is reappropriated by every generation in the style of their singing. This singing tradition shapes the event by linking the faith and endurance of the slave to the contemporary African American confronting the racism of his or her culture. The people in the white church do not have this legacy to inform their singing. Their traditions are formed in other ways. Thus their singing will not have the echoes of the drum in it.

Hymns also carry a more private and idiosyncratic form of a community's past. Anyone at all familiar with a church community knows that favorite hymns evoke memories of past events and the people who sang them. Hymns have bits of the past stuck to them. A man remembers the occasion when the pastor's child was buried when he sings the hymn used at the funeral; the treasurer recalls the long meetings leading up to the building of the new sanctuary every time she sings the hymn used to open the dedication service.

Thus the hymns a community sings transmit their experience, their values, their history from one generation to another. Each time a community stands to sing a hymn, it recreates its identity anew, carrying the past forward into the present but changing it slightly by shifting its meaning and intentions through present circumstances. Perhaps this time the hymn is sung, the man's wife is pregnant with her first child, and he understands in a much deeper way what the pastor lost in the death of his child; or perhaps the treasurer has been transferred to another town, and this is the last time she will sing this hymn in the sanctuary she spent so many long hours helping to build. Perhaps an ecumenical gathering brings the two churches from the city and suburb together, and they sing "Let My People Go" together. The meaning of the images in the hymns shifts ever so slightly to accommodate the present; the events of the present stick to the hymn, altering and rearranging the other bits of life clinging to it.

From this description of the way hymns function in a community and how they carry meaning it is easy to see how hymns might transmit aspects of a denomination's identity. As a prolonged illustration of this idea I would like to turn to a study of the favorite hymns in two denominations, a small but significant part of the Music in Churches project undertaken by the School of Theology at Boston University.[1] From a more philosophical approach to the matter of the transmittal of religious identity we turn to an actual description of this phenomenon. A look at the data of the study suggests that this transmittal process is highly complex. Yes, hymns *do* carry meaning from one generation to another, but what kinds of ideas, beliefs, patterns of feeling are transmitted in that way? Does anything of the original spirit or meaning of the hymn endure over long periods of time through many generations of churchgoers? What of the fact that many congregations are peopled with "switchers"—those who were not raised in the particular traditions of the denomination of which they are now members?

The Boston University Study

In a Boston University study, a questionnaire was passed out at the end of worship one Sunday in twenty-four representative United Methodist and Episcopal churches in southern New England in the late fall of 1988. One of its questions asked people to name their favorite hymn. Here are the "Top Ten" in each denomination:

United Methodist [447 responses]

How Great Thou Art [74]
Amazing Grace [41]
On a Hill Far Away (The Old Rugged Cross) [20]
In the Garden [19]
Are Ye Able [14]
O for a Thousand Tongues [11]
A Mighty Fortress Is Our God [10]
What a Friend We Have in Jesus [9]
Holy, Holy, Holy [8]
Nearer, My God, to Thee [8]
Onward, Christian Soldiers [8]

Episcopal [388 responses]

Amazing Grace [25]
A Mighty Fortress Is Our God [13]
For All the Saints [11]
Lift High the Cross [9]
Eternal Father, Strong to Save [8]
I Sing a Song of the Saints of God [7]
Onward, Christian Soldiers [7]
The Church's One Foundation [7]
How Great Thou Art [6]
O God Our Help in Ages Past [6]

I have chosen to concentrate on the hymn "Amazing Grace" because it appears prominently in each list and because of its historical
roots in the Methodist camp meetings in the early 1800s. By examining the data through the "lens" of this hymn we can see how hymns
transmit faith and the extent to which the original meaning of the
hymn has endured to the late twentieth century.

Amazing Grace!

Amazing grace! how sweet the sound
That saved a wretch like me!
I once was lost, but now am found,
Was blind, but now I see.

'Twas grace that taught my heart to fear,
And grace my fears relieved;
How precious did that grace appear
The hour I first believed!

Through many dangers, toils, and snares,
I have already come;
'Tis grace hath brought me safe thus far,
And grace will lead me home.

The Lord has promised good to me,
His word my hope secures;
He will my shield and portion be,
As long as life endures.

UM: [Yea, when this flesh and heart shall fail,
And mortal life shall cease,
I shall possess, within the veil,
A life of joy and peace.]

When we've been there ten thousand years,
Bright shining as the sun,
We've no less days to sing God's praise
Than when we'd first begun.

The version above is taken from the new United Methodist hymnal (1989). The bracketed verse only occurs in the United Methodist hymnal. The order of the verses is that of the United Methodists; in the new Episcopal hymnal (1982) verses 3 and 4 are reversed. This is the first time that the hymn has been included in an *official* Episcopal denominational hymnal.

According to the United Methodist *Companion to the Hymnal*, the text to this hymn appeared first in *Olney Hymns* (published in England in 1779) and was entitled "Faith's review and expectation." John Newton (1725–1807) wrote it. According to popular legend, he was converted to the Christian faith while plying the African slave trade; this hymn grew out of that experience. The text entered Methodist hymnals through *Zion Songster, A Collection of Hymns and Spiritual Songs Generally Sung at Camp and Prayer Meetings,* and in *Revivals of Religion* compiled by Peter D. Myers (New York, 1829). The last verse is not by Newton but by John P. Rees. These lines were printed as a separate text in the second appendix of the 1859 edition of *The Sacred Harp*. They were attached *in print* to the Newton hymn for the first time in E. O. Excell's *Coronation Hymns* (Chicago, 1910). The tune, which has had various names attached to it, originally appeared in *Virginia Harmony* (1831).

This brief history of "Amazing Grace" recounts its origins and shaping in the camp meetings and revivals of the nineteenth-century

American frontier. Although it appeared in many Methodist hymnals in the nineteenth century, it undoubtedly thrived in the oral tradition, too, since hymnals were in short supply at camp meetings and would have proved an encumbrance in the midst of the "heat" of conversion. Indeed the editors of *Companion to the Hymnal* conjecture that the verse by John Rees was just one of many that became attached to Newton's text as the hymn was used to spur people on to "Canaan's shores." This particular verse happened to stick, whereas the others floated off to join other texts! The hymn remains in the oral tradition today and is one of the few hymns that people from differing denominations can sing impromptu at ecumenical gatherings.

The images of the text are quite striking. There is an opposition set up between states before and after conversion:

> lost/found
> blind/see
> death/life
> dangers, toils, snares/joy and peace

The "wretch" of the text, relying on the promises of "the Lord," journeys toward "home" trusting in the grace of God that is truly "amazing"—grace that "saves" and "secures" the singer. The first line refers to the "sound" of grace as sweet, a description which speaks to the experience of salvation as well as to the song itself. God is pictured as Lord above all yet close, reliable, trustworthy, worthy to be praised, a savior, the source of good yet whose portion includes "dangers, toils, and snares." The tune, a simple folk song, is capable of elaborate treatment in almost every kind of arrangement. Singers and communities develop patterns of performing the hymn; improvised versions abound, and settings are written down and published. On occasions of great moment and sentiment anyone can start the hymn, assured that most people will join in. It is truly "populist" sacred music but is not limited to that style, since many a composer has set the hymn in elaborate style. In the last several decades it has enjoyed great popularity in circles wider than the church community. Many "pop" and folk artists have performed and recorded it—Aretha Franklin and Judy Collins, to name just two.

What can this hymn and its popularity at this time in the history of American mainline Protestantism reveal to us about religious identity and its transmittal? One would surmise that the text and tune—in short, the event—of this hymn would have some effect on belief about God, people of faith, and the nature of the church. How does the conversion experience described in the text influence the beliefs of these people? Does the fact that this version of the hymn was born in the midst of the Methodist camp meeting have any bearing on its ability to form the identity of people of faith today? What clues about this process can we find in the data of the project? Let us turn to the data of the study and see what there is to learn.

Summary of the Data

I divided the responses into four groups or cohorts and compared them: those United Methodists for whom "Amazing Grace" is their favorite hymn (MAG); those Episcopalians for whom "Amazing Grace" is their favorite hymn (EAG); all other Methodists (M-O); and all other Episcopalians (E-O) (see table 4–1 for a summary of some of the comparisons).

1. There are many similarities among Episcopalians and Methodists whose favorite hymn is "Amazing Grace." Their median age is the same, forty-five or more years. They began coming to their particular churches at approximately the same time, since 1979. They come to a church and remain there for many of the same reasons; taking part in worship and the friendliness of the people rank high among them. They have the same level of education and financial security. They would agree that any style of music is appropriate in worship so long as the congregation can use it to praise God. There are no significant differences between them on what constitutes worship at its best and the role of the church in the world. Their differences are found mainly in their religious practice. The Episcopalians are more likely to meet in small Bible study groups and to go on retreats. The Methodists feel closer to God singing in church and at worship.

2. There is little difference between those Methodists for whom "Amazing Grace" is their favorite hymn and other Methodists. They (MAG) tend to be younger and have fewer of their close, personal friends among members of the congregation; they are less likely to be raised in the Methodist church (37 percent compared to 49 percent). They are more likely to have had powerful "spiritual" experiences that seemed to lift them out of themselves. In describing the interrelationship of God, Jesus Christ, and people, they would more likely see Jesus as a mediator between themselves and God (41 percent compared to 27 percent).

3. There are many differences between those Episcopalians for whom "Amazing Grace" is their favorite hymn and other Episcopalians. These differences run across almost all the categories in the survey and therefore are difficult to summarize briefly. One of the most significant ones comes from the percentage of people raised in the denomination: among "Amazing Grace" people only 16 percent of them were raised Episcopalians as compared to 47 percent of all other Episcopalians in the sample. The other "cradle" denominations represented among this group are Methodist, Baptist, United Church of Christ, Presbyterian, Unitarian, and a lone Roman Catholic. Other differences grow out of their adherence to more evangelical forms of piety and belief, many of which are congruent with the images of the hymn but incongruent with the more formal style of public worship in the present-day Episcopal church. I will discuss three findings in the data to support my conclusions.

First, as regards the view of the church and its mission to the world, the "Amazing Grace" people differ significantly from their denominational colleagues in three categories. In two categories they consider the activities mentioned to be *more* important to the mission of the church than their denominational counterparts: (a) "Opening members' hearts and minds to the spiritual gifts of miracles, and healing, and to the baptism of the Holy Spirit;" (b) "Preparing church members for a world to come in which the cares of this world are absent." In a third category they consider the activities to be *much less* important: (c) "Encouraging church members to reach their own decisions on issues of faith and morals even if this diminishes the church's ability to speak with a single voice on these issues." These characterizations of the mission of the church to the world are focused on the members of the congregation themselves who have the tendency to view the world as somewhat hostile and uncaring. They grow out of an evangelical piety that emphasizes the movement of the Holy Spirit.

Secondly, their religious experience is centered in the intimacy of a small group. They are more likely to meet for prayer and Bible study and to discuss religious beliefs with others, to image God as a close companion and emphasize God's presence rather than a symbol or idea. They are likely to go on retreats and to have powerful "spiritual" experiences more frequently than others of their denomination. They are more likely to characterize the interrelationship between God, Jesus Christ, and people—with Jesus as a mediator between themselves and God (40 percent compared to 28 percent).

Thirdly, affiliation with the people in their congregation is more significant to them. More of them are attached to the church (80 percent compared to 66 percent), consider their communities closely knit, and would be upset if they had to leave (42 percent compared to 32 percent).

These findings suggest that "Amazing Grace" embodies for these Episcopalians a variety of religious experience epitomized by the evangelical prayer group and characterized by intense personal experience of God and the building of strong bonds of affection and intimacy among its members. Not only because of its images and melody but also because of its informal style—the fact that people know it by heart and can sing it anywhere—"Amazing Grace" can provide a vehicle for the expression of the small group ethos within a congregation even though the intimacy implied would seem out of place intermixed with the more austere and objective cadences of the Book of Common Prayer.

Systems of Belief

In light of the similarities and differences between the two denominations and the two groups within each denomination, it is interesting to compare their ideas of God. (See table 4–1.)

TABLE 4–1

The numbers in the following table represent the percentage of respondents who scored high on the question which read, "As you read each of the following phrases, indicate how true it is for you." The answers ranged from (1) Not true at all, to (5) Extremely true. The percentages shown are the combined figures for those answering with a 4 or 5.

God is:

	EAG	E-O	MAG	M-O
Faithful	92%	93%	100%	95%
Dependable	88	89	100	93
Forgiving	100	97	100	98
Mysterious	84	76	50	73
More present in relationships with others than in an individual's life	17	18	18	14
Distant	13	15	13	12
Permissive	17	18	15	19
A creative force in history	74	83	78	85
Aware of everything I think	88	74	82	80
Close	92	76	82	83
Vindictive	0	3	5	4
My constant companion	83	64	77	73
Strict	48	30	42	43
Clearly knowable	67	45	74	61
In my life more as a symbol or an idea than as a real presence I can feel	17	27	16	22
All-powerful	96	81	95	89
Awesome	87	77	84	78
Fascinating	78	72	71	71
Judgmental	50	34	32	37
Indifferent	0	2	13	3

Again one can see in comparing these lists, the "Amazing Grace" people are somewhat more likely to adhere to a set of feelings or feeling attributes generated by an intense personal and immediate encounter with God. The status of the attribute "a creative force in history," a more abstract principle rather than a feeling, also bears this out. Among EAGs, it ranks tenth, among MAGs eighth, whereas with the others it ranks in the top five.

I compared the percentage scores across the four groups to see what patterns emerged. Were there instances where the two "Amazing Grace" groups fell together rather than remaining with their denominational cohorts? Were there extreme differences among the scores that might indicate something?

Those attributes of God in which the two AG groups fell together at the higher end of the scale are the following: forgiving, aware of everything I think, my constant companion, clearly knowable, all powerful and awesome. Those on the lower end of the scale are: permissive, a creative force in history, and in my life more as a symbol or an idea than as a real presence I can feel. Again we can see a pattern emerging based on the images of God in the hymn. It is the experience of God's presence in a highly personal fashion that is compelling.

Given the unanimity about the immediacy of God's presence it is interesting to note where the two "Amazing Grace" groups diverge. There are two attributes where the difference between the two groups is larger than fifteen percentage points: mysterious (E-84, M-50), and judgmental (E-50, M-32). Why would such differences exist? Since I cannot interview these people, I am left with conjecture. The clues to this discrepancy may lie in the differing worship styles of the two groups, their differing ecclesiologies as given in their views of ordination, or perhaps in the social location of the group within their respective communities. This discrepancy may indicate that the context in which one experiences God as immediate has influenced the images one might ascribe to God. Without more conclusive evidence, however, one is left with speculation.

The styles of assembly of the two denominations are considerably different. In the churches in the sample most Episcopalians observed a weekly celebration of the Eucharist, whereas most United Methodists took part in some form of service dominated by the sermon. Thus most Sundays the Episcopalians participated in a symbolic act that is highly objective and carefully delimited in meaning by the words and rubrics of the *Book of Common Prayer.* Penitence and praise alternate in these texts. The people kneel to pray and read a fixed set of prayers out of a book. Furthermore, at this period in history, most kneel to receive the bread and wine at the Eucharist. This is a posture one takes before someone high and lifted up—a judge or a king; it is the posture of humility. The central act of worship is a highly complex ritual accompanied by language both formal and metaphorical.

The patterns of worship of New England Methodism are much less formal and ritualistic. In many communities there is a high premium placed on informality and spontaneity in worship. In others worship follows a set pattern week in and week out with prayers and responses written by the pastor or a lay leader. The focus of worship is the sermon, an expository rhetorical form for which people sit and listen. United Methodists generally sit, and sitting can mean almost anything. The focus of attention in worship is often another human being who preaches and prays as one listens. Here God implicitly becomes less high, not quite so lifted up, less mysterious, more approachable. The Methodists' traditional emphasis on class meetings, Sunday school for all ages and Bible study undergirds the belief that a close, personal relationship is possible with a God who is both accessible and intimate. The emphasis on fellowship and the "down home" quality of American Methodist worship practices as opposed to the more formal and symbolic nature of the liturgy of the Episcopal Church may account for some of the discrepancies among the two "Amazing Grace" groups.

A second source of these differences may lie in the patterns of governance implied in the two views of ordination. One calls the clergy by different names: an ordained Episcopalian is called a priest and the Methodist a pastor. The Episcopal Church entertains a more sacerdotal definition of ordination. In the sample, several of the ordained Episcopal clergy were referred to as Father, thereby highlighting their affinity with their Roman Catholic brothers as opposed to their Protestant brothers and sisters. Their Methodist counterparts were invariably called by their first names. Leadership among United Methodists is more egalitarian; the clergy are not set apart from or above the laity.

A third source of the differences may lie in the social location of the two groups in their denominations. When the United Methodists stand to sing "Amazing Grace" they are firmly rooted in their heritage; when the Episcopalians sing it, they are an anomaly. Perhaps imaging God as Judge and as the mysterious Other is a symptom of their own precarious position among their peers. The fact that these people are anomalies in their chosen denomination would also account for the fact that the Episcopalians are more likely than their Methodist cohorts to meet in small groups. They are more likely to gather in small groups for prayer and Bible study because in these groups their religious experience can be sustained in the face of the hostility evinced from their colleagues for whom the formality of Sunday worship is perhaps the strongest link to *their* heritage. Too much can be made of this more psychological understanding of the differing views of God and their source in the social location of these two groups. However, such an understanding fits with the anger that greeted me in some of these communities when the popularity of "Amazing Grace" became the topic of conversation! As one person exclaimed, "I left the Methodist church and joined this one just so that I would never have to sing 'Amazing Grace' again!"

Conclusions

What conclusions can be drawn from these data concerning the transmission of denominational identity through the hymn "Amazing Grace"?

The power of the hymn to transmit the attitudes and feelings of an enduring aspect of the Methodist religious tradition is clearly in evidence among the people in this sample. "Amazing Grace" was born in Methodist assemblies in the midst of conversion experience, entered the oral tradition, and was handed along at camp meetings where conversion was both *context and content.* Although at some point it was written down in hymnals and is often sung in Sunday morning worship, it has not lost its place in the oral tradition and therefore maintains the spontaneity and power of singing "by heart." Its text and style are closer to those denominations where more informal styles of worship prevail. Its natural habitat is the camp meeting or its modern counterparts—informal prayer meetings and Bible study groups. Patterns of assembly that grow out of that "path of faith" will welcome it. Those for whom "Amazing Grace" is their favorite hymn fit into the style of most United Methodist assemblies in the sample.

In Episcopal churches it will find a home among those for whom small, informal group meetings are common and where the congregation is more active in charismatic renewal, a modern-day movement within the church which promotes and thrives on more informal and affect-laden expressions of religious experience in public worship. Indeed it may be that their use of the hymn "originated" in *Cursillio* or its antecedent, "Faith Alive!"—two para-ecclesial, ecumenical renewal movements popular among Episcopalians in New England. At this point in the history of the Episcopal Church, "Amazing Grace" and hymns like it may carry the force of religious revival similar to the one of the Wesleys in eighteenth-century England whose patterns of worship at that time served as an antidote to what the Wesleys considered to be the arid practice in the Church of England. Charles Wesley's hymns, though much more complex rhetorically and theologically than "Amazing Grace," were a powerful vehicle for the spread of "methodism" throughout the English countryside. They, too, were sung in open air meetings, at class meetings and at small, informal worship settings. Many of them were committed to memory and therefore survived and were passed down through the oral tradition. Those Episcopalians for whom "Amazing Grace" is their favorite hymn are an anomaly among the people in the sample and would not generally fit without some tension into those Episcopal congregations where the more formal and ritualistic patterns hold complete sway over Sunday worship.

One of the more interesting and intriguing conclusions to be drawn from this segment of the data of the Boston University project concerns those aspects of identity actually transmitted by aesthetic objects like hymns. Although there are many similarities among the "Amazing Grace" groups about their ideas of God, there are also crucial differences. The conclusion to be drawn from this fact is that the hymn may mean different things under different circumstances! There is a multivocal quality to aesthetic forms that allows a variety of meanings to be carried by them.

In my view, rather than necessarily expressing *doctrines* of God, this hymn above all else expresses *structures of faith* that are consistent with although not limited to the experience of conversion. It functions as a symbol for *an intensity of personal experience* of faith which spills out of the singers, pushing them to become the means of conversion for those around them. Many but not all images of God can work in its milieu. It also functions as a symbol for the experience of the nearness of God. The God who is near might be loving or judging, comforter or confessor, known or mysterious, strict or permissive; nevertheless God is near. This knowledge of God's presence occasions the outpouring of praise and wonder on the part of the singers so that grace has a "sweet sound."

This hymn transmits this intensity of personal experience as much through its style as the content of its verbal and musical images. The subject matter chosen is a personal account of the experience of salvation through "amazing grace." The hymn starts with an exclamation: "Amazing Grace!" The style of the hymn grows out of that phrase. Not only does grace save, the manner in which the singer tells of his or her experience of that grace also saves. The highly personal quality of the images intensifies the message of the saving grace of the Lord. The emotional aura of the text is bound up not only in the content of the story but the images chosen and the rhetorical manner in which the author presents his theme. The singer speaks to the heart of everyone who stands in the assembly to sing the hymn. The sound is sweet, and it saves. As for the execution of the hymn, here, too, the style communicates the subject matter. The folk quality of the melody allows everyone to sing it. Most people know the verses by heart, and therefore people do not have their noses buried in the hymnbook while they are singing. The tune begs for improvised counter-melodies and flourishes, which intensify affect as the verses succeed one another. It fosters religious enthusiasm.

"Amazing Grace" corresponds with the criterion enunciated by the woman who described her favorite hymn: "It sounds the way following Christ is like." "Amazing Grace" transmits through its "sounds" religious experience that is more compatible with the informal worship styles of American Methodism and is more central to its history. It is anomalous to the Episcopal Church because the hymn conflicts with the style of the most significant transmitters of its history and tradition: the rituals and prayers of the *Book of Common Prayer,* which dominate public assemblies. These assemblies are characterized by formal symbolic activity rather than religious enthusiasm.

As for the issue of the transmission of a denomination's culture, it is easy to see from the data that hymns carry the culture of the denomination from one generation to another but that they also may provide the means whereby that denomination can be modified in significant ways. In the case of the Episcopalians, this group of "outsiders" has brought this hymn with them into the denomination where it continues to provide them with the means to express religious experience that is not necessarily characteristic of their colleagues. Yet they remain attached to their church! They would be more upset than their fellow church members if they had to leave their church! What will it mean to these Episcopal churches to have proponents of more evangelical religion singing their hearts out in their midst over several decades?

The transmittal of the religious identity of a group is accomplished through artistic forms, such as hymns, which require that each generation appropriate anew the meanings evoked in their singing. This process of appropriation takes place under myriad and unpredictable circumstances which control to a certain extent the meaning that is transmitted. Thus, in the case of "Amazing Grace," when Methodists stand to sing it, they are reinforcing their denominational identity. However, we have seen in this example that such is not the case among Episcopalians. These highly loyal members of their denomination have brought the hymn with its emphasis on religious enthusiasm into the more formal and ritualistic precincts of modern-day Episcopalianism. Whether it will have an effect on the context, for example, resulting in the renewal of enthusiasm in the denomination, remains to be seen. What can be said is that the context in which they sing this hymn has had some effect on its meaning.

A more personal and polemical note: a denomination ignores its musical traditions, past and present, to its peril. Not only are its roots in the past severed but also its ability to refashion those roots in contemporary religious terms is diminished. If it is true that denominational reform and renewal are needed, one effective means of bringing them in is through song. Charles Wesley understood this; the civil rights marchers of the 1960s understood this; and the women fighting for inclusive language in hymnals understand this. In singing one "makes faith." The songs our mothers taught us—those that come to us" out of our historic traditions—are powerful vehicles for faith-making, and because they are art forms they provide us not only with the means to understand the faith that enlivened our foremothers and forefathers, but also the means to refashion it with our own insights and experiences. They should exist alongside the contemporary hymns which grow out of the imaginations of artists living at the end of the twentieth century.

NOTES

1. This project was made possible by a grant from the Lilly Endowment as a part of its focus on mainstream Protestantism.

REFERENCES

Dulles, Avery
    1974   *Models of the Church.* Garden City, N.Y.: Doubleday & Co.
Kroeber, A. L.
    1957   *Style and Civilizations.* Westport, Conn.: Greenwood Press.
Langer, Susanne K.
    1957   *Philosophy in a New Key.* Cambridge, Mass.: Harvard University Press.
Meland, Bernard.
    1976   *Fallible Forms and Symbols.* Philadelphia: Fortress Press.

5

Women's Organizations: Centers of Denominational Loyalty and Expressions of Christian Unity

Barbara Brown Zikmund

Any attempt to look at questions of denominational identity in U.S. religious history cannot ignore the fact that there are more women than men in most churches. This is true now, and this has been true for over two hundred years. Therefore, to discern the ways in which denominational identity is shaped and preserved in Protestantism in this country it is important to examine the experiences of women. In fact, some believe that only by surveying the women's organizations within major denominations will the most significant distinctions between denominations become evident.

At the same time, a close examination of the historical record shows that Protestant church women's organizations are rarely narrowly denominational. Although women's organizations emerged to serve the needs of women in particular denominational traditions, Protestant church women's organizations consistently transcended denominational ties and broke new ecumenical ground. Women's organizations are self-consciously denominational but refuse to be limited by many of the confessional, cultural, and racial divisions that separate Protestant denominations in this country. Even as Protestant church women's organizations strengthened denominational loyalty, they also helped form crucial new organizations dedicated to building ecumenical bridges between denominations.

The Rise of Women's Organizations

There are several ways to describe the rise of women's organizations in U.S. Protestantism. One might go back to the gatherings of women in the home of Anne Hutchinson in the 1630s. Hutchinson was an outspoken critic of the theology preached in Puritan Boston. She invited women into her home to discuss sermons, and she challenged political and religious authorities. Unfortunately, her meetings with women were not understood or appreciated, and eventually she was banished from the Massachusetts Bay Colony.

As the United States developed, more formal structures appeared within Protestant churches to serve the needs of women. Nevertheless, it is important to note that the establishment of women's organizations built upon an emerging ideology that women's roles in the home as wife and mother were especially important. In her private "separate sphere," women were natural keepers of goodness and virtue. Men and women believed that women needed support for their maternal instincts and their innate abilities as nurturers. And church women had a special calling to preserve Christian values and to raise children to be faithful Christians and good citizens.

By the nineteenth century, many middle- and upper-class white Protestant women embraced what is now called the "cult of true womanhood." As individuals and within the churches women accepted an ideal that they should be pious, pure, and domestic, submitting to the dictates of their spouses. They agreed that by staying home they could keep the true faith and preserve high morals. While men were necessarily drawn into the sordid public world to earn money to support their families, women had a responsibility to provide a peaceful haven within the home and church. Common sense claimed that preserving "women's place" was best for women and good for society (Welter 1966; Cott 1977).

In the early nineteenth century when New England women first began to form voluntary associations, their motives were in keeping with their understanding of women's role. Organizations for women were natural extensions of the family. "Maternal associations" helped young women develop proper religious and moral influence over children. Sunday schools extended their influence as teachers, and associations to meet the needs of poor widows and orphans served the wider human family.

Christian women also founded "moral reform societies," groups committed to reforming the behavior of men by launching open attacks on prostitution in the growing cities of America and by rescuing young women from the sex trade. The phenomenal growth of the Women's Christian Temperance Union in the late nineteenth century was grounded in the conviction that women had to change men in order to protect the home.

Throughout the nineteenth century hundreds of so-called voluntary associations or "benevolent" societies were organized by Protestants in this country to serve diverse social and religious causes. Men and women from many denominational traditions banded together to support each other, to educate the public about an issue, and to raise money. From the beginning, however, the ideal of women's separate sphere limited women's participation in these organizations. It is well documented that discrimination against certain women in the antislavery crusade sparked the beginnings of the women's rights movement in 1848.

Most church women, however, did not become activists. They continued to believe that a woman's place and work was grounded in her role as wife and mother and that separate organizations for women within the churches were helpful.

Types of Women's Organizations

At the risk of oversimplification it is possible to document five different types of women's organizations which have emerged within mainline Protestant church history in the United States from the early nineteenth century to the present: the separate order, the mission board, the ladies aid society, the altar guild, and the prayer or support group. Not all of these appear as distinct bodies or as organized structures in all periods of history. Not all of them are found in every denominational tradition. Taken together, however, they encompass the unique ways in which women relate to the churches and provide specific channels through which women express denominational loyalty.

The Separate Order

In the early nineteenth century there were no women clergy in U.S. Protestantism. Certain women in the free church denominations and among the Quakers may have "served" in local settings from time to time as "evangelists" or "female laborers," but generally speaking Protestant women could not make a "vocational" commitment to the church. The growth of pietism in Europe and revivalism in the United States began to change things.

In the 1830s a young Lutheran pastor, Theodore Fliedner of Kaiserswerth, Germany, decided to open a hospital and to invite young unmarried women to serve as "deaconess sisters" in a ministry of mercy. The idea had great appeal, and Kaiserswerth became a center of new vocational service for Protestant women. Deaconesses were "consecrated" by the church; their promises, however, were not considered vows for life. They lived and worshiped together in a common house, but they were free to leave if they wished to get married or were needed at home. Such a "Protestant" religious order for women, based upon the biblical tradition of *diakonia* (service), spread throughout the world (Bancroft 1890; Golder 1903; World Council of Churches 1966).

Within Lutheran, Methodist, and Protestant Episcopal (Anglican) churches the Kaiserswerth model extended to the United States. In 1849 four Kaiserswerth-trained deaconesses came to work at a new Lutheran Protestant hospital in Pittsburgh, Pennsylvania (Lee 1963, 28). In 1852 the Sisterhood of the Holy Communion (Episcopal) was organized in New York City. It supported communities of Christian women devoted to works of charity and held together by commitments to personal holiness and spiritual discipline. Later the formation of the Community of St. Mary followed a more Roman Catholic pattern, involving lifetime vows and obedience to the order (Donovan 1986, 31–38). These sisterhoods, and many others founded to support institutions for orphans, girls, widows, aged, and the poor did not attract large numbers of women, but they built strong denominational ties among those women who took the vows, and they established nursing as a legitimate female career.

Following the Civil War, Lutheran, Methodist, Episcopal, and German Evangelical women formed special deaconess orders and expanded their vocational vision to include social welfare work as well as hospital service. In 1885 Lucy Rider Meyer founded the Chicago Training School for Women, and the office of deaconess was formally recognized by the Methodist Episcopal Church a few years later (Lee 1963, 36–37). In 1889 the German Evangelical Deaconess Society began its work in St. Louis (Rasche 1984, 95–109). And in 1890 and 1891 the Episcopal Church opened two schools to train deaconesses (Donovan 1986, 106–122).

For over one hundred years the distinctive vocational role of a Protestant deaconess sister attracted many Christian women. As other options for service became available, however, deaconess orders were modified, or even phased out, in some denominations. In some cases deaconesses have been aligned and absorbed into the clergy "orders" of the churches.

In a few denominations, such as the Episcopal Church, separate orders for women remain a special type of church organization for women. As members of one of these orders, lay women commit themselves to a way of life and to regular retreats, while sometimes remaining vocationally grounded in their families and nonchurch careers. The Episcopal Order of the Daughters of the King and the Society of the Companions of the Holy Cross are examples of this type of women's organization (Cavert 1948, 37).

The Mission Board

The participation of U.S. women in organized mission work began in 1802 when a Baptist woman in Boston established the Boston Female Society for Missionary Purposes to raise additional funds for the Massachusetts Missionary Society. She took her inspiration from the biblical story of the widow's two mites, noting that every woman could contribute an extra "cent" to the salvation of souls if she denied herself some little thing. Other women agreed, and the idea spread. Soon many women organized "female cent societies" to support missions (Beaver 1968, 14–16).

Originally these organizations were "auxiliaries," raising money for mission boards run by men. Most of them were ecumenical, because the pioneering work of many mainline Protestants in the foreign mission field was through the American Board of Commissioners for Foreign Missions, founded in 1810. The ABCFM benefited from the monies of the "female societies," and received sizable bequests and legacies from committed Christian women. In 1839 the board's annual report showed contributions from 680 "ladies associations" (Goodsell 1959, 154–155).

Gradually, however, denominations wanted more direct control over their mission efforts and broke away from the ABCFM. Furthermore, women learned from returning missionaries that there was a special need for single women in the mission field to meet the needs of women and children. In cultures where male missionaries could not even speak with women, and missionary wives were too burdened with their own family obligations to render much help, single women were needed. Most church officials and mission boards, however, viewed women on the mission field "as necessary but subordinate and secondary" (Beaver 1968, 54). Women did not agree, and slowly they began to look for ways to agitate and promote mission programs and personnel to meet the needs of women and children not being reached by missionaries and programs sponsored by the male-dominated mission boards.

In 1837, a Methodist Female Missionary Society founded in 1819 in New York sent a woman missionary to Liberia. In 1861 an interdenominational society, the Women's Union Mission Society of New York, began recruiting and sending single women to the mission field. By 1883 it had supported forty-three women (Bliss 1952, 36).

Changes in mission work and structures follow different patterns in different denominations. However, during the decade after the Civil War women in practically every major Protestant denomination reorganized themselves for mission work. Perhaps women discovered their own strength during the Civil War when they ran effective organizations to oversee welfare programs for Union soldiers and their families. But for whatever reason, during the post-Civil War era there was a virtual explosion of new forms of women's associations (Scott 1984, 13).

In 1868 a group of Boston Congregational women organized the Woman's Board of Missions (WBM). Within a year Congregational women in Chicago followed the WBM example, organizing the Women's Board of Missions of the Interior (WBMI). And within the decade Congregational women organized women's boards in California and Hawaii (Zikmund 1984, 140–153). Also in 1869 Methodist Episcopal women created the Woman's Foreign Missionary Society (Wheeler 1883). Soon thereafter women in the American Baptist, Presbyterian, and Reformed denominations joined the Congregationalists and the Methodists in establishing separate women's boards (Beaver 1968, 90–92).

Each case was different. Usually the newly organized national women's mission organizations agreed to cooperate with the general boards of their denominations while maintaining a measure of financial and administrative independence. They put their energies into raising money and recruiting single women to work among women and children. The general denominational mission boards arranged details of passage, the living situations, and the supervision of the women in the field, but the primary link between local churches and women missionaries was through the women. As one male mission secretary wrote, "Ladies will write to each other as they will not write to me, [although I] do the best I can to win their confidence." The object of these new boards was to "diffuse information, to call out and sustain a loving, active interest in behalf of our female missionaries, and to raise funds for the support and constant enlargement of our work" (Davis 1926, 9).

Initially the women's boards in all denominations had to overcome great resistance. Looking back at their beginnings women recalled how "it was not supposed that women were capable of doing such work outside the home. The idea of their conducting a business, keeping books, or carrying on the work of a large organization was unheard of" (Davis 1926, 6). Some women's boards encountered so much opposition from male church leaders that they lasted only a few years. The Woman's Foreign Missionary Society of the Methodist

Protestant Church, organized in Pittsburgh, Pennsylvania, in 1879, was dissolved by a vote of the General Conference in 1884. Women had no voice or vote in that body (Beaver 1968, 105–106).

Most of the national women's boards thrived, however, supported by the existence of thousands of local women's mission societies. The boards benefited from the work of many groups of women in local congregations who gathered regularly to study and learn about "mission" and to raise money for the work. These women became deeply involved in the world. They studied each mission project carefully. They learned about their own faith and forged very personal connections to their church. They wrote letters and educated themselves about "heathen lands." They read missionary literature filled with human stories of salvation and transformation. They entertained returning missionaries on furlough and sent care packages to meet special needs. Within women's mission societies the eyes of church women were raised to new horizons, and the pettiness and parochialism of the average church was transcended. In the 1930s the *Christian Century* noted the positive impact of these organizations: "For many a woman the missionary society lifted her membership in the church above the level of mere perfunctoriness, and above the level of what might be called kitchen labor, to the plane of cultural and spiritual enrichment" ("The Churchwoman" 1930, 300–303). Women's missionary societies pressed the churches and the clergy to deal with the larger issues and obligations of their Christian faith.

Second, women's missionary societies raised great amounts of money, often above and beyond the regular benevolences of the church. In fact, the tradition of the "women's gift" or the "second offering" for mission flows directly out of women's concern for the special needs of women and children in the mission field. The women revealed repeatedly "the power of small offerings frequently collected from large numbers of contributors." Whereas the general mission boards asked for large contributions, "the women asked for two cents per week—asked it from door to door; devised mite boxes, formed small local circles, held frequent meetings, looked after children, old women, poor people, hand-picked their own fruit, and astonished the world with their success" (Montgomery 1914, 38).

Ladies' Aid Societies

A third form of women's organization developed in the churches out of many of the same needs which shaped women's mission societies. A major difference, however, was that ladies' aid societies were usually concerned with matters closer to home. If women were expected to be homemakers and the caretakers of families and of institutions which were natural extensions of the family such as the school and the church, ladies' aid societies were the voluntary organizations within local congregations concerned about local families, local schools, and the health of the local church.

Women realized that as individuals they did not have a great deal of power to change things. They learned, however, that together they could raise money, and money gave them power. Generally speaking, ladies' aid groups in local congregations sought to deal with the practical business of helping the church meet expenses. Women worked at many things to make money "to supplement the church's budget or its building fund, to purchase a new carpet or a new organ, or to pay off the debt." Through the "making of quilts and rag carpets, the serving of dinners and oyster suppers, the holding of rummage sales, bazaars and fairs, the promotion of lectures and entertainments," women raised incredibly large sums of money for church and local community needs. Many small churches depended upon this type of financial support ("The Churchwoman" 1930, 300–303).

Involvement in the work of ladies' aid societies was always time-consuming. What the women lacked in resources they made up for with time. As with any activity involving a great deal of time, participation in the fund-raising and local service projects of ladies' aid societies nourished deep feelings of belonging and identity. Women poured themselves into their churches, giving time and money and discovering in return that the church could not survive as an institution without them and their financial support. For these women, "feeling needed" became a legitimate way to forge congregational and denominational loyalty. Even when churches no longer needed the money, women's organizations continued to sponsor fund-raising activities and events in order to nourish their sense of belonging and to provide opportunities for fellowship. Ladies' aid societies often rendered community-wide local social services, providing fellowship and wholesome recreation under church auspices in small communities (Cavert 1948, 32).

By the 1930s the earlier distinction between mission societies and ladies' aid societies became blurred. Efforts were made to merge the various organizations for women in local congregations into overall women's auxiliaries, women's fellowships, women's societies, or women's guilds. In small congregations missionary programming became one part of the ladies' aid structure. In large congregations women divided into "circles," which focused upon specific tasks, serving the needs of a specific constituency. Generally speaking, the materials prepared by denominational "women's" offices came to cover all areas of women's work and life in the church: spiritual life, Bible study, missionary education, social outreach, local church needs, stewardship, fund-raising, and ecumenical relations (Cavert 1948, 28–32).

The Altar Guild

In more liturgical churches there is another women's organization which is sometimes separate from both the missionary society and the ladies' aid society. Also, in small congregations even when there is no formal women's organization there is invariably a group of women who take responsibility for the care of the church altar. Altar guilds are responsible for arranging the flowers for the altar, preparing the elements for the Lord's Supper, polishing the silver used in the service, cleaning up after worship, and seeing to it that the altar cloths are kept in good condition. In some denominations there is a national committee to support altar guilds and to deepen the devotion and reverence of altar guild members.

Serving on the altar guild may be an elected responsibility tied up with lay oversight of congregational worship and music. In other cases its tasks simply fall to an older woman or to the women who sing in the choir, because they are "up there" anyway. For the women who do these things, however, care for the altar deepens loyalties and allegiances to the clergy, the local church, and the denomination. This is especially true when the identity of a denomination is closely aligned with its sacramental life, as in the case of the Episcopal Church. The women who carry out these activities have strong denominational loyalties.

Prayer and Women's Support Groups

This final category of women's organizations in church life is difficult to describe. In one sense women have gathered in groups for prayer under the sponsorship of the church since the first century. In the nineteenth century the conviction that women should not pray publicly in "promiscuous assemblies," that is, in meetings where men and women met together, led to the institutionalization of separate women's prayer and Bible study groups. Women came together to pray for each other, for their families and communities, and for the world. Because prayer is a personal act, women in prayer groups often came to know each other well and through that knowledge to care more deeply for each other and for their church. Inasmuch as more self-conscious loyalty to the local congregation often carries with it denominational identity, these women developed stronger denominational allegiance.

On the other hand, in more recent years the women's liberation movement has emphasized the importance of support groups for female health and well-being. Feminists argue that women are often isolated in their families and thus find it difficult to trust their own thoughts and feelings. It is important, therefore, for women to come together to discover themselves. Through "consciousness raising" groups women learn that they have common experiences of doubt and faith. And in these supportive groups women begin to imagine new ways in which churches can become life-giving, rather than life-draining, communities for women.

Membership in women's organizations in the churches has always provided a certain amount of special support and "networking" for those women who were active enough to hold regional or national offices and responsibilities. Whether at the annual meeting of a denominational woman's mission board or a regional "school for mission" or an ecumenical gathering for worship, women cherished these experiences. Among many church women there was a mystique about such gatherings. By attending conferences, fellowship days, and state rallies women nourished friendships across the miles and shaped denominational identity.

In more recent decades women have rediscovered the power of networking beyond local congregations. New creative task forces, commissions, and regional and national structures attract younger church women who find traditional women's organizations unappealing or stifling. These younger women acknowledge that the existing "circles" and "fellowships" in their local congregations may serve the needs of older women, but they are looking for something else. They want to relate to women in the church, but they do not have the time or desire to seek out local women's organizations in their churches. These women find that they can strengthen their feminist commitments and sustain their denominational loyalty through contacts they make serving on special task forces and commissions beyond the local church. Furthermore, these "new church women" have strong convictions about inclusive language and commitments to racial and social justice in the churches.

The character and purposes of women's organizations in the churches change with the times, the denomination, and with the current issues and crises in the wider church and society. Historically, Protestant women's organizations have tended to be outwardly motivated. Church women organized to serve the needs of others. They wanted to share the gospel with women and children around the world; they wanted to meet the needs of the ill, the poor, the broken and hurting; they wanted to strengthen their local church so that it could do its work better; they wanted to support women who felt called to unconventional forms of faithfulness; they wanted to take care of details so that people could be free to get on with important tasks and decisions. Women have usually considered it unseemly for women to organize to serve their own needs.

In recent years traditional women's organizations in the churches have been shrinking. Some of this is because existing women's societies, fellowships, and organizations have not recognized the changing responsibilities of women employed outside the home. Others would say that women have become more self-centered and self-serving, finding traditional service-oriented women's organizations unattractive. Still others point out that the power once held by women's organizations in the churches is gone, and modern women will not give their time and money unless they feel they can make a difference.

Women's Organizations in Relationship
to Denominational Structures

By the second decade of the twentieth century American Protestantism was well organized into denominational bureaucracies with national staffs. Decision-making was more and more centralized and national legislative bodies had become symbolic centers of denominational identity. Not surprisingly, with increased denominational centralization the arguments against separate women's organizations increased. Denominational leaders worried that independent women's organizations undermined denominational unity.

Helen Barrett Montgomery, a popular Baptist author of a book about the history of women in foreign missions, *Western Women in Eastern Lands,* countered this thinking. Montgomery insisted that women's boards were not diverting money from the general mission offerings but tapping "a new vein of contributions that would not and could not be reached by the methods of the general boards." The development of a unified board might be logical, but it would never work because, she wrote, men did not know how to work "easily with women, unless they be head and women clearly subordinate." In spite of the rapid strides made toward one "tremendous organization" of men and women working side by side, Montgomery quipped, "We have still a long stretch of unexplored country to be traversed before the perfect democracy of Jesus is reached." She also believed that total contributions would decrease under a unified board. Montgomery was especially worried about the work among women and children. "It is only natural and right that the work of establishing churches, training ministers, educating the future leaders, should absorb the energies of men." However, she added, when funds are limited, without separate women's boards the work for women and children will not be a priority. Finally, Montgomery believed that women's organizations could make a distinctive contribution, out of their "feminine viewpoint." "Certain methods are tried out, certain experiments made that [do] not appeal to men." Women can cooperate all the better by doing their separate work alone, she wrote. The way out of the slight tension which existed between women's organizations and the denominational structures, she concluded, was not to say: "These women are doing too well, they are raising four million dollars a year, let us absorb them," but rather to cultivate new forms of cooperation (Montgomery 1914, 266–272).

The new forms of "cooperation," however, failed to preserve most of the separate women's organizations in mainline Protestantism. In 1910 the Methodist Episcopal Church, South, merged its women's boards and general boards. Northern (American) Baptist women began participating in a cooperative "joint council" in 1915 leading to a 1955 integration of the woman's board into regular denominational structures (Beaver 1968, 184–187).

In 1920 the northern Presbyterians consolidated several women's boards to form a united Women's Board of Foreign Missions. Soon thereafter (1922) the Presbyterian General Assembly, where women were not voting members, combined all benevolent groups in the church into four major boards dealing with foreign missions, home missions, Christian education, and ministerial pensions. Presbyterian women at the time were convinced that consolidation would serve the best interests of the church (Boyd and Brackenridge 1983, 59ff.). In retrospect, however, some Presbyterian women came to lament the loss of the "one power base developed by women in the Presbyterian Church" (Verdesi 1976, 77).

By the 1920s there were four independent Congregational women's mission boards, one based in Boston, one in Chicago, one in California, and one in the Hawaiian islands. As Congregationalism moved toward more centralized denominational decision making and unified fund-raising, pressures to merge these women's organizations into the American Board of Commissioners for Foreign Missions (by that date the denominational structure for Congregational foreign mission outreach) increased. Arguments were made that the need for separate boards was over, that missionaries would be better served, that the Nineteenth Amendment ushered in a new day for women, and that bureaucratic efficiency was important. In 1927 three of the four Congregational women's boards ceased independent existence and became part of the American Board. Only the Woman's Board of Missions for the Pacific Islands remained independent. A recent assessment of that story asserts that the consolidation was really counterproductive. It "reinforced trust in bureaucratic solutions, and it furthered a system of male-dominated leadership in the church. Women gave up autonomy, and their unique contributions to foreign missions strategy were lost. It was a high price to pay" (Stuckey-Kauffman 1987, 100).

Methodist women were the only major Protestant group that retained real power in the denominational consolidations of the twentieth century. Although the Methodist Episcopal Church, South, and the Methodist Protestant Church had streamlined their women's organizations earlier, in 1939 when they merged with the Methodist Episcopal Church, North, to create the Methodist Church, the Woman's Division of Christian Service preserved its independence from the general denominational mission boards and assumed the oversight of a unified women's service organization created out of earlier women's mission bodies and ladies' aid societies. Methodist women continued to secure and control their own funds, generate programs, establish separate mission institutions, and recruit and deploy their own commissioned workers from 1940 to 1964 (Stevens 1978).

In the early sixties efforts were mounted again within the Methodist Church's General Board of Missions to eradicate dual mission structures. This time the direct responsibility of the Women's Division for home and foreign mission work was eliminated, along with its mission education programs for children, youth, and students. The Women's Division, however, continued its responsibility for Christian social relations and most importantly, the division kept control over its financial assets. Administration of mission work for women and children was moved into other structures of the church, with the understanding that the Women's Division would continue to contribute designated funds to the budgets of the general mission boards for those programs. After the formation of the United Methodist Church in 1968, women's organizations of the Evangelical and United Brethren (EUB) Church merged into the Women's Division and a new organization was founded, United Methodist Women. Finally, the Women's Division survived yet another reorganization in 1972 and moved through the 1970s into the 1980s as an aggressive advocate for the well-being of women in the church (Hoover 1983, 25–35; see also Campbell 1975; Fagen 1986).

Women's Organizations, Denominational Identity, and Interdenominational Creativity

What is the relationship of this history of women's organizations to denominational identity? On the one hand the establishment of women's mission boards and national denominational organizations for women drew women out of their isolation in home and family and engaged them in the wider world. Because women's mission studies and educational activities with children depended upon tracts, lessons, magazines, and many resources published by national and regional bodies and denominational publishing houses, women in these organizations became highly informed about denominational priorities, emphases, and programs. Furthermore, women's participation in district, regional, and national meetings of these denominational women's organizations further shaped and strengthened their denominational loyalty. Meeting women from distant places and building friendships within denominational families kept active church women committed to the same denomination even when their families moved.

In denominations or communities where there were frequent changes in local pastoral leadership, sometimes formalized through an itinerant system (Methodism), women's organizations provided important stability and continuity for local congregations. Women were the "pillars of the churches" who kept the Baptist, Presbyterian, Methodist, or Congregational faith, even when a local congregation lacked stable pastoral leadership. There is no doubt that separate women's organizations in major Protestant denominations strengthened and shaped denominational identity.

On the other hand, women's organizations in these same Protestant denominations were also highly ecumenical and interdenominational. When the male leadership in many Protestant denominations refused to relate constructively or to acknowledge the legitimacy of different sacramental practices and theological understandings of Christians in other faith traditions, women's organizations transcended denominational pettiness.

As far back as 1887 an early president of the Women's Board of Home Missions of the Presbyterian Church, U.S.A., looked at the needs of the immigrants flooding American cities and asked that Christian women set aside a day for prayer for home missions, when there could be "confession of individual and national sins with offerings." In 1890 two Baptist women, Helen Barrett Montgomery and Lucy Waterbury Peabody, suggested a day of prayer for world missions. In their travels they discovered Christian women in all corners of the globe praying for the needs of the world. Convinced that it was sensible and spiritual for sisters to pray for sisters, they moved out to spread the dream of a World Day of Prayer for missions.

The idea was inspired. Anglican women in Canada already had set aside such a day for prayer. By 1916 Canadian Methodist and Presbyterian women joined them, and they organized a Women's Inter-Church Council to sponsor a national World Day of Prayer. In 1919 church women in the United States celebrated a similar day, and several interdenominational mission boards took responsibility for worship materials. Finally, in 1921 it was decided that the first Friday of Lent would become the annual time for women around the world to observe a World Day of Prayer.

The most significant thing about this women's World Day of Prayer was its inclusiveness. Until 1930 services were written by North American women. Soon thereafter committees were formed in many countries, and responsibility for preparing the services passed from country to country. In segregated societies white women and black women worshiped together long before local congregations or denominational organizations would entertain such an idea. After World War II the yearning of women for peace and reconciliation gave the World Day of Prayer new power, bringing together six hundred German women and women from Britain, France, and other allied nations for the 1947 service in a large Berlin church.

In 1961 the World Day of Prayer celebrated its seventy-fifth anniversary, with thirty-seven prayer fellowships of fifty women each on five continents. Since that time it has become the most universal expression of Christian unity in the world. In fact the annual distribution of its published materials is second only to the Bible. Its informal grass-roots translation projects, ensuring that women participate in the service in their own language, is the largest in the world. In 1987, on the centennial of the World Day of Prayer, women affirmed that the "Day" was a gift "passed from heart to heart by mothers and sisters in Christ who dared to live beyond the limits of creed and race, daily circumstance and tradition." Through the organization of the International Committee for the World Day of Prayer the Holy Spirit continues to lead women to move beyond the limits of denominational identity (International Committee for the World Day of Prayer 1986).

It has already been noted that from the early years women organized for missions interdenominationally as well as denominationally. In 1888 thirty-two women from United States mission boards and four Canadians joined British women to create the first international ecumenical missionary agency intended to be universal in scope, the World's Missionary Committee of Christian Women. Although there were strong pressures to organize denominationally and nationally, the women "kept their sense of solidarity, and conversed, discussed, corresponded, and acted together." This World's Missionary Committee coordinated women's contributions to the 1893 Columbian Exposition in Chicago, the 1900 Ecumenical Missionary Conference in New York, and the Central Committee for the United Systematic Study of Missions." (Beaver 1968, 145–150).

Once women organized themselves locally and denominationally it was a natural step to create and support ecumenical councils, federations, and international committees. Women were key forces behind the Sunday School Union, the YWCA (Young Women's Christian Association), the Cooperating Committee for Women's Christian Colleges in Foreign Fields, the Committee on Christian Literature for Women and Children in Missions Fields, and other organizations which eventually came together to form Church Women United. They were convinced that confessional differences should not stand between them and their sisters, nor erode the impact of their shared calling to teach, reform, or spread the faith (Bennett 1944; Calkins 1961).

Most interdenominational organizations of church women began with local and functional concerns. Women gathered for specific tasks in their own cities and towns. Alongside the World Day of Prayer for missions, women celebrated May Fellowship Day, a day to stress unity in the local community. Councils of church women were organized for community service, working with juvenile courts, welfare agencies, and for parental education. Through these councils it was common for women from different denominations and different races to speak out together "against racial discrimination," and to discover the rich varieties of black and white worship traditions. In certain instances local councils were "interfaith," stretching to learn about the lives and concerns of Jewish women and contributing to the overseas relief of Jewish refugees (Cavert 1948, 51–52).

By 1928 a National Commission of Protestant Church Women was formed, and in 1932 a more independent body reorganized itself into the National Council of Federated Church Women. The organization remained small during the depression years, but its official magazine, *The Church Woman,* was widely circulated. Soon the magazine was the official organ for two additional bodies coordinating interdenominational work by women, the Foreign Missions Conference and the Home Missions Council. Its editorial policies upheld world peace and racial justice in a world churning with war and filled with racial prejudice (Shannon 1977, 12–15).

In 1941 the three organizations came together officially to establish the United Council of Church Women, today known as Church Women United (CWU). The creation of this "united," in contrast to

"interdenominational," organization was an extraordinary development consistent with the history of women's organizations in the
churches. Its mixture of formally accredited representatives from denominational and interdenominational agencies, and the participation
of women from more loosely organized local and state councils of
church women, linked it to national trends and kept it in touch with
the grass roots. Throughout the 1950s and 1960s the United Council
of Church Women exercised important leadership, especially on questions of racial injustice (Shannon 1977, 5–21; see also Calkins 1961).

As the modern women's movement dawned, the women in Church
Women United began to recognize that women were victims of injustice also. Earlier feminist campaigns for voting rights, temperance,
and mission outreach had depended upon the leadership of a few
strong-minded women, but the new women's liberation movement
was different. It started *within* women and spread through small
groups. It followed patterns understood by church women for
decades. Therefore, in 1966 CWU affirmed a new vision—a commitment to "releasing the full potential of every person, . . . and [to]
working toward the wholeness of women and of society." Church
women from many denominations knew that religious faith was essential to being a whole person and they needed to be involved. As
Margaret Shannon, executive director of CWU from 1966 to 1975,
put it: "Church women need to remember that reconciliation and
righteousness go hand in hand. We are not asked to agree on every
issue, but to understand what fears and facts are of serious concern to
our sisters" (quoted in Edens 1978, 9).

Women's Organizations in
Contemporary Mainline Protestantism

With the publication of Betty Friedan's *The Feminine Mystique*
(1963) a new era dawned in the history of women's organizations in
American Protestant churches. Protestant women were deeply involved in the civil rights movement of the 1960s. Yet even as women
worked to promote racial equality, active church women also became
aware of their own limitations. When Friedan argued that education
and the right to participate in all aspects of society were women's
greatest needs, many church women said "amen." They became critical of what Friedan called the "feminine mystique," a mid-twentieth
century idea that women ought to find complete fulfillment in their
female roles as wives and mothers. By the mid-1960s many young
women began to search for new ways to express their Christian faith
and discipleship.

Christian women criticized the "Christian mystique." They argued that it "sells women short" by promoting a theology that claims that women are mysteriously different and implying that women cannot live life in its fullest sense. It uses scripture to convince women that they should limit themselves to "feminine roles." It endorses marriage as an exclusive profession to be chosen above all other vocations, when in truth marriage is only one part of life. In pastoral counseling it tries to "adjust" women to their "feminine role," rather than challenging them to full discipleship. And, finally, it limits women's work in the church to housekeeping, teaching, and calling functions while denying women access to ecclesiastical policy-making and liturgical leadership. The "Christian mystique" blesses the fact that the church fails to see women as full persons, "though their work, money, and prayers are most acceptable" (Suthers 1965, 911–914).

At first most Christian women were ambivalent and even hostile to the women's liberation movement. Older church women often protested that church organizations were precisely where they felt the most liberated. Yet younger women were less sure. By the late 1960s Protestant denominations which had downplayed separate women's organizations for several decades began organizing special women's task forces and commissions. Efforts were made to increase women's presence in general denominational structures. Furthermore, as more women claimed their call to ordained ministry, denominations which had long denied ordination to women (such as the Lutherans and Episcopalians) finally voted approval (see Zikmund 1986, 339–383).

By the 1970s women's organizations in local congregations, in denominational structures, and as vehicles of interdenominational encounter began to wane. The reasons were complex: Younger women who were trying to put family and career together no longer had the time to "give" to church work (or any other voluntary organization). Some women became totally disillusioned with the church once they became aware of its sexist habits and theology, and they simply dropped out. Other women continued to be involved in church work, serving as new female members of general structures, boards, and organizations, rather than putting their energies into women's organizations. The enrollment of women in theological seminaries increased dramatically. Key women who had been, and might have continued to be, active in women's organizations enrolled in seminaries to prepare for pastoral ministry.

It is possible to summarize developments in the recent past by noting the situation of women's organizations in the 1980s: (1) Many local women's organizations continue to function as they always have. In larger congregations women's associations, guilds, and fellowships are alive and well. (2) In the average church, however, women's organizations have decreased in size and influence. Groups shrink as their members get older. The church bazaar is scaled down. Mission projects are less ambitious. And although older women members eagerly invite younger women to join them, few do. (3) Some congregations have done away with all specific "women's" organizations. They have been able to accomplish the same things with short study courses, special outreach activities, and spiritual enrichment seminars. Younger women are more critical of the church and more demanding. When they choose to get involved, they refuse to be limited by the entanglements of an organization. As a result many regional and national women's structures have been recast into "resource centers" and "coordinating offices" that support women's spiritual journey, plan special events, and link women ecumenically.

The most important expression of this development is the Ecumenical Decade of Churches in Solidarity with Women (1988–1998). Coming as a Christian response to the United Nations Decade on Women (1975–1985), it provides a long-term framework for church people all over the world to grow in their understanding and support of women. It grows out of the recognition of the World Council of Churches that women "make up over half of the constituents of the member churches and half of the human family." And it affirms the principle that partnership between men and women ought to mean "equal participation" in the churches.

There was great hope that the UN Decade would result in improvements in women's condition throughout the world. In reality, however, most women today face *more* difficult conditions than they did fifteen or twenty years ago. Military spending and developing economies have worsened the situation of women and children. Patriarchal assumptions are still accepted as "natural" by most of the world's peoples, men and women.

Today, women are the first to lose their jobs, women workers are consistently paid less than men, many women in rural areas engage in an endless struggle for sufficient water and food to support their families. Women of color often carry double and triple burdens related to their gender, race, and poverty. Pregnant women suffer increased health risks as a consequence of nuclear testing. Finally, when socioeconomic conditions deteriorate, levels of sexual abuse and violence against women rise, even among affluent populations (*Ecumenical Decade* 1988).

Women in churches around the world care about these things. "Solidarity" is the word which captures the essence of the Ecumenical Decade for women. In the past, women's organizations assured women that they were not alone. In the 1990s women are confident that through more intentional worship, programs, communication, and outreach during the coming decade, women will grow in knowledge about themselves and God.

Women's organizations in American Protestant churches have been ends unto themselves, *and* they have functioned as the means to greater ends. At times they have been simple organizations, focusing upon one task such as preparing the altar. At other times they have been quite complex, bringing together women of incredible diversity around social issues and religious questions which have kept male ecclesiastical and political leaders apart for years. Women have always recognized that they needed each other in order to be faithful. In fact, a vision of unity always informed their denominational *and* their interdenominational organizations.

> This sense of the necessity of "unitedness" did not keep women from being loyal to the individual church *and* the denominational communion in whose tradition they were reared. . . . But it was never a cramped or narrow denominationalism which such women supported. Their loyalty to the larger conception was strengthened rather than undercut by the conviction (or intuition, if you will) that the church as the Body of Christ was the richer for the gifts that all groups within it, including women, could bring to it. Unity can be seen in the light of particularity. Neither need destroy the other (emphasis added, Calkins 1961, 2–3).

REFERENCES

Bancroft, Jane M.
  1890   *Deaconesses in Europe and Their Lessons for America.*
         New York: Hunt and Eaton.
Beaver, R. Pierce
  1968   *American Protestant Women in World Mission: A History of
         the First Feminist Movement in North America.* Rev. ed.
         Grand Rapids: Wm. B. Eerdmans Publishing Co.
Bennett, Mrs. Fred S. et al.
  1944 *The Emergence of Interdenominational Organizations
         Among Protestant Church Women.* New York: United Council of Church Women.
Bliss, Katherine
  1952   *The Service and Status of Women in the Churches.* London:
         SCM Press.

Boyd, Lois A., and R. Douglas Brackenridge
    1983   *Presbyterian Women in America: Two Centuries of a Quest for Status.* Westport, Conn.: Greenwood Press.
Calkins, Gladys Gilkey
    1961   *Follow Those Women: Church Women in the Ecumenical Movement.* New York: National Council of Churches of Christ.
Campbell, Barbara E.
    1975   *United Methodist Women: In the Middle of Tomorrow.* New York: Women's Division, Board of Global Ministries.
Cavert, Inez M.
    1948   *Women in American Church Life.* New York: Friendship Press.
"The Churchwoman"
    1930   *Christian Century* 47 (March 19): 300–303.
Cott, Nancy F.
    1977   *The Bonds of Womanhood: "Women's Sphere" in New England, 1790–1830.* New Haven, Conn.: Yale University Press.
Davis, Grace T.
    1926   *Neighbors in Christ: Fifty-eight Years of World Service by the Woman's Board of Missions of the Interior.* Chicago: James Watson.
Donovan, Mary Sudman
    1986   *A Different Call: Women's Ministries in the Episcopal Church 1850–1920.* New York: Morehouse-Barlow Co.
Ecumenical Decade: Churches in Solidarity with Women 1988–98.
    1988   A pamphlet published by the World Council of Churches' Sub-unit on Women in Church and Society.
Edens, Martha
    1978   "Speaking the Truth in the Spirit of Love." *The Church Woman* (November):4–10.
Fagan, Ann
    1986   *This Is Our Song: Employed Women in the United Methodist Church.* n.p.: Women's Division, General Board of Global Ministries, United Methodist Church.
Friedan, Betty
    1963   *The Feminine Mystique.* New York: Dell Publishing Co.
Golder, C.
    1903   *History of the Deaconess Movement in the Christian Church.* Cincinnati: Jennings and Pye.
Goodsell, Fred Field
    1959   *You Shall Be My Witnesses.* Boston: American Board of Commissioners for Foreign Missions.

Hoover, Theresa
  1983 *With Unveiled Face: Centennial Reflections on Women and Men in the Community of the Church.* New York: Women's Division, General Board of Global Ministries of the United Methodist Church.
International Committee for the World Day of Prayer
  1986 *Come and Rejoice: Centennial Celebration of the World Day of Prayer, 1887–1987.* New York: Riverside Church.
Lee, Elizabeth Meredith
  1963 *As Friends Among the Methodists: Deaconesses Yesterday, Today, and Tomorrow.* New York: Women's Division of Christian Service, Methodist Church.
Montgomery, Helen Barrett
  1914 *Western Women in Eastern Lands.* New York: Macmillan Co.
Rasche, Ruth
  1984 "Deaconess Sisters: Pioneer Professional Women" in *Hidden Histories in the United Church of Christ,* edited by Barbara Brown Zikmund, 95–109. New York: United Church Press.
Scott, Anne Firor
  1984 "On Seeing and Not Seeing: A Case of Historical Invisibility," *Journal of American History* 71:7–21.
Shannon, Margaret
  1977 *Just Because: The Story of the National Movement of Church Women United in the U.S.A., 1941–1975.* Corte Madera, Calif.: Omega Books.
Stevens, Thelma
  1978 *Legacy for the Future: The History of Christian Social Relations in the Women's Division of Christian Service, 1940–1968.* New York: Women's Division, Board of Global Missions, United Methodist Church.
Stuckey-Kauffman, Priscilla
  1987 "Women's Mission Structures and the American Board" in *Hidden Histories in the United Church of Christ, 2,* edited by Barbara Brown Zikmund, 80–100. New York: United Church Press. Based on a master's thesis by the same author, "For the Sake of Unity: The Absorption of Congregational Woman's Boards for Foreign Missions by the American Board, 1927: With Special Attention to the Woman's Board of Missions for the Pacific." Berkeley, Calif.: Pacific School of Religion, 1985.
Suthers, Hannah Bonsey
  1965 "Religion and the Feminine Mystique," *Christian Century* (July 21): 911–914.

Verdesi, Elizabeth Howell
  1976   *In But Still Out: Women in the Church.* Philadelphia: West-
         minster Press.
Welter, Barbara
  1966   "The Cult of True Womanhood, 1820–1860." *American
         Quarterly* 18(2): 151–174.
Wheeler, Mary Sparkes
  1883   *First Decade of the Woman's Foreign Missionary Associa-
         tion of the Methodist Episcopal Church, with Sketches of its
         Missionaries.* New York: Phillips and Hunt.
World Council of Churches
  1966   *The Deaconess: A Service of Women in the World Today.*
         WCC Studies no. 4. Geneva: World Council of Churches.
Zikmund, Barbara Brown
  1986   "Winning Ordination for Women in Mainstream Protestant
         Churches" in *Women and Religion in America: A Documen-
         tary History, vol. 3:1900–1968,* edited by Rosemary Rad-
         ford Ruether and Rosemary Skinner Keller, 339–383. San
         Francisco: Harper San Francisco.
Zikmund, Barbara Brown, and Sally A. Dries
  1984   "Women's Work and Woman's Boards" in *Hidden Histories
         in the United Church of Christ,* edited by Barbara Brown
         Zikmund, 140–153. New York: United Church Press.

PART TWO

Denominations as
Translocal Institutions

While today we first encounter denominations in their local manifestations—as congregations, church schools, and so forth—most of us probably think of them as those institutions, regional or national, that exist beyond the local community. Earlier in the history of the nation, there were no such translocal institutions. Congregations were either independent entities, ordering their own life and calling their own ministers, or they had ties with ecclesiastical bodies in the "mother country," for example, England, Scotland, or Holland.

Not until the nation achieved independence from Britain did translocal religious bodies begin to form. In the first instance this was a recognition of a need for coordinating the training and ordination of clergy. As the nation developed, translocal organizations were required to carry out or coordinate activities that local congregations were not well-positioned to do—for example, the education of clergy, the administration of foreign and home missions, the coordination of abolitionist activities, the promotion of the Sunday school movement, or the campaign for temperance. While some translocal organizations were nondenominational in origin, they later were incorporated into denominations. As the denominations grew and assumed greater structural definition, they also created other translocal institutions: youth camps, summer assemblies and conferences, campus ministries, and so forth. The roles of the various translocal institutions varied. Some were more or less directly concerned with education and cultural transmission; others were not. Most, however, provided occasions for transmitting aspects of the denomination's culture, as clergy and laity involved themselves in their activities as leaders or participants. In the chapters that follow, we examine four of these translocal institutions in which many continue to participate and also the role of ordination in transmitting denominational culture and identity.

Focusing primarily on Southern Presbyterians, Gwen Kennedy Neville draws on her training as a cultural anthropologist to examine the roles of summer assemblies and conference centers and, in contrast, youth camps. After first providing a perspective on the creation and transmission of culture, she analyzes the spatial arrangements, patterns of interaction, and programs of the summer conference center of the former Southern Presbyterian Church in Montreat, North Carolina. She shows how it and other centers like it function as settings where the denomination's culture is created and transmitted in sacred space and time. While summer youth camps have a different role from that of the conference centers, they too transmit and reinforce identification with the denomination's culture.

A second type of translocal institution is the denominational college. Handing on the sponsoring denomination's culture was not the primary purpose of these institutions, but their founders often had this as a secondary aim. Dorothy C. Bass traces the history of church-related colleges in the United States. She examines the impact of secularizing movements within higher education on church-related colleges. Some of these colleges have given up their church relationship; others have adapted and thrived; yet others have been pushed to the margins of the educational enterprise. For all of them, achievement of the secondary aim of transmitting the denomination's culture has become problematic; most view it as incompatible with the central mission of higher education. In reviewing these developments, Bass raises probing questions about what distinctive role mainline Protestant and other church-related colleges and universities might play in the future of American higher education.

Continuing the theme of the church's relation to higher education is Allison Stokes's examination of the other higher educational strategy developed by mainline Protestants: denominational campus ministries. Confronted by the rapid growth of state and secular private universities that were attracting increasing numbers of their students, the denominations followed their students by establishing campus ministries. Stokes chronicles these developments and the changing character of campus ministry. The challenge that faces contemporary campus ministries, she says, is not transmitting a denomination's culture but "remedial religion."

In contrast to the problems facing denominational colleges and campus ministries in transmitting denominational cultures, one might suspect that theological seminaries would be far more effective in this task. Relative to colleges and campus ministries, this is the case—but only as a matter of degree. Examining some of the formative studies of theological education of the first two-thirds of this century, W. Clark Gilpin concludes that the assumptions undergirding theological education, whether denominationally related or not, have worked against the transmission of denominational cultures. While affirming the ecumenical vision that characterizes these assumptions, Gilpin argues nevertheless that the persistence of denominations as primary religious forms creates a need for a "critical ecclesiology of denominations," and he suggests some of the issues that such a task requires.

In the final chapter of Part Two, J. Frederick Holper ties together the local and translocal dimensions of denominational culture and identity with a focus on ordination, using Presbyterian ordination practices as a case study. Arguing that ordination practices are ways that denominations attempt to guard and transmit their traditions through selecting and authorizing leaders, Holper traces important developments in Presbyterian ordination practices. From early in its American experience, Presbyterian ordination practice reflected a dialectical tension between discipline and democratization. The former, derived from its European heritage, emphasized the tradition and boundary-maintenance role of ordained ministers, elders, and deacons (the latter two being lay offices). Their task was to maintain the God-given identity of the church. The democratization pull is a particular fruit of the American experience, with its more sociological emphasis on the church as a society whose identity is shaped by those who participate by free choice. Holper shows how these two emphases have played themselves out in changing views of ordination. In particular, he examines six "democratizing" developments—not exclusive to Presbyterians—that have had a profound impact on ordination practices and have weakened the role of ordination in transmitting a distinctive denominational identity and have led to "an increasingly less boundaried and disciplined community of faith and witness." He concludes with a brief summary of a recent report by the Presbyterian Church (U.S.A.) that sets forth a new understanding of ordination, one that seeks to reclaim a peculiar Presbyterian communal identity within the ecumenical context of the church catholic and in ways appropriate to contemporary culture. As such, it might be thought of as an example of the kind of critical ecclesiology for which Gilpin calls in the preceding chapter.

6

Places and Occasions in the Transmission of Denominational Culture: The Case of "Southern Presbyterians"

Gwen Kennedy Neville

Cultures and communities worldwide and throughout history have defined themselves as separate entities distinct from other cultures and communities. It is not surprising that in American religious life we find expressions of this boundary formation, one aspect of which is the creation and continuity of denominations within Protestant Christianity. Our society has been described by historians of religion as one based in denominations, those multiple realities within Protestantism that seem so singularly suited to our emerging pluralistic identity as a nation. In colonial times and in the days of the early American nation, denominations were closely associated with northern European cultural communities—the Congregationalists with English and continental Christian movements rooted in communities; the Presbyterians with the Scots and Scots-Irish; and the Reformed Church with German and Dutch settlers. Today denominations are reluctant to be closely associated with these kinds of "ethnic" identities and are more likely to lean toward a new self-definition based on either doctrine or practice. And as our society becomes increasingly mobile, thereby breaking up local communities that once provided roots for local church meanings, denominations appear to be in danger themselves, possibly on the verge of breaking up to make way for umbrella organizations with broader self-definitions that are personalistic and atomistic. Within this seeming crisis of denominational life—in which some social analysts cry that denominations are in danger of disappearing altogether—I have chosen to focus on the ways and means through which I have observed one regional denomination, the "Southern Presbyterians," going about the business of creating and recreating their world of meanings over the generations.[1]

My focus on this one regional denomination—now merged with the "northern" branch of Presbyterianism into the Presbyterian Church (U.S.A.)—is not to single out this group as unique. On the contrary, I use it as one example of the ways in which all denominations within the American experience have constructed their cultural worlds through repeated regatherings in ritual and symbolic spaces and times. These sacred places and occasions form temporary enactments of central symbols and meanings for each denomination and in so doing provide a way of passing along the culture of that group, a way of teaching its own self-fashioning of its boundaries and its separateness. I have described elsewhere an elaborate series of these kinds of regatherings in the Southeast and in Texas and labeled the complex as a pilgrimage system. The gatherings include—in addition to the summer conference centers and family cottage communities of which Montreat in this chapter is an example—family reunions, church homecomings, cemetery association days, and camp meetings. In each of these types of assemblies (which I call "kin-religious gatherings" and also "folk liturgies") people who live in scattered nuclear families and who move about in response to the demands of a modern society return to a homeplace, church, or cemetery to reaffirm their sense of cultural, community ties and meanings with kin and co-believers (Neville 1987; Neville 1973).[2] The assemblies are religious and kin-based, and often the participants are all members of either Methodist, Baptist, or Presbyterian churches. On the one week or weekend of the reunion or homecoming, clusters of related families come "back home" to the location of their childhood or of their parents' childhood as a way of return to older, safer values and cultural worlds. It is a pilgrimage to sacred places and meanings by persons who as Protestants view their individual lives as a pilgrimage, a wandering about in search of their individual fulfillment or "contribution," their expression of their "selves" as members of the elect, or as children of providence, or as those who have been "saved." The vernacular will differ in the ways that Presbyterian, Methodist, and Baptist pilgrims express their personhood, yet within each of these, as in the "mainline" of general denominational life in the United States, there is an emphasis on the person as an individual whose worth before God is unquestioned and whose selfhood is in part created by the fact that as a Protestant she or he must be free to *move*. It is just this imperative, I maintain, that has given birth to the pilgrimage of return and of reunion, one that is directly contrastive structurally to the pilgrimage of the Catholic world in which persons see themselves in fixed positions and whose pilgrimages are enacted in journeys away from home in search of good works and visions. A full discussion of these contrasts is beyond the scope of this chapter; I have chosen here to spotlight only one of the kinds of gatherings I have studied in detail, the summer conference center and family cottage community at Montreat, North Carolina. At this place and within the occasion of summer assemblies, one finds an expression of the Presbyterian self-definition as a "covenant community."

Montreat: Symbolizing Community

The summer conference center of the Southern Presbyterians, known as Montreat, is set apart from the world by a narrow gate set across a straight and narrow road leading into an isolated mountain cove. Houses dot the ridges high above the central artery, their wide porches overlooking the valley below.[3] Other houses lie along the main thoroughfare that finds its way beside the tumbling rapids of Flat Creek, where children wade and fish for crawdads and splash in the pools that punctuate the forward line of water. At the center of the cove is a clearing where tall stone buildings provide harbor for collective life, gatherings, and services of worship and where other buildings advertise their functions as recreation center, bookstore, craft shop, post office, laundromat, and general store. The "cottage people," those who are summering in the houses, mingle with the "conference people," those who are attending week-long organized religious programs, as both groups move in and out of the village center to get mail, buy supplies, wash clothes, and chat at the playground or by the creek. The rhythms of life from day to day at Montreat echo those of the ongoing cycles of nature—sunrise, morning chill calling for jackets while drinking coffee on the porch, rounds of errands or meetings or conference sessions before lunch, clearing away the dishes as the afternoon rains begin, visiting with old friends in the evening by the fire or in the protected corners of the lobby in the conference hotel. All generations are here together—the old people rock and chat with longtime friends; the children go to the "clubs," those day-camp-like organizations where planned age-graded activities and crafts are supervised by college students handpicked for their Presbyterianness; young parents visit as they supervise the very young; and the middle-aged take walks, rides, or shopping trips, attend conference meetings, or sit quietly on a porch and read or rest from the rush of the city.

A cultural web is woven here each summer, which holds the members tightly in a cyclic routine, a periodic community of the kind that cannot be constructed in the urban spaces of a modern American world. It is a community that enacts a drama summer after summer, a story told of what life *is* and *ought to be,* an alternate world of meanings paralleling the meaning world of individualism and atomization. It is a world into which the members enter, play their parts in the performance of this sacred time and space, and leave again refreshed and renewed for their lives in the more secular territories of day-to-day routine. Within this place and this occasion, the culture of being Presbyterian—and more specifically, "Southern Presbyterian"—is created and transmitted once again. The power of ritual has done its work, and a whole symbolic universe is passed along.

The Montreat community started as a vision shared by the denominations of U.S. Protestantism in the late nineteenth century—that of an ideal "city of God" that could be created in little summertime utopias known variously as Chautauquas, camp meetings, conference centers, "encampments," and summer communities. Many of these survive today. Modeled on the great open-field camp meeting preachings of early frontier America, the more permanent versions took shape between 1870 and the century's turn at Ocean Grove, New Jersey; Northfield, Massachusetts; Oak Bluffs on Martha's Vineyard; Craigville on Cape Cod; and at numerous other locations and in various shapes and sizes. Montreat was chartered in 1897 by a partnership composed of ministers and businessmen from Connecticut and New York who, according to Montreat's local historian (Anderson 1949), hoped to fashion a community modeled on Ocean Grove, New Jersey, an early example of the open-air camp-meeting-turned-to-summer-community. It was purchased by the Presbyterians in 1907. Its central meeting building, the auditorium, took on a series of forms from open-sided tent on a platform to the large stone structure it is today. Cabins and temporary shelters of the early days gave way to substantial summer houses and family "cottages" numbering over four hundred by the 1980s. The year-round population of about one hundred families, mostly church and college professionals and retirees, swells in summer into the thousands when a large conference is in session. Then individual Presbyterians from throughout the southern states meet in the classroom buildings and stay in the dormitories for conferences on the Bible, church music, women's concerns, world mission issues, and so on.

Montreat draws its conference attenders and its cottage owners from across the region served by the former Southern Presbyterian Church. This encompasses a fourteen-state area, with the majority of cottage owners and transgenerational family groups coming from North Carolina, South Carolina, Virginia, Georgia, and Florida. A "colony" of Southerners in East Texas in the late nineteenth century created a strong Presbyterian pocket in Marshall, Tyler, and Houston, and this area has continued to contribute cottage families over the years (and, incidentally, to draw its ministers from the seminaries in Richmond, Virginia, and to send its sons and daughters to colleges in North Carolina, Georgia, or Virginia). Other parts of Texas were sparsely dotted with Presbyterian churches and were early locations of "union churches" and combined work with either the Cumberland Presbyterians and/or the Northern Presbyterians (UPCUSA). This drawing into Montreat of people scattered over a wide region is comparable to the zone for drawing pilgrims to a pilgrimage center; the Turners refer to this as a "catchment area" (Turner and Turner 1978). By drawing them together for repeated participation in strongly charged symbolic events, the annual assemblies at Montreat serve continually to resocialize streams of attenders and to forge a regional denominational identity among these participants.

Certain features are shared by the denominational centers and family communities of all the mainline denominations—a permanent conference facility with a central assembly building known as an "arbor," "tabernacle," or "auditorium"; a number of permanent houses or cottages owned by private families who hand them down through the generations and often owned in clusters by families who are related to one another; a conference office run by a director and staff paid by an incorporated "association" or "conference center." The location is in the mountains or near a lake or an ocean beach, or removed into a rural spot, associated with natural beauty and recreational pleasures. There exists in each of the centers, in addition to the cottages and the central meeting hall, a set of buildings or converted houses or, as at Montreat, college dormitories, to be rented by those who do not own houses or cottages and come to attend conferences on special topics with denominational emphases. The topics of the conferences are in some way also often organized by or connected to the overarching denominational boards and agencies. In the case of Montreat, various boards have traditionally used the center for denomination-wide meetings; in the case of other centers, the denomination may lease the conference facility from the owning "association." In each of the communities, there is a separation of the cottage people from the conference people. Both are there because of ties to religious denominational life, but the two groups are there for different purposes. The conference people are temporary residents attracted by meetings; the cottage people are ongoing, transgenerational inhabitants attracted by kinship and continuity.

In the North Carolina mountains within a short drive from Montreat, centers of denominational family life have been built by the Methodists (Lake Junaluska) and the Baptists (Ridgecrest). Each exhibits the features outlined above. If this is so, one asks, how is it that Montreat can teach Presbyterianism to its participants; and how can the others teach Methodist and Baptist lifeways? The answer to this question is embedded in the nature of ritual as a learning environment and in the nature of symbols as communicators of culture. Each denomination speaks in its own dialect of the Protestant tongue. Each of these three major segments of Southern religion is bounded off in symbolic ways from the others. It is these kinds of markers that must be encoded through ritual and taught to successive waves of Methodists, Baptists, and Presbyterians. They include the symbolism of the worship service—the use of spatial arrangement and order of worship as well as choice of hymns, the manner and content of the preaching, and the presence or absence of an "altar call." Markers also include the style of family and kinship—whether "lateral" with an emphasis on one's living relatives on both sides, or "lineal" with an emphasis on descent from a common ancestor at the head of a long line of Christian ancestors. Also, boundaries are taught regarding beliefs and social practices. Toleration for differences, for instance, is often mentioned as a strong marker in the United Church of Christ denomination, while insistence on one way to heaven through salvation is given as a powerful belief in other denominations, notably the Baptists. Another way of bounding off group life and expressing denominational identity is transmitted in and through the very process of reassembling annually or periodically with the same people one has seen in happy and relaxed summertime camaraderie over the unfolding succession of summers that mark one's life. Friendships made at Montreat in childhood are lifelong friendships, and kin groups forged through ritual participation establish networks of obligation and of awareness that contrast sharply with the isolated or "disconnected" world of day-to-day urban life. Within the symbolic community of Montreat, worlds of belief and behavior of the Presbyterian "denominational culture" can be expressed and invented in ways that complement the secular routine; and these can be taught and learned.

Symbolic Worlds and Boundaries

The Presbyterian "denominational culture"—essentially this particular construction of theological and social reality—is centered on three significant social-theological themes: the doctrine of God as sovereign over a community of believers; the idea of the covenant;

and the idea of a family of faith. The centrality of God as authority is reflected in the first question in the catechism memorized by the proper Presbyterian child: "What is the chief end of Man?" with the answer printed below: "The chief end of Man is to glorify God and enjoy Him forever." The individual person answering the outsider's question about Presbyterian belief boundaries will sometimes refer to "predestination"—and it is often this answer that is given by knowledgeable receivers of other denominational cultures, even though neither the member nor the "other" knows exactly what the doctrine of predestination is all about. Predestination, or the doctrine of the elect, is the notion of having been chosen by God as *a people.*

This doctrine is closely connected to a second definitional feature of the Presbyterian landscape of belief: the doctrine of the covenant, that transgenerational contract between God and the people that creates on earth a resulting social entity known as "the community of faith" or the "covenant community." It is the locus of God's active love and the place where humans can respond to that love. It is also the earthly expression of a heavenly city. Often on earth it is not, in fact, a city but a town, a small church in the countryside, or a subculture of interactive Christians in large congregations.

The third theme that appears repeatedly in Presbyterian belief and group self-definition is that of the "family of God," or of the "family of faith." The image of God as the father of a large descent group starting with Abraham and coming down to the people of the church today is an image that is found in the words of infant baptism, of the marriage service, and of the funeral. It is an image that finds its way into sermons, announcements, and church materials directed at the "church family." It is given shape and form in the "family night supper" and in the great summertime family reunions so well known in the American South and so important in the kin groups that comprise historical Presbyterianism in this region.

God as king of a kingdom expressed in the civic notion of town and church, covenant life as community expressed in communal ideology and behavior, and "family" as an extended transgenerational kin group handing down the tradition are the three dominant themes constructing the belief and behavior of the Southern Presbyterians as a denomination. These three themes of town, church, and family laced together into covenant life are given full expression in the celebration of the annual sacred community, the summer-long performance of meaning-in-action that is Montreat.

In the small-town South, people are clear about their church affiliation and their denominational identity. Presbyterians, Baptists, and Methodists use subtle definitional language to set themselves off from the others. Baptists define *themselves* as a separate nonreformed group with a deeply historical belief system composed of followers of Jesus and of the preachings of John the Baptist. Their world places the experience of salvation at center stage, and the idea of "personal decision" is emphasized. When answering the question "What is the difference between Baptists and other Protestants?" non-Baptists seeking definitional markers will say that the "Baptists dunk you under the water." This practice, "immersion," is congruent with the emphasis on individual decisionmaking at the time of joining the church. Immersion and also the practice of adult decision and adult baptism are critical features in the symbolic setting apart of Baptists from "others" and in constructing a world in which persons as *individuals* are the focus of preaching and teaching, in contrast with the Presbyterian focus on transgenerational community. Deep South and Texas Baptists are also often defined by others as "the ones who don't believe in drinking or dancing" (a definitional feature often accompanied by jokes and derision from individuals affiliated with more permissive groups or with no group at all).

Methodists define themselves as "fellowship-centered" and take pride in *not* being narrowly doctrinal or behaviorally proscriptive. They are proud of their ties to John Wesley and to frontier outdoor preaching. Methodists are said by others to be theologically liberal, the ones who "will let you believe anything you want as long as you are a good person and live a good life." Methodists depict themselves as personalistic, interpreting Jesus' words of invitation as calling people to be followers or disciples in the most practical, life-oriented sense. They ask for forgiveness of "trespasses" and seek to be methodically good, faithful persons. Yet, within this denomination of tolerance and individual discipleship, worshipers continue to kneel at the altar rail for Communion and to accept ministers appointed by bishops, symbolic and ecclesiastical emblems of deep historic cultural ties to the English church. In contrast to Baptists, Methodists and Presbyterians baptize infants, signifying their birth *into* the family of faith. In contrast to Methodists, Baptists and Presbyterians receive Communion in their pews from the hands of deacons or elders, signifying the "priesthood of believers." These examples of customary practice indicate some of the subtle ways of stating denominational identity.

In defining themselves and shaping their cultural reality, Presbyterians call on a vocabulary emphasizing legacy, tradition, heritage, kinship, and community. Methodists' vocabulary is more likely to focus on words such as "individuality," "personhood," "discipleship," "response," and "fellowship." The words of Baptists as they speak of their Christian world might include "personal decision," being "saved," or being "born again." In contrast to the Presbyterian's General Assembly and their representative bodies of presbyteries, Methodists have General Conference (but only every four years!) and an annual conference on the administrative territorial level, while Baptists hesitate to affiliate at all among congregations, and when they do, it is called an association or convention. The occasions and places giving expression to these vocabularies—in what might be called the vocabularies of ritual and symbolic constructions—include such commonplace and often neglected arenas as morning worship service; ceremonies marking life events in baptism, weddings, and funerals; picnics, all-church suppers and "dinners-on-the grounds"; anniversaries and homecomings; vacation church school; Christmas and Easter pageants; congregational meetings; annual or other district, state, or national assemblies and conventions, and summer camps, conferences, and cottage communities.

The "culture" of a denomination, I suggest, is a complex construction of symbolic material into meaningful sequences or "programs-for-action." The denominational culture makes this group or network of groups recognizable to itself and others and also bounds it off in a systematic way to preserve internal integrity and prevent invasion from outside. Denominational culture is preserved and transmitted, I offer, through marking devices, separate continuous worldviews, beliefs that are both written and unwritten, and through sacred places and sacred occasions that provide opportunities to perform cultural forms central to the denomination's vision of itself.

Montreat provides such a place for the Southern Presbyterians. Places like Lake Junaluska and Ridgecrest may do the same for "Southern Methodists" and Southern Baptists—each forms a locus for enactment of meanings within a ritual space in the sacred time of summer. Other places within each of the mainline denominations provide the same opportunity for intense cultural transmission—a process and a result connected with a condition that Victor Turner calls *communitas*.[4] At the conferences or cottage communities at Luddington, Michigan; Ocean Grove, New Jersey; Martha's Vineyard; Lake Tahoe; Ghost Ranch, New Mexico; Mo Ranch in Hunt, Texas; and the old Presbyterian Westminster Encampment at Kerrville, Texas, as well as at numerous other locations, transgenerational loyalty and ongoing communal life can be found.

"Camps": Symbolizing Individualism

In addition to Montreat and the other transgenerational summer communities, denominations in the South and throughout the United

States operate "camps" for youth and children in a purposeful program of religious education that is age-graded and nature-centered. In
the Presbyterian tradition these are owned and run at the level of the
presbytery and so reinforce local networks and ties among the
churches in a territory. Young people who regularly attend presbytery
camps form friendships with others in the presbytery, and ministers
and laypersons who serve as counselors forge ties of friendship with
one another, on a local rather than denomination-wide basis. Within
the recurrent gatherings of the youth camp, each denomination packages its own version of its religious reality through Bible studies and
discussion groups. In the same way as the older and more kin-based
communities do, camps share together a certain regularity of pattern
and structure. In the structure of the youth camp one finds individual
young people in attendance on their own, without families; one finds
rustic cabins or even tents as housing, where groups of youngsters are
supervised by counselors; a central building with multiple functions
serves as a simple dining hall; and worship is outdoors on a hillside,
by a lake, or in some other spot focused on the natural world. The curriculum of camps includes, in addition to Bible study or discussion or
both, arts and crafts skills, hiking, swimming, and team sports. One of
the stated goals of camp experience is to emphasize nature and the
outdoors and to enjoy Christian fellowship. Denominational identity
may be constructed in and through the definitional markers of language, hymns, preaching and especially through co-participation with
other Presbyterians or Methodists; and it is certainly marked clearly in
camp names (for example, "Westminster" and "John Knox" for the
Presbyterians, "Wesley Woods" for the Methodists, and "Camp Cal-
vary" for the Southern Baptists). In spite of these markers, however,
one finds a similarity among youth camps that is more striking than
that among the kin-based conference communities. This similarity
communicates a certain personalistic and individualistic emphasis in
which the "faith journey" of the person is central as opposed to the
handing down of tradition through a "long line of Christians." In fact,
denominational camps for youths and children resemble closely the
initiation rites in nonindustrial societies which, as Victor Turner has
pointed out, serve to move the participant into a new "stage" in the
social order, serving here as a kind of rite of passage for the person's
Christian experience (Turner 1965). It is possible that the similarity of
camp curricula and the uniform emphasis on these kinds of personalistic and nature-based experiences have served over the years to de-
emphasize denominational identity in camps in unexpected ways,
while the kin-based communities and camp-meeting style centers
have in fact served to transmit that identity more successfully. This

much can be said with certainty: the boundaries formed within the two different settings are different sorts of boundaries. A young person coming away from an age-graded camp without having had a moving personal experience may feel bounded *out* of the clustering of one's age-mates who "made a personal decision" or experienced "being saved" (especially at the Baptist version of the youth camp) or who, in more general terms, had a "significant religious experience" (spoken of by Methodist and Presbyterian youth). Meanwhile, the person most likely to feel bounded *out* of the kin-centered transgenerational community is the one who is the most "individual," the newcomer, the first-time attender, or the in-law, however deep that person's level of faith and reality of conversion might be.

In both types of places and occasions—the denominational summer conference and kin-based communities and in the camps run by presbyteries and other local territorial entities—culture is created symbolically and is taught and learned. One type, the kind represented by Montreat, is an example of a pilgrimage center for a set of connected groups of culture-bearers who find this setting to be a way for constructing and continuing a sacred cultural world that alternates with the secular one. The second type, the kind represented by the presbytery camp, is an example of an age-graded ritual process expressing themes of individuality and personhood in and through a denominational language in sacred space and time. Both are held in summer, itself a sacred time in our culture, a kind of *liminality* of time—a time out of time, time suspended, in which unexpected experiences are expected to occur. And both are held in rural, nature-focused settings away from the hubbub of the city—a sacredness of place that creates the same kind of separation as summertime, endowing the place itself with semimagical power.

The two themes of kinship and of individual person-as-pilgrim are twin themes central to Protestant cultural worlds and as such are central themes in the making of the United States. The Protestant person is caught between two poles of requirement: to be a member of a family, a kin group, a church, a community and/or to be an individual, a person, a self, an autonomous and achieving citizen. The kinds of summertime group life I have described make life bearable and do-able under such opposing cultural demands. Within the winter, urban, everyday world, the ritual expression of *communitas* and of temporary resolution of contradiction finds symbolic enactment in the weekly worship services, the Sunday school, the local church family night suppers, and other denominational social forms. In Protestant theology of all varieties the individual is at the forefront as a target of God's message and God's grace, without intervening intermediaries; and this individualism, as pointed out by Weber and others, is a significant factor in the construction of a modern, capitalistic world. The individual, however, is set within community by various Protestant theologies in various ways. The person is, within ritual processes, encased in the web of kinship and of denominational identity that shield and protect while she or he travels through the chilling territories of the secular universe as a pilgrim travels outward on a journey of selfhood.

Summary and Conclusions

Protestantism in the United States is segmented by separate denominational worlds marked not only by patterns of social interaction measured and described by sociologists but also by the expression of meaning through the powerful medium of symbols. Symbols and symbolic constructions of the kinds I have described here create separate worlds within which separate social entities live and move, even as they live together under the umbrella of "Protestant culture" and the more overarching, generalized umbrella of democratic individualism. The cognitive separateness of the internal segments of Protestantism in the United States can and might fruitfully be conceptualized as separate "dialects of meaning" within one overall language of the Protestant tradition, dialects of belief and practice that are mutually intelligible but distinctive. A "native speaker" or actor, for instance, of Methodism or Presbyterianism is able to converse readily in the Protestant tongue and the Protestant behavioral idiom; but two Methodists or two Presbyterians will have certain inflections, constructions, and shared nuances of interpretation around which, and within which, they can form an "identity."

One of the main processes in making these separate symbolic worlds concrete and immediate is that of ritual. In the recurrent, patterned expression of sacred ceremonies, occasions, and assemblies, groups of people enact a performance with themes that give shape and form to their common language and common world of understanding. It is these occasions and places, these sacred enactments, that I have chosen as my focus in the exploration of denominational cultural expression and its transmission from generation to generation of believers. Events such as the ones to which I refer serve as windows into denominational culture and serve as appropriate, even ideal, entry points for the ethnographic description and the ethnological explanations of denominational culture because they are examples of what anthropologists have labeled "paradigmatic human events." These types of events, by their structure and process, their use of material paraphernalia, and their placement of human actors in carefully patterned sacred spaces in special periods of time and rhythmicity, state all the crucial meaning-features of the symbolic landscape. They provide a model for the way the world *is* in the same way that models of buildings provide a concrete sample of ideas in the head of an architect or city planner; they also provide a model for the way the world *should be,* as "model cities" give expression to a vision of possibilities. It is within sacred occasions and at sacred places and gatherings, I maintain, that the most powerful transmitter of culture exists and works its magic on participants. It is therefore on one such place—sacred to the "Southern Presbyterians"—that I have trained my lens of analysis in order to provide an ethnographic example of the way in which I believe these symbols and meanings take on social form.

In summary, I have attempted in this chapter to present the idea that denominational culture is taught and learned most fully within special cultural locations in each denomination where the full symbolic inventory can be called out in particular sequences and structured patterns for each denominational entity. I have called on examples from the southern United States and from three mainline denominations in that region—the Presbyterian, Methodist, and Baptist. It is within the kin-based summer community, assembling annually over the generations, that I find the clearest example of cultural transmission in action. Within communities of this type, the values, beliefs, doctrinal emphases, and socially prescribed actions and behaviors can be expressed in visible form and made accessible to the successive waves of newcomers to the covenant community. This type of transgenerational, kin-based community most classically found at Montreat, North Carolina, is especially efficacious in the process of passing along a tradition of a covenant people being the elect of God. Other forms and shapes and symbolic orderings of conferences and of camps will teach other messages and transmit other traditions, as in the example of the youth camp which symbolizes aspects of individualism and teaches generalized democratic values within a denominational setting.

Throughout this chapter I have relied on images of culture-as-language and ritual-as-text. This mode of seeing and of understanding symbolic worlds of Protestantism in the United States is, I am convinced, a mode of analysis and interpretation that allows the creative exegesis of social texts. It suggests possible alternate interpretations of meanings, alternate readings and understandings to those previously suggested by social description from the rational, positivistic, or straight-out functional methods of analyzing denominational life. While studies of patterns and rates of behavior and belief are instructive in the total configuration of the sociological study of religion, these approaches are limited. I have suggested here that the study of symbol, ritual form, dramatic process, and the language of self-definition provide a rich field of possibility in the search for the meanings of denominational cultures and for the ways these are passed on to new generations.

NOTES

1. The denomination informally known for over a hundred years as "Southern Presbyterian" is the former Presbyterian Church in the United States, or PCUS, which split off from its northern affiliation at the time of the American Civil War and reunited only recently to form the Presbyterian Church (U.S.A.), a reconstituted national Presbyterian Church. The denomination in the American South has remained culturally separate from its northern sister denomination over the years. For more information on Presbyterian history in the South, see Thompson (1963). For information on doctrinal matters, see Guthrie (1967 and 1984). On the transformation of ethnic groups and on the question of boundaries, see Anderson (1970); also Barth (1969).

2. For a discussion of the models and methods I have chosen in this paper, see Geertz (1965); Schneider (1976); and Turner (1965). Also see Turner and Turner (1978).

3. My studies of Southern Presbyterian cultural expression began in 1970 and have continued to the present. My research began with the ethnographic study of the summer community described here. I wish to thank the people of Montreat for their assistance and also the agencies which have funded parts of my research over the years. These include the National Endowment for the Humanities, the Emory University Research Council, the Candler School of Theology, and the E. R. Paden Chair at Southwestern University, which I have held since 1979, endowed by the Brown Foundation of Houston, Texas.

4. Turner (1965) explains *communitas* as a condition of closeness and communal identification characterized by the equality and good feelings associated with the shared participation in ritual.

REFERENCES

Anderson, Charles
  1970 *White Protestant Americans: from National Origins to Religious Group.* Boston: Little Brown & Co.

Anderson, John Campbell
  1949   *The Story of Montreat from Its Beginning 1897–1947.* Published privately at Montreat, N.C.: John C. Anderson.
Barth, Frederick
  1969   *Ethnic Groups and Boundaries.* Boston: Little Brown & Co.
Durkheim, Emile
  1965   *Elementary Forms of Religious Life.* New York: Free Press. (Originally published in 1915.)
Geertz, Clifford
  1965   *The Interpretation of Cultures.* New York: Basic Books.
Guthrie, Shirley
  1967   *Christian Doctrine.* Richmond: John Knox Press.
  1984   "Calvinism." In *Encyclopedia of Religion in the South,* edited by Sam E. Hill, 125–127. Macon, Ga.: Mercer University Press.
Neville, Gwen Kennedy
  1973   "Kinfolks and the Covenant: Ethnic Community Among Southern Presbyterians." In *The New Ethnicity: Perspectives from Ethnology,* edited by John W. Bennett. Proceedings of the American Ethnological Society. Chicago: West Publishing Co.
  1987   *Kinship and Pilgrimage: Rituals of Reunion in American Protestant Culture.* New York: Oxford University Press.
Schneider, David
  1976   "Notes Toward a Theory of Culture." In *Meaning in Anthropology,* edited by Keith Basso and Henry Selby, 197–220. Albuquerque: University of New Mexico Press.
Thompson, E. T.
  1963   *Presbyterians in the South,* vols. 1–3. Richmond: John Knox Press.
Turner, Victor
  1965   *The Ritual Process.* Chicago: University of Chicago Press.
Turner, Victor, and Edith Turner
  1978   *Image and Pilgrimage in Christian Culture.* New York: Columbia University Press.
Weber, Max
  1958   *The Protestant Ethic and the Spirit of Capitalism.* New York: Charles Scribner's Sons. (Originally published in 1905 as *Die protestantische Ethik und der Geist des Kapitalismus* and translated in 1930 by Talcott Parsons.)

7

Church-Related Colleges: Transmitters of Denominational Cultures?

Dorothy C. Bass

Together, the seven denominations of "mainline" Protestantism are related to well over two hundred colleges.[1] It might be imagined that this array of institutions, devoted by their very nature to the transmission of culture and supported in a variety of tangible and intangible ways by denominations, would make major contributions to the transmission of denominational cultures. And perhaps they often do so, through the ineffable communication of ethos or the subtle hints of local traditions. If they do, however, the contribution is a subtle one that has been discussed rarely by either the friends or the critics of church-related colleges for at least the past generation. When the church-related colleges of mainline Protestantism are discussed, the question is not, "Are they Presbyterian, or Baptist, or Episcopal?"; the question is, "Are they Christian?" or even more broadly, "In what sense do they contribute to the mission of the church?"

Sociologist Robert Wuthnow has recently argued that changes in the U.S. system of higher education since 1960 have been of crucial importance in the "restructuring" of religion in this country. Since this religious restructuring has prominently featured decline in the institutional strength of mainline Protestantism, decline in individual loyalty to denominations, and decline in the religious commitment of highly educated persons, the church-related college would seem to stand near the eye of the storm. Before it is charged with failure in some imagined mission to contribute to the strength of mainline Protestantism, sustain individuals' loyalty to denominations, and promote specific religious beliefs, however, two caveats are in order. First, few if any prominent voices have been raised to support such a mission for mainline Protestant church-related colleges. And second, these institutions have not so much failed as they have been overwhelmed by massive changes in the structure, purpose, and ethos of twentieth-century higher education.

What follows is an account of the displacement of church-related colleges from a central position in the system of higher education in the United States. With that historical background in hand, we shall then turn to the question of how the mission of church-related colleges, within a system of higher education where they are marginal, has been conceived. Whether distinctive denominational cultures within mainline Protestantism have much relevance to that conversation appears doubtful. Yet, as the many supporters of church-related higher education would surely affirm, the irrelevance of denominational specificity is not necessarily a problem.

The History of Church-Related Colleges in the United States

English settlers in the New World began to build institutions of higher education during the colonial period. Indeed, the energetic Protestants of Massachusetts Bay did so only six years after their arrival, as soon as they had "builded our houses, provided necessaries for our liveli-hood, reard convenient places for Gods worship, and setled the Civill Government." The need to prepare a new generation of learned ministers was a particularly strong motive—they "dread[ed] to leave an illiterate Ministery to the Churches, when our present Ministers shall lie in the Dust" (Miller and Johnson 1963). But the commonwealth also needed leaders of other sorts, and the college founded in 1636, which became Harvard University, was meant to educate those as well. In keeping with Western civilization's long tradition, religion and higher learning were closely intermingled at colonial Harvard. Strong ties to churches would also characterize almost all other colleges founded during the colonial period. During the Enlightenment, the assumption that higher learning had to be associated with religious institutions came into question, and some colleges, such as the College of Pennsylvania (now the University of Pennsylvania) were founded independently of churches. Even so, the tradition of church sponsorship was strong, and well into the nineteenth century most colleges had close ties to churches.

The rapid, and often haphazard, expansion of Protestant culture and its institutions into the transappalachian West between the War of Independence and the Civil War was a period of rapid, and often haphazard, expansion for church-related higher education. Seen from one point of view, the hundreds of colleges that sprang up represented serious efforts to embody the coherent religious and moral visions of the church groups that founded them; one thinks of Alexander Campbell's Bethany College, the Congregationalist Oberlin College, Southern Presbyterianism's Davidson, and dozens of others. Yet many more were founded than survived, and historians agree that competitive boosterism on the part of denominations and towns gave rise to many now-extinct institutions that were colleges in name only. An outstanding example of this educational type was provided by the fiction-writer Garrison Keillor in his "history" of Lake Wobegon. Originally founded as "New Albion, the Boston of the West," the young town was home to "New Albion College, World Revered Seat of Learning Set in This Mecca of Commerce and Agriculture. Dr. Henry Francis Watt, Ph.D., Litt.D., D.D., President. Choice Lots Remain For Purchase, $100" (Keillor 1985, 34). The Unitarian school in this story lasted only a few months. Though even the weakest schools fared better than New Albion, Keillor's caricature does highlight some of the real challenges of planting new institutions of cultural transmission on the frontier.

The dozens of respectable church-related colleges founded during the nineteenth century, however, embodied important ideals and accomplishments, shaping the ethos of higher education in this country and contributing substantially to the overall system of education for Protestants in the United States. Together with the church, the common school, the Sunday school, the seminary, the family, publications, and voluntary associations, church-related colleges were part of an ecology of education that sustained the culture of Protestantism. Some elements of the ecology emphasized denominational distinctiveness, while others transcended it; colleges probably did both, as they were attended by denominational loyalists from a wide region together with locals of mixed denominational backgrounds. Some denominations held their colleges to strict denominational rules, while others did not (Douglas Sloan in Parsonage 1978, 178).

Religion and education mingled comfortably at "the old-time college," as this nineteenth-century institution came to be known after other models emerged in later years (Ringenberg 1987, 77). Located in "college towns" of manageable size and drawing students and faculty from a like-minded social group, these schools rarely had more than a few hundred students. The curriculum was fixed, capped by a course in "moral philosophy" usually taught by the president, who most likely was a clergyman familiar with each student's career. Clergy were also strongly represented on the board of trustees and the faculty. Communal life was strong, featuring required attendance at worship services and involvement in voluntary associations (literary, antislavery, missions, temperance) that reflected the ethos of the institution. The specific provisions for accountability to and support from the affiliated denomination varied widely.

Until the Civil War, the church-related college was the normative institution of higher learning in the United States. During the last third of the nineteenth century, however, the emergence of the modern university introduced a quite different model of what higher learning was and how it ought to be pursued. The great private and state universities that grew so impressively during this period emulated the research universities of Germany and explicitly sought to differentiate themselves from "the old-time college." Harvard's influential president Charles W. Eliot, for example, declared in 1891 that "it is impossible to found a university on the basis of a sect," and when Johns Hopkins University opened in 1876, the founders took the radical step of having no prayers of invocation or benediction offered at the inaugural ceremonies (Hawkins 1971, 354–358). The university's model of the academic enterprise was specialized, secular, and attuned to national and international communities of scholarship rather than to denominational or regional constituencies. After 1900, such universities rarely chose clergymen as trustees or presidents. Professors shifted their attention away from the development of student character and toward scholarly productivity within the newly founded disciplinary guilds that corresponded to the segmented departments of the university. For students, the elective system, the introduction of professional studies and the practical sciences, and the larger size of the university added elements of freedom and vocational utility to the college years (Noll 1984, 29).

At the turn of the century, church-related colleges still boasted a healthy share of the action in American higher education. Almost half of all undergraduates attended church-sponsored schools, the majority of which were affiliated with mainline denominations (Ringenberg 1984, 132; Patillo and Mackenzie 1966, 21). Yet the modern university had already seized the lion's share of cultural and intellectual authority in matters of higher learning. Henceforth, church-related higher education would be on the defensive.

During the first two decades of the twentieth century, the initiatives of reform-minded leaders in higher education extended the influence of the modern university's distinctive norms far beyond the walls of the large research institutions. Accreditation agencies were developed, and powerful foundations used funding incentives to persuade old-time colleges to begin conducting themselves in the new way. For example, to participate in a pension program established by the

Carnegie Foundation, colleges had to renounce denominational ties and ensure that a key group of professors possessed a doctoral degree. And strategists at Rockefeller's General Education Board, which dispensed millions of dollars to help build college endowments, were ruthless (though not always successful) in their efforts to weed out weak denominational colleges (Bass 1989, 52–56). In large part, these initiatives were fueled by desire to bring order and standards to a system of higher education that was full of internal contradictions, as long as no agreement existed about what constituted secondary, undergraduate, graduate, and faculty levels of attainment.

Some of the changes that occurred as the university took over leadership from the church-related college, however, were encouraged by motives that were intellectual and religious in nature. A new cultural era was arriving in which the relationship between religion and higher learning would become increasingly difficult to define. The secularization of higher education in an institutional sense—its removal from ecclesiastical control as the state-supported and nonecclesiastical independent sectors continued to grow—was only one aspect of the story; another aspect was intellectual. Within the world of mainline Protestant church-related higher education, the norms and values of the modern research university possessed a strong appeal to leaders and professors of liberal bent. They were excited by the contributions of modern science and historical criticism, familiar with the potential restrictiveness of sectarianism, and enlivened by a modernist theology that saw itself as a friend, not an opponent, of new ideas and structures. Thus President William Rainey Harper of the University of Chicago made the newly founded and still Baptist-controlled research university a place that was open to persons of all faiths and encouraged it to take on a mission of free inquiry and nonsectarian public service. President Henry Churchill King of Oberlin, an active denominational leader in Congregationalism, welcomed the disaffiliation of Oberlin and other church-related colleges from church bodies in full confidence that their religious mission— which his own theological liberalism led him to define very broadly—would not fade as a result (Bass 1989, 52–53).

By 1910, the official separation of the leading U.S. universities from denominational ties was complete, including the great colonial colleges founded by religious groups and the few state universities that owed their founding to churches. What was more important, however, was the new authority of university standards and values to shape perceptions about what higher education should be throughout the nation. The reach of this authority was greater in some subcultures than others, to be sure; it had far less impact where ethnic identity or regional self-consciousness prevailed, as they did among most

Lutherans and in the Deep South, for instance. Moreover, some conservative religious groups resisted these values through separatist strategies, while others—such as Roman Catholics—found that persistent ethnic ties and the discriminatory practices of even the "independent" institutions continued to provide their colleges with distinctive missions. During the 1920s and 1930s, pressures arising out of the fundamentalist-modernist controversy led some Presbyterian and Baptist colleges to privilege ecclesiastical demands more highly than those set forth by the larger academic world. But for many mainline Protestant colleges, the new context seemed to be one in which other kinds of schools prospered and grew, while their own particular gifts were not rewarded. Sensing crisis, the denominations began to consult with one another in 1910 in the Council of Church Boards of Education (Limbert 1929, 226).

The Contemporary Pattern Takes Shape

In many regards, the main contours of the contemporary situation of church-related colleges were already in place during the middle years of this century. Their share of American higher education continued to decrease. They began to report haziness of purpose and to conduct studies into their identity. At most schools, strict rules regarding chapel requirements and moral behavior began to ease. Some institutions, to be sure, maintained sharply delineated notions of their distinctiveness: Southern Presbyterian colleges required doctrinal affirmations from faculty members, and many Lutheran colleges served ethnic constituencies that were still far from assimilated into the dominant culture. In general, however, denominationally affiliated colleges' interest in religion had lost its sectarian flavor, Merrimon Cuninggim reported in 1947 (1947, 57).

Between 1920 and 1960, some ways of thinking about religion and higher education that still carry much weight emerged. In one significant development, a constituency of concerned Christian educators that cut across denominational lines came of age. They gathered through the Yale-based National Council on Religion and Higher Education, beginning in the 1920s, and later through the Faculty Christian Fellowship or programs sponsored by the Hazen or Danforth Foundations. This constituency was likely to share in the liberal celebration of many aspects of the modern university, while also expressing concern for intellectually responsible ways of restoring a religious presence there. In these circles, and in dozens of books on church-related colleges or on religion in higher education more generally, almost no attention was paid to denominational differences.

Also attaining great influence was the idea that the most significant contribution of the denominations to higher education and the persons within it would most likely not come through church-related colleges. Changes in the overall shape of higher education in the United States, argued Clarence P. Shedd of Yale in 1937, had removed much of the former importance of church-related colleges. In view of massive gains in state-supported higher education, ministries at secular schools were needed more than religious colleges were; it was now time, as the title of Shedd's most influential book put it, that *The Church Follows Its Students.* The demographic arguments advanced by Shedd, the key figure in the development of the professional campus ministry, captured the imagination of many key leaders, in church and academy. Although the denominations were not about to abandon their colleges, a 1959 report that there were four times as many Methodists in Iowa's three state schools as there were in Iowa's four Methodist colleges—a statistic that represented the situation outside Iowa as well—could hardly have been received as encouraging news by the colleges' advocates (Michaelsen 1960, 306).

The shifting educational arrangements that removed church-related colleges from the center of higher education to its margin had particular importance for predominantly African American institutions of higher education. The black community's need for educated leaders after emancipation had fueled the founding of most such colleges in the late nineteenth century, so that today even many state-supported and independent colleges that serve the black community can be traced to religious origins. And religious affiliation seems in general to have been a positive force in the longer history of African American higher education. For example, in spite of limited financial resources, the black and white missionary founders of the late nineteenth-century colleges brought an egalitarian vision to the enterprise, which the philanthropists and governmental reformers of the early twentieth century forsook on behalf of more "pragmatic" vocational programs (Peeps 1981, 265).

In effect, financial restrictions kept most predominantly black colleges in the age of "the old-time college" long after that model had lost esteem and power. Black colleges long continued to be far more likely than predominantly white ones to be small institutions with clergymen presidents and a dearth of professors with Ph.Ds. During the 1940s, the great majority were not accredited at the highest level (McKinney 1945, 21–25). In 1965, 58 out of 123 were church-affiliated, and accreditation continued to be a widespread problem. Affiliation with mainline denominations seems to have brought some institutional benefits: as of 1978, all of the eighteen predominantly black colleges affiliated with the

United Church of Christ or the United Methodist Church were fully accredited, although half of those under other sponsorship were not. More important, those who know these colleges attest that their vision of the liberating qualities of education, which they once held up virtually alone, is still alive. In this, they provide an example of a distinctively religious (though still not particularly denominational) contribution to higher education in the United States during a period when such examples are increasingly difficult to find (Cook 1978, 149–150).

Since the '60s: A Time of Uncertainty

If the emergence of the modern university around 1900 marked the qualitative displacement of the church-related college, the immense growth of higher education during the 1960s sealed its quantitative displacement. The total numbers of students enrolled in all institutions of higher education in given years reflect that enormous expansion: 2.6 million in 1950, 3.6 million in 1960, 8.6 million in 1970, 12.1 million in 1980.[2] Of this increase, almost all was outside the church-related sector. In 1965, two-thirds of all undergraduates were enrolled in government-supported institutions. Only half of the remaining third were in church-related colleges, and of those the greatest number were Roman Catholic. In 1987, the U.S. government estimated that 80 percent of all students were in public institutions (Wuthnow 1988, 154; Harris 1972, 269; Patillo and Mackenzie 1966, 21; *Digest* 1988, 142).

"A society which once hinged around the church is now more and more pivoting around the university, and the church is marginal to that university," the Presbyterian educator Robert Lynn declared in 1966. One of the implications of this reorientation, Lynn argued, was that church-related colleges had become an institutional drain with little relevance to the current situation (1969, 20). On campus, a distinctly religious tone (much less a distinctly denominational one) was increasingly difficult to sustain during the 1960s, when "secularization" seemed to be the watchword even of Christian theology. Students protested successfully against remaining chapel requirements and social regulations, and an important 1965 study sponsored by the Danforth Foundation reported that such relics at "colleges related to large Protestant denominations such as the Methodist and United Presbyterian churches" tended to be "minimal." Since only 26 percent of all church-sponsored Protestant colleges required weekly or daily chapel attendance, "minimal" must have really meant just that (Patillo and Mackenzie 1966, 148).

Moreover, the Danforth study argued, church-sponsored higher education as a whole (including evangelical, Roman Catholic, and

Jewish) was troubled from within as well as pressed from without. The study discovered widespread unclarity of purpose, which must surely have been farthest advanced at "mainline" institutions. The most basic problem facing all religiously sponsored colleges, the report argued, was theological: "The shifting sands of religious faith today provide an uncertain foundation for religiously oriented educational programs." Although the authors concluded with an exhortation to reclaim "the great tradition of liberal education infused with the Christian faith," they conceded that there was "no way to manufacture agreement on fundamental questions" (Patillo and Mackenzie 1966, vii, 214).

The Danforth Commission report, while critical, was basically sympathetic to the historic vision represented by the church-related college; in essence, the report was one step among many by which the Foundation sought to renew that vision in the contemporary situation. Several years later, however, a more modest study conducted under the auspices of the Carnegie Commission on Higher Education painted a bleaker picture of the characteristics and prospects of this educational sector. Comparisons among "universities," "liberal arts colleges," "mainline denominational colleges," and "evangelical-fundamentalist colleges" provided little basis for a favorable report on the third group, the author implied. "Lacking strong commitments to the church and to spiritual experience, as well as to scholarship and the world of ideas, some of these Protestant colleges emerge from our array of data as tepid environments," the study reported. "Neither warmly spiritual nor coolly intellectual, they are essentially without vigor and sooner or later, perhaps, will become nonviable" (Pace 1975, 44). There is much to question about the methods and biases of this study, and even the author conceded that few generalizations about mainline denominational colleges would hold up, in view of these institutions' great diversity. Yet the general picture presented matched the impressions and the fears of enough other observers to be troubling.

Articulating a Mission: Beyond Denominationalism

However corrosive on colleges the forces of marginalization, secularization, and diversity have appeared to some observers, strong support for these institutions has continued to come from many of the most thoughtful leaders of mainline Protestantism. The support has not always taken the generous financial form the colleges' administrations might most desire, but it has articulated a credible rhetoric that may succeed in sustaining the vision of church-related higher education

through yet another generation. In liberal tones characteristic of mainline Protestantism itself, these supporters have characteristically argued that the point of church-related colleges is not to advance
denominational empires but rather to serve "the public good," as a
1969 symposium put it (Magill 1978). Also characteristically, these
mainline Protestants have sought to win the respect of the establishment (in this case the secular university) while also criticizing it (in
this case for deficiency in "values"). Thus the small independent liberal arts college, which long ago grew away from its Protestant roots,
is often the implicit model to which mainline church-related colleges
are urged to aspire, and the preservation of the liberal arts themselves
is often claimed as a prominent aspect of their mission. Further, it is argued, church-related colleges add a much-needed element of diversity
to America's huge system of higher education.

Within this antisectarian rhetoric, denominations are discouraged
from seeking to make a worldly profit from their support of these institutions. As a longtime participant in this conversation put it recently,
"The genius of Christian higher education has been the recognition by
the churches that the gift of autonomy to the schools makes possible
one of the highest forms of the love of God, namely, the intellectual
love of God." Responding in *The Christian Century* to a conservative
critic who had urged church-related colleges to be more distinctively
Christian, this United Methodist university president called the denominational college or university "the church's gift to the world. The
Christian tradition, celebrating, as it does, the beauty and complexity
of the world, has liberated persons to explore that world without constraints of ideology or doctrine" (Trotter 1988, 1099).

For the most part, the denominations have thus far been persuaded
by this position. A 1978 survey of denominational policies summarized the denominations' goals for church-related higher education in
this order: concern for the development of individuals' mental, physical, and spiritual resources; provision of opportunities for exposure to
Christian faith and teachings; commitment to value-centered inquiry;
affirmation of the importance of the liberal arts; and commitment to
improving society (Parsonage 1978, 283). Separate reports on the policy statements of each of the mainline denominations disclosed some
denominational particularities, but they had to do with the churches'
rationales for being related to colleges, not with expectations that the
colleges would themselves reflect the particularities. The theological
justifications for higher education set forth by denominations, in other
words, characteristically referred to such notions as "the Reformed tradition" of scholarship or the "Wesleyan heritage" of joining vital piety
with knowledge. There was little expectation, however, that the col-

leges would promote Reformed or Wesleyan religious views among students and faculty. Almost all of the denominations had conducted major evaluations of the identity of church-related colleges within the past decade. Even in the rare instance when a particularistic claim was asserted—as in the Lutheran Church in America's fourth expectation of colleges, that they demonstrate "the centrality of Christianity to a life perspective"—it was counterbalanced by a call for "religious diversity within a Christian orientation" (Parsonage 1978, 217). Far more common in the statements are references to "the wholeness of persons," the liberal arts, and the importance of "values."

Although the denominations have been reluctant in recent years to claim that the furtherance of denominationalism is a goal of their related colleges, it seems likely that a notable minority of students nonetheless are confirmed in their own denominational identities by good experiences at these colleges. Here the evidence is impressionistic: many church-college graduates, some of them with strong adult denominational loyalties, express deep gratitude to their colleges. No studies have explored the ineffable process by which such formation occurs, however. The presence of important teachers, the greater likelihood of marrying within one's birthright denomination, and the influence of excellent chapel programs may all play a part where such denominational strengths persist, as they surely do in some places.[3]

The mixture of forces at play—the demands of the larger system of American higher education, the ecumenical consensus that colleges are not primarily agents of denominationalism, the widely varying schemes for financial support, the personnel and traditions of each college, and so on—mean that the denominational culture of any specific college needs to be assessed on its own terms. On the diversified terrain of contemporary American higher education, the specific definitions that govern a given college's understanding of its own church-relatedness, or that of its sponsoring denomination, include a wide and various set of options. In the 1978 study, Merrimon Cuninggim urged that assessing colleges' church-relatedness with reference to ideal types be abandoned in favor of an approach that would situate colleges along a spectrum. Some colleges, he argued, are best understood as "consonant" with their sponsoring denomination's vision; they are "allies" of the denomination. Others, at mid-spectrum, "proclaim" the vision, serving as "witnesses" for the denomination. At the far end are those colleges that "embody" denominational vision; these eschew pluralism to "reflect" specific ecclesiastical characteristics with a firmness that would preclude the inclusion of almost all mainline Protestant colleges in this category (Cuninggim in Parsonage 1978, 17–89).

Cuninggim's spectrum helps make sense of one of the paradoxes of church-related higher education. On the one hand, the transmission of distinctive denominational cultures is not a major goal or accomplishment of these colleges in part because shaping denominational identity is not central to the mission in higher education that this stream in American religious life has proclaimed as its own. On the other hand, anyone with a wide acquaintance among mainstream Protestants is likely to suspect that attending these colleges has had an impact on many persons. The paradox has to do with the difference between explicit purposes and implicit results: thus, a college of the United Church of Christ, in being "consonant" with the educational vision of the denomination, might welcome a religiously diverse student body and faculty and celebrate their efforts in social action without needing to articulate them in distinctively Christian form. Or a United Methodist college might "witness" to its denomination's principles through its commitment to racial inclusiveness and global consciousness, even though many students and faculty members were cold to the presence of Methodism *per se*. In other words, when colleges are assessed with reference to the guiding visions of their sponsoring denominations, a finding that they are not central agents for the transmission of distinctive denominational identity is not, in the view of influential mainline Protestant leaders, a negative finding. But if in the meantime they have shaped some students through processes that are hard to pin down, all the better.

Today, dozens of genuinely excellent church-related colleges are succeeding as liberal arts institutions, though the future meaning of their denominational affiliation is often unclear. The changing character of denominationalism in this country has impact at certain points, as for example in recruitment strategies: since mainline Protestants are highly assimilated into the general culture and reportedly possess only limited denominational loyalty in any case, these colleges face increasing difficulty in sustaining the edge on a specific recruitment pool that they once had. The strongest colleges now succeed in competition with other liberal arts colleges by sustaining their admissions pools less through denominational ties than by appealing to students of diverse backgrounds. These are unlikely to move in the direction of greater denominational distinctiveness. In addition, stronger and weaker colleges have come under pressure to relinquish particularistic practices since restrictions on state and federal aid to institutions and to students were adopted during the 1970s (Trotter 1988, 1098).

It remains to be seen whether the complex relationships between colleges and denominations will continue to win support on both sides, as the economic and cultural pressures felt by all private educational institutions and by all agencies of mainline Protestantism continue to mount during the 1990s. Perhaps there will be a new call to highlight denominationalism, echoing that which is currently issued to the seminaries. The history and character of mainline Protestant higher education would offer scant resources for effectively answering such a call, however. Indeed, today even the denominational ethos that persists at certain schools may eventually be overpowered by the contemporary culture in which faculty and students are formed.

The transmission of specific denominational cultures has not been a guiding purpose of church-sponsored higher education for quite some time, and it is unlikely that it will become so again. Yet it is possible to conceive of a renewed effort on the part of some mainline Protestants to make the contributions of their own religious position more explicit within the educational institutions they are able to influence. It is inherently difficult to develop an explicitly Christian character without abandoning hard-won and cherished beliefs in tolerance, publicness, and critical thought, to be sure. But it is not impossible, and it is a development that would deliver a much-needed word to the realm of higher education in the United States.

As an ever larger proportion of U.S. citizens enter institutions of higher learning—and as the knowledge developed there has great significance for a shrinking world—the question of what cultures are transmitted in these institutions becomes ever more important. The constituents of a thriving cohort of evangelical and fundamentalist institutions know this (Carpenter and Shipps 1987). So do many Roman Catholic educators, though the openness of the last twenty years has led some of them to wonder about the enduring distinctiveness of their colleges and universities (*Daedalus* 1988, 16–25). As mainline Protestants reflect upon their own identity and the identity of the many kinds of institutions they have nurtured over the years, they would be wise to refrain from hoping that changes in "their" colleges and universities could change the course of U.S. higher education. They would also be wise, however, to include in their reflections a serious inquiry into how to nurture colleges that represent the best insights of the traditions they bear. Such colleges would be nonsectarian and intellectually sound, but in crucial aspects of ethos and content, they also would be striving to grow into worthy communities able to take a vital part in the churches' ongoing task of rediscovering the meaning of the Christ for the contemporary world.

NOTES

1. The problems of definition encompassed in this short sentence are multiple. My use of the term "mainline" for the variety of Protestantism I intend to discuss defers to ordinary language; it is not meant to imply that this religious family is central to American religious life. I include the seven denominations identified in the Lilly Endowment's workplan on "mainstream Protestantism": the Presbyterian Church (U.S.A.), the United Church of Christ, the Episcopal Church, the United Methodist Church, the American Baptist Churches, the Christian Church (Disciples of Christ), and the Evangelical Lutheran Church in America. A case for seeing these as a coherent group is made in *Between the Times: The Travail of the Protestant Establishment in America, 1900–1960,* edited by William R. Hutchison (1989). To arrive at the figure of "more than two hundred," I have added together the college affiliations reported in the *Digest of Education Statistics* (1988), which total 246, and allowed a considerable leeway for errors.

2. The increased size of the college-aged cohort contributed to the expansion, to be sure, but the proportion of this cohort that enrolled was also rising dramatically (Wuthnow 1988, 155).

3. The hypothesis that higher education is the major formative experience shaping adult religious commitment is advanced by sociologists Robert Wuthnow in *The Restructuring of American Religion* (1988) and Dean Hoge in work in progress. Considerable further research is needed to test this hypothesis. Attention to the influence of church-related colleges on religious commitment should receive major attention in such a study.

REFERENCES

Bass, Dorothy C.
    1989   "Ministry on the Margin: Protestants and Education." In *Between the Times: The Travail of the Protestant Establishment in America, 1900–1960,* edited by William R. Hutchison. New York: Cambridge University Press.
Carpenter, Joel A., and Kenneth W. Shipps (eds.)
    1987   Making Higher Education Christian: The History and Mission of Evangelical Colleges in America. Grand Rapids: Christian University Press.
Cook, Samuel Dubois
    1978   "The Church-Related Black College: Ambiguous Past and

Uncertain Future." In *The Church's Ministry in Higher Education,* edited by John H. Westerhoff. New York: United Ministries in Higher Education.

Cuninggim, Merrimon
1947   *The College Seeks Religion.* New Haven, Conn.: Yale University Press.

Daedalus
1988   "Religion and Education" 117, no. 2 (Spring).

Digest of Education Statistics.
1988   Washington, D.C.: U.S. Department of Education.

Harris, Seymour E.
1972   *A Statistical Portrait of Higher Education.* New York: McGraw-Hill Book Co.

Hawkins, Hugh
1971   "The University Builders Observe the Colleges." *History of Education Quarterly* 11 (1971): 353–362.

Keillor, Garrison
1985   *Lake Wobegon Days.* New York: Viking Penguin

Limbert, Paul M.
1929   *Denominational Policies in Support and Supervision of Higher Education.* New York: Teachers College, Columbia University.

Lynn, Robert W.
1969   "A Ministry on the Margin." In *The Church, the University, and Social Policy: The Danforth Study of Campus Ministries,* edited by Kenneth Underwood. 2 vols, Middletown, Conn.: Wesleyan University Press.

Magill, Samuel H. (ed.)
1978   *The Contribution of the Church-Related College to the Public Good.* Washington, D.C.: Association of American Colleges.

McKinney, Richard I.
1945   *Religion in Higher Education Among Negroes.* New Haven, Conn.: Yale University Press.

Michaelsen, Robert
1960   "Religious Education in Public Higher Education Institutions." In *Religious Education: A Comprehensive Survey,* edited by Marvin J. Taylor. Nashville: Abingdon Press.

Miller, Perry, and Thomas H. Johnson (eds.)
1963   *The Puritans.* New York: Harper & Row, II: 701.

Noll, Mark A.
1984   "Christian Colleges, Christian Worldviews, and an Invitation to Research." In *The Christian College: A History of*

Protestant Higher Education in America, edited by William
C. Ringenberg. Grand Rapids: Wm. B. Eerdmans Publishing Co.

Pace, C. Robert
   1975   *Education and Evangelism: A Profile of Protestant Col-
          leges.* New York: McGraw-Hill Book Co.

Parsonage, Robert Rue (ed.)
   1978   *Church Related Higher Education.* Valley Forge, Pa.: Jud-
          son Press.

Patillo, Manning M., and Donald M. Mackenzie
   1966   *Church-Sponsored Higher Education in the United States:
          Report of the Danforth Commission.* Washington, D.C.:
          American Council on Education.

Peeps, J. M. Stephen
   1981   "Northern Philanthropy and the Emergence of Black Higher
          Education—Do-Gooders, Compromisers, or Co-Conspira-
          tors?" *Journal of Negro Education* 50.

Ringenberg, William C.
   1984   *The Christian College: A History of Protestant Higher Edu-
          cation in America.* Grand Rapids: Wm. B. Eerdmans.
   1987   "The Old-Time College." In *Making Higher Education Chris-
          tian: The History and Mission of Evangelical Colleges in
          America,* edited by Joel A. Carpenter and Kenneth W. Shipps.
          Grand Rapids: Christian University Press/Eerdmanns.

Rudolph, Frederick
   1962   *The American College and University: A History.* New
          York: Alfred A. Knopf.

Shedd, Clarence P.
   1937   *The Church Follows Its Students.* New Haven, Conn.: Yale
          University Press.

Trotter, F. Thomas
   1988   "The College as the Church's Gift." *Christian Century* (No-
          vember 20, 1988): 1098–1101.

Veysey, Lawrence R.
   1965   *The Emergence of the American University.* Chicago: Uni-
          versity of Chicago Press.

Wuthnow, Robert
   1988   *The Restructuring of American Religion.* Princeton, N.J.:
          Princeton University Press.

8

Denominational Ministry on University Campuses

Allison Stokes

The young Baptist campus minister at Ohio State was addressing a group of fellow Baptist campus ministers when he observed, "Out of the eclipse of religion on the modern campus there has come to all participating religious groups the consciousness that the religious problems of the campus are one." Admitting that he was on shaky ground because he did not know personally to what extent campus religious groups had cooperated in the past, he said he nevertheless had been told that in previous generations student work was primarily denominationally centered rather than religion-centered. The chief responsibility of campus ministers was to their particular denomination rather than to "the effectiveness of religion in the total life of the university."

All that had changed, though, because "religion is much more on the defensive today. . . . We feel that we must work together if religion is to 'rate' at all upon the modern campus." The pastor noted that in his brief experience with students, what most impressed him was that "the denominational mind is fast disappearing." He described a lack of concern about denominational pride and superiority. "The students whom I have talked to on both state and denominational campuses do not seem to be interested in Baptist, Presbyterian, or Congregational denominations as such."

These observations may strike readers as contemporary. Not so. The year was 1937. In 1938, Professor Clarence Shedd, teacher of courses on religion and higher education at the Yale Divinity School, quoted this speech by the Rev. George Davis in his comprehensive study, *The Church Follows Its Students* (Shedd, 216–217). Shedd's book, a history of denominational ministries at state and large independent universities, is an invaluable resource for persons interested in the transmission of denominational identity. If we assume that the decline of "the denominational mind" on campuses is a relatively recent phenomenon, occurring since the 1960s, perhaps, a reading of Shedd gives a different perspective. For almost a century, clergy appointed by the denominations to minister on university campuses — folks like George Davis at Ohio State—have observed *and* encouraged diminished sectarian consciousness.

The intriguing question, of course, is Why? Is it that campus ministers value interdenominational cooperation and unity above denominational competition and division? Has a spirit of ecumenism caused an eclipse of denominational identity and influence on campus? In part, yes. In the early decades of campus ministry, when the mainline groups were committed to a common, cooperative enterprise, *ecumenism* powerfully contributed to the fast-disappearing denominational mind. Within the past generation, however, the forces of *pluralism* and *secularism* have rendered nearly irrelevant the task of transmitting denominational identity, while challenging mainline Protestant ministers to educate for Christian discipleship.

This chapter tells the story in brief of the changing shape of denominational campus ministry from its inception at the turn of the century to its present state of upheaval and disarray. We will see that a historical perspective surfaces some ironies. Whereas denominational campus ministries were ecumenically initiated on the premise of following high school students to college campuses, today many denominational leaders have interpreted this to mean preserving students as loyal members of the denomination—a situation that has led to serious conflicts between ministers on university and college campuses and church leaders. Another irony is that the concern for mainline denominational survival may be, in fact, one of the forces supporting the conservative, nondenominational resurgence.

Ecumenism and Campus Ministry

Campus ministry began as a denominational enterprise. When it became clear around 1900 that future growth in higher education belonged to the large state schools, pioneering efforts began in earnest as the churches perceived a new missionary field. The Presbyterians, Congregationalists, Baptists, Methodists, Lutherans, Episcopalians, and Disciples of Christ all began to establish what Clarence Shedd called "university pastorates," or what we now call "campus ministries" or "ministries in higher education." Shedd judged this movement to be equal in importance and significance to the church-related college movement (described by Dorothy Bass in chapter 7). Because some state universities feared sectarian rivalries and some church-related colleges feared decreased financial support from their denominations, initially there was not a little antagonism to the work. After about a decade, however, the need in the new large universities for a diversity in religious ministries, which apparently could be carried forward without sectarian rivalry, was evident. There seemed "'little danger of over-doing religion with a half dozen university pastors' in a university where 'a faculty of several hundred was required to take care of students scholastically'" (Shedd 1938, 29). Furthermore, the conviction was growing that the great home mission field of the church lay in the public university.

What is remarkable is that the founding of denominational ministries on university campuses coincided with interdenominational (later interfaith) cooperation between them; thus, from the beginning campus ministry had an ecumenical thrust. In the first decades of the century cooperative efforts took three forms: local university clergy associations, national university pastorate conferences, and a council of education secretaries representing the denominations.

Campus clergy organized the first local university pastors' association at the University of Michigan in 1905. Ann Arbor also provided the site in 1908 for the first "Interdenominational Conference of Church and Guild Workers in State Universities." Conveners of the gathering believed that "such union of efforts will strengthen each separate denomination, especially by enabling the delegates to lay before their annual church gatherings more definite and careful methods of work in student fields" (Shedd 1938, 69).

In 1912, secretaries from the national offices of the various denominations established the Council of Church Boards of Education. A subcommittee on "Religious Work in State and Denominational Institutions" took responsibility for cooperative guidance of university work. Leaders agreed that the university must not be made a field of competition. Dr. Richard C. Hughes, secretary of the Presbyterian Department of University Work, warned in 1914, "The churches that enter this field must understand at the outset that any emphasis upon sectarianism, any attempt to use this enterprise to build up the church as an end in itself, will be a source of almost fatal weakness" (Shedd 1938, 72).

After 1920, denominational leaders increasingly coordinated their work. Reflecting the views of national university secretaries of denominations, Dr. M. Willard Lampe wrote:

There is something peculiarly anomalous about purely sectarian effort in a university atmosphere. One of the high functions of religion anywhere is to enable one to see life as a unit, but nowhere is this function needed, and nowhere does its absence tend more to disparage religion than in a modern university. Moreover, the purpose of the university religious work is altogether too large for any denomination to achieve by itself (Shedd 1938, 167).

From the beginning of campus ministry, then, a balance obtained between denominational ministry and ecumenical vision.

In a thorough sociological analysis of changes in students' religious attitudes and values over five decades (1914–1969), Dean R. Hoge discovered a long-range trend toward overall liberalization of religious attitudes and reduction of traditional religious behavior. Hoge's book, *Commitment on Campus,* documents an exception to this gradual weakening of traditional religious participation when in the late 1940s and early 1950s a remarkable rise in religious commitment and orthodoxy occurred. A careful examination of a great deal of data indicated to the sociologist of religion that this was a discrete occurrence; thus, falling indicators of religious participation in the late 1950s and 1960s, however disheartening, could be seen as a return to the normal trend (Hoge 1974, 186).

It is not surprising that sentiments favoring ecumenism declined during the period of orthodoxy. For example, between the years 1948 and 1968 statistics showed a *drop* in the percentage of students at Harvard, Radcliffe, Williams, and Los Angeles City College who *agreed* with the proposition that "denominational distinctions, at least within Protestant Christianity, are out of date and may well be eliminated as rapidly as possible" (Hoge 1974, 38).

This was the "Golden Age" of campus ministry, the incredible growth and expansion of the church's presence on campus (McCormick 1987, ch. 2). The number of full-time professional workers in campus ministry grew from about two hundred in 1938, to one thousand in 1953, to fifteen hundred in 1963. More money than ever before flowed into this specialized ministry as denominational centers flourished— Wesley Foundations (Methodist), Westminster Foundations (Presbyterian), Canterbury Clubs (Episcopal), Pilgrim Clubs (Congregational), Luther Houses, Baptist Student Unions, and Disciples Student Foundations. And outside the Protestant mainline, Newman Centers (Roman Catholic) and Hillel Foundations (Jewish) were established.

In the 1960s, individual denominational work developed into ecumenical cooperation, largely in the form of the United Ministries in Higher Education (UMHE). The story of the UMHE as it evolved to become in 1979, the United Ministries in Education (UME), and in 1989, the Higher Education Ministries Team (Barker 1989) is a sad story of the steady decline of Protestant mainline support of campus ministry.

I write about campus ministry, not college chaplaincy, a distinction which one must be careful to make when discussing religious work in higher education. Nevertheless, the influence upon denominational ministers by the particular identity and work of chaplains must be taken into account in any consideration of the eclipse of denominational identity on campus.

Chaplains—whether in hospitals, prisons, the military, or higher education—are ordained by denominations and accountable to them (often nominally), but they are not employed by them. Chaplains are employed by nonecclesiastical agencies to take responsibility for the religious dimensions of the common life. In the words of Donald G. Shockley, chaplain of Emory University, "a college chaplain is engaged in ministry to and through the institution itself." A chaplaincy ministry, Shockley explains, is "based upon an extraordinary assumption: that a minister may serve in a meaningful way persons who do not share his or her religious affirmations and who are often total strangers" (Shockley 1989a, 42).

Consider, for example, the ministry of the Rev. William Sloane Coffin, Jr. During his seminary days at Yale Divinity School, Coffin served as a campus minister at Yale: he was pastor to Presbyterian students (Coffin 1977, 125). After ordination and year-long stints as chaplain at Phillips Academy, Andover, and Williams College, he was appointed in 1958 by Yale University President Whitney Griswold to be university chaplain and "Yale's conscience" (Coffin 1977, 133). In fact, during his seventeen-year tenure, Coffin became conscience to the nation and in that capacity exercised powerful influence as a role model for campus ministers.

Given his expansive interpretation of his calling, how important to others was his denominational affiliation? How many knew that he was ordained in the United Church of Christ (UCC)? or that he switched from his early Presbyterianism? Did it make a discernible difference? No. When scores of alumni called upon President Griswold to rebuke Coffin after his arrest and jailing in Montgomery, Alabama in 1961, Griswold replied, "The chaplain apparently acted out of Christian convictions. This leads me to believe that these are the grounds on which one should argue with him" (Coffin 1977, 163).

Christian convictions, not Presbyterian, not UCC convictions. It may be argued that Coffin's Christian witness (dare one say, generic Protestantism?) contributed to the erosion of denominational allegiance among campus ministers, who by the very nature of their placement already stand outside daily dealing with denominational agencies and agendas. (It seems natural that after he left Yale, Coffin pastored an interdenominational—American Baptist/UCC—congregation, the prestigious Riverside Church in Manhattan.)

As we have seen, ecumenism was the earliest factor in the fast-disappearing denominational consciousness, but since World War II the increasing pluralism and secularism in higher education have contributed most powerfully to the eclipse. These two sociocultural forces are the most formidable challenges to Protestant campus ministers today. In light of them, the task of transmitting denominational identity takes low priority, if it is viable at all.

Pluralism and Campus Ministry

The entry of returning World War II veterans into public higher education under the G.I. Bill brought enormous changes in colleges and universities. In an important and engaging study of campus ministry which updates Clarence Shedd's early work, Thomas R. McCormick describes the vets:

> They were older and more mature than college students of former generations. Many had traveled widely during the war years. Others had received excellent education from top universities to prepare them for military service. Some had developed language skills, particularly in German or Japanese . . . They came from diverse backgrounds, and in distinction from earlier generations of students, many of these were married (McCormick 1987, 30).

This influx of students brought numerous changes, among them an enlargement of educational opportunity through federal assistance for the economically deprived and otherwise disadvantaged. In 1947–48 a commission on higher education appointed by President Harry Truman published a lengthy report emphasizing a need to remove all barriers to educational opportunity and recommending that economic, racial, religious, and geographical restraints to education be addressed. McCormick writes, "Such concern for social justice in opening access to all capable students to the powers and privileges of higher education had an important beginning which would develop in the forth- coming years" (McCormick 1987, 31–32).

As blacks, Jews, and members of the working class began to be a presence on campuses and a challenge to the hegemony of white, Protestant, middle- and upper-class student bodies, campus clergy were called upon to be community builders. Since the '60s, a primary task of ministry has been to foster tolerance, understanding, and unity where diversity is increasingly normative.[1]

One campus minister tells of his experience in challenging students to wider experience and interaction with the diverse community:

> Unusual and often intolerant beliefs abound among the students to whom I talk. For example, one told me I should not "consort with Catholics," and another that a prayer that "does not invoke the name of Jesus is not heard by God." I suffer the greatest condemnation for "tolerating homosexuality." Angry parents write to me threatening to report me to the university's president for corrupting students' morals—as if promoting tolerance will promote bad morals! (Olson 1988, 381)

His efforts to promote tolerance, however, have brought him some extraordinary satisfaction. He writes:

> To see that young person who had trouble acknowledging that Catholics are Christians holding hands at a Martin Luther King, Jr. celebration not only with Catholics but with blacks, Jews, and humanists is a miracle.

Ministry in a diverse religious community challenges leaders to provide resources that will facilitate and promote interfaith understanding, particularly through liturgies. Yale University chaplains John Vannorsdall and Harry Baker Adams have responded to the challenge by calling together a committee of clergy and musicians to produce a *New Hymnal for Colleges and Schools*. Published by the Yale University Press in 1992, the book contains not only Protestant hymns but also music from Roman Catholic, Jewish, African American, and ethnic traditions for use in ecumenical and interfaith worship.

Pluralism in the university environment provides opportunity for communication and mutual understanding that otherwise might not take place. It also provides opportunity for ugly expressions of racism, sexism, classism, anti-Semitism, xenophobia, and homophobia. When campus ministers confront prejudice and conflict, they do so not as representatives of their own denominations but of the entire religious community. Dealing pastorally with the pain and alienation inflicted by ignorance, suspicion, and bigotry leads clergy beyond denominational particularism to the universal moral and ethical claims of one human family under God.[2]

Observers of U.S. culture suggest that our society is becoming ever more uniform outwardly and more diverse inwardly. In an insightful study of the country's pluralism E. Allen Richardson writes, "This increase in actual diversity has combined with the long-standing

American emphasis on individualism to produce an ethic that rejects the outward expression of differences in public life but upholds the right of the individual to maintain them privately" (Richardson 1988, 199). What is needed, he says, are mediating institutions that provide a middle ground between public and private life and between values of homogeneity and diversity. The function of mediating institutions is to provide:

> a secure atmosphere in which traditions, values, and patterns of life often experienced only in the private home, can be made known in public life and thus help reduce the schizophrenic division between the inside and outside realm. Mediating institutions deal with the question of identity by maintaining a balance between the competing ideologies of pluralism and assimilation . . . and they assist the society in making sense out of the experience of diversity in public life (Richardson 1988, 202).

Universities serve as mediating institutions. And so do campus ministries. The clergyman quoted above describes his work as "trouble-shooting:"

> Students use campus ministers to let off a lot of steam in a safe context. We hear stories not told to other churchpeople or to family members. . . . I hear of the church's inadequacies concerning the role of women, the poor, the homeless, the oppressed. I hear the complaint that the church is too supportive of the military and the establishment, that it is too caught up in materialism and wealth, in real estate and budgets, and that it does not care about its young people. I hear of the pain the church has inflicted upon gays and lesbians; and on and on goes the list (Olson 1988, 381).

In their concern for mediating between public and private worlds, for cultivating civility, for forming students who can make humane, knowledgeable, rational choices, educators and campus ministers share a common goal: education for citizenship. During his presidency of Yale University, the late A. Bartlett Giamatti acted as an eloquent spokesperson for the function of the university in educating for citizenship. What he said of the university applies equally to campus ministry in our time. Both affirm a diversity of values and backgrounds and peoples. Both envision a culture "where pluralism is ordered so that it can be nourished and where diversity is defined as a good." Both know that "it is in everyone's interest to listen and learn from each other and to cherish the powerful pluralism, and all it implies, that is the unique instinct and strength of our country" (Giamatti 1981, 11, 14).

But campus ministry parts company with the university in that its purpose is more than education for citizenship. It is education for *discipleship* as well.[3] Here the forces of secularism in our culture become problematic for campus ministers.

Secularism and Campus Ministry

When Wayne C. Olson, director of the Metropolitan Indianapolis Campus Ministry, described to a clergy friend his disappointment as campus minister in seeing students ill-prepared to meet the challenges that the secular university presents to their faith, he was engaging in a conversation repeated countless times on countless campuses. Olson's frustration about students' spiritual immaturity and lack of biblical knowledge, his sense that he is doing "remedial religion" (Olson 1988, 382), is a common experience for university pastors.

United Methodist Bishop Calvin McConnell, a former campus minister, explains that today one is relating to second and third generation "unchurched," "unfaithed" students, faculty, and administrators, "who have not experienced the church or participated in Christian community personally enough to result in commitment" (Lamar 1989, 6). This secular environment—in which students have neither the background of faith to cause them to seek out the church, nor interest enough to desire it—calls for missionary approaches, indeed, for remedial Christian education.

Fred Lamar, chaplain and professor at DePauw University in Greencastle, Indiana, concurs. His twenty-four years in campus ministry have convinced him that "we need 'remedial religion for the spiritually disadvantaged' in our colleges as much as we need remedial education for the economically disadvantaged in our classrooms" (Lamar 1989, 6).

Recalling his ministry at Yale, William Sloane Coffin wrote in his memoir, "I remember one evening asking a group of faculty if they thought the existence of God was a lively question. 'It's not even a question,' replied a political scientist, 'let alone a lively one.'" To which Coffin comments, "Such was my mission field in academia!" (Coffin 1977, 136). College chaplains and campus ministers everywhere know the story, for they function in a social setting in which, according to sociologists, "the norms are to question all that is holy, to rationalize, to categorize, and to dissect" (Wiley and Carroll 1971, 23).

If in a pluralistic environment *education for citizenship* is a responsibility shared by the university and church, in a secular environment *education for discipleship* is solely the church's responsibility. And if, as John A. Coleman suggests, neighbor love is the key to any correlation, or dialogue, between citizenship and discipleship, then from the church's point of view, discipleship must be the starting point in the dialogue (Coleman in Boys 1989, 51, 54).

Operating as they do in intensely secular environments where folks act "as though we speak in an unknown tongue" (Lamar 1989, 6), Protestant ministers must focus on educating for Christian discipleship. It is easy to see that lifting up nuanced denominational boundaries makes little sense in a situation where remedial instruction is essential.

The marginalization of mainline Protestant denominations—their removal from "the mainline to the sideline," to use *Newsweek's* inimitable phrase—is a component in the secularization process with fallout for campus ministry. As the denominations have increasingly focused their national energies and resources upon church growth and the local congregation, they have drastically slashed budgets for higher education, sharply reducing the number of denominational clergy on campus.

With the funding squeeze of the past thirty years it has been common for several denominations to come together to establish local or regional united ministries boards to employ one campus clergyperson to represent the several groups. Now we are witnessing a retreat from genuine ecumenical commitment as groups cut back, or cut altogether, funding to these boards. At the national level the United Methodists pulled out of ecumenical partnership in 1979 and the American Baptists in 1989, leaving the UCC, Disciples, Presbyterians, Episcopalians, Moravians, and Brethren to go it without them in the reconstituted Higher Education Ministries Team. The Team's program budget in 1989 was less than one hundred thousand dollars (Barker 1989, 2). It appears that promoting denominational identity-building at the expense of ecumenical partnership is an intentional growth strategy. (Daniel Olson's essay in this volume about shared religious identity is suggestive here [see ch. 1].) In recent years denominational executives responsible for higher education ministries have channeled much creative energy and considerable financial resources into writing independent position papers and organizing independent national student gatherings. Hughes's caveat of 1914, that any attempt to use campus ministry to build up the church as an end in itself could be fatal, seems to be long forgotten.

Donald Shockley, who has researched the history of campus ministry and brilliantly interpreted the challenge it presents (Shockley 1989a), has seen major breakthroughs on the ecumenical front (Shockley 1989b). He once called attention to a nationwide meeting of Christian students in December 1990, in which some four thousand delegates gathered in Louisville, Kentucky, to "CELEBRATE! Many Gifts; One Spirit." I was more skeptical than he was, however, about the cooperative mood. The original name of the event—"A National Ecumenical Student Conference"—was changed to "A National Ecumenical Gathering of Student Christian Conferences"—a significant change which recognizes the denominational emphasis of the meeting. Because denominational dinners opened the long weekend and denominational meetings stretched over three full days (plenary sessions were in the evenings), much time was clearly designated for denominational identity-building. The response of one ecumenically minded observer regarding this event was to my mind prophetic: "All of this confirms my long-held hunch that the current denominationalism stems from the bureaucrats and self-appointed leaders who seem to believe they can stem membership decline by a resurgence of denominational hype. It isn't working; it won't work, but who will blow the whistle and make us deal with reality?"

Given the limitations of this chapter, the development and decline of student ministry on the university campus cannot be explored; however, some provocative thoughts may be raised. When Clarence Shedd published his study of university pastorates in 1938, he meant for the volume to be a companion to his *Two Centuries of Student Christian Movements,* which had appeared in 1934. As difficult as it may be to comprehend in our day, when mainline Protestant campus ministry—by students and clergy—is collapsed into a single, clergy-led venture, in Shedd's time student Christian associations operated independently. Denominational clergy ministry and student ministry were parallel enterprises with distinct histories.

There are observers who believe that the demise of the student Christian movement was inevitable once denominational clergy began to take over ministry on campus.[4] One may ask, is the phenomenal growth of *non*denominational student groups like the Inter-Varsity Christian Fellowship, Campus Crusade for Christ, Navigators, and Fellowship of Christian Athletes the predictable response of young people who refuse to be co-opted by denominationally appointed clergy, who prefer to focus on universal Christian identity and set aside denominational divisions, and who, in character with their developmental lifestage, insist on exercising autonomy? If so, then are not denominational, "top down" efforts to resurrect a student movement out of the Protestant mainline doomed to self-destruct? Is the concern of liberal mainline denominations for their own survival ironically fueling the commitment of theologically unsophisticated students who choose conservative orthodoxy in a struggle to maintain Christian identity in a cultural context where peers profess other religious beliefs (Jewish, Muslim, Hindu, Buddhist) or, indeed, no religious belief at all? These are promising psycho-social research questions.

Arthur E. Holt, professor of social ethics in the Chicago Theological Seminary for many years, remarked in an Earl Lecture in 1940 that "in proportion as the church loses its power to dictate, it must enlarge its power to educate" (Holt 1941, 160). That Protestant mainline religion has lost its power to dictate is a well-documented fact: the forces of pluralism and secularism have bumped it from its accustomed place on the public square. Nevertheless, Protestant mainline religion has shown little recognition that not only must it enlarge its power to educate, it must do so ecumenically, in partnership, if it is to be effective in the pluralistic, secular world of academe.

Today denominational commitment to the mission field of campus ministry is anemic, if not self-seeking. Even so, there are educators who are working mightily to change that, people like the Rev. Ansley Coe Throckmorton, the executive who carries responsibility for all education in the United Church of Christ. She wrote in 1988:

> All is not well with teaching in the church. The message of reconciliation and transformation is not heard, and its implications are not understood. The suffering of human existence remains unrelieved by grace and truth for too many. The church, the churches, including many of the ministers, have lost touch with the language, symbols, and texts of faith. Many persons tell us that they feel illiterate and inarticulate about their faith (UCCBHM 1988, 3–4).

Concerned for a holistic approach to Christian educational mission, Throckmorton led the way in the eighties in calling for profound and creative reforms that acknowledge "the inadequacy of current educational theory and practice, and of over-reliance on church schools often as the sole provider for education." She and clergy educators who share her vision look to the nineties as a decade of reform and renewal of the Protestant mainline church's approach to its educational ministries.

Throckmorton's colleague, Dr. Verlyn L. Barker, shares her concerns. He recently told a gathering of campus ministers that a passion for survival has clouded our minds:

> My conviction is that the survival of the church's ministry in higher education has to do with understanding how it is the mission and ministry of the church in the setting of higher education, not with how many students and faculty and staff from *our* churches we manage to recruit for programs, and not with the number of good causes and activities with which the minister in higher education is identified. Ministry is a calling of preaching and teaching, not of being busy-bodies who believe exhaustion is a sign of fulfilling their calling. (Barker 1989)

Campus ministers take heart.

NOTES

1. On private college and university campuses, administrators seek to achieve pluralism through vigorous minority recruiting, need-blind admission policies, generous financial aid packages, and aggressive affirmative action.

2. Douglas Sloan, professor of the history of education at Teachers College, Columbia University, is studying the role of the church in educating for a public vision. He sees the church as a forum in which we "can seek together our common purpose out of the richness of our different identities, in which healing can take place and conflict can be creative" (Sloan 1989, 13). This, I believe, is especially true of campus ministry.

3. For their seminal thinking about the distinction/relationship between these two pedagogies, I am indebted to the National Faculty Seminar. This interdisciplinary and ecumenical group of eleven scholars met from 1983–1986 under the auspices of the Center for Congregational Education in Indianapolis with funding from the Lilly Endowment. Members of the seminar initially tackled the question, "How shall we interpret the Christian faith to educate for the future good of the world?" Their conversations led them first to an exploration of, and then to a volume of essays about, *Education for Citizenship and Discipleship* (Boys 1989). For his chapter I owe particular thanks to John A. Coleman, S.J., professor of religion and society, Jesuit School of Theology and The Graduate Theological Union.

4. David S. Wiley and Jackson W. Carroll offer some sociological reflections on the University Christian Movement and its demise in their unpublished study, "Process '67 and the University Christian Movement," June 1971.

REFERENCES

Barker, Verlyn C.
    1988–89 "Moving the Tents Again." In *Resume,* the United Ministries in Education 1988–1989 Annual Report. Albuquerque, N.M.
    1989 "The Minister in Higher Education: Theologian, Mentor and Educator." Southwestern Campus Ministers' Conference, Texas Christian University, June 1989.

Boys, Mary C.
  1989   *Education for Citizenship and Discipleship.* New York: Pilgrim Press.
Coffin, William Sloane
  1977   *Once to Every Man, A Memoir.* New York: Atheneum Publishers.
Coleman, John A.
  1989   "The Two Pedagogies: Discipleship and Citizenship." In *Education for Citizenship and Discipleship,* edited by Mary C. Boys, 33–75. New York: Pilgrim Press.
Giamatti, A. Bartlett
  1981   *The University and the Public Interest.* New York: Atheneum Publishers.
Hoge, Dean
  1974   *Commitment on Campus, Changes in Religion and Values Over Five Decades.* Philadelphia: Westminster Press.
Holt, Arthur E.
  1941   *Christian Roots of Democracy in America.* New York: Friendship Press.
Lamar, Fred
  1989   "Getting a Head Start in Being the Church," *Circuit Rider* (June 1989), 6–7.
McCormick, Thomas R.
  1987   *Campus Ministry in the Coming Age.* St. Louis: CBP Press.
Olson, Wayne C.
  1988   "Campus Ministry as Remedial Religion." *Christian Century* (April 13, 1988): 381–382.
Richardson, E. Allen
  1988   *Strangers in This Land: Pluralism and the Response to Diversity in the United States.* New York: Pilgrim Press.
Shedd, Clarence Prouty
  1938   *The Church Follows Its Students.* New Haven, Conn.: Yale University Press.
Shockley, Donald G.
  1986   "The College and University Chaplaincy: A Theological Perspective." In *Invitation to Dialogue: The Theology of College Chaplaincy and Campus Ministry.* New York: Education in the Society, National Council of Churches.
  1989a *Campus Ministry: The Church Beyond Itself.* Louisville, Ky.: Westminster/John Knox Press.
  1989b "Rattling the Dry Bones of the Student Christian Movement." *The Christian Century.* (November 22, 1989): 1087–1089.

Sloan, Douglas
  1989   "Educating for a Public Vision," *The Chicago Theological Seminary Register* 69 no. 1 (Winter 1989): 4–13.
United Church Board for Homeland Ministries (UCCBHM)
  1988   "The Educational Mission of the United Church of Christ." New York: Division of Education and Publication.
Westerhoff, John H.
  1978   *The Church's Ministry in Higher Education.* New York: United Ministries in Higher Education (UMHE) Communication Office.
Wiley, David S., and Jackson W. Carroll
  1971   "Process '67 and the University Christian Movement, A Report and Interpretation of a Survey of Conference Participants." June 1971. Unpublished.
Wiley, George
  1979   "Toward Parish and Community, Unreflectively: Visions of Campus Ministers in the Mid-Seventies." *The NICM Journal* 4, no. 2 (Spring 1979): 12–23.

9

The Theological Schools: Transmission, Transformation, and Transcendence of Denominational Culture

W. Clark Gilpin

A century ago, in the 1880s, the theological school played a central role in forming denominational identity, and it played that role in a double sense. First, it sought to form individual students by inculcating the particular configuration of beliefs, moral norms, and patterns of worship and polity that made the denomination a recognizably distinct fellowship within the larger Christian tradition. Second, as custodian of this denominational lore, the theological school contributed significantly to the formation of the denomination itself, molding corporate practices and habits of mind by providing "expert" interpretation of the tradition. Each of the mainstream Protestant churches can point to a period in its history when a particular theological school, by exercising these formative roles, decisively influenced the denomination's theological outlook, liturgical practice, or sense of social responsibility.

To be sure, the nineteenth-century theological schools did not intend to be sectarian in their educational aims. They understood the Bible, theology, and church history as the legacy of the whole church. Nevertheless, exegesis, doctrine, and the historical development of Christianity all received interpretations that directly reflected the confessional standards, theological controversies, and patterns of worship that comprised the denominational culture of the parent church. Faculty members were recruited from the ordained ministry of the sponsoring denomination, and they pledged to uphold the denomination's doctrinal standards and form of government in pursuing their professorial duties. In these ways, a distinctive denominational culture permeated the theological school and its curriculum; the school's governing educational purposes included faithful transmission of this culture in a way that would shape the religious identity of each student generation and the church at large.

The present situation presents a marked contrast. One might say that the theological schools of mainstream Protestantism share a corporate memory of their historic formative roles with respect to students and denominations, but they are uncertain whether or how to exercise those roles in the contemporary setting. They are uncertain whether the formation of denominational identity should be numbered among the central aims of theological education, because it stands in tension with the major religious and intellectual commitments of mainstream theological schools in the twentieth century. They are uncertain how formation of denominational identity should occur, because the increasing diversity of seminary students and faculty coupled with the decreasing importance Americans attach to denominational affiliation have rendered the very notion of denominational identity perplexing. Yet, the perceived plight of the mainstream denominations enforces the notion that these questions about formation cannot be deferred to some later day.

In sum, at a time when the mainstream churches are actively seeking new avenues for reestablishing the vigor of denominational identities, they find the seminaries generally sympathetic but not much help. The reason, it seems, is that seminary faculties have given little systematic consideration to the formative tasks involved in the transmission of denominational cultures within their own sphere of work. In denominational seminaries and university divinity schools alike, denominational traditions of theological reflection appear to be largely inert, in the sense that they exert little influence upon the active imagination of theologians, upon the interests that motivate students, or upon the subjects of inquiry that order the theological curriculum.

In an effort to interpret this situation, the present chapter will argue that, through two-thirds of the twentieth century, the assumptions that guided ministerial education for the mainstream churches militated against the development of a rationale for the transmission of denominational culture within schools of theology. Hence, the initial task will be to sketch the twentieth-century history of attitudes toward denominationalism and denominational identity in mainstream theological education. Two major studies of theological education, the first directed by William Adams Brown and Mark A. May in the 1930s and the second directed by H. Richard Niebuhr, Daniel Day Williams, and James M. Gustafson in the 1950s, will be used as "windows" through which to see the characteristic features of this history.

The chapter will also argue, however, that embedded in this history are significant resources for understanding and transmitting denominational culture. A second task, therefore, will be to draw out and reconfigure those resources in relation to the quite different context in which mainstream theological schools now find themselves. This reconfiguration will require something quite different from the current tendency toward "neo-denominationalism" that pressures students to attend the seminaries of their own communion. What is missing is not simply "close encounters" with patterns of denominational life but a rationale that would explain the relationship between such experiences and the central educational tasks of the theological school.

Transformation of Denominational Culture

During the first third of the twentieth century, the liberal theologians of American Protestantism developed a characteristic interpretation of the relations of the theological school to the denomination, the university, and American society. This interpretation was codified in four volumes, *The Education of American Ministers* (Brown and May 1934), based upon five years of research directed by William Adams Brown of Union Theological Seminary and Mark A. May of Yale University. The Brown-May study, which provided the rationale for the formation of the American Association of Theological Schools in 1936, represented the culmination of liberal thinking about the aims of theological education, a line of thought that decisively influenced the Protestant churches and that, therefore, is pivotal for understanding the role that twentieth-century theological schools have played in the formation and transmission of denominational cultures.

The director of the study, William Adams Brown (1865–1943) epitomized the ecclesiastical portfolio that the liberal theologians carried in their various denominations and on behalf of Protestant ecumenical Christianity. Throughout his forty-four year tenure on the Union faculty, Brown vigorously engaged in the life of American Presbyterianism, in social gospel causes, in the interdenominational programs of the Religious Education Association, and in the beginnings of the world ecumenical movement. The range of Brown's influence was unusual, but the orientation was characteristic of his generation. Liberal theological educators committed themselves to the proposition that federated action by the denominations could influence positively both church and society, and their watchword was "efficiency" in the conduct of matters religious. It was, to borrow a phrase from H. Richard Niebuhr, the epoch of "the institutionalization of the kingdom."

Brown and May began their assessment of ministerial education by lamenting the modern displacement of the church from its traditional social role. The church was no longer what once it had been: the organized fellowship charged with "the releasing and directing of energies which are to bear fruit not only in the development of Christian character in individuals but in the creation of a Christian society" (Brown and May 1934, 6–15, 96). The church's failure to maintain its moral leadership and status in society, said Brown, had been detrimental not only for the church but, more fundamentally, for society and its institutions. Further, the entire problem had been exacerbated by excessive denominationalism, that "narrow view of life" which, by identifying Christianity "with the form of religion represented in one's own communion," was a chief reason for "the failure of the church to command the whole-hearted allegiance of many thoughtful men" (Brown 1919, 168–169). Thus, Brown set education for ministry in a broader context of reform and recovery: the ecumenical renewal of the church's proper sense for "its mission to organize society as a whole in accordance with the religious principle" (Brown 1906, 58).

Given this emphasis upon the public moral responsibility of the church, Brown and other liberal theologians emphasized the church's instrumental or mediating role. Its task was to adjust, adapt, or interpret the Christian gospel in order that this message might serve as a unifying spiritual force amid the diverse currents of modern social and intellectual life. This mandate required federated action by the denominations that found its justification beyond the churches themselves in the society for which they sought to establish a renewed cultural synthesis. "In addressing ourselves to the tasks that we face in our own country and in our own church," Brown stated at the centennial of Lancaster Theological Seminary, "we are not merely doing our immediate duty; we are fitting ourselves to co-operate with our fellow-Christians of other churches and of other lands in that co-operative study through which alone the church of Christ can be put in the position to fulfil its ecumenical function as the teacher of the nations" (Brown 1926, 383). The liberals experimented with incorporating this social mission of the church directly into theological studies, adding sociology courses to the curriculum and involving students in urban settlement houses as a part of their seminary education.

Congruent with this view of the church's responsibility within society was the liberal commitment to align theological studies with the modern university and its methods. They conceived the task of theological scholarship in relation to the canons of free, critical inquiry that characterized university scholarship. Theology properly proceeds, they proposed, by a method of empirical investigation, for which no presuppositions are in principle reserved from criticism. Writing in

1916 on the relation of critical scholarship to ministerial "efficiency," the Baptist philosopher of religion George Burman Foster of the University of Chicago concluded that the inherited view of religious authority, "rooted in God's dictation and donation of truth," was "no longer tenable." Theological scholarship must therefore be revised; "the study of a deposit of truth must give way to the search for reality," and "theology must come to terms with the scientific and philosophical theories which are current" (Foster 1916, 175).

This shifted the balance of theological studies from inquiry about the nature and substance of the tradition to inquiry about the meaning and plausibility of the tradition in the modern world. The earlier ministerial education had emphasized the transmittal of tradition and had built upon doctrinal studies refracted through the specific confessional standards of the churches; the newer approach made the study of theology an interdenominational enterprise aimed at reinterpreting tradition for the modern world, the common theological pursuit of the mainstream churches. From this perspective, the liberal educators regularly contrasted modern theological inquiry with the catechetical indoctrination into denominational theology that, they believed, had typified the nineteenth-century denominational seminary. Liberal rhetoric commonly compared the rural, parochial, and rather sleepy denominational seminary with the urban, ecumenical, and progressive vigor of the university-related divinity school. Indeed, they were convinced that the very creation of the denominational seminary had served to separate theology and the ministry from the forefront of higher learning and thereby had directly contributed to the declining influence of the Protestant churches in American society. Their reforming mission, as Charles Briggs summarized it in 1904, included taking the side of science "against a common foe, ecclesiastical domination, the greatest foe of theology, as it is also of all learning" (1904, 435).

Perhaps the most accurate designation of the characteristic liberal stance is "liberated denominationalism." They aimed not to reject their denominational heritages but to open them toward modern American society and toward one another. They aligned themselves with movements of social reform and with university scholarship in order to have the independence to carry out this opening of the denominational mind. The involvements of Northern Baptist and Disciples of Christ professors at the turn of the century illustrate this reformist perspective on denominational identity. Among the Baptists Walter Rauschenbusch was instrumental in forming the Brotherhood of the Kingdom, an organization of pastors and educators committed to "infusing the power of religion into social efforts" (White and Hopkins 1976, 72–79). Similarly, Disciples professors at the University of Chicago, especially Edward Scribner Ames, guided development of the Campbell Institute, an association of ministers with graduate degrees who promoted theological discussion and contributed to "the literature of the Disciples of Christ" in ways that soon made this group a wide-ranging forum for liberal theology within the denomination (Willett 1917).

Their goal for individual students was not unlike their goal for the denominations: to reorient them away from the preservation of traditional ideas toward an active engagement with public life. Chicago's Foster aptly summarized the liberal attitude:

> It may be said that usually the candidate for the ministry—young though he may sometimes be—enters the divinity school as a finished religious and theological product, but that in consequence of his studies there he departs, unfinished, growing, aware that his personality, with its religion and its theology, are alike in the making. A divinity school that achieves such a result has fulfilled its function in the life of the human spirit (Foster 1916, 178).

What, then, was the liberal legacy with respect to the transmission of denominational culture in seminaries and divinity schools? In one sense, the situation was and has remained unchanged. At no point have the theological schools of mainstream Protestantism simply "handed on" the cultures of their respective denominations. In addition to denominational culture, they have also participated in and expressed a long series of interdenominational religious and theological movements from anti-slavery and the social gospel, to theological liberalism and neo-orthodoxy, to feminist and liberation theologies. The liberal scholars were distinctive in the degree to which they self-consciously attempted explicit correlation between inherited denominational culture and contemporary religious and theological movements.

For the denomination, the most important consequence of this correlation was its more or less deliberate intent to transform denominational identity through interaction with larger cultural movements. Such transformations, to the extent that they were persuasively achieved, argued for the continuing pertinence of the denomination's tradition within the larger context of American religious life. From the liberal vantage point, in other words, effective transmission of denominational culture included the transformation of that culture.

For the student, such transmission by transformation established and sustained immediate engagement between denominational culture, especially the inherited denominational theology, and those intellectual questions and social commitments that had originally led the student toward the ministry. Harry Emerson Fosdick wrote for his student generation when he observed:

What present-day critics of liberalism often fail to see is its absolute necessity to multitudes of us who would not have been Christians at all unless we could thus have escaped the bondage of the then reigning orthodoxy. Of course the revolt was not the whole answer! Of course it left out dimensions of Christian faith which would need to be rediscovered! Despite that, however, it offered a generation of earnest youth the only chance they had to be honest while being Christian. (Fosdick 1956, 66)

Finally, the liberal theologians helped "invent" the twentieth-century form of mainstream Protestantism. Although terms such as "mainstream" or "mainline" did not figure in their rhetoric, this more recent terminology nicely captures their sense of responsibility to a "central" spiritual tradition within the American commonwealth and their tacit assumption that others—notably fundamentalist Protestants and Roman Catholics—had either rejected or stood outside of this central tradition. They regarded their own denominations as "open" institutions, committed to federated action in the public sphere and willing to transform a religious heritage in order to achieve a broader religious and social consensus. Likewise, they conceived of theology less as doctrinal studies grounded in specific confessional traditions than as an ecumenical inquiry into common human experience and the transpersonal forces that challenged and sustained that common experience. They were institution builders who believed in the power of institutions to better the human lot. This confidence arose not so much from a sense of their own righteousness as from the conviction that the values to which they aspired were congruent with the heart of things. These commitments to a tolerant consensus around which a plural Protestant tradition could sustain its religious hopes and cooperatively institutionalize its moral influence within the nation went far to define the modern self-conception of the mainstream.

Transcendence of Denominational Culture

From 1954 to 1957, H. Richard Niebuhr, Daniel Day Williams, and James M. Gustafson collaborated on a major study of issues and trends in the schools of theology and reported their findings in *The Advancement of Theological Education* (Niebuhr, Williams, Gustafson 1957). The Niebuhr study documented important continuities in the development of institutional patterns during the twenty years since the report by Brown and May. Among these continuities, the strongest was the advancement of genuinely graduate education in theology as prerequisite for ministry in all the mainstream churches, especially as part of the general expansion of American higher education following World War II. This development powerfully reinforced and extended what had begun in the liberal era: the pursuit of research and teaching according to issues framed by interdenominational professional organizations, such as the Society of Biblical Literature. Questions or issues arising from specifically denominational concerns occupied a decidedly secondary place on the research agenda of theological faculties, even though faculty members generally remained active as preachers, teachers, and theological consultants for the churches.

Ecumenical relations had also advanced, but unevenly. On the one hand, Niebuhr and his colleagues did not find that the schools had become significantly more interdenominational in the composition of their faculties and student bodies. Faculties of the separate schools continued to be isolated from one another "behind denominational walls," and the report therefore emphasized that "the life of the whole Church should become the context for all theological studies" and called for interdenominational exchanges of faculty as a way of combating the tendency of schools to become "ingrown" (Niebuhr, Williams, and Gustafson 1957, 77, 89, 215). On the other hand, a development with significant implications for the transmission of denominational identity was the breaking of what Brown, twenty years before, had called "the ecclesiastical circle" of faculty education, in which seminary faculty members received their educations entirely within the affiliated schools of their own denomination. By the 1950s, a review of the educational backgrounds of assistant professors clearly indicated that the pattern had shifted toward more pluralistic, interdenominational educations (Niebuhr, Williams, and Gustafson 1957, 17–19, 23). This trend, like the growing prestige of specialized research in the various academic disciplines, cut across denominational lines and reinforced the growing independence of scholarship from explicitly denominational convictions and questions.

In addition to tracing these continuities of institutional development, the Niebuhr study also displayed some pronounced changes in the assumptions that governed the theological school's relations to denomination, university, and society. These changed assumptions were particularly evident in *The Purpose of the Church and Its Ministry* (Niebuhr 1956), Niebuhr's theological appraisal of the state of theological education, written in consultation with his colleagues on the study team. In its portrait of church and denomination, the book drew upon themes from Niebuhr's earlier writings, especially *The Social Sources of Denominationalism* (Niebuhr 1929) and *The Kingdom of God in America* (Niebuhr 1937). In those works he had dramatized the conformity of denominational differences, ostensibly based upon different creeds or doctrines, to a caste system based instead upon class, race, or economic power. "The evils of denominationalism," he asserted, arose from "the failure of the churches to transcend the social conditions which fashion them into caste-organizations, to sublimate their loyalties to standards and institutions only remotely relevant if not contrary to the Christian ideal, to resist the temptation of making their own self-preservation and extension the primary object of their endeavor" (Niebuhr 1929, 21). This failure reflected a far-reaching entanglement of the church in the worldliness of civilization and led Niebuhr to seek a point of view that, while inevitably within history, nevertheless provided moral and theological leverage upon that historical situation. He therefore insisted upon the dynamic or dialectical character of the church's life, in which loyalty to a God sovereign over history made the church critical of even its own best efforts to institutionalize that loyalty in particular historical forms. Niebuhr had vividly stated his perspective in his preface to *The Kingdom of God in America* (1937), arguing there that the true church was not an organization but the organic movement of a people in pilgrimage toward a kingdom and an eternity that can be represented in no one society and no single time. The "dilemma of constructive Protestantism" arose from the fact that the necessary task of creating institutions to embody the life of this movement always and necessarily falsified its fundamental meaning as a journey prompted and sustained by confidence in God.

In *The Purpose of the Church and Its Ministry* (Niebuhr 1956), this dialectical analysis of the church provided the background against which Niebuhr put forward his well-known characterization of the theological school as "intellectual center of the church's life." What, he asked, was the community within which the theological school carried out its work and whose aims and values it represented? Niebuhr rejected as superficial the answer that this communal context consisted of the various denominations that had created and funded the theological schools. Instead, he concluded that despite "their denominational affiliation and their service of denominational purposes the theological schools usually give evidence of sharing in a community of discourse and interest that transcends denominational boundaries" (1956, 6). Although denominational organization and U.S. public life are both "conditioning elements" in the work of theological schools, Niebuhr argued that "the primary context in which the ministry and theology do their work is neither denomination nor nation but the Church in its wholeness" (1956, 11, 12). He found this interdenominational context of study apparent in courses in Bible, church history, and theology: "With few exceptions teachers and students do not engage in a denominationally restricted discussion but participate in a Protestant and a Christian conversation or debate about the ultimate problems of faith and life" (1956, 15).

Even if, however, "the Church in its wholeness" had replaced the denomination as the primary context of theological education, neither the church catholic nor the denomination, in Niebuhr's view, should be confused with the primary object of theological study. "The confusion between part and whole is not to be avoided by denying the reality of the parts," he insisted, "but only by the acceptance of diversity and limitation and the corollary recognition that all the parts are equally related in the whole to the ultimate object of the Church" (Niebuhr 1956, 40–41). Hence, for mainstream Protestantism at mid-century a greater danger than the confusion of denomination with whole church was the confusion of church, considered as a whole or in its essence, with the ultimate object of theological education (1956, 41). Instead, that ultimate object consisted, for Niebuhr, of an inquiry into the final sovereignty of God over a creation in which the church's purpose was the exercise and the extension of the love of God and neighbor.

From this perspective, ecumenical Protestantism no less than the individual denominations stood under judgment, since the exaltation of church or of Christianity led to the mistaken—indeed, idolatrous— effort "not to reconcile men with God or to redirect their love and ours toward God and the neighbor but rather to convert them to Christianity" (Niebuhr 1956, 42). Whenever it prevailed, such an exaltation of church undercut the theological school's striving genuinely to be theological, since education that presumes the church as its ultimate context "necessarily becomes indoctrination in Christian principles rather than inquiry based on faith in God; or it is turned into training in methods for increasing the Church rather than for guiding men to love of God and neighbor" (1956, 43).

As "intellectual center of the church's life," therefore, the theological school bore religious responsibility for direct, independent, intellectual inquiry into life before God: "Such a movement of the mind toward God and the neighbor-before-God is characteristic of the Church in all its parts but it is the first duty and a central purpose of the theological school" (Niebuhr 1956, 112). This exercise of the intellectual love of God then ordered the second function of the theological school, to bring critical reflection to bear upon the church's other activities of worship, teaching, pastoral care, and social service.

Theological differences between William Adams Brown and H. Richard Niebuhr are, of course, striking. Both considered the relationships between Christianity and society and asked about the place of theological study in those relations. But where Brown had seen adaptation and correlation, Niebuhr saw accommodation and entanglement. Where Brown had sought to reform society by applying the ideals of Christianity, Niebuhr hoped for the repentance of the church itself, believing that it had lost its bearings in the midst of the "polytheistic" loyalties of a fragmenting culture. Nevertheless, from their different vantage points, the liberal and the realist movements in Protestant theology directed fundamental challenges to those who would make the theological school an instrument for the transmission of denominational culture. First, the task of theological education is inquiry, not indoctrination, and the denomination must be prepared to have its heritage placed under scrutiny and judgment. For both the liberals and for Niebuhr, the theological school had a necessary independence with respect to the church, whether that independence is thought of as primarily grounded in its alliance with the university or in its orientation in faith toward God. Second, theological education is directed toward the public realm, toward "God and the neighbor," and therefore is inimical to any construal of the transmission of denominational culture that would make the church the ultimate object of its work. These criticisms have militated against thorough consideration of the appropriate place of denominational formation in theological education. They are serious criticisms and demand full and continuing attention. Yet, if students are genuinely to be educated to serve God and the neighbor in and through these denominations, some such thorough consideration seems required in the current situation of uncertainty about the identity of the mainstream churches.

Denominational Culture and
the Agenda of Theological Education

Mainstream theologians of the twentieth century criticized denominationalism as a problem to be overcome, by commitment to the critical inquiry of the university, by an ecumenical vision of the church, and by a theocentric interpretation of human history that exposed the ways in which denominationalism constricts the religious power of the church by confusing it with the power of race, class, and caste. This criticism was not only cogent but also consistent with the developing religious and ethical commitments of the mainstream churches. Its cumulative force has been such that, in combination with broader social factors, it has profoundly affected mainstream denominational identities in the closing decades of the century. To summarize the results in a sentence, this criticism has deflected attention from the denominations' inherited integrity as coherent and distinctive traditions of piety bearing directly upon the destiny of the soul, the just society, and the community of faith.

In the current situation of "denominational switching" and the eclectic personal fabrication of religious orientations, this lack of attention to denominations as coherent traditions of piety has meant that students enter seminaries poorly informed about denominational traditions and that they perceive these traditions as having a declining significance for personal religious identity. Significant numbers of mainstream Protestants inside and outside the seminaries would be prepared to argue for the importance of gender, race, or class experiences for shaping personal religious identity. They would be far less persuaded that denominational affiliation has a comparable shaping role. Denominational identity has become increasingly incidental, an epiphenomenon of the religious life. Denominations are no longer among the principal interpreters of legitimating myths in the private, the public, or even the churchly sphere. As a result, these mainstream traditions of piety not only have been difficult to sustain but also, by relative inattention to them, have appeared lacking in spiritual energy. As Martin E. Marty has observed, mainstream Protestantism "misread" the "passionate hunger for personal experience" in the contemporary American environment, and "when religious groups forget this individual locus and focus they lose power," power both in the sense of public influence and of religious potency (Marty 1982, 29; 1985, 20–21).

Within this context, the seminaries and divinity schools are by no means disinterested in the historic task of the formation of students. If anything, this has become an area of increasing concern. Theological students, like others in this country, have been influenced by the individualistic tendencies in contemporary religious life, which emphasize personal religious quest, diminish the formative power of community, and encourage "religion a la carte," an eclecticism based on individual preference (Bellah et al. 1985, 219–249; Roof and McKinney 1987, 40–71). Further, since the late 1960s, student bodies have become increasingly diverse, as women, ethnic minorities, and older "second career" students have overturned the inherited image of the seminarian as a white male recently graduated from college. Within this new situation, it becomes difficult to imagine "formation" that is sufficiently open to accommodate a sought-after diversity without in the process losing all coherence. Hence, the title of an influential book by Joseph C. Hough and John B. Cobb, *Christian Identity and Theological Education,* signals the widespread view among theological educators that "what is needed today as a basis for reformlng theological education is a strong conviction about who we are as a Christian people" (Hough and Cobb 1985, 4).

This heightened concern for the Christian identity of the student, consistent with the twentieth-century trends of mainstream theological education, leaves uncertain the matter of the student's denominational identity. If, in previous decades, faculty viewed formation in terms of students who entered seminary with relatively distinct denominational identities and, in the course of education, had their religious horizons expanded to encompass the wider Christian tradition on behalf of which they would minister, this is no longer the case. Increasingly, theological educators perceive the formative process less in terms of "expansion" than of "consolidation." They encounter students with eclectic religious identities and multiple communities and are struck by the task of nurturing their understanding of the unifying religious realities that have undergirded the historic tradition. The place of specifically denominational identity in this consolidation of a Christian identity is an unresolved question. It is, of course, not simply a question of forming the student's personal religious stance but also preparing the student for the complexities of transmitting denominational culture within a mainstream congregation, where this same eclecticism and decreasing sense of denominational tradition are prominent features.

The relationships of theological faculties to the denominations themselves exhibit similarly unresolved questions. On the one hand, several observers have noted that, over the past two decades, theological seminaries have increasingly identified themselves as "institutions within the orbit of the church" or as "instruments of the church." Indeed, their administrative leaders have regularly counted among the achievements of the immediate past the strengthening of relations with denominational church constituencies and the "renewed ecclesiastical identity of theological schools." As Leon Pacala, president of the Association of Theological Schools, commented in 1981, "the absence of alternate interpretations, significant qualifications, challenges or counter claims concerning this identity of theological schools is startling and can only be understood as evidence of the extent to which theological schools adopted their newly defined identity" (1981, 14).

This strengthened alliance between school and denomination includes interest, on the part of seminaries, in the relation between denominational identity and the current plight of mainstream Protestantism. For example, the March 1989 conference at Louisville Presbyterian Theological Seminary, titled "The Presbyterian Predicament," was only one of many such conferences on seminary campuses during the 1980s. Advertisements for the Louisville conference posed three questions of the sort that have bedeviled all the mainstream churches and their theological schools:

Why is the Presbyterian Church experiencing membership decline?
What is happening to mainstream Protestant denominations?
What is the theological identity of American Presbyterianism?

On the other hand, this recent interest in their own ecclesiastical identities and responsibilities does stand in tension with the inherited scholarly and theological commitments of mainstream theological schools. For this reason, the transmission of denominational identity is not integral to the formal structure of theological education and is peripheral to current proposals for revision and reform. In *Christian Identity and Theological Education,* for example, professors Hough and Cobb specifically identify denominational studies as a "neglected topic" in their proposals for reform. They find that concern for denominational identity is "legitimate but dangerous," and they directly oppose approaches to the history of Christianity in which "identity as a member of a particular denomination is exaggerated" or the contemporary scene is "viewed only through denominational eyes" (Hough and Cobb 1985, 100–101, 116–117). Similarly, in those recent assessments of theological education which have focused on relationships to the institutional church, it has been the local congregation not the denomination that has been the subject of attention (Hauerwas and Willimon 1986; Hough and Wheeler 1988; Sweet 1984).

Thus, mainstream theological schools display considerable uncertainty about the contemporary meaning of two legacies: the nineteenth-century commitment to the transmission of denominational culture and the twentieth-century commitment to the pursuit of an ecumenical culture. Both of those earlier positions had assumed denominationalism as a potent force within personal piety, American society, and the wider church. In the present century, the liberal theologians sought to reinterpret denominational identity by bringing it into transformative correlation with wider intellectual and religious movements. H. Richard Niebuhr sought to redirect denominational identity by focusing theological attention on the sovereign God whose presence in history challenged the permanence of all human institutions. But in the current situation of greatly weakened denominational cultures, one can no longer assume the presence of a prior denominational identity, which it is the task of theological study to transform or redirect. The possibility and appropriateness of denominational identity has itself become a question. In other words, the seminaries may be said to have entered the contemporary context lacking a critical "ecclesiology of denominations," an understanding of church that would make the case for the formation of denominational identity as an appropriate and integral feature of theological study.

Reflection leading toward a critical ecclesiology of denominations would need to build upon the twentieth-century criticisms of denominationalism and would have at least three implications for mainstream theological studies. First, it would entail a richer encounter for students with the nature of the church. "Movement" has long been a favored metaphor for "the true church" within mainstream Protestantism, and it remains an image to be cultivated. Yet, the church is also an institution. And the only institutional form of church beyond the local congregation that the average theological student encounters is the denomination. Robert Wuthnow has argued that the concrete interaction between religious movements and religious institutions tends powerfully toward increased bureaucratization, as "the religious marketplace generates not only a single charismatic, feminist, or peace movement, but proliferates distinct denominational brands of each" (Wuthnow 1985, 115). It is also the case, however, that not all constituency groups have simply been co-opted by denominations; some have substantially redirected denominational culture and denominational resources. Critical assessment of this varied interplay between the church as "movement" and as "institution," and of the implications of that interplay for understandings of church, represents an important subject in practical theology for the mainstream theological schools.

Second, inquiry leading toward a critical ecclesiology of denominations recalls an easily forgotten dimension of the identity of the mainstream as a whole. Such terms as "mainstream," "mainline," or "old-line" are misleading if they are taken to imply that the role of a community of churches within American culture has devolved upon them simply by longevity, numerical strength, or financial resources. Those are factors, without question, but the consolidation of the mainstream at the beginning of this century also occurred by virtue of corporate moral decisions by the denominations as they decided to relate to one another and to the society in particular ways. To return to Niebuhr's observation on the broadly Protestant and Christian "conversation or debate about the ultimate problems of faith and life," one may say that the mainstream arose as a conversation about the possibilities and limits of churchly engagement in the central issues of American public life. The mainstream, in other words, is not merely a collective term for inherited cultural privilege, it is also the result of moral decision and, hence, is subject to theological scrutiny and evaluation. Here, too, is an important subject in practical theology for the mainstream theological schools.

Third, and finally, reflection leading toward an ecclesiology of denominations includes recognition that responsible formation included critical distance. A school too closely identified with the denomination cannot exercise a formative influence. As was clear both to William Adams Brown and H. Richard Niebuhr, correlations of denominational culture with contemporary interpretations of Christianity and of human existence are part of a critical inquiry. Whatever judgments a scholar reached were achieved, in George Burman Foster's phrase, in pursuit of "the truth interest," which guided university and religion alike; inquiry had not been launched with denominational interests paramount. In Niebuhr's language, when denominational purposes become paramount they confuse a proximate aim with the ultimate aim that guides all Christian institutions, denominations as well as schools, namely, "the increase of the love of God and neighbor." Within the theological school, transmission has the character of transformation because critical inquiry implies change, both for the knower and the known. Hence, Brown, Niebuhr, and their peers insisted that the independence in relation to the church of the theological school, through its alliance with the university or through its religious orientation toward the sovereign God, was a crucial condition for the school's capacity to serve the purposes that the church serves.

REFERENCES

Bellah, Robert N., Richard Madsen, William M. Sullivan, Ann Swidler, and Steven M. Tipton
    1985   *Habits of the Heart.* Berkeley, Calif.: University of California Press.

Briggs, Charles A.
    1904   "A Plea for the Higher Study of Theology." *American Journal of Theology* 8:433–451.

Brown, William Adams
    1906   *Christian Theology in Outline.* New York: Charles Scribner's Sons.
    1919   "The Seminary of Tomorrow." *Harvard Theological Review* 12: 165–178.
    1921   "The Common Problems of Theological Schools." *Journal of Religion* 1: 282–295.
    1926   "A Century of Theological Education and After." *Journal of Religion* 6: 363–383.

Brown, William Adams, and Mark A. May
    1934   *The Education of American Ministers.* 4 vols. New York: Institute of Social and Religious Research.

Fosdick, Harry Emerson
    1956   *The Living of These Days: An Autobiography.* New York: Harper & Brothers.

Foster, George Burman
    1916   "The Contribution of Critical Scholarship to Ministerial Efficiency." *American Journal of Theology* 20: 161–178.

Hauerwas, Stanley, and William H. Willimon
  1986   "Embarrassed by the Church: Congregations and the Semi-
          nary." *Christian Century* 103 (Feb. 5–12, 1986): 117–120.
Hough, Joseph C., and John B. Cobb
  1985   *Christian Identity and Theological Education.* Decatur, Ga.:
          Scholars Press.
Hough, Joseph C., and Barbara G. Wheeler (eds.)
  1988   *Beyond Clericalism: The Congregation as a Focus for Theo-
          logical Education.* Atlanta: Scholars Press.
Marty, Martin E.
  1982   "Religious Power in America: A Contemporary Map." *Crite-
          rion* 21 (Winter): 27–31.
  1985   "Transpositions: American Religion in the 1980s." *Annals of
          the American Academy of Political and Social Science* 480
          (July): 11–23.
Niebuhr, H. Richard
  1929   *The Social Sources of Denominationalism.* New York: Henry
          Holt.
  1937   *The Kingdom of God in America.* New York: Harper & Brothers.
  1956   *The Purpose of the Church and Its Ministry: Reflections on the
          Aims of Theological Education.* New York: Harper & Brothers.
Niebuhr, H. Richard, Daniel Day Williams, and James M. Gustafson
  1957   *The Advancement of Theological Education.* New York:
          Harper & Brothers.
Pascala, Leon
  1981   "Reflections on the State of Theological Education in the
          1980s." *Theological Education* 18:9–43.
Roof, Wade Clark, and William McKinney
  1987   *American Mainline Religion.* New Brunswick, N.J.: Rutgers
          University Press.
Sweet, Leonard I.
  1984   "Seminary and Congregation: Uneasy Alliance." *Theology
          Today* 40: 426–430.
White, Ronald C., and C. Howard Hopkins
  1976   *The Social Gospel: Religion and Reform in Changing Amer-
          ica.* Philadelphia: Temple University Press.
Willett, Herbert L. (ed.)
  1917   *Progress: Anniversary Volume of the Campbell Institute on
          the Completion of Twenty Years of History.* Chicago: Christ-
          ian Century Press.
Wuthnow, Robert
  1985   "The Growth of Religious Reform Movements." *Annals of
          the American Academy of Political and Social Science* 480
          (July): 106–116.

10

Presbyterian Ordination Practice as a Case Study in the Transmission of Denominational Identity

J. Frederick Holper

Compared to such matters as organizational patterns, cultural location, religious education programs, and worship practices, the ways in which "mainline" denominational traditions understand and order their offices of public ministry would appear to be marginal to the process of shaping and transmitting denominational identity. The reasons for this assumption are two: first, unlike those other matters, ordination is limited to relatively few members of a denomination; and second, those who seek ordination as authoritative teachers (those who are formally charged with passing on the tradition) ordinarily must earn specific academic credentials in a denominationally approved seminary or divinity school, thus confusing the "traditioning role" of ordination practice with the traditioning role played by theological institutions.

This chapter will question the legitimacy of that assumption, arguing that, since ordination practice is driven by the need to discern and authorize those called to be "representative leaders," it functions as a laboratory within which denominational traditions test, explore, and shape their particular identities and mission orientations.

Though the issue could be addressed across denominational lines,[1] the focus here is upon a case study of a single denomination—the Presbyterian Church (U.S.A.) (PC(USA)). The choice is made for two primary reasons.

First, the PC(USA)—the largest Presbyterian denomination in the United States—has been engaged in a formal process of reinterpreting and refocusing its denominational identity for nearly twenty years, both before and after it was formed in 1983 as the result of a union/reunion between the so-called "northern" United Presbyterian Church in the U.S.A. and the so-called "southern" Presbyterian Church in the U.S.[2]

Among the very first denominational-identity issues to be identified by the new denomination was the meaning and practice of ordination to office. Following a three-year study by a representative task force of the reunited church, the denomination's General Assembly (its highest governing body) sent a major report on ordination to every congregation and governing body in the denomination in June 1992.

Second, Presbyterian polities in general (and the polity of the PC(USA) in particular) insist upon the necessity of *ordaining* (as distinct from merely *electing*) "sociologically lay" men and women to two of its three offices of representative leadership within the church. This characteristic, particularly in the late twentieth century when rotation of "lay" leadership is normative, calls into question the relationship between ordination and traditioning noted above: that ordination's role is marginal because it is an event/process of concern primarily to clergy; and that the most important link between ordination and traditioning arises as a by-product of the role played by theological institutions.

The specific thesis advanced here is twofold: First, the "tradition" of American Presbyterianism represented by the PC(USA) in 1992 is grounded in a necessary and appropriate dialectical tension between an ethos of "discipline" inherited from the denomination's European Reformed roots and an ethos of "democratization" absorbed as a result of its early historic role as an arbiter of culture in the American context. Second, (because of the emphasis placed upon the representative character of office-bearers) ordination practice shapes and gives expression to that tension at every level of the church's faith and life.

Given the importance of the terms "representative," "discipline," and "democratization" in the argument being made, some description of what is meant by those terms is needed.

In general, persons may be perceived as "representative" in at least the following three ways. First, persons elected to political office by particular constituencies (such as political parties, sociological or ethnic communities) are elected or reelected to the extent that they represent their constituents' wishes in some legislative or executive position. Second, persons singled out for recognition on the basis of their achievements or potential for achievement (such as Nobel prizewinners or valedictorians of graduating classes) are honored not merely because of what they have done as individuals but also for who they are perceived to be, that is, persons whose lives and work represent the values or commitments shared by the communities (such as scientific, academic) from which they were chosen. Third, individuals may be sent or commissioned by some competent authority (for example, president, sovereign) to exercise representative authority on that person's or group's behalf (for example, as an ambassador). For Presbyterians in this country, the term "representative" has not conformed to any single one of these traditional definitions, but has—at different times—been understood in all three ways.

The term "discipline" functions in several distinct ways within Presbyterianism in the United States. In its most narrow sense, it refers to the processes by which the church as a whole holds members, officers, and governing bodies accountable for alleged offenses against the good order of the church. One major part of the Presbyterian Church's constitution is, in fact, known as "The Rules of Discipline." In a broader sense, "discipline" refers to the assumptions, commitments, and processes around which a distinctive, boundaried denominational community is created, upon which it orders its life and mission, within which it forms new members and calls old members to renewal, and by which it tests its identity and vitality. Finally, "discipline" is the term historically used to denote the distinctive ministry of elders within the denomination's ordered public ministry.

"Democratization" is used here primarily to refer to the ways in which certain U.S. political, social, and cultural values have helped to reshape or reinterpret the communal assumptions, commitments, and processes that undergird and flow from Presbyterianism's understanding and practice of ordination.

Because U.S. political, social, and cultural values tend to accord priority to individual initiative, choice, and rights (Bellah et al. 1985), a clear tension has developed within the PC(USA) between the tradition's Reformation-era commitment to the church as a disciplined, boundaried community whose identity (gift), mission (task), and order (means) are God-given (Calvin 1960, IV.1.i) and a more sociologically defined model of the church as a democratic, voluntary society whose identity, mission, and order are determined by the free choice of those who associate themselves with Presbyterian congregations.

In what follows, it is assumed that this tension functions dialectically within the PC(USA)—not in the Hegelian sense of thesis, antithesis, synthesis, but in the more Chalcedonian sense which undergirds classical Christology. Just as orthodox theology insists that Jesus Christ is both indivisibly and inseparably human and divine, so the PC(USA) lives and functions within a dialectical tension in which the duality of discipline and democratization can neither be obscured nor separated (Presbyterian Church (U.S.A.) 1992, 25). Ordination practice serves the critical function of keeping the denomination from fleeing the tension of this dialectic. In so doing, it plays a key role in the task of handing on tradition.

Signs of Dialectical Tension in Early American Presbyterian Ordination Practice

Building upon and adapting prototypes first developed in sixteenth- and seventeenth-century European Reformed contexts, the PC(USA) and its predecessor denominations have for nearly three hundred years ordained persons to three public, representative offices of ministry: *ministers,* whose ministry is focused around teaching, worship leadership, and pastoral care; *elders,* whose ministry is centered in functions of discipline and governance; and *deacons,* whose ministry is focused around care for those in need.[3] Though the denomination's constitutional standards had—until the 1982 reunion—referred to all three offices as distinct, necessary, and perpetual, the denomination's reflection on ministry has tended to focus on one or another of them at different times: the office of minister during the first century of its existence, the office of elder during the second century, and the office of deacon (at least tentatively) for the future.

Two European ministerial patterns in particular, the model John Calvin borrowed from Martin Bucer for the church in Geneva (Wendel 1942) and the model Andrew Melville put forth in the *Second Book of Discipline* of the Church of Scotland (Kirk 1980), became the basis and pattern in this country for Presbyterianism's understanding and practice of ordination to office. The principal distinction between the two models lay not in the type of ministers each proposed for a well-ordered church, for those were essentially the same. Rather, they differed on the functional starting point for reflecting on the church's ordered ministry.[4] For Calvin, the starting point was the pastor's ministry of edification: building up the body of Christ on the basis of the Word rightly preached and the sacraments rightly celebrated. Other ordained officers shared responsibility with the pastor for specific functions within that primary ministry. For Melville, the functional starting point was the presbyters' shared ministry of jurisdiction: joint oversight by pastors, doctors, and elders in the formation of a disciplined church (Holper 1988, 44–70; 88–96). For both, a central task of all ordained officers was the governing task of forming and sustaining disciplined communities of faith and witness; the significant difference lay in how the means to that end were to be emphasized and utilized.

These two models were brought together in the Westminster Assembly's form of presbyterial church government in 1645, with the Calvinian model forming the basis for ministry at the local level, and the Melvillian model at all other levels. This blended model, modified somewhat by Presbyterians in this country to reflect their experience during the colonial and revolutionary periods, was adopted as the model for ordained ministry in the first constitution of the Presbyterian Church in the U.S.A. (PCUSA) in 1789.[5]

Two things are striking about the early American Presbyterian model for ministry: its overwhelmingly local focus and its tilt toward the "discipline" side of the dialectic described above.

The local focus is clear. The first PCUSA form of government assumed that all ordained officers—ministers, elders and deacons—would carry out their responsibilities primarily within the confines of particular congregations, except for those occasions when it was necessary to meet in regional, state, or national church courts with representatives of other local congregations. Mission was primarily a local matter. The higher church courts had few specific mission responsibilities. Moreover, the denomination's new constitution assumed that nearly all elders and deacons, as well as some ministers, would probably serve a single congregation continuously for life. The process for calling and training persons for the offices of elder and deacon took place within a congregation under the oversight of a local pastor. Though responsibility for testing candidates for the office of bishop or pastor (that is, minister) fell to the regional presbytery rather than to the congregation, no one could be ordained to any office without having tested his gifts within, and being elected by, a particular congregation. The only exception to this pattern was a frontier context-induced provision allowing presbyteries to ordain some candidates as evangelists rather than as pastors. But even this exception was granted in order to "plant" new congregations and ordain new elders and deacons.

The tilt toward the "discipline" side of the dialectic is only somewhat less apparent. The constitutional descriptions of the ministers', elders', and deacons' responsibilities were, without exception in 1789, focused around functions of building and sustaining boundaried communities of faith and witness: preaching and teaching the Word of God, overseeing and disciplining members, and caring for the human and financial resources of the congregation. The "democratization" side of the dialectic, on the other hand, was more embryonic. No one could be ordained to any office without having been called through the voice of the church, and elders (or ruling elders as they were then known) were described as "the representatives of the people," but those provisions merely echoed the initial moves toward lay involvement in church leadership undertaken in the European contexts from which American Presbyterians had come.

This original emphasis on the "discipline" side of the dialectic was soon challenged, however. The "settled congregation" model worked as intended only in populated towns and cities large enough to produce sufficient numbers of traditioned and gifted officers for all three offices, and only in contexts in which the church's proximity to other culture-mediating institutions on the public square implicitly supported its disciplinary ethos. Since neither of those circumstances was realistic during periods of rapid change, Presbyterians were constitutionally ill-equipped to respond to the demands of ecclesiastical disestablishment and westward frontier migration during the nineteenth century, both of which demanded a new openness to democratizing influences. All three of the church's ordained offices were to feel the effects of that openness.

Democratizating Influences on Offices of Ordained Ministry in American Presbyterianism

At least six "democratizing" developments helped produce change in Presbyterian ordination practice during the last two hundred years. Though each of them has affected all three offices to some extent, the first three are responsible primarily for changes in the office of minister, the fourth and fifth for changes in the office of elder, and the sixth for changes in the office of deacon. In order, they are:

1. the emergence of entrepreneurial models of ministry;
2. the development of ministry as a profession;
3. the societal trend toward specialization in the workplace;
4. the triumph of Jacksonian democracy;
5. the emergence of civil rights and liberation movements;
6. the development of social service entitlement programs.

At the beginning of the nineteenth century, ecclesiastical disestablishment and the unsettled character of frontier society put a premium on entrepreneurial rather than edification models of ministerial leadership for extending the claims of the gospel to scattered populations. Two developments in particular make this clear.

First, nondenominational or interdenominational agencies (which were, by definition at the time, nontraditional) emerged to fill the vacuum created by denominational disestablishment: for example, the American Home Missionary Society, the American Bible Society, and others (Ahlstrom 1972, 422–428). These agencies' effectiveness and economic survival depended upon at least two things: downplaying distinctions (in faith and order) among Christians and rewarding the accomplishments (such as making converts, setting up educational institutions, building hospitals) of those commissioned to carry out the agencies' work. Denominations, including the Presbyterian Church in the U.S.A., responded to this challenge in different ways, but in time nearly all were forced to accommodate the entrepreneurial model within their own understandings of ministry. This, in turn, mandated a fundamental rethinking of the nature of the U.S. church and its ministry, and particularly of the fundamental context within which ordained officers (particularly ministers) were to function. The hegemony of the congregation as that fundamental context was under siege.

> The Presbyterian mission enterprise in the United States and [later] overseas found itself in need of persons to perform specialized tasks that the traditional ordering of ministry for congregations . . . did not comprehend. Administrators, doctors, and nurses were needed for hospitals. Teachers were needed for schools; presidents, deans, and professors for colleges and universities. Book, tract, and magazine publishers were needed for production of a vast Christian literature. Salesperson-evangelists were needed to sell and distribute that literature to its intended market; they were called colporteurs. Talented managers were needed to run large-scale enterprises, both in board home offices and in the fields. (Wilkins 1990, 15–16)

The growing importance of entrepreneurship in reshaping the office of minister was not limited to the influence of voluntary agencies. As noted earlier, the original PCUSA form of government had provided for the exceptional ordination of some men as evangelists rather than bishops or pastors in order to settle new congregations on the frontier. This exception served the denomination well in helping it respond to westward migration, but it encouraged the emergence of revivalist entrepreneurs: ministers like Charles Grandison Finney who moved from place to place in order to "preach up a revival" before moving on (McLoughlin 1978).

These parallel developments are noteworthy for at least three reasons. First, in permitting ministers to engage in these forms of ministry, the tradition began to redefine its self-identity and its understanding of church office in increasingly transcongregational or extra-congregational terms. Second, by freeing some representative ministers to work in contexts in which they were either geographically or ecclesiastically less accountable to the denomination's discipline, the tradition implicitly gave increasing value to individual initiative. This had the effect, certainly unintended, of undercutting the importance of communal discipline—not merely for officers, but for members as well. Third, by ordaining persons who had never been called by a congregation or even by a higher church governing body, but rather by agencies organized along the lines of voluntary societies, the fundamental rationale for ordination to the office of minister began to shift. Persons earlier had been ordained primarily because the people of God (congregations) were perceived to have the right and responsibility to choose communal leaders who would represent to them, and reinforce for them, the beliefs, values, commitments, and ministries they shared together. The emergence of entrepreneurial forms of ministry, by contrast, shifted the baseline requirement for ordination, or continuance in office, to employment by an approved agency of the church (nondenominational, interdenominational, and denominational).

The second major shift, the emergence of the ministry as a profession, acquired critical mass during the middle years of the nineteenth century (Smith 1962). The shortage of adequately prepared and tested ministers for the frontier (and worries about doctrinal orthodoxy occasioned in part by the success of the camp-meeting movement) led the PCUSA to establish denominational seminaries beginning in the early nineteenth century. This development brought to an end the option of preparing candidates for ordained ministry under the tutelage of respected local pastors. The emergence of denominational seminaries certainly helped the denomination to confront the problems which had made them necessary, but it also had the effect of hastening the redefinition of ministers as "professionals."

The office of minister has always been accorded pride of place within the ordered ministry of the Presbyterian church in this country. Indeed, until reunion, nearly all the tradition's forms of government had referred to the office of minister as "first in the church, both for dignity and usefulness." The importance of the shift under discussion, therefore, should not be seen in terms of a change in the status or importance of the minister, but in terms of a shift in the foundations upon which that status or importance was based. *Professional* status and importance depends upon having earned publicly certified credentials attesting to possession of particular specialized knowledge and skills. Because professional credentials depend upon certification by a publicly chartered institution or agency rather than a congregation or governing body of the church, the professional identity of the minister began to be seen as portable, that is, as something which accompanied him or her regardless of the context in which it was exercised. Indeed, a later, twentieth-century development in the former Southern Presbyterian church—permitting persons to be ordained as ministers in order to attend graduate school—suggests the absurd lengths to which portability of professional credentials had been carried.[6] The traditional identity of the minister, by contrast, had rested upon a quite different foundation: namely, functioning as a communally-representative and accountable leader within and for a particular community. In the latter case, ministerial identity was not nearly so portable. Once ministry began to emerge as a profession like other professions, it was a fairly short step to seeing the necessity and perpetuity of ordained office as a property attached to persons rather than as a functionally representative ministry without which the church *as a whole* could not carry out the commission God has given it.[7]

The third "democratizing" shift—a trend toward ordering representative ministry in more specialized and bureaucratic forms—was built upon the foundations of those earlier shifts but reflected a broader societal trend toward specialization and bureaucratization in the workplace. During the nineteenth century, specialization in ministry had been driven by the development of voluntary agencies to meet the challenges of the western frontier. During the late nineteenth century and continuing through most of the twentieth century, however, new "frontiers" (mission foci)—worldwide missions, suburban sprawl, inner-city renewal and racial-ethnic concerns—emerged one after another, each spawning new bureaucracies and new forms of professional ministry (Wilkins 1992).

As suburbs developed around major urban centers, old-style "collegial" pastorates (in which two or more ministers served together as pastors of large urban congregations) gave way to program-driven, bureaucratically influenced models of pastoral leadership. Particular program competencies became the foundations for determining a minister's role and influence (such as, assistant pastor, associate pastor, senior pastor). Post-World War II expansions in such fields as higher education and social services made it possible for increased numbers of ordained ministers to serve as teachers, chaplains, therapists, and social workers—first in denominational agencies and institutions, then later in contexts not under the jurisdiction of the denomination at all. The demand for denominationally provided interpretation and support systems for all these forms of ministry provided still further opportunities for specialized forms and contexts for ministry.

In 1992, ministers serving congregations in some pastoral connection still outnumber those serving in specialized contexts, but the gap is diminishing. Indeed, in urban presbyteries (regional groupings of ministers and congregations) where large numbers of educational and social service agencies are located, the numbers are nearly identical.

The effects of these three shifts have not been limited to the office of minister. Both the ministry of elders and the ministry of deacons has been affected. A few instances may be cited by way of example. The shift from a congregational mission focus to transcongregational and extracongregational foci has required a corresponding shift in the involvement of elders in the mission of the local church beyond the congregation (in committees and commissions of governing bodies, as well as in stipendiary or voluntary service to denominational entities). The emphasis upon knowledge and skills arising out of the professionalization of ministry has led to the emergence of "professional" elders (elders who function in ministry leadership positions once held only by ministers). The trend toward management models of church organization has encouraged an understanding of the elder's ministry more in terms of managing congregational programs than of exercising communal discipline.

The ethos of rugged individualism appropriate to the rigors of frontier existence, the emergence of Jacksonian democracy, and a shortage of theologically educated ministers to serve frontier congregations combined to produce a fundamental rethinking of the role of the "laity" in the church's public ministry, beginning in the middle of the nineteenth century. Though Presbyterians in the United States had followed the example of earlier Reformed bodies in ordaining "sociologically lay" men to the offices of elder and deacon, and had built parity in governance for ministers and elders into their constitution, the ministry of elders and deacons—until well into the nineteenth century—had been described as derivative from and auxiliary to that of ministers (Holper 1988, 274–293). By the end of the nineteenth century, however, the influence, role, and function of elders at all levels of the church's life and mission had begun to expand.

Congregations in the West began to demand the right to limit the lifetime tenure of elders' service on the local governing body known as the session, a right which was finally granted, beginning with the northern stream of the church, in 1875.[8] Governing bodies beyond the level of the congregation (presbyteries and synods) began to elect elders (and not merely ministers) as moderators. A requirement that elders be present in order to establish a quorum for conducting governing body business was codified in the denomination's constitution. Elders began to take responsibility—and were held accountable—for preaching and leading worship in churches without pastors. And elders began to participate with ministers in the ritual act of laying hands on those to be ordained to all offices of ministry (Holper 1988, 304–374).[9]

Perhaps the most important result of these developments was a shift in the understanding of the representative character of church office. Though elders had been described constitutionally as "the representatives of the people" in the governing bodies of the churches, they were interpreted theologically as representatives set over the church by the risen Christ. Beginning in the late nineteenth century, however, congregations on the western frontier (for example, Illinois, Michigan) began to chafe at the notion that they could not replace recalcitrant elders on the local church session. During debates urging term limitations for elders, proponents (led by a prominent Chicago layman and magazine publisher) argued that "the people" to be represented were the current members of a particular congregation, not some anonymous invisible church. They insisted that their representatives needed to be responsive to the concerns of the constituency which had elected them. Though its immediate effect was to break the stranglehold on entrenched leadership within particular congregations, the church's acceptance of this principle laid the foundation for later debates on the admission of women to church office and on providing for fair representation of youth, older adults, and racial-ethnic persons in the composition of church governing bodies.

Moreover, the debates on the nature and extent of parity between ministers and elders, which had been occasioned by reflection on the tradition's insistence upon parity between them in *governance,* inevitably led to a new focus for the tradition's understanding of ordained ministry in general. For a variety of reasons, the PCUSA in the beginning had seen the minister's office as the necessary starting point for reflection on the nature of the church and its ministry. It alone was part of the *esse* of the church. The other offices were important for the "good order" (*bene esse*) of the church, but they were clearly derivative and auxiliary. When the functions exercised by ministers were no longer ordinarily and integrally related to those exercised by elders and deacons at the congregational level, the ministry of governance exercised jointly by ministers and elders in higher governing bodies became the primary starting point for reflection on ministry. The question of who had "the vote" became more important for thinking about the representative character of church office than who could teach and preside at the sacraments. Nor were ministers the only persons whose office was affected by this development. Deacons, who have no jurisdictional authority and no constitutionally defined role beyond the congregation, began to become dispensable.[10]

Much attention has been paid recently to the fifth democratizing shift, namely the effects of civil rights and liberation movements, including those working for the ordination of gay and lesbian persons. The focus in the secular press has been on the effects of these movements on ordination to the office of minister. However, these movements had a far earlier and—because of the growing tendency to think about ministry in terms of "the vote"—structurally more important influence on the office of elder. The decision to admit women to church office (beginning in 1922 for the Northern stream, in 1964 for the Southern stream),[11] and the adoption, at the time of reunion, of constitutional provisions meant to ensure fair representation by women and racial-ethnic persons on church governing bodies and their agencies, committees, and commissions[12] have been momentous. These developments, in turn, have helped sensitize the denomination to the ways in which—through the language it uses to describe God and human persons, through the style and language of its worship, through its presuppositions about which historical practices have pride of place in helping define Presbyterianism in this country—the "tradition" to be handed on has in the past been construed too narrowly. To cite but one example of the way in which this provision has helped shape the transmission of denominational identity, the PC(USA) recently adopted a new hymnal (Presbyterian Church (U.S.A.) 1990). The committee which produced it and the denominational agency whose staff advised it were chosen so as to reflect the racial, ethnic, and gender diversity of the denomination as well as its traditional theological and liturgical commitments. In terms of its use of inclusive language (as to race, gender, and physical ability) and its attempt to represent non-Euro-American texts, melodies and harmonizations, the new hymnal represents an enormous step forward from its predecessor published a mere twenty years earlier (Joint Office of Worship 1972).

The final democratizing shift to be considered is the emergence of social service entitlement programs, with the state as the primary provider. Though this shift has produced opportunities for new forms of professional ministry for those ordained as ministers and elders, the most profound result has been the marginalization of the office of deacon. From the origins of the Reformed tradition, the office of deacon has been charged with caring for the needs of those for whom government-funded entitlement programs are targeted, namely the poor, the elderly, the sick, and those in need (McKee 1984). Though a slim majority of Presbyterian congregations continue to elect and ordain persons to serve on boards of deacons, the original function of deacons as "social service safety nets" has been usurped by state-sponsored entitlement programs. In response, recent studies show, Presbyterian congregations have tended either to merge the functions of the diaconate with those of the session or to carve out a limited pastoral care/visitation role for their deacons. Though these strategies—particularly the latter—are not without value, the fact remains that the "representative" function of the office in forming communities whose tradition includes particular concern for social justice concerns is in danger of being lost.

These democratizing shifts have, of necessity, been described primarily in terms of their effects upon the nature and purpose of ordination. But they have also fundamentally reshaped both the denomination's communal identity and mission (that is, its "tradition") and the ways in which that tradition is passed on. To begin with, these shifts did not occur solely because individual ministers decided that the mission focus of the denomination needed to change. They occurred because the denomination found itself required to rethink its identity, refocus its mission priorities, and redefine its leadership needs in order to "be Presbyterian" in new historical contexts. Furthermore, because officers are ordained to "represent" to the church *as a whole* its own God-given calling, identity, values, and commitments, shifts in ordination practice to reflect the denomination's mission strategy beyond the congregation inevitably reshaped and refocused the ministry of church members *ad extra* as well. On the other hand, the effects of these democratizing trends—entrepreneurial leadership, professional identity, specialization of tasks, constituency-based understandings of representation, and the strategic embrace of government entitlement programs as the primary means for providing social services—has resulted in an increasingly less boundaried and disciplined community of faith and witness. The need to reclaim a disciplined Presbyterian communal identity, mission, and order *within the ecumenical context* of the church catholic clearly lies behind the report on ordination going to the denomination in 1992.

Trajectories for the Future: Ordination as a Vehicle for Reclaiming Communal Discipline

In *A Proposal for Considering the Theology and Practice of Ordination to Office in the Presbyterian Church (U.S.A.)* (Presbyterian Church (U.S.A.) 1992), a special task force of the denomination challenges its congregations and governing bodies to consider the need for a new understanding of the ministry of ordained officers and of how their ministry grows out of and shapes the ministry of the whole church. Though the report is comprehensive in scope, setting forth dozens of proposals relating to the preparation, admission, and support of those ordained to all three offices, its most significant and controversial contributions may be: first, its insistence that, while diversity and specialization in ministry needs to continue, it is time to reclaim the norm that the ministry of ordained officers arises from, remains integrally related to, and is ordered solely for, the empowerment of the ministry of the whole people of God as servants of God's reign in the world; and second, its emphasis upon reclaiming communal identity and discipline as distinctive and essential dimensions of Presbyterianism's tradition of ministry in this country.

The report's insistence upon relating the ministry of its officers to the ministry of the whole church is clear. Though arguing for retention of the three traditional ordained offices of Presbyterian church order—minister of the gospel, elder, and deacon—the report defines each of them in relationship to the personal, collegial, and communal dimensions of ministry set forth in recent ecumenical convergence documents (World Council of Churches 1982; Consultation on Church Union 1985), but emphasizes the communal dimension first. It does so on the grounds that ordained officers are chosen in order to "represent to the church and before the world the ministries of God Service to which the whole church is called: that is, telling the good news, making disciples, caring for those in need or distress" (Presbyterian Church (U.S.A.) 1992, 60).

The report seeks to address the importance of discipline and communal identity in two important ways: first, by rejecting the notion that ordination decisions should revolve around lists of "ordainable" and "nonordainable" specialized occupations and insisting instead that ordination should rest upon whether the form of service engaged in is focused around the six core functions which are distinctive to each office; and second, by identifying those core functions as essential leadership tasks in the formation, discipline, and outreach of distinctive communities of faith and witness. For ministers, those core functions include: (1) authoritative proclamation of the Word, (2) community formation, (3) leadership in governance, (4) prophetic witness to God's reign and purpose in the world, (5) edification of the body of Christ, and (6) service of font and table (Presbyterian Church (U.S.A.) 1992, 69–71).

For elders, the six core functions are: (1) exercising authoritative discipline within communities of faith, (2) strengthening and nurturing the life and faith of congregations and governing bodies, (3) oversight of the mission and work of the church at all levels, (4) participation in the governance of the church, (5) providing for and guarding the integrity of the church's worship, and (6) representing, in liturgical events, the ministry of discipline.

For deacons, the six core functions are: (1) exhibiting the exemplary moral authority of sympathy, service, and witness after the manner of Jesus Christ, (2) discerning and embodying the presence of the church in the world and the world in the church, (3) caring for the needs of God's people in crisis, (4) challenging structure and conditions which keep persons and groups powerless and voiceless, (5) voluntarily assuming official powerlessness for the sake of empowering others, and (6) representing, in liturgical events, the church's presence in the world and the world's presence in the church.

Moreover, the emphasis upon communal identity and discipline are further underscored in the report's insistence that the authority of ministers, elders and deacons to act depends upon and is strengthened by their willingness to be accountable to the scriptural, constitutional, and contextual standards of the communities they serve (Presbyterian Church (U.S.A.) 1992, 60–61). When it turns its attention to the personal dimension of ordination, the report argues that—while there are some gifts and character traits which are proper to each office,[13] most of the necessary gifts and character traits are shared by all of them, precisely because they represent the whole church.[14]

Conclusion

Because ordained officers represent to the church and before the world the distinctive identity and sense of purpose of those they lead, the processes, norms, and rites by which a particular denomination orders those leaders in office become occasions for it to test and transmit its culture. For the PC(USA) and its predecessor bodies, ordination practice has expressed and shaped a continuing dialectical tension between the denomination's inherited commitment to discipline as a mark of the church and its appropriated commitment to the democratic values and forces of the culture in which it lives. As it wrestles with the implications of the recently released report of the task force on ordination, one thing seems clear. As the denomination attempts to transmit its culture faithfully, neither side of the dialectic can be allowed to "win," and neither side can be allowed to "lose."

NOTES

1. Ordination-related questions continue to be the most significant stumbling blocks in ecumenical discussions. Two of the most inclusive ecumenical convergence statements—*Baptism, Eucharist and Ministry* (World Council of Churches 1982) and *The COCU Consensus: In Quest of a Church of Christ Uniting* (Consultation on Church Union 1985)—have produced less agreement in their chapters on the ordering of ministry than in other areas. The resulting denominational uneasiness, however, was an important factor in convincing several American denominations (including the Presbyterian Church (U.S.A.), the United Methodist Church, the Church of the Brethren

and the Evangelical Lutheran Church in America) to undertake formal re-examinations of their own distinctive understandings of ministry and ordination in light of these ecumenical statements.

2. These geographical designations are more reflective of the Civil War origins of the division than of the spread of the two denominations at the time of reunion. For example, though the former PCUS was largely concentrated in the states of the Confederacy and the border states around them, the former UPCUSA had established presbyteries in every state of the union following the end of the Civil War.

3. A fourth ordained office characteristic of Reformed church orders in Europe—the doctor, whose ministry was neither liturgical nor disciplinary but rather focused upon the doctrinal purity of the church's teaching—was proposed but later rejected when the denomination adopted its first indigenous constitution (Synod of New York and Philadelphia 1786, 7–8).

4. The social, economic, and political context clearly played a significant role in their differences. Calvin forged his model at a time when his influence with the Genevan magistracy was at its peak. The magistracy (from which Genevan elders were derived) generally supported the reform movement socially, economically, and politically. By contrast, Melville had to lead during a period when Presbyterians in Scotland were trying to reform the church in the face of political and economic opposition from the crown and its episcopal allies (Donaldson 1960, 183–202; Kirk 1980, 82–87).

5. Even before its evolution into a full-fledged American denomination, the Presbyterian Church USA had used the Westminster Confession of Faith as its doctrinal standard, had commended Westminster's Directory of Public Worship in matters liturgical, and had been guided in most other matters by a Scottish-redacted prototype form of government modeled on the Westminster form.

6. Though this provision was carried into the constitution of the reunited church in 1983, objections from former Northern presbyteries led to its removal a few years later.

7. This shift of emphasis can lead to clericalism, to be sure. But the issue is larger than even that. Persons ordained to other offices—particularly elders—are now moving into stipendiary forms of service in church agencies beyond the congregation (thus mimicking the migration of ministers from the pastorate to other forms of service in the nineteenth century). As a result, the communally-representative character of all ordained offices is in danger of being obscured because of the emphasis being placed upon the personal characteristics of the persons holding them.

8. This Northern church permissive provision gave way in 1955 to

one mandating rotary-term service. The Southern church did not grant permission for rotary-term service until 1932 and never did require it (Holper 1988, 339–342; 367–374).

9. These developments did not all take place at one time, but over a period of some fifty years. Some, like the provision for rotary-term service, began in the Northern stream of the church but were resisted in the Southern stream for decades. Others, like the inclusion of elders in the laying on of hands in ordination, began in the Southern stream and were not introduced in the Northern stream until the second half of the twentieth century.

10. The function of deacons has never been very clear in Presbyterian polities in this country. Indeed, the Northern and Southern streams of the tradition assigned quite different responsibilities to them: responsibility for acts of sympathy and service within the Northern stream, responsibility for property within the Southern stream. Within the reunited church, the trend has been to merge the responsibilities of the deacons with those of the elders on the session.

11. The process by which women were admitted to office within the two streams of the tradition is instructive regarding the differences in their understanding of ordination. Within the Northern church (Presbyterian Church USA), which saw the *rite* of ordination as an exercise of the power of order by *persons* previously ordained to the office, women were admitted to the office of deacon in 1922, to the office of elder in 1930, but not to the office of minister until 1956. In the Southern church (Presbyterian Church in the U.S.), which saw ordination strictly as an exercise of the power of jurisdiction by church *governing bodies* (including elders as well as ministers), women were not admitted to any office until they were admitted to all of them (Holper 1988, 347–350; 421–423; 466).

12. The PC(USA) Form of Government not only describes fair representation as a norm for the church's life and work, it also provides for "Committees on Representation" in all the higher governing bodies (presbytery, synod, general assembly), the majority of whose members must be drawn from racial-ethnic groups within the particular governing body. In addition, the total membership of the committee must include persons from the following categories: majority male, majority female, racial-ethnic male, racial-ethnic female, youth male and youth female. "Its main function shall be to advise the governing bodies with respect to their membership and to that of their committees, boards, agencies, and other units in implementing the principles of participation and inclusiveness to ensure fair and effective representation in the decision making of the church." (Presbyterian Church (U.S.A.) *Constitution* 1991, G.-9.0105).

13. The gifts cited as necessary for ordination as minister are: (1) an ability to discern and communicate the gospel in light of the context; (2) "personal presence" in a variety of relationships for ministry; and (3) "disciplined passion" in following Jesus Christ. For elders, the gifts needed are identified as an ability to discern and interpret the context for the church's ministry and mission in light of the Word; and the courage to order the life and mission of the church in light of the Word. For deacons, the distinctive gifts are the ability to discern and communicate the presence of Christ in the person of those who are hungry and thirsty, sick and imprisoned, poor and homeless; and a willingness to exhibit the scandal of the gospel in the corridors of power. The distinctive character traits noted for each office are: for ministers—truthfulness; for elders—prudence; for deacons—openness and vulnerability to others (Presbyterian Church (U.S.A.) 1992, 76–78; 95–97; 109–111).

14. The gifts shared in common are: maturity in faith, sound judgment, healthy self-awareness, sensitivity toward the needs of others, and ability to work with others. The character traits shared in common are: a manner of life which manifests the truth of the gospel, personal integrity in all aspects of life, evidence of the "fruit of the Spirit," and disciplined use of the means of grace. The bases for personal authority shared in common are: call to office, faithfulness to constitutional standards, and openness to the Spirit (Presbyterian Church (U.S.A.) 1988, 61–65).

REFERENCES

Ahlstrom, Sydney E.
   1972   *A Religious History of the American People.* New Haven, Conn., and London: Yale University Press.
Bellah, Robert N., Richard Madsen, William M. Sullivan, Ann Swidler, and Steven M. Tipton
   1985   *Habits of the Heart.* Berkeley, Calif.: University of California Press.
Calvin, John
   1960   *Calvin: Institutes of the Christian Religion,* edited by John T. McNeill; translated by Ford Lewis Battles. Philadelphia: Westminster Press.
Consultation on Church Union.
   1985   *The COCU Consensus: In Quest of a Church of Christ Uniting.* Princeton, N.J.: Consultation on Church Union.

1989 *Churches in Covenant Communion.* Princeton, N.J.: Consultation on Church Union.

Donaldson, Gordon
1960 *The Scottish Reformation.* Cambridge: Cambridge University Press.

Holper, J. Frederick
1988 "Presbyteral Office and Ordination in American Presbyterianism: A Liturgical-Historical Study." Ph.D. Diss., University of Notre Dame, Notre Dame, Ind.

Joint Office of Worship
1972 *The Worshipbook: Services and Hymns.* Louisville, Ky.: Westminster/John Knox Press.

Kirk, James
1980 *The Second Book of Discipline.* Edinburgh: Saint Andrew Press.

McKee, Elsie Ann
1984 *John Calvin on the Diaconate and Liturgical Alms-giving.* Geneva: Librairie Droz.

McLoughlin, William G.
1978 *Revivals, Awakenings and Reform: An Essay on Religion and Social Change in America—1607–1977.* Chicago: University of Chicago Press.

Presbyterian Church in the United States
1981 *The Plan for Reunion of the Presbyterian Church in the United States and the United Presbyterian Church in the United States of America to Form the Presbyterian Church (U.S.A.).* Atlanta: Office of the Stated Clerk of the Presbyterian Church in the United States.

Presbyterian Church (U.S.A.)
1990 *The Presbyterian Hymnal: Hymns, Psalms, and Spiritual Songs.* Louisville, Ky.: Westminster/John Knox Press.

1991 *The Constitution of the Presbyterian Church (U.S.A.).* Part Two: The Book of Order. Louisville, Ky.: The Office of the General Assembly.

1992 *A Proposal for Considering the Theology and Practice of Ordination to Office in the Presbyterian Church (U.S.A.).* Manuscript copy of report approved for transmittal to the 1992 General Assembly. Louisville, Ky.: Theology and Worship Ministry Unit.

Smith, Elwyn A.
1962 *The Presbyterian Ministry in American Culture: A Study in Changing Concepts, 1700–1900.* Philadelphia: Westminster Press.

Synod of New York and Philadelphia
   1786   *A Draught of the Form of Government and Discipline of the Presbyterian Church in the United States of America.* New York: S & J Louden.
Wendel, Francois
   1942   *L'Eglise de Strasbourg.* Paris: Presses Universitaire de France.
Wilkins, Lewis, Jr.
   1990   "Renewing the Office of Deacon: Sign of Hope or Waste of Time?" In *Ordination: Past, Present, Future,* edited by Jack Rogers and Deborah Flemister Mullen. Louisville, Ky.: Denominational Resources/Presbyterian Publishing House.
   1992   "The American Presbytery in the Twentieth Century." In *The Organizational Revolution,* edited by Milton J Coulter, John M. Mulder, and Louis B. Weeks, 96–121. Louisville, Ky.: Westminster/John Knox Press.
World Council of Churches
   1982   *Baptism, Eucharist, and Ministry.* Faith and Order Study Paper #111. Geneva: World Council of Churches.

PART THREE

Denominational Identity
and Culture: Case Studies

Having considered the transmission of denominational cultures by examining particular plausibility structures, local and translocal, we turn in this final section to several case studies of denominations. One of the themes common to these chapters is their focus on denominational identity, that is on the distinctiveness of a particular denomination's culture.

Lawrence N. Jones provides us with a look at denominational identity and loyalties among African Americans. In black denominations, he argues, denominational loyalties have long been secondary to racial considerations. A legacy of institutional separation and racist attitudes and practices have helped to create a distinct religious ethos more important to blacks than denominational ties themselves. Jones traces the rise of the historic African American denominations and details distinctive aspects of congregational life among blacks. He observes that ethnic identity is of far greater importance than other social and economic factors in shaping the religious and spiritual concerns of African Americans. More so than for whites, the black community functions as a plausibility structure undergirding the black church.

Donald A. Luidens' chapter provides a case study of a denomination whose historic ethnic identity—*Dutch* Reformed—has undergone change over the years. Luidens focuses on various efforts of the denominations' leaders to respond to its identity crisis and its crisis of membership loss. After providing a brief history of the denomination, Luidens examines three stages of the developing crises and efforts by leaders to define them and respond at each stage. He questions the leaders' strategies and is particularly critical of their lack of attention to external changes that have contributed to the denomination's difficulties. He makes it clear that leaders who attempt to reclaim an old identity, forge a new one, or turn around declines will ignore external conditions at their own peril.

For United Methodists, identity historically was found in the denomination's close relation to U.S. nationalism. The denomination and the nation grew up roughly together. As Russell E. Richey points out, this linkage served the denomination well for the first century of its existence. But with increasing cultural and religious pluralism, the denomination's identity was severely damaged. Using the writings of Methodist historians, Richey shows the transformations of Methodist identity, as the writers responded to the changing context of U.S. society and to changes within the denominations. They reinterpreted Methodist identity to themselves and to others. How these interpretations inform congregational life and mission is an important but not fully resolved issue.

Denominational mergers have been common among mainline Protestants, especially since mid-century. Under the best of circumstances, mergers have an unsettling effect on denominational culture and identity. While some mergers are in essence family reunions—for example, recent Presbyterian and Lutheran mergers—in the case of the United Church of Christ (UCC), the two merging partners had little in common in theology, polity, or historic traditions. William M. Newman describes the United Church of Christ merger experience and uses data from UCC congregations to examine members' understanding of their identity. Newman's analysis reveals important insights about how mergers happen, how congregations meld old and new identities, and how a new identity is formed. As he shows, mergers typically occur from the top down under the leadership of denominational officials. Identity, however, is formed from the bottom up.

The Presbyterian Church (U.S.A.) is another example of a denomination created by a merger. Unlike the United Church of Christ, however, theirs is a union of two groups with a common heritage. The merging denominations had a common religious history; yet, as Louis B. Weeks describes, contemporary Presbyterian identity lacks strong focus. Weeks discusses Presbyterian Church history leading up to the merger and the style of leadership that has emerged in the new church. Based on interviews with denominational executives, Weeks describes a recognizable Presbyterian culture. The executives interviewed also expressed concern about the future of a distinctive Presbyterian culture. Like most mainline Protestant denominations, the Presbyterians are torn by competing loyalties to denominational, parachurch, and ecumenical concerns.

Finally, Creighton Lacy, longtime ecumenist, missionary, and professor of world missions, writes about a world beyond denominationalism. Unlike most of the other authors, Lacy argues that denominational identity has little continuing relevance in the world church that has come into being through missionary outreach. Lacy surveyed a number of missionaries, local church pastors, and laity about denominational identity and missions. He and many of his respondents argue that denominations make little sense pragmatically or theologically. Western in origin, denominations have little relevance in Third World settings and cultures. Even more damaging than the pragmatic problems that denominational identity creates for non-Western cultures is its negative impact on Christian unity.

11

Timeless Priorities
in Changing Contexts:
African Americans
and Denominationalism

Lawrence N. Jones

To understand fully the relationship of African Americans to denominationalism as an aspect of religious life in this country requires that one confront the pervasive presence of racism. The experience most frequently shared by individuals of African descent in U.S. society is that of being reminded that they are, in fact, persons of African descent. Sometimes these reminders are subtle, sometimes direct and violent, sometimes cloaked in good intentions, sometimes condescending and paternalistic, sometimes incorporated in a variety of institutional structures—but always a fact of life. Race, more than any other human attribute, is the one constant factor in the relationship between African Americans and members of the majority group. The fact of being made conscious that one's racial lineage may be traced to Africa is not in itself racist. Racism, rather, is embedded in the psyche of many if not most non-African individuals who believe that African Americans, with acknowledged exceptions, are inferior human beings destined to be subordinate to members of the white race.

The virus of racism has affected every aspect of U.S. society, including organized denominational groups. In spite of the concerted efforts that have been exerted by individuals and groups to eradicate it, the virus of racism is healthy and is being incubated in the minds of each new generation. No social institution has been immunized against the infection of racism. As contradictory as it may seem in light of the gospel, Christian communities are frequently strongholds of racism.

There is no possibility of understanding the religious history of this country if one ignores the role of racial attitudes in giving contour and texture to religious institutions. Religious communities have been shaped not only by the attitudes of whites toward blacks but also by the way in which blacks perceive whites, their institutions, and their societal structures.

The majority of studies which have sought to define denominations or denominationalism have had to devote special chapters to African Americans because neither they nor their religious institutions fit into the typologies being employed or created.[1] The task of locating blacks in the denominational landscape is further complicated by the fact that they did not fully participate in the creation, ratification, nor validation of the denominational culture.[2] Blacks were grafted into a Protestantism which was already well established when they encountered it and to which they came as strangers. Religious bodies were the first public institutions to which blacks related. Blacks were never fully assimilated into the churches even in those early days, nor has the passage of time significantly modulated their historic marginality.

The major premise of this chapter is that unconditional loyalty to a particular denomination has never been a realistic option for African American Christians. The principal reason accounting for blacks' reluctance to commit themselves to any denominational structure is that they rarely have had the experience of being fully incorporated into the institution's life. The term which best describes this situation is "marginalization," that is, the experience of being excluded from centers of power, from the formulation of policy, from the exercise of leadership outside racially circumscribed enclaves, and from having their ideas and visions received on their own merit. This has been the case since the first encounters of African slaves with Christianity early in the seventeenth century, and it is still the case today. The assumption that African Americans were an inferior people destined by God to be subordinate to Europeans was the undergirding rationale for nearly 350 years of slavery. This assumption was ratified in law and custom until forty years ago when the *Plessy* v. *Ferguson* decision of 1896 was reversed by the Supreme Court in the case of *Brown* v. *Board of Education* (17 May 1954). However, neither a change in the law of the land nor the pronouncements of the Supreme Court of the United States have eradicated the long-held and widely shared belief in black inferiority nor have they neutralized it as a determinative factor in ordering much interracial life in the United States.[3] It is the effectual marginalization of blacks in this country that has inhibited, and in some instances prohibited, the development by African Americans of unqualified loyalty to most U.S. institutions (including religious institutions)—with the critical exception of the Constitution of the United States. Institutionalized religion in the United States has mirrored, save in some limited instances, the racial attitudes and practices of the larger society with respect to blacks. Even where structural changes have been made in religious institutions for the purpose of rectifying blatant injustice and discrimination, blacks continue to experience the consequences of attitudes which assume their inferiority and which are reflected in the implementation of policy.

James H. Smylie observed that "the Church of Jesus Christ, mainline Protestants decided, is a fellowship that transcends racial, national, and economic barriers"(Smylie 1979, 80). This assertion is true if it is understood as a statement of intention, but this intention has yet to be made concrete in any consistently visible reality. The Protestant church continues to be one of the most segregated public institutions in U.S. society.[4] While this essay will be devoted primarily to a discussion of the recent past and the present, one cannot understand either period without reviewing the history of African Americans as it relates to their participation in the Protestant churches.

The Africans who were brought to this land beginning in 1619 and who within a half-century had been consigned by law and custom to be slaves *durante vita* (for the duration of their lives) were strangers to Christianity.[5] After slavery was established, the colonists found themselves facing a fundamental conflict. This conflict had its origins in the religious requirement that they seek to convert the "heathens" and their fear that conversion would confer freedom upon the Africans and therefore destroy their investment in these valuable properties. Both church and state dealt with this problem effectively by deciding that the conversion of slaves to Christianity and even church membership would not alter their civil status. However, laws establishing the legality of slavery, and church decrees which held that the maintenance of the institution was not contrary to divine decree, did little to mitigate the fear that "Christian" slaves would be less tractable servants. In New England there was the further problem that church membership was the basic qualification for inclusion in the political process.

With the way cleared by the civil authority and with the endorsement of the Church of England, there remained the disturbing question as to whether or not exposure to the gospel would undercut the authority of the masters by conveying the impression that human bondage was inherently wrong. This debate raged at length in the South where the majority of slaves were concentrated. The matter was partially dealt with when religious leaders were able to convince some slaveholders that "religious instruction" would, in fact, make slaves more accepting of their bondage. It is notable that the objective was the "religious instruction" of the slaves, not their "Christianization," nor was it that of proselytizing on behalf of a particular denomination. Little that was done in these earliest years of exposing African Americans to Christianity had as an operative premise that blacks would enjoy status equal to that of whites in religious institutions.[6] This is a critical point because it meant that denominational loyalty was neither cultivated nor desired. Prior to the Civil War the affiliation of African Americans with a particular denomination was an accident of geography, polity, missionary zeal, and the religious affiliation of masters and mistresses. The congregational polity of the Baptists, the simple statement of the gospel message, and the missionary zeal of the Methodists in the South are largely responsible for the fact that most African Americans are today members of these denominations. It is noteworthy that both of these church bodies emphasized the religious experience of conversion, being saved for eternity and moral living, rather than doctrinal or creedal particularities. To be sure, the Baptist emphasis on "believers baptism" and congregational polity set them apart from the Methodists, but these were matters of limited interest to the slaves and freedpersons of color. Baptist polity made possible the proliferation of congregations, and Methodist discipline provided organizational models and worship patterns which lent distinctiveness to denominational identity.

It was not accidental that blacks were not indoctrinated into the distinctive aspects of the denominations to which they belonged. Charles Colcock Jones, perhaps the most notable among white clergymen who dedicated their lives to the religious instruction of African Americans, helped to write a plank in the Constitution of the Association for the Instruction of Negroes in Liberty County, Georgia, which stipulated that

> the instructions of this association shall be altogether oral, embracing general principles of the Christian religion as understood by orthodox Christians, avoiding in the public instruction of Negroes, doctrines which particularly distinguished the different denominations in this County from each other.[7]

It is clear that here the primary consideration was to assure the financial support of various denominational groups in Liberty County. Care was taken that the religious instruction provided to African Americans was sanitized of denominational bias.

When African Americans began to organize themselves into separate congregations or, in the case of the Methodists, into denominations, the denomination of choice usually was the one from which they were withdrawing or in which they had been nurtured. Richard Allen, founder of the African Methodist Episcopal Church (A.M.E.), refused to align himself with the Anglican Church or with the Quakers for several reasons:

> The Methodists were the first people that brought glad tidings to the colored people. I feel thankful that ever I heard a Methodist preach. We are beholden to the Methodists, under God, for the light of the Gospel we enjoy; for all other denominations preached so high-flown that we were not able to comprehend their doctrine. Sure am I that reading sermons will never prove so beneficial to the colored people as spiritual or extempore preaching (Allen 1960, 80).

Allen makes it eminently clear that the emphasis upon religious experience and the simplicity of the preaching as well as the evangelical zeal of the Methodists were the sources of his loyalty to that body. Later on, it was the willingness of the Methodist elder in Philadelphia and the support of the venerated Bishop Asbury that caused the Africans to refer to themselves as Methodists, even though they had gathered themselves in separate congregations. After the African churches were formally severed from the white body in 1816, they still retained their "Methodist" identity.

In virtually every instance where Africans separated themselves from white congregations or from white denominational judicatories, there were three basic reasons given: (1) that they had become aware that their presence in significant numbers in the churches was an offense to the white members; (2) that their predilection for emotional expression in worship was unsettling to whites, and (3) that they were not able effectively to preach to other blacks because they, the unconverted blacks, could not reconcile the conduct of whites toward persons of color with the gospel being commended to them.

Though the overwhelming majority of blacks were either Baptists or Methodists, there were a few who joined Presbyterian, Congregationalist, Anglican, Quaker, Dutch Reformed, or Unitarian congregations. As in the cases cited, the reasons were not denominational distinctiveness but the affiliation of the master or mistress or the kindness that a member or a congregation had extended to the blacks who became nominal members. Several groups of Christians in the South spent significant sums of money to provide religious instruction for blacks and to enroll them as members in the churches. Even so, an examination of the patterns of assimilation of blacks into individual churches shows that they were either seated in the balcony during regular services, constituted as separate congregations pastored by white clergy, worshiped in the same building but at different times than did whites, or were permitted to have their own places of worship provided whites were present to monitor what was being preached and to control the business aspects of the congregation's life. The palpable reality in these arrangements was fear. This fear appeared to be rooted in a fundamental consciousness that no person had a moral or religious right to enslave another and that the person enslaved would have a "natural instinct" to revolt against their oppressors. This fear also accounted for the police-state character which permeated the institution.

Several other factors operated to inhibit the development of denominational loyalty among blacks. For example, segregated African American congregations were organized by whites in virtually every major denomination. This had the effect of restricting interracial contacts. Sometimes the "for-negroes-only" congregations were created at the instigation of blacks, but most often the initiative originated among the whites. A consequence of the establishment of separate congregations was that blacks were precluded from participating in majority group denominational matters. In addition, they did not participate in the theological and doctrinal debates that took place in the early nineteenth century. African Americans were generally excluded from colleges where training for ministry was a primary mission. In sum, all of the normal channels through which denominational nurture was provided were closed to slaves and freedpersons. It was the case that blacks and whites frequently participated in some of the voluntary societies, but even here the dominance of whites was evident, and blacks frequently felt themselves to be more "tolerated" than accepted on a basis of equality (see Allen 1960). African Americans who maintained their membership in congregations of the majority group churches found themselves relegated to second-class citizenship without any hope of rising in the hierarchy of the denomination (Weatherford 1924, 314).

When the Civil War ended, the freed men and women in the South left the major denominations in great numbers. Many joined the Colored Methodist Church, now the Christian Methodist Church, South. Other Methodists and freedpersons responded to the missionary activities of the A.M.E. and the A.M.E. Zion churches. Today the concentration of the memberships of these churches in certain states reflects the fact that missionaries from the respective denominations "got there first."

The major problem confronting the black denominations following the Civil War was how to accommodate the massive numbers of blacks who now were coming into the ranks. The defection of the African Americans from the churches of their former masters is mute testimony to their desire for freedom and respect which they had harbored for generations. The enjoyment of freedom, the gathering in community, and the attainment of personal affirmation were the experiences most prized, and with emancipation no institution existed to provide these experiences except the churches. For blacks who remained in the prewar denominations, the solution was to organize them into racially defined judicatories. This was the strategy of the Cumberland Presbyterians and of the Methodist Church, North and South. In view of these demeaning actions it would have been a contradiction in terms for persons of color to have developed strong denominational loyalties. To have done so would have been to affirm the community which was the instrument of their oppression.

The primary mission of the northern churches to the recently freed men and women was the founding of schools and the provision of other forms of home missionary activity with the intention of helping blacks make the transition from slavery to "ostensible freedom." The schools, colleges, and universities which the churches established proved to be a fertile source of black recruits for the denominations. Numerous African Americans joined the ranks of their northern church benefactors after having been exposed to their worship styles and preaching in the college chapels. In this instance, it was not denominational difference but alternative worship styles that served to attract students and faculty. For the first time class, culture, and education became critical considerations informing the choice of a denomination with which freedpersons affiliated.

Prior to 1890 the central mission of the church had social, educational, and economic dimensions. Four million ex-slaves needed to be assimilated into the larger culture precisely at a time when that culture was institutionalizing patterns of segregation and discrimination relative to persons of color.

The last decade of the nineteenth century marked the beginning of the largest intranational migration in the nation's history. Blacks, 90 percent of whom had traditionally lived in the rural areas of the South, began in ever-increasing numbers to move from the farms to the cities and from the South to the North. There was a "push and pull" effect observable in this massive relocation of African Americans. Among the "push factors" were discrimination, segregation, and racial injustice. In addition, the severe devastation of Southern crops by the boll weevil and a series of bad crop years contributed to an agricultural depression. These social and economical realities created a floodtide that was further accelerated by a rising tide of lynchings across the South.

Among the "pull factors" in the movement to the North was the labor shortage exacerbated by the cutting off of migration from Europe during World War I. Consequently many industries sent recruiters into the South to gather blacks to work in the mines and factories of the North. Added to this was the lure of a better life fueled by reports of families and friends who had migrated to the cities. The passage of legislation in 1924 restricting migration from Europe opened the way for blacks to become a permanent part of the Northern industrial labor scheme. This mass movement of individuals created an immediate problem for African American congregations in the North. Only in infrequent instances were these church bodies ready to accommodate the rapid influx of newcomers. Several consequences followed hard upon these realities. First, many new congregations came into existence, housed in storefronts and other available space. Second, many of the migrants defected from the churches and became lost in the maze of the city. Third, a spate of new churches came into existence which were not within the traditional denominational affiliations, such as the "Black Hebrew," the Moorish Temple, the African Orthodox Church, and other "exotic" bodies which emerged in the cities. Later in the century substantial numbers of blacks left the historic black churches and joined the ranks of the so-called "Black Muslims."

The most noteworthy religious phenomenon during this period was the emergence of the Pentecostal and Black Holiness bodies as major features in the black religious landscape. Originating in the rural South, these church bodies began to claim more and more adherents. A lineal descendant of the perfectionist and holiness churches of the late nineteenth century, these churches, the most prominent among which is the Church of God in Christ, began to attract more and more adherents in the urban areas and became the direct competitors of the more historic black churches. These churches emphasized the religious experience of "receiving" the gift of the Holy Spirit, accompanied by "glossolalia" or speaking in tongues. The Church of God in Christ was founded in rural Mississippi, and it was brought to the cities by the migrating members. There are many Pentecostal religious bodies which are more "movements" than ordered denominations—that is, they have not developed highly structured centralized governance and polity. Pentecostalism continues many of the traditions of nineteenth-century evangelicalism, including a pietistic lifestyle, emphasis upon moral living, biblical literalism, the requirement of definite, unambiguous conversion, and the expectation of the gifts of the Spirit, particularly the gift of healing. There are some persons who would argue that Pentecostalism is a truly original creation within the African American religious community. However the debate is resolved, it is clear that Pentecostalism, and to some degree the holiness churches, had no immediate antecedents in white Protestantism nor did they proliferate by fission from some larger majority group denomination. It is something of a paradox that the major Pentecostal groups among whites had black ancestors.[8]

For the purposes of this discussion, it is significant to note that the distinctive appeal of the Pentecostal movements was their capacity to respond to the needs of their constituents. Like the older African American churches, they provided the centers of community for the new migrants and functioned as strongholds of religious and family values. These urban congregations were worshiping cells in which individuals could participate in an uninhibited way. They were *de facto* "southern oases in a northern wilderness." While these bodies frequently differentiate themselves from each other by subtle doctrinal definitions, they are not marked so much by distinctive doctrine as they are by worship style, charismatic leadership, and an insistence upon authenticated religious experience. As will be apparent, Pentecostalism has sustained its appeal and has grown in membership over the years. Its future was not tied to a continuing influx of members from the rural or urban South.

African American denominations were relatively untouched by the controversies that swirled around the American churches during the 1920s. They also have not been separated theologically into "liberal" and "conservative" wings. There are several rather obvious reasons for this. Blacks have not been included in those constituencies in the major denominations which concern themselves with theological orthodoxy. As indicated above, they have been more concerned with issues relating to life and work rather than faith and order.

Following the end of World War II most American churches experienced short-lived accelerating growth in membership, and then an erosion in membership began which continues unabated. While no accurate membership statistics are available among black churches, there does not seem to have been declines in membership but rather a realignment or redistribution of some of the members.

In the realignment and relocation of membership among black churches in the last three decades, denomination has been largely a moot element. We shall examine the effect upon black participation in denominations by looking at several changes occurring in the larger culture. The decision of the United States Supreme Court in *Brown* v. *Board of Education* was an event of signal importance because it destroyed the legal construct of "separate but equal" in public education. Following this precedent, discrimination in public accommodations, housing, employment, and education were officially declared to be illegal, and legislation was passed to ensure appropriate conformity in the nation. Though the hopes fueled by these official actions have not been fully realized, processes of change were instituted that have altered the social and demographic profile of the nation. They contributed to a climate in which some attitudes were changed and in which the level of consciousness among blacks was raised. In the mainline Protestant churches, black members became more vocal about racial practices, representation, levels of inclusion and employment, and about de facto racist policies within national and regional church structures. Virtually every major denomination has a "black caucus" or its equivalent, whose principal agenda is to mount the barricades against racist policies, programs, and structures within the churches. It does not appear that the minority membership of these churches has grown significantly, other than through the accidental growth that results when minority persons become the majority in a congregation as a result of "white flight." Most national denominations have given their blessing to this kind of transformation. The Evangelical Lutheran Church in America and the Reformed Church in America, along with the United Methodist Church, have many examples of this accidental growth. When whites abandon membership in inner-city parishes, blacks may fill the void. It is the geographic location of the church and its racial character rather than its denominational label that influences an individual's decision to become a member.

Another demographic trend that has had an impact upon some of the mainline churches is the movement of blacks from the inner city into the suburbs. "White flight" has precipitated the changeover to minority membership in many congregations. This phenomenon had occurred earlier as blacks began to move into the inner city in the early 1900s. As a consequence, majority group "city" church members relocated to the suburbs or to white enclaves in the city. Sometimes long-established black congregations purchased these buildings. Sometimes churches serving the newly arrived migrants occupied them and established new congregations.

There are several other observable trends that are affecting membership in black churches at the present time. One of these trends is the decline in the membership of some historic black churches, largely due to the failure to retain the young adults who grew up in the church. There is evidence that many of these individuals abandon the church because of its apparent irrelevance to contemporary issues. An article entitled "Black Churches Losing Historic Role" in the *Washington Post* (20 August 1988) pointed out that many historic churches have failed to restructure their programs to meet the needs of persons in the inner city and thus have experienced a decline in membership.

Other factors also contribute to the declining membership of some long-established black congregations. Frequently families who can afford it move to the suburbs and elect not to make the trip back to their home church in the inner city. This may be an indication of the lack of potency of their faith commitment and/or the failure of the church to engage them in critical ways in the life of the institution. It often happens that such individuals do not attend any church.

The conclusion should not be drawn from the above observations that inner-city churches, historic or relatively new, inevitably have suffered from a loss of membership. Some churches have experienced dramatic growth in membership in recent years. Among those that have been accorded wide public notice are congregations in San Diego, Chicago, New York City, and metropolitan Washington, D.C. Certain programmatic, structural, worship, and leadership characteristics are shared by these congregations. These characteristics include multiple social ministries for members and special programs for "singles," professionals, young people, children, and senior citizens. In addition, they offer diverse educational opportunities tailored to meet the religious and secular needs of specific constituencies.[9] Some of the more successful churches sponsor Christian academies, kindergarten through twelfth grade, where black history, culture, and church history are emphasized. They frequently employ dynamic young assistant ministers with special responsibilities for youth and young adults. Invariably, the ministerial leadership in these churches is relatively young and has high visibility, not only within church circles but also in the secular community. Community involvement is common to all these thriving congregations and encompasses such concerns as homelessness, housing, employment, hunger, and a variety of services available to individuals and communities.

There is a connection between the "spiritual" ambience within a church and its drawing and retentive power where membership is concerned.[10] In a perceptive article entitled "The Black Church in the American Society: A New Responsibility," C. Eric Lincoln pointed to this aspect of the attracting and holding power of the churches:

> From its inception the Black Church has nurtured a distinctive spiritual ambience which has been unique to its own traditions. Much has been written about the alleged "hortatory boisterousness" or "flamboyance" in the pulpit, or about "exhibitionism" in the pews. Observers have been much exercised in their efforts to find the proper antecedent patterns in the African bush or in the frontier churches of America. Generally they have missed the point, for what they have been searching for is style rather than quiddity (the essence of the thing), *mode* rather than mood. In consequence, the essence of Black worship has slipped through their fingers, and the inferiority of the Black Church is improperly appreciated beyond its communion because it is improperly understood (Lincoln 1979, 91).

Lincoln goes on to observe that as

more and more racial shibboleths have lost their relevance and their potency, and as more and more blacks have matured into the security of self-appreciation, the uniqueness and the particularity of the Black Church as a valued spiritual heritage has become a major factor in Black identity.[11]

I am presently engaged in a study of one of the thriving and growing churches to which I have referred above and have discovered the following relevant, though as yet unpublished, data. This growing church possesses all the characteristics listed above, with the following additions: it is family-oriented; its worship involves all who are present as participants; it has multiple staffs; its leadership is trained and charismatic; it makes the employment of religious language normative within and away from the church; conscious attention is paid to cultivation of the gifts of the Spirit; the worship style has a "Pentecostal flavor," with spirited music accompanied by drums, guitars, cymbals, and tambourines; it has multiple musical organizations; there is active social concern and community involvement; accepted management and business practices are followed; there is emphasis upon tithing for mission and as an expression of gratitude for the goodness of God; and there are multiple members of the staff with specialized responsibilities.

In former times it was widely accepted that Pentecostal and holiness membership and worship were confined to the "disinherited" or underclasses. This generalization no longer holds. Blacks from all classes and age groups may be found as active members in these revitalized historic African American congregations that have appropriated a more Pentecostal worship style. A majority in these congregations are women, most of them young, commonly given to expressing their faith in some physical gesture, such as lifting the hands and arms and waving the arms and singing with vigor and conviction. This style of worship is communal in character, and no opprobrium attaches to the participant for his or her conduct. There is frequent verbal expression in the service, such as the utterance of "praise the Lord," "hallelujah," and the like. Services of worship feature contemporary gospel music as substitutes for the warm evangelicalism of the hymns of Watts and Wesley which has dominated worship in the black church for so long. Sometimes traditional evangelical hymns have been arranged to conform to the gospel music style. There is much extemporaneous prayer and testimony.

The most rapidly growing congregations have a high percentage of younger, upwardly mobile "buppies" (black yuppies). These African Americans, who have had a taste of the "American Dream," have found material and social success to be a bittersweet experience. These thriving churches have provided worship experiences and a style of congregational life that compensate for the lack of satisfaction which their daily experiences do not supply. These younger African Americans, who have matured in the post-Vietnam War era and who have "escaped" from the grinding despair of the ghettos, have felt the absence of living in true residential communities. They suffer from the fragmentation of their lives precipitated by the distribution of children into area schools established to accommodate differing grades, and the dispersion of the employed family members over wide urban areas. In addition, many of these individuals are confronted daily with the presence of negative racial attitudes and behaviors in the workplace and know, as a consequence, the loneliness of pervasive anonymity in the midst of relative affluence. A central fact of their lives is the absence of sustaining and affirming community. It might be observed that in many respects their lives do not differ to any radical degree from that of many majority group persons. But there is a crucial difference: blacks perceive that their isolation is attributable primarily to the fact of race. They live under the tension of being a racially hyphenated part of the culture in the workplace and in the social life of the community. Many of these individuals have found in the African American churches religious experiences which return them to their roots and locate them in the midst of caring communities where race is not a decisive element in their acceptance.

Dr. Joseph Roberts, pastor of the Ebenezer Baptist Church in Atlanta, has delineated in other terms several reasons for the return of upwardly mobile blacks to long-established churches with progressive ministries, contemporary worship patterns, and charismatic leadership. Among these are the vacuity of life at the upper echelons of business and industry, the diminishing class and economic stratification in the churches, the failure of human-potential preaching to address pressing personal and group problems, the decline in the appeal of biblical literalism, and the greater capability of persons in the pews to provide leadership within the institutional church (Bonds and Frank 1988, 6).

The previous discussion is not meant to give the impression that all is right with the black churches. It is to assert that blacks who participate in the churches do so on bases other than denominational label and in disregard of previous church membership. It is a sobering fact to learn that in statistical terms, African Americans are no more religious than are whites. Forty percent of African Americans are not affiliated with any religious organization. Indeed most are not affiliated with any social organization at all (Turner 1989). This is part of the continuing challenge to the entire religious community.

This chapter has been concerned primarily with Protestantism in the

United States, but many of its generalizations are equally applicable to blacks in the Roman Catholic Church. Approximately one million blacks are Roman Catholics, but as in the Protestant churches there is a persistent concern among blacks for social issues as demonstrated by the presence of black caucuses insisting upon the church's being accountable in these matters. There is an effort too to indigenize the worship, and more and more congregations with black priests are doing so. The declining importance of denomination is once again in evidence. The Islamic groups also have an intense involvement in social matters and are conspicuous for their efforts to contribute to the control of drugs in black communities, through a ministry of physical presence and through the exertion of political pressure.

Black religious groupings have borrowed from whites some institutional forms, some patterns of worship, some core theological tenets, but they have lived with a different view of the world which has sharply modified their view and practice of the Christian faith. The racial identity of blacks is the one constant reality in their lives, and their view of the world is both defined by them and for them by this reality. With the exception of their brothers and sisters who have been fully indoctrinated in liberal white theologics, African American Christians hold to Protestant evangelicalism as it prevailed in the first half of the nineteenth century. There has been a pivotal aspect of this theology which has always been at variance with that of their white counterparts. This pivotal aspect has been the insistence that God is for the oppressed and that faith involves the pursuit of justice in this life, even as one looks forward to life with God in eternity. Visions of the "sweet bye and bye" have always been seasoned by a clear awareness of the "nasty now and now." William C. Turner identifies the essential elements of black evangelicalism as follows:

> The evangelicalism of the Black church is a case study of how a crisis conversion or a subsequent religious experience can yield an outlook that challenges the prevailing social order: it need not produce a right-wing radical, and conservative social and political ideas are not necessarily prerequisite for evangelical or charismatic faith (1989, 41ff.).

Turner argues that the main streams of the black church (Baptist, Methodist, Holiness-Pentecostal) flow in a common course: "They make a vigorous effort to preserve a spirituality that is not intellectualized to an extent that would diminish direct and immediate witness of the Spirit" (Turner 1989, 42). Turner asserts that the experience of conversion leads to the appropriation of a worldview common to the community and guarantees the participation of the convert in the sustentation of that community (Turner 1989, 49–50).

The Afro-Christian world view helped Blacks order their religion in a manner that was consistent with the Afro-Christian understanding of God [the sovereign God who is no respecter of persons], and the divine relationships willed for God's people. Hence, conversion among Blacks holding evangelical faith was not merely a transaction between a solitary soul and the Lord. It was also a spiritual birth into a community engaged in a quarrel with parts of the wider religious community and the American culture as a whole. It was a personal experience of reckoning with the truth that the Lord justified and sanctified the poor Black slaves without requiring that they first become white or give up the desire and quest for freedom.

Turner is on solid historical ground. For though the rhetoric of some black Christians will not be the same as the language conventionally used by the Pentecostal and holiness groups, the core affirmations of their faith are the same.

In important respects black religious communions, with some conspicuous exceptions, share a single religious tradition which they have labeled with names derived from the larger religious culture. They are "de-nominated" as a way of distinguishing their historic lineage but not to denominate any basic difference. All share the basic tenets of evangelical religion. They are devoted to a faith in the sovereignty of God over human existence, and as congregations they exhibit a distinctive spirituality which is a response to the experience of being black in this society and a consciousness of having "no other helper" but God. This is a timeless faith which has been creatively expressed in changing contexts.

NOTES

1. See Russell Richey (1977) for a discussion of the various perspectives within which Protestant churches are classified by sociologists, historians, and others who have tried to develop inclusive typologies.

2. One might very well conclude that there are no black denominations if one attempts to use the criteria that have been used to designate them in contemporary research. Jackson Carroll describes denominations in terms of their culture. He speaks of "a persistent set of beliefs, values, norms, patterns, symbols, stories and style that makes denomination distinctive." He elaborates his definition by quoting Clifford Geertz's observation that culture includes both "worldview" and "ethos." Worldview is a "people's picture of the way things in sheer actuality are, their concept of nature, of self, of society. It contains their most comprehensive ideas of order." Geertz defines ethos as a people's "tone, charac-

ter, and quality of life, its mores and aesthetic style and mood; it is the underlying attitude towards themselves and their world that life reflects." This way of defining a denomination or denominationalism comes closest to being useful in discussion of religious movements among blacks (See Jackson W. Carroll 1988, 3; also Richey 1977).

3. David Bryon Davis (1975, 1–84) provides an encapsulated summary of the evolution of western attitudes toward Africans from the classical period of Greek philosophy till the end of slavery.

4. There were eleven "caucuses" in majority group denominations at the height of the civil rights movement in the late '60s and early '70s.

5. A Virginia Act in 1667 decreed that "Christian Baptism does not confer freedom upon the slaves" (cited in Joseph C. Hurd, *The Law of Freedom and Bondage in the United States,* 1858 [reprint New York: Negroes University Press, 1968], p. 232). This legal statute received confirmation from the Anglican Bishop of London who wrote, in a "Letter to Masters and Mistresses of Families in the English Plantations Abroad" in 1727, "Christianity and the embracing of the Gospel, does not make the least Alteration in Civil Property, or in any of the duties which belong to Civil Relations." (cited in Withrop D. Jordon, *White Over Black: American Attitudes toward the Negro, 1550–1812* [Chapel Hill, N.C.: published for the Institute of Early American History and Culture at Williamsburg, Va. by the University of North Carolina Press, 1968], p. 191).

6. In a chapter such as this it is impossible adequately to deal with the exceptions to many of the generalizations one makes. There were lively and often courageous minorities within the Methodist and Baptist bodies in the South who stood in opposition to the institution of slavery and argued for its extirpation. It was rare indeed to find Christians of any denominational label who argued for the equality of whites and blacks or who followed their convictions to their logical political and religious consequence.

7. "Constitution of the Liberty County Association for the Religious Instructions of Negroes," Article VI, included in the "Seventh Annual Report of the Association for the Religious Instruction of Negroes in Liberty County." Savannah, Ga.: Thomas Purse, 1842 (reprint New York: Kraus Reprint Co., 1969), p. 25.

8. With the onset of World War I the Church of God in Christ achieved recognition as a bona fide denomination and could certify clergy persons for exemption from military service and admit them to certain other privileges involving clergy discounts on railroads and in other business establishments. As a consequence, white Pentecostals went to blacks for clergy credentials. It would not be until 1914 that whites would establish their own separate "Assembly of God" and

would join the ranks of other major denominations in bowing to the separation of the church along racial lines. The final break came at the meeting of the "Pentecostal Assemblies of the World" in 1924 when the whites withdrew and subsequently organized The Pentecostal Ministries Alliance in Jackson, Tennessee, in 1925 (Jones 1975).

9. *New York Times* (August 24, 1988), A2/18. Cf. *Washington Post* (August 20, 1988), A1.

10. The *Yearbook of American and Canadian Churches, 1988* reports that for a second straight year church membership has remained stable according to a report in the *Washington Post,* (August 20, 1988), D1.

11. There has been concern expressed by some church leaders about the "pentecostalization" of worship in traditional middle-class black churches. Dr. Larry Mamiya of Vassar College has observed this debate and in an unpublished paper (1986) has written:

> There appears to be two major factions regarding . . . (neo-pentecostalism): those who support it (traditionalists) and those who oppose it (reformists). There is a large third group of members who take a neutral, wait-and-see attitude. The traditionalists emphasize "order and decorum" in worship. According to one pastor, the charismatic style of worship tends to adulterate [historic worship patterns created by the Church's founders]. . . . Other critics think that the movement is a "fad" that will pass with time. Moreover, traditionalists think that the use of "high-spirited instruments" like guitars, drums, and cymbals and the phenomenon of people "being slain in the spirit" are pure emotionalism. . . .
>
> For the . . . reformist, the present "neo-pentecostalism differs from the older pentecostalism because it combines both "Letter and Spirit." The charismatic movement goes beyond the emotionalism of the past because many of the pastors and some of the laity who are involved are "highly educated." Many have had college and/or formal theological education in seminaries. Another difference from the past is that the present movement tends to emphasize "progressive politics," a reaching out to the community rather than the conservatism and inward withdrawal which characterized the older phase.

REFERENCES

Allen, Richard
    1960   *The Life Experience and Gospel Labors of the Rt. Reverend Allen.* Nashville: Abingdon Press.

Biersdorf, John E.
   1975   *Hunger for Experience.* New York: Seabury Press.
   1988   "Black Church Losing Historic Role," *Washington Post,*
          (August 20, 1988): A1.
Bonds, Diane S., and Thomas E. Frank
   1988   "Professional Mobility and the Black Church: A Conversa-
          tion with Joseph A. Roberts, Jr., and Luther E. Smith." *Min-
          istry and Mission* 14, no. 1 (Fall). Atlanta: Candler School
          of Theology, Emory University.
Carroll, Jackson W.
   1988   "Mainline Protestant Identity: Has It A Future?" Unpub-
          lished paper. Hartford, Conn.
Clark, Kenneth E.
   1965   *Dark Ghetto.* New York: Harper & Row.
Davis, David Byron
   1975   *The Problem of Slavery in Western Culture.* Ithaca, N.Y.:
          Cornell University Press.
Dubois, W. E. B.
   1967   *The Philadelphia Negro: A Social Study.* New York:
          Schocken Books.
Erskine, Noel Leo
   1978   *Black People and the Reformed Church in America.* Grand
          Rapids: Reformed Church Press.
Gregory, Chester W.
   1986   *The History of the United Holy Church of America, Inc.
          1886–1986.* Baltimore: Gateway Press.
Hoge, Dean R., and David A. Roozen
   1979   *Understanding Church Growth and Decline.* New York:
          Pilgrim Press.
Jones, Lawrence N.
   1975   "The Black Pentecostals." In *The Charismatic Movement,*
          edited by Michael Hamilton. Grand Rapids: Wm. B. Eerd-
          mans Publishing Co.
   1976   "In God We Trust." In *Minorities and the American Dream:
          A Bicentennial Perspective,* edited by Warren Marr and
          Maybelle Ward. New York: Arno Press.
   1977   "The Early Black Societies and Churches: Matrix of Com-
          munity and Mission." In *The Black Church: A Community
          Resource,* edited by Dionne J. Jones and William H.
          Matthews. Washington, D.C.: Institute of Urban Affairs and
          Research, Howard University.
   1979   "The Black Churches: A New Agenda." *The Christian Cen-
          tury* 96, no. 14 (April 18, 1979): 434–438.

Lewin, Tamar
  1988   "Black Churches: New Mission on Family." *New York Times* (August 24, 1988): A 1–2.
Lincoln, C. Eric
  1979   "The Black Church in America: A New Responsibility," *The Journal of the Interdenominational Theological Center* 6 (Spring 1979).
  1988   C. Eric Lincoln and Lawrence N. Mamiya, "In the Receding Shadow of the Plantation: A Profile of Rural Clergy and Churches in the Black Belt," *Review of Religious Research* 29 (June 1988): 349–384.
Mays, Benjamin E., and Joseph W. Nichols
  1933   *The Negro's Church.* New York: Institute of Social and Religious Research.
Murray, Andrew E.
  1966   *Presbyterians and the Negro—A History.* Philadelphia: Presbyterian Historical Society.
Nelson, Hart M., and Anne Kusener Nelson
  1975   *Black Church in the Sixties.* Lexington, Ky.: University Press of Kentucky.
  1988   "Unchurched Black Americans: Patterns of Religiosity and Affiliation." *Review of Religious Research* 29 (June 1988): 398–412.
Nickels, Marilyn Wenzke
  1988   *Black Catholic Protest and the Federated Colored Catholics 1917–1933.* New York: Garland Publishing.
Niebuhr, H. Richard
  1957   *The Social Sources of Denominationalism.* New York: Meridian Books.
Perkins, Benjamin Paul Sr.
  1972   *Black Christians' Tragedies: An Analysis of Black Youth and Their Church.* New York: Exposition Press.
Reimers, David M.
  1965   *White Protestantism and the Negro.* New York: Oxford University Press.
Richey, Russell E. (ed.)
  1977   *Denominationalism.* Nashville: Abingdon Press.
Smylie, James H.
  1978   "Church Growth and Decline in Historical Perspective: Protestant Quest for Identity, Leadership, and Meaning." In *Understanding Church Growth and Decline,* edited by Dean R. Hoge and David A. Roozen. New York: Pilgrim Press.

Spear, Allan H.
  1967   *Black Chicago: The Making of a Ghetto.* Chicago: University of Chicago Press.
Synan, Vinson
  1971   *The Holiness-Pentecostal Movement in the United States.* Grand Rapids: Wm. B. Eerdmans Publishing Co.
Taylor, Robert J.
  1988a "Correlates of Religious Non-Involvement Among Black Americans." *Review of Religious Research* 30 (December 1988):126–139.
  1988b "Structural Determinants of Religious Participation Among Black Americans." *Review of Religious Research* 30 (December 1988):114–125.
Turner, William C.
  1989   "Black Evangelism: Theology, Politics, and Race." *Journal of Religious Thought* 45 (Winter-Spring), 40–56.
Washington, Joseph R., Jr.
  1972   *Black Sects and Cults.* Garden City, N.Y.: Doubleday & Co.
Weatherford, Willis D.
  1924   *The Negro from Africa to America.* New York: George D. Doran and Co.
Willson, Joseph
  1841   *Sketches of the Higher Classes of Colored Society in Philadelphia.* Philadelphia: Historic Publication No. 246. The document can be found at Historic Publications, 302 N. 13th Street, Philadelphia, PA 19197.
Yinger, J. Milton
  1957   *Religion, Society, and the Individual.* New York: Macmillan Co.

12

Between Myth and Hard Data: A Denomination Struggles with Identity

Donald A. Luidens

Sociologists of the American religious scene have developed a rich literature on the peculiar religious structure known as the "denomination." In general, this type of structure has been described as dependent upon social and cultural factors which make and shape its experience. With few exceptions, sociologists perceive these molding forces to originate *outside* the denominations, and see the denominations as relatively powerless to govern them. In effect, denominations *react* to the forces rather than *control* them.

It is the contention of this chapter that, by and large, denominations fail to recognize their dependent status. Instead, they understand the consequences of the external challenges—whether positive or negative—as originating from within their own ranks. Accordingly, they feverishly reshape their own, internal structures and ideologies in an effort to "remedy" the crises which descend upon them.

As an example of such denominational self-criticism and remolding, this paper will look at the recent experiences of one Protestant denomination in the throes of a self-defined "identity crisis." Having been founded by Dutch Calvinists, the Reformed Church in America is a classic ethnic/national denomination—referred to by H. Richard Niebuhr as an "immigrant" denomination (1968, 200ff.). Along with other mainline denominations, it experienced the twin threats of structural and ideological upheaval that swept through the church during the 1960s and 1970s. In the midst of the Reformed Church's struggle with "denominational identity," there are clear cues about the future of denominationalism in the United States.

This study of the Reformed Church in America (RCA) will proceed as follows: a brief historical overview will bring the reader up to the watershed year of 1968. Discussion will then focus on three "stages of crisis": early indications of crisis (1968–74); deepening crisis (1975–84); and full-fledged crisis (1984 to the present). At each stage, an analysis will be undertaken of the components of the struggle: How is the crisis perceived by members of the denomination? What ideological and structural factors do they see as being involved? Which of these factors are internal and which external to the denomination?

Data for this discussion and analysis will be of two kinds: quantitative information drawn from two questionnaire studies of the denomination undertaken by the author in 1976 and 1986 (with the assistance of Roger J. Nemeth), and qualitative material culled from a reading of the principal publications of the denomination since 1968.

A Brief History of the Reformed Church in America

The Reformed Church in America traces its roots to the Calvinist Reformation in the Netherlands. Its first arrival in the New World was aboard Henry Hudson's *Half Moon* in 1609. By 1628, the first congregation of the Dutch church had been established by the Dutch West India Company in New Amsterdam—later to be New York City. The church grew in subsequent generations, as the Dutch became the principal settlers of the Hudson and Mohawk Valleys as well as of the rolling hill country of New Jersey. At the time of the American Revolution, ninety-eight congregations of the Dutch Reformed Church—as it had come to be known—served forty-five thousand parishioners throughout New York and New Jersey (Brouwer 1977, 34).

In his discussion of the vagaries of immigrant religious life, Niebuhr pointed to a crisis in the 1750s regarding the use of English in Dutch Reformed worship services (1968, 224f.). This initial tussle with "Americanization" has been frequently repeated in the life of the Reformed Church in America (as the Dutch Reformed Church was renamed after 1867—following just such an Americanizing clash). The most recent manifestation of this struggle has been with "minority"—nonwhite—components of the membership and their full integration into the judicatories of the denomination.

While the initial growth of the denomination took place throughout the Middle Atlantic states, the most lasting growth began in the mid-1800s as new waves of Dutch immigrants arrived in Michigan, Iowa,

Wisconsin, and other sections of the Midwest. These Dutch settlers came primarily from among religious schismatics who had opposed the establishment in 1816 of the official Reformed Church of the Netherlands (Brouwer 1977, 110–111).

Shortly after arriving, these new immigrants further divided into two groups: one group affirmed its new citizenship and allied itself with the Eastern denomination, the Reformed Church in America; the second group wished to remain aloof from the perceived heresies of that Americanized denomination and formed the Christian Reformed Church.

Subsequent growth of the Reformed Church in America was largely around the initial immigrant sites (the mid-Atlantic and Midwestern states). Beginning in the early 1950s, however, new efforts took the church into Canada, California, Arizona, Colorado, and elsewhere in the country. In particular, new church extension has been active in Texas and, most recently, throughout the "Bible Belt" (from Virginia and Georgia to Alabama and Oklahoma). In all of these efforts, new membership has been characterized by non-Dutch ethnicity and non-Reformed culture.

For much of the twentieth century the RCA has been an active participant in various ecumenical endeavors. As a charter member of the Federal, World (WCC), and National Councils of Churches (NCC) and the World Alliance of Reformed Churches, it has been well represented in governing boards and agencies—as well as on staffs. While union with other denominations has been problematic—the catastrophic near-merger with the Presbyterian Church U.S. in 1968–69 is a vivid part of the collective memory—a list of the churches with which the RCA is in dialogue is an expansive one: the Christian Reformed Church, Lutherans, Reformed Churches in Hungary and South Africa, Disciples of Christ, and Methodists. Questions regarding other alliances, such as full membership in the National Association of Evangelicals (who refused RCA participation because of its NCC/WCC ties) and the Council on Church Union (COCU, in which the RCA has observer status), elicit continual debate at General Synod each year (*GS Minutes* 1989, contents). While the RCA has been a regular participant in ecumenical activities, it has done so against the vocal opposition of a minority and with strong reservations about more than collegial cooperation.

While currently numbering fewer than a quarter of a million active members, the RCA stretches from coast to coast and from the North to the South. In that respect it is a national church in the "mainline" tradition. The exact theological and cultural location of the RCA has been much discussed. Elsewhere the author has argued that the RCA ought to be considered a "moderate Protestant" denomination:

Together with other such denominations the RCA has experienced a recent history of membership decline, it has endorsed "liberal" positions on social issues from Central America to women's ordination, and it was a founding member of both the World and National Councils of Churches. On the other hand, it has labeled abortion and homosexuality as sins needing repentance. (Luidens and Nemeth 1987e, 453, fn. 1)

Early Indications of Crisis: 1968–74

During 1968–69 the "Plan of Union," a proposal for merger between the RCA and the Presbyterian Church U.S., was rejected in the Reformed Church after a bitter campaign. While a majority of the RCA classes voted in favor of the merger, the constitutionally required two-thirds did not. In the wake of this defeat, a motion was introduced to the 1969 General Synod calling for the appointment of "a joint committee of 24 with 12 representatives of the divergent views within the RCA to be assigned the task of drafting a plan for the orderly dissolution of the RCA to be reported to the General Synod of 1971" (*GS Minutes* 1969, 201). While this extreme motion was waylaid in committee, it provided the impetus for the establishment of a "Committee of 18" to develop the means for reconciliation throughout the denomination. The storm clouds were gathering.

Parallel to this struggle over ecumenism and theology, the RCA found itself at the end of the 1960s in the midst of organizational turmoil. It was this organizational turmoil that overwhelmed other issues during the next few years. In response to the tremendous growth in membership and programs which came about during the 1950s and early 1960s, there was strong concern—especially among lay leaders—that the denomination be placed on firmer managerial footing. Its several organizational branches had developed autonomously in response to special interest groups within the church. Specifically, boards of world mission, domestic (U.S.-based) mission, Christian education, ministers' pensions, and others had been instituted. It was felt that these autonomous groups—often in direct competition for financial and human resources—would be more efficient if they were amalgamated under a single organizational rubric (Brouwer 1977, 177 f.).

In response, an umbrella agency (the General Program Council, GPC) was established to oversee the on-going programmatic activities of the denomination (*GS Minutes* 1968, 141). The GPC supervised the activities of a General Program Council Staff (referred to hereafter as "the staff"). So important was the corporate model of operation in this setting that the principles of "management by objectives" were soon established as the guidelines for the staff's day-to-day functioning. At its most extreme, denominational leaders were heard to refer to local congregations as "franchises of the national corporation."

It was in the midst of considerable personnel upheaval—attendant upon the development of the GPC staff and a simultaneous reorganization within both of the denomination's seminaries—that the RCA began to suffer a membership decline. While this decline was initially attributed to short-term causes—such as the denomination's "preoccupation" with the Vietnam War, black activists, and other social issues; the natural fallout of a denomination in organizational transition; or the temporary drop in recruiting that any organization suffers from time to time—it became increasingly alarming to staff members.

In an interview with this author in 1976, the General Secretary of the RCA said he was convinced no denomination could continue to function if its membership fell below 200,000. For several years he had been fearful that the RCA might arrive at that breaking point (in 1976 the RCA had 216,000 "active communicants"). However, more immediate matters absorbed the staff, so they did not respond right away to the declines. It would appear, furthermore, that at this early stage the membership drop was not perceived as a major issue in the rest of the denomination.

In 1972 Dean Kelley used the drop in members in the RCA as an example of the decline of a "liberal" church in comparison to the growth of the "conservative" Christian Reformed Church (CRC). As Kelley demonstrated, the overall membership of the RCA had begun to level out in the early 1960s; by the late 1960s, the denomination was losing numbers. By contrast, the CRC had grown throughout the post–World War II period, and it had continued to show consistent growth patterns up to the time of Kelley's writing (Kelley 1977, 29). The drop in RCA membership was accompanied by a fluctuation in membership contributions—a pattern which was initially confusing to evaluate because it involved the merging of several, formerly autonomous, bookkeeping systems.

These unstable patterns elicited responses from the staff and leadership that displayed two characteristics: (1) the "trends" were perceived to be temporary ones which could be corrected with the proper institutional adjustments; and (2) while there was general recognition that the RCA was experiencing patterns also visible in Presbyterian, Methodist, and Episcopal quarters, their impetus—and therefore their remedy—was understood to be *internal* to the RCA and to have primarily a *structural* (in this case, organizational) basis.

In response to their analyses of the declining membership trends, the staff launched several "corrective" initiatives intended to fine-tune the organization of the denomination. In particular, regional centers were established throughout the RCA, ostensibly to "decentralize" operations and to provide more immediate contact between denominational members and the national staff. This resulted in a variety of national officers being posted in quarters outside New York City (where the denominational headquarters are located). However, since the staff continued to function as a single unit, the amount of actual decentralization of authority was limited. Policies had been, and continued to be, guided by the GPC, and programmatic implementations were articulated and executed by the staff in close cooperation with the GPC *(GS Minutes* 1972, 146–147, 274; 1973, 68, 280).

While the operations of the staff were being formalized, streamlined, and otherwise rationalized, the workings of the governing General Synod annual meeting were similarly being subject to the organizational microscope. Long the denomination's governing and policy-setting agency, the General Synod had functioned with a significant informal structure. Composed of equal representations from lay and clergy members of the denomination, the General Synod had relied on personal networking, family connections, and "the good old boys"—especially clergy—to hold sway. However, as it became increasingly clear that the unpredictability inherent in such informal relations would undermine the functioning of a rationalized denomination, the General Synod was itself transformed. Beginning with the establishment of a General Synod Executive Committee to function throughout the year in lieu of the annual meeting, the General Synod came under increasing formalization and structure *(GS Minutes* 1964, 169–172, 175–177). In its current manifestation it is highly standardized with an active lexicon of its own ("committees" versus "commissions," "advisory" versus "implementing," "reference" versus "action") (Hoff 1985, cf. 111ff.).

At about the same time, efforts were underway to consolidate the theological education of the denomination's future ministers in one site. This direct threat to the RCA's two historic theological centers was hotly contested. In the ensuing debate, it was suggested that *both* seminary sites should be relinquished and replaced by a new one, which would be in closer proximity to the national offices. Again, the underlying intentions were to promote efficiency and integration of the denominational program. It was expected that a more intentional exposure of the RCA's future ministers to the program agencies of the denomination would help to ensure the ministers' long-term support for the GPC's programs.

Proposals went so far as to suggest that the seminaries should come under the presidency of the chief executive of the General Program Council. However, after almost two years of debate and acrimony on this possibility, "the plan proved to be unacceptable to the church. Many letters and overtures opposing the plan were received. The search for a president [of the seminaries] is being renewed" (*GS Minutes* 1972, 25). The bitter feelings left in the wake of this consolidation effort served to alienate the theological institutions from the staff of the denomination.

In all of these efforts, the expectation was that the times of trouble were of short duration and the problems manageable. Adaptive measures—principally organizational—that were taken within the denomination were expected to be sufficient to respond to the perceived crisis. These measures were intended to address matters of efficiency, of communication and promotion, and of control and decentralization. There seemed to be little effort to define the crisis in terms either as *external* to the denomination (that is, as a consequence of broader structural or cultural influences which were sweeping through all of mainline Protestantism) or as *ideological* (as Kelley had been arguing).

The Crisis Deepens: 1975–1983

In his presidential address to the General Synod of 1975, Rev. Bert E. Van Soest brought the issue of membership decline out into the open. For the first time, numbers became a major issue to the laity and the bulk of the clergy. In response to the problem, Van Soest proposed a new formulation of the matters at hand. As had been the case with the earlier formulation, he placed the crisis firmly in the lap of the church: "The real crisis, however, is not in the world; it is in the church." While acknowledging that the crisis was widespread in U.S. Protestantism, Rev. Van Soest saw it as peculiar to the RCA as well:

> At this point we as a denomination also face a real crisis. Although we are about to celebrate our 350th anniversary, we remain not only small, but a denomination that has a negative growth rate! We have a membership that is growing older. And the particular synods are reporting from east to west that the gains within their constituency [*sic*] as far as church growth is concerned are insignificant or negative. (*GS Minutes* 1975, 243)

Having identified the symptom of the RCA's "crisis" as a declining membership, and having argued that the failing lay within the church itself, Rev. Van Soest predictably moved to a remedy which was internal to the denomination:

> When we examine our national program expenditures, we do not see the high priority on evangelism, missions and church growth that our Reformed commitment demands. It seems to be that at this point we are caught in an agony as to how to express this high priority in program dollars. (*GS Minutes* 1975, 244–245)

In effect, Rev. Van Soest saw the denomination as having lost faith in its ideological roots—its theological priorities of evangelism, mission, and church growth. This loss of faith had resulted in misapplication of resources to other tasks. Van Soest's conclusion was to redirect the problem of membership decline away from structural issues and onto ideological ones. To rectify the perceived shortcoming, Van Soest called on the denomination to make greater programmatic efforts to reaffirm "Jesus the Master Evangelist" and to promote church growth. The twin pillars of evangelical zeal and membership outreach should form the heart of the RCA's theological thrust for the next few years.

This new formulation was quickly adopted by the church. In the wake of Van Soest's call to arms, the denomination engaged in an aggressive promotion of church growth. At the heart of this program was a document entitled "Reformed Church Growth: Perspectives and Proposals" (*GS Minutes* 1977, 122ff.). Throughout the denomination, local and regional judicatories developed strategies for "church extension" (Koopman 1987). Representatives from the Church Growth Institute of Southern California were hired as consultants to various RCA agencies. Among the most successful church extension efforts was the denomination's foray into Texas. Within two years, several young pastors had been dispatched to the Dallas area to lay the groundwork for five new churches. By late 1980, three of the congregations had been officially organized (*GS Minutes* 1981, Appendix 1:108–109).

Additional—though minimal—growth was experienced among minority communities. During the 1970s, the Black Council had become an established participant in the life of the RCA. Its objectives of serving the African American constituents (estimated at less than one percent of the entire membership) were drawn up in 1970 in response to the heightened awareness of racism in the church (*GS Minutes* 1970, 62). Together with the Native American, Hispanic, and Pacific and Asian-American Councils, the Black Council worked to create a climate of greater self-sufficiency for minority congregations in the RCA and to alert the rest of the RCA to the biblical injunction to reach out to all peoples.

The most significant membership increase was experienced in the West. A strategy carefully tailored to reflect the "homogeneous unit" principals espoused by the Church Growth Institute, and enthusiastically fostered by the RCA's Rev. Robert Schuler, bore notable fruit in California and Arizona (Droog 1987, 16–17). Between 1975 and 1983, RCA membership in California churches increased 21 percent, from 16,183 to 19,583 (*GS Minutes* 1976, Appendix 1:94, 98; 1984, Appendix 1:98, 102).

However, despite its aggressive efforts to respond to the problem of membership decline with a renewed resolve to attract new members, the RCA found itself on the threshold of 1984 with little evidence of denomination-wide "success." Indeed, given the data in table 12–1, the membership trends continued to be downward—in the face of continued growth in the sister Christian Reformed Church.

TABLE 12–1

Reformed and Christian Reformed Churches; Membership Trends, 1960–89

	Reformed Church Total Baptized/Actual		Christian Reformed Church Total Baptized/Actual	
1960	326,633	222,523	236,145	124,268
1961	324,413	225,927	242,593	127,646
1962	332,534	230,210	250,934	131,332
1963	340,574	232,196	256,015	133,870
1964	378,242	228,934	263,178	137,049
1965	384,065	230,731	268,165	140,179
1966	385,754	232,414	272,461	142,961
1967	386,835	233,020	275,530	145,472
1968	384,751	232,978	278,869	147,738
1969	383,166	230,519	281,523	149,812
1970	380,133	228,620	284,737	152,670
1971	379,505	226,830	285,628	154,276
1972	375,546	223,317	286,094	155,547
1973	378,279	220,959	287,114	157,667
1974	366,381	216,356	287,533	159,658
1975	359,637	214,303	286,371	160,660
1976	360,227	215,827	287,503	163,185
1977	356,181	215,188	288,024	164,583
1978	354,218	214,266	287,656	167,353
1979	353,621	215,384	289,011	169,545
1980	353,968	214,389	292,379	172,786
1981	352,773	214,500	294,354	176,275
1982	352,695	214,090	296,706	179,518
1983	353,184	214,981	299,685	182,513
1984	351,356	215,521	302,436	185,406
1985	348,585	213,812	305,228	188,111
1986	348,836	213,228	306,309	189,239
1987	346,846	211,890	308,993	191,680
1988	344,836	207,474	310,159	192,442
1989	340,284	204,545	313,868	185,606
1990	333,681	201,283	315,055	187,329

Furthermore, the very successes which could be pointed to—the growth in nonwhite, non-Dutch membership, and the shift of the denomination's numerical center further to the West—seemed to spell future disruption for the traditional RCA. As the chief architect of the church growth movement in the West argued in a 1985 *Church Herald* article, the newcomers from the Southwest were a different breed and would take some getting used to:

> The youth of the churches and the great opportunities for growth forced the churches [in the Southwest] to be highly creative, innovative, and daring. The use of the drive-in worship service was popularized by the Reformed churches in California. The setting aside of denominational labels and calling themselves "community churches" was innovative and daring, but in spite of criticism, was seen as the price that had to be paid if the RCA were to reach people unfamiliar with the Reformed Church. The use of Christian entertainers was an attempt to bring people into the church and under the preaching of the Word. (Droog 1985, 16)

These innovations were a far cry from the traditional themes and patterns of the Reformed Church in America.

Crisis as Identity Issue: 1984–Present

In 1984, the definition of the RCA's crisis was once again shifted in a subtle, yet significant, way. In his presidential address, the Rev. Leonard Kalkwarf recounted the variety of persons and congregations he had met during his year as General Synod president. While he generally applauded this variety, it raised for him a troubling question:

> It is this very diversity, which can be a positive factor in the life of our denomination, that has created a problem for us. I repeatedly heard individuals raise the question about our identity. The issue seems to be, "What is the glue that holds us together?" Early in our history, the answer to this question might have been our Dutch heritage. As one visits different congregations, one is struck by the variety of worship forms, vestments, liturgies, architectural styles, and even theological emphases. Surely these are not what we have in common, and perhaps they ought not to be. Perhaps it is to be found within that beloved old document [the Heidelberg Catechism] which affirms that our only comfort in life and death is that we are a people who belong [to God]. (Kalkwarf 1984, 14)

Thus, for Kalkwarf at least, the traditional marks of the RCA—its Dutch composition, its worship forms and theological perspectives, even its symbolic accoutrements—had been transcended as "the glue that holds us together." Rather wistfully, he speculated that the RCA's confessional heritage—embodied in the Heidelberg Catechism—may be the last universal link among RCA members.

In response to his recommendation that the denomination undertake a three-year study of its identity, the General Synod established an Ad Hoc Task Force on RCA Identity. Once again, the RCA was perceived to be in the midst of a crisis; once again the crisis was perceived to be generated from internal factors; and once again the crisis was perceived to be a matter of ideology and culture ("identity") rather than polity and structure. While Kalkwarf hinted that external cultural factors might be playing a role (he suggested that "contributing to the confusion is a trait we have adopted from our American culture . . . individualism"), he felt that the heart of the problem was internal to the denomination (having to do with priorities, with intention); presumably, external forces such as U.S. individualism were incidental (Kalkwarf 1984, 15).

Under the aegis of the Identity Task Force, a wide range of activities were instigated. Two principal purposes were served by these activities: on the one hand there was an enthusiastic effort to promote the RCA as a solid, unified, healthy institution; on the other hand, there was a parallel effort to discover what the RCA's identity was (RCA n.d., 166–168).

Among its promotional activities, the Task Force orchestrated events at the 1986, 1987, and 1988 General Synods around the theme (adopted from the first question in the Heidelberg Catechism[1]), "A People Who Belong" (Mulder 1984, 6–7). Included were the viewing of video presentations, the composition and production of a religious musical, the simulcasting of regional gatherings of RCA members, the development and distribution throughout the RCA of promotional and historical materials, and the production and display of a "patchwork quilt" composed of embroidered panels contributed by 500 of the RCA's 960 congregations.

In each of these promotional undertakings, the intended message was that the unifying characteristic of the members of the RCA was their common "belonging" to Jesus Christ—an assertion readily applicable to any "Christian" group. Beyond this general affirmation, however, there was no claim to the primacy of one or another tradition, belief, or group as "typical" of the RCA. In fact, in each of these promotional endeavors, the dissimilarity of the membership was readily apparent and even stressed as a matter of some pride.

The Identity Task Force's effort to discover denominational identity included several ventures. A series of regional conferences was held in

October and November of 1987 to solicit lay and clergy perceptions of the identifying characteristics of the denomination. In January 1988 representatives from these conferences met together to pool their perceptions. While not empowered to issue any official directives, the "St. Louis Consultation"—as the joint gathering was called—served to reaffirm the collective commitment of the participants to the diversity and viability of the denomination. As the *Church Herald* put it:

> The RCA's ethnic diversity received numerous endorsements from the consultation's small groups. Similarly, there was recognition of the diversity of members' ages and diversity of worship styles in the church, together with calls that the diversity be appreciated and incorporated. (RCA 1988b, 25)

However, despite issuing a lengthy list of characteristics and commonalities in the RCA, the lasting impact of the gathering was unclear. According to the *Church Herald,* "Most participants finished the consultation without knowing how their weekend activities would contribute to the RCA's articulation of an identity" (RCA 1988b, 25).

The Task Force also engaged the current author and a colleague[2] to execute a nationwide KAP (knowledge, attitude, practice) study of the RCA's laity and clergy. This study was carried out during 1986 and 1987. Reports were presented orally to the Task Force and to the leadership of the national staff. In addition, a series of articles appeared in the denominational journal, the *Church Herald* (Luidens and Nemeth 1987a–d). Rather than clarifying the denomination's identity, however, the Luidens-Nemeth[3] study seems to have demonstrated how much the traditional identity factors had been undermined in the Reformed Church.

Historically, the principal distinguishing characteristic of the RCA had been its Dutch ethnic composition. In 1976 it was still possible to say that "over half [54 percent] of the entire membership claims Dutch heritage" (Luidens 1978a, 4). However, even at that date, there was wide variety across the country. While only 22 percent of East Coast members could claim any Dutch ancestry, that number contrasted with 68 percent for the rest of the denomination. By 1986, the denomination-wide proportion of Dutch background had dropped to 48 percent. Again, the patterns differed depending upon region: the East Coast composition had held steady at 23 percent; the Midwest (in the 1986 survey, separated from the Far West) continued at 69 percent; however, the Far West—the center of RCA growth during the intervening period—was only 24 percent Dutch (Luidens and Nemeth 1987b, 6).

While there has been a decreasing emphasis on the Dutch ethnicity of the RCA, there has not been a total cessation of the debate around ethnicity. This has been in part because of the role that the Dutch have played in South Africa. In a recent address to the United States Senate Foreign Affairs Sub-Committee on Africa, the General Secretary of the RCA made the following claim:

> The RCA's relationship with South Africa is somewhat unique, in that the architects of apartheid are members of that country's Dutch Reformed Church, a church which shares virtually an identical theological and ecclesiastical heritage with the RCA in that both denominations can be traced back to the Reformed Church in the Netherlands. In fact, until 1867 my denomination was officially known as the Protestant Dutch Reformed Church. (Mulder 1988, 1)

Indeed, the involvement of the white Dutch Reformed Church in fostering apartheid has been of considerable embarrassment to the majority of the white members of the RCA—and a point of constant accusation from the denomination's Black Council. Since the early 1960s there has been a lively exchange between the RCA and the white, colored, and black branches of the Dutch Reformed Church in South Africa. The decision to discontinue communication with the white branch was conjoined with a denominational policy of divestiture in the early 1970s. Furthermore, the issue of South Africa has been the premier topic of consideration for almost twenty years in the Black Council. Since June 1984, three-quarters of the council's newsletters have referred to some aspect of the South African situation. In sum, the issue of South Africa has been a challenge to the historic Dutch ethnicity of the RCA, rather than an affirmer of it.

Perhaps as threatening to the identity of the RCA as its ethnic dilution has been the increasing theological heterogeneity of its membership. Rev. Kalkwarf had noted that he found little uniformity of theological, liturgical, and worship approaches across the denomination. This perception has been echoed in each subsequent presidential address (Brownson 1985, 14–15; Leestma 1986, 12–13; Neevel 1987, 8; Wise 1988, 15). However, it was Kalkwarf's expectation (hope?) that the creeds and confessions of the denomination had retained their allegiance, and therefore their unifying power. As a "confessional" denomination, the RCA had long centered its theological formulations on several Reformation era confessions and ecumenical creeds. Prominent among these were the Apostles' and Nicene creeds and the Heidelberg Catechism.

In order to ascertain the strength of continued commitment to these confessions, Luidens and Nemeth asked their lay and clergy respondents to indicate how important they felt each one was in their own religious lives. The data in table 12–2 serves as evidence that among both lay and clergy respondents, support for these historic affirmations varied considerably. Only the Apostles' Creed received strong support from both constituencies. On the other hand, two of the major faith statements—considered parts of the denomination's constitution and sworn to by each member and pastor—received affirmation from fewer than 30 percent of either group. Clearly, these statements are not the center of denominational commonality.

TABLE 12-2

Support for Historic Creeds Among Laity and Clergy
(Percentages reflect the number of people answering
"Extremely Important" or "Quite Important")

	Laity	Clergy
Apostles' Creed	81%	86%
Heidelberg Catechism	50	75
Nicene Creed	47	53
Belgic Confession	28	29
Canons of Dort Synod	20	20

Response in the denomination to the findings of the sociologists included this despairing letter from Rev. Earl Kennedy to the editor of the *Church Herald:*

> Perhaps historic Calvinism is becoming a dead letter in the RCA, inspite [sic] of our lip service to it. . . . Catechism sermons are almost a thing of the past, instruction of the young in catechism is waning, and knowledge of the Belgic Confession and the Canons of Dort is almost nonexistent, even among the clergy. (Kennedy 1988, 24)

While deploring the results of the survey, Kennedy acknowledges their reflection of the current state of affairs.

John Stapert, the editor of the *Church Herald,* greeted the findings with ambivalence:

> According to the sociological research of Drs. Donald Luidens and Roger Nemeth of Hope College, there's no commonly held belief that characterizes members of this denomination. The search for the glue that presently holds us together has come up empty; further scratching won't detect it. (Stapert 1988, 5)

In the face of this evidence of theological divergence, Stapert called for the RCA "to set forth a singular purpose around which all its members will rally."

Theologian Paul Fries, while acknowledging that "much valuable information can be gained from" sociological research, feels that "it does not address the question of denominational unity." Instead, Fries argues that the RCA must engage in actively "confessing" its faith, thereby recapturing its identity. In effect, the RCA has been led astray in its efforts to discover identity by using analytic skills. True religious identity can only be found in making and acting upon theological affirmations, as was the case during the Reformation when "confessing confessional statements was a matter of the heart as well as of the head; of affect as well as intellect. Confessing in this way carried existential urgency and often risk" (Fries 1988, 5–6).

In sum, the results of the sociological studies raised the level of denominational malaise and increased the sense of urgency that the RCA must *do* something to find, or create, a common sense of identity.

One recent effort to create such an identity through a denomination-wide activity has been the initiation of a major fund drive. Entitled "Putting People in Mission" (PPIM), this undertaking has been the principal project of the General Secretary of the RCA (Mulder 1989, 6). Initiated in 1987, it hopes to fund over one hundred projects from around the denomination and thereby to present a unified image of the RCA membership pulling in collective harness (Jappinga 1988, 11). According to its official description, PPIM is intended to be "helpful in strengthening the life of the denomination and in developing a sense of unity in mission" (*GS Minutes* 1988, 328).

While PPIM is a programmatic response to the identity crisis, the denomination has initiated several efforts to rework its undergirding theological formulations. Two statements of belief have been composed. An "Identity Statement" (with longer and shorter versions) was written by the Task Force on RCA Identity, and was affirmed for denomination-wide distribution and use at the 1988 General Synod (RCA n.d., 173–174). Beginning with the refrain, "We are a people who belong, . . ." this statement reaffirms broad, general tenets of Christianity; as one elder has observed, "One of the most important features of the short statement of RCA identity is that it distinguishes us from practically nobody" (Westphal 1988, 3).

A second theological statement has been proposed by the PPIM governing committee. This "mission statement for the proposed fund drive" is a trinitarian call to maximize spiritual, human, and fiscal resources in response to God's call to ministry. While not submitted for adoption beyond the PPIM committee, this statement has had wide dissemination among those actively engaged in the larger fund drive.

On another track, the RCA's Theological Commission has recently launched a project to retranslate and revitalize the Heidelberg Catechism. The Heidelberg Catechism is supposed to be a central tenet in the preaching of the RCA clergy. According to the denomination's constitution, the Catechism's major doctrinal points are mandated to be "explained by the minister at regular services of worship on the Lord's Day, so that the exposition of them is completed within a period of four years" (RCA 1988a, 13). Thus, a rephrasing of the Catechism is intended to make it more accessible to contemporary experience.

The latest in this series of efforts to reaffirm a common identity occurred when the General Synod of 1989 enthusiastically endorsed the following measure:

> To instruct all classes to direct their congregations to identify themselves as congregations of the RCA in places such as signage, newsletters, letterhead, and bulletins. (RCA n.d., 154)

In a bold stroke, the earlier plea for "innovative and daring" measures to reach potential newcomers in the South and West was effectively undermined.

Commentary and Conclusions

The Reformed Church in America perceives itself to be in the midst of a major crisis, a crisis which began in the late 1960s and which continues apace. Along with other mainline Protestant denominations, the RCA has accepted the conclusion that declining membership is symptomatic of a deep failure within the churches. This self-perception began among denominational staff members who first observed the numerical decline and had to live within the consequent fiscal constraints. Subsequently, the crisis became a preoccupation of the clergy and lay leadership as well as the wider membership.

Remarkably, this self-critical analysis persists in the face of classic and ongoing sociological explanations of denominational formation and transformation. The evidence clearly shows that the sources of denominational transformations are largely (although not exclusively) external to the respective denominations, and they rest in the structural and ideological crosscurrents of the day. Summarizing the combined findings of a team of sociologists and historians who were studying denominational growth and decline, Hoge and Roozen concluded the following:

> The main explanations for the recent denominational trends are to be found in the social context more than in the institutional churches. They are more cultural than demographic in nature, as shown by our research . . . indicating the weakness of demographic explanations (looking at numbers of persons in various age, education, and regional categories)

in explaining trends. *It seems that a broad cultural shift has occurred that has hit the churches from the outside,* and it has hit the affluent, educated, individualistic, culture-affirming denominations hardest.... The value shift was in the direction of greater individualism, personal freedom, tolerance of diversity, and distance from many traditional institutions. (Hoge and Roozen 1979b, 328, emphasis added)

The shift was particularly harsh on mainline denominations, such as the RCA. While some denominations may be able to weather particular swells better than others do, that success has less to do with their capacity to make internal *adjustments* and more to do with their differing, preexisting compositions. The RCA was especially vulnerable.

In sum, while the sociological and historical evidence strongly suggests that the RCA, along with mainline Protestantism in general, is largely helpless in face of grand social and cultural changes, the members of the denomination cling resolutely to the assumption that their fortunes, for good or for ill, are within their own control. Their task, as a consequence, is to read the signs of the times and then position themselves—that is, adapt their internal cultural and structural forms—to take advantage of those signs.

In effect, the RCA has found itself in the midst of a marketing struggle. Its identity crisis revolves around the search for a descriptive handle which can be used to capture the essence of the denomination—to affirm those within it and to lure those who might be attracted to join. Accordingly, the denomination can be expected to continue to try various adaptive modes until it finds one which is perceived to reverse the membership trends—and thus lift the denomination out of the crisis mode. This adaptive response, at the core of the denominational type, may be too constrained by history and tradition to allow for complete "success" in the denomination's efforts.

Ironically, the membership trends of the RCA are likely to be reversed under only two conditions: (1) If the external social and ideological circumstances remain as they currently are (that is, if they remain as crisis-creators for mainline Protestantism), then the RCA will have to be significantly transformed in order to make the requisite membership gains. Under such a condition, the "new" RCA will be sharply different from the "old" RCA, thereby divesting itself of any traditional underpinnings. (2) On the other hand, if the external circumstances change dramatically (such as might happen if increasing numbers of upper-middle class, baby-boom-era adults begin to approximate traditional families, complete with marriages, children, community commitments, and religious affiliations), then the RCA can expect to grow, as long as it does nothing to change its current structures or ideologies (Luidens and Nemeth 1988).

If the first scenario of growth is to be accomplished, however, it will be "over the dead bodies" of the RCA's most stalwart members, those who make up the heart of this denomination's aging membership. The RCA will be so transformed that its long-term adherents will find themselves on totally unfamiliar social and cultural turf. Growth will be in the face of their alienation. On the other hand, if the second scenario is to come about, it will require that the denomination ascend to a level of self-analysis that rises above its internal circumstances and acknowledges the larger social and cultural tides which swirl around it. This analysis may necessitate uncharacteristic sectarian behavior, for members might have to agree that they would not accept further change, even if their numbers continued to fall.

Unfortunately for the future of mainline Protestantism, and for denominations as culture preservers and transmitters, neither course is pleasant: the first route requires submerging the historic denominational traditions in the face of ongoing demands, and the latter course is inimical to a denomination.

NOTES

1. The first catechetical question in the Heidelberg Catechism, together with its answer, are as follows:

> Q: What is your only comfort in life and in death?
> A: That I am not my own, but belong—body and soul, in life and in death—to my faithful Savior, Jesus Christ.

2. At the same time that the Task Force on RCA Identity was deliberating its assignment, Luidens and Nemeth were planning to replicate Luidens's 1976 study. The happy coincidence was not without strain. There was some misgiving on the part of Task Force advisors about the advisability of doing both sociological and programmatic research in the same study. Despite these initial reservations, the relationship has been a symbiotic one.

The results of the research have been widely disseminated and studied by members of the denomination, but their very sociological nature make them difficult to use for program planning. Indeed, while the descriptive data have been absorbed as part of the denomination's "story," the implications of the data (that there are wider social patterns involved in the denomination's fate) have not been fully comprehended or adopted as the above analysis indicates. In any case, the involvement of sociologists as analysts and consultants has introduced a peculiarly modern note into the life and planning of the RCA.

3. The discussion of the 1976 and 1986 studies draws from 1978 and 1987 *Church Herald* articles (see References) as well as from unpublished data. The 1976 study of the RCA was conducted by Luidens. Questionnaires were sent to samples of more than 1,800 lay and 600 clergy members; lay members responded at a 43 percent rate, while 60 percent of the clergy filled out the questionnaires. For the 1986 Luidens and Nemeth study, 44 percent of 4,000 lay questionnaires and 66 percent of the 950 clergy mailings were returned in useable form.

REFERENCES

Berger, Peter L.
    1986   "American Religion: Conservative Upsurge, Liberal Prospects." In *Liberal Protestantism: Realities and Possibilities,* edited by Robert S. Michaelsen and Wade Clark Roof, 19–36. New York: Pilgrim Press.
Brouwer, Arie
    1977   *Reformed Church Roots.* New York: Reformed Church Press.
Brownson, William
    1985   "President's Report to General Synod: A Pilgrim Journey." *Church Herald* 42, no.12 (June 28): 13–18.
Droog, Chester
    1985   "The RCA: Growing in the Southwest." *Church Herald* 42, no. 11 (June 7): 8–12.
    1987   "Lessons from RCA Church Growth." *Church Herald* 44, no. 9 (May1): 16–17.
Fries, Paul
    1988   "Confession Is Identity." *Perspectives: A Journal of Reformed Thought* 3, no. 6 (June): 4–7.
Greeley, Andrew M.
    1972   *The Denominational Society.* Glenview, Ill.: Scott, Foresman & Co.
Hageman, Howard
    1986   "Immigrant Faith." *Church Herald* 43, no. 16 (September 19): 23.
    1989   "Dutch Wasn't Much in His Ministry." *Church Herald* 46, no. 3 (March): 23, 51.
Hoff, Marvin
    1985   *Structures for Mission.* Grand Rapids: Wm. B. Eerdmans Publishing Co.

Hoge, Dean R.
   1979   "National Contextual Factors Influencing Church Trends."
          In *Understanding Church Growth and Decline,* edited by
          Dean R. Hoge and David A. Roozen 94–122. New York:
          Pilgrim Press.
Hoge, Dean R., and David A. Roozen (eds.)
   1979a *Understanding Church Growth and Decline.* New York:
          Pilgrim Press.
   1979b "Some Sociological Conclusions About Church Trends." In
          Understanding Church Growth and Decline, edited by
          Dean R. Hoge and David A. Roozen, 315–333. New York:
          Pilgrim Press.
Hutchinson, William R.
   1986   "Past Imperfect: History and the Prospect for Liberalism."
          In *Liberal Protestantism: Realities and Possibilities,* edited
          by Robert S. Michaelsen and Wade Clark Roof, 65–82.
          New York: Pilgrim Press.
Jappinga, Jeffrey
   1988   "The $25 Million Vote." *Church Herald* 45, no.13 (July
          22): 11.
Johnson, Benton
   1986   "Winning Lost Sheep: A Recovery Course for Liberal
          Protestantism." In *Liberal Protestantism: Realities and
          Possibilities,* edited by Robert S. Michaelsen and Wade
          Clark Roof, 220–234. New York: Pilgrim Press.
Kalkwarf, Leonard
   1984   "Meeting at the Summit: President's Report to General
          Synod."*Church Herald* 41, no. 12 (June 15): 14–21.
Kelly, Dean
   1977   *Why Conservative Churches Are Growing.* Updated Edi-
          tion. New York: Harper & Row.
Kennedy, Earl William
   1988   "Letter to the Editor: Resist COCU." *Church Herald* 45, no.
          4 (February 19): 24.
Koopman, LeRoy
   1987   "Ten Marks of a Growing Church." *Church Herald* 44, no.
          9 (May 1): 12–15.
Leestma, Kenneth
   1986   "President's Report to General Synod: God Provides Where
          God Leads." *Church Herald* 42, no. 12 (June 27): 9–13.
Luidens, Donald A.
   1978a "Portrait of a Denomination." *Church Herald* 35, no. 18
          (September 8): 4–5.

1978b "Variety in Action and Belief." *Church Herald* 35, no. 19 (September 22): 10–12.

Luidens, Donald A., and Roger J. Nemeth

1987a "Reformed Church in America Identity: The Struggle for Unity Amid Diversity." Unpublished report presented to the RCA Task Force on Denominational Identity. (January): 20 pages.

1987b "The RCA Today: Painting a Portrait." *Church Herald* 44, no. 3 (February 6): 5–7.

1987c "The RCA Today: Beliefs and Behaviors." *Church Herald* 44, no. 4 (February 20): 12–14.

1987d "The RCA Today: Unity Amid Diversity." *Church Herald* 44, no. 6 (March 20): 11–14.

1987e "'Public' and 'Private' Protestantism Reconsidered: Introducing the 'Loyalists.'" *Journal for the Scientific Study of Religion* 26, no. 4 (December): 450–464.

1988   "The RCA and the Baby Boomers." *Church Herald* 45, no. 3 (February 5):10–13.

Marty, Martin E.

1970   *Righteous Empire: The Protestant Experience in America.* New York: Dial Press.

Michaelsen, Robert C., and Wade Clark Roof (eds.)

1986   *Liberal Protestantism: Realities and Possibilities.* New York: Pilgrim Press.

Mulder, Edwin

1984   "People Who Belong." *Church Herald* 41, no.17 (October): 6–7.

1986   "Seeking the Denomination's Identity." *Church Herald* 43, no. 1 (January 3): 12–13.

1988   Statement to Senate Foreign Relations Committee's Sub-Committee on Africa. Black Caucus RCA Newsletter 16, no. 5 (May 31):1–4.

1989   "There Are Stories to Be Told." *Church Herald* 46, no. 3 (March): 6.

Neevel, James

1987   "Christian Adventurers: President's Report to General Synod." *Church Herald* 44, no.12 (June 19): 8–14.

Niebuhr, H. Richard

1968   *The Social Sources of Denominationalism.* Cleveland and New York: World Publishing Company.

Reformed Church in America (RCA)

1988a *Book of Church Order, The Reformed Church in America.* 1988 edition. New York: Reformed Church Press.

n.d.   Minutes of the General Synod (GS) of the Reformed Church in America. Acts and Proceedings.

1988b "Reformed Church News: RCA Pursues Identity." *Church Herald* 45, no. 4 (February 19): 25.

Roozen, David A.
1979   "The Efficacy of Demographic Theories of Religious Change: Protestant Church Attendance, 1952–1968." In *Understanding Church Growth and Decline,* edited by Dean R. Hoge and David A. Roozen, 123–143. New York: Pilgrim Press.

Stapert, John
1988   "Reformed Glue." *Church Herald* 45, no. 2 (January 15): 4–5.

Westphal, Merold
1988   "Editorial: Identity and Belonging." *Perspectives: A Journal of Reformed Thought* 3, no. 6 (June): 3.

Wise, Robert
1988 "President's Report to General Synod: A Vision of Fullness." *Church Herald* 45, no. 12 (June 24): 12–19.

Wuthnow, Robert
1976   "Recent Pattern of Secularization: A Problem of Generations? *American Sociological Review* 41 (October): 850–867.

1988 *The Restructuring of American Religion.* Princeton, N.J.: Princeton University Press.

13

History as a Bearer
of Denominational Identity:
Methodism as a Case Study

Russell E. Richey

So it was that Methodism, with a system more mobile than that of any other church, with a message more democratic and inclusive, and with a ministry which was part and parcel of the life of the frontier, came over the mountains with the great rush of emigration, and took over the spiritual command of the commonwealths which men were hewing from the wilderness—a command which it maintains to this day (Luccock and Hutchinson 1926, 270).

Well into the twentieth century, Methodists held several propositions about themselves and their role in society. The propositions, still implicit in the above, are (1) Methodism was/is a child of providence; (2) providence made Methodism and the Methodist connection (i.e. polity) especially for American society; (3) Methodist response to and stewardship of that providential calling had benefited both church and nation, blessing the church with great numbers and the nation with troops of true believers in the U.S. system; (4) the purposes and ultimately the health—spiritual and physical—of Methodism are bound up in this linked mission of nation and church.[1]

Thereby, Methodists conflated the kingdom of God with the nation, construed denominational purposes in terms of those of a Christian United States, and in making the church subservient to Christian nationalism, intimately tied the former's health to the latter's; or so the propositional or ideational evidence suggests.[2] Important and further implications follow, namely that the demise of the Christian United States, the event that Robert Handy called "the second disestablishment" (1984, 159–184), shattered this mission that the church had taken as its own, that no comparable purpose of such energizing dimensions has arisen to take its place, and that the present malaise of mainline denominations in general and Methodism in particular is rooted in this loss of purpose. This analysis locates mainline Protestantism's problem not in present agendas so much as in a faulty earlier purpose. The wedding of denomination to nation, however stimulating it proved to denominational growth, built a fundamental flaw into denominational foundations. When the promises of the First Amendment and the realities of pluralism exposed the fault line in the Christian United States, Methodists, and perhaps also other mainline denominations, suffered structural damage.

These propositions about denominational identity were widely shared. The Methodist pattern then is but an instance of a common story. So also their use in denominational history—the ideological use of history was not unique. The premium Methodists put on a historical fabrication of identity allows us to use them as a case study, an illustration of how in the quest for a Christian United States, Methodists (and other Protestants) wrought fundamental changes in their purpose and perhaps in their character.

Why History?

At a recent General Conference of the United Methodist Church, individuals and groups concerned to redirect the denomination and to return it to full health chose a curious vehicle for renewal. They recast the history of Methodism. They rewrote the "doctrinal history" in the *Book of Discipline* (1988, 40–60) so as to accent those aspects of Methodism which, if reemphasized, would rejuvenate the church. The strategy was an obvious and well-tried maneuver for Methodists.

From the earliest *Disciplines* down to the most recent, Methodists have begun these formal, official self-presentations with a history of the movement. The first word that Methodists have wanted to say about themselves was a historical one. For the most part, these historical statements functioned to state and hence transmit the received Methodist identity. For long periods they would be carried over intact from one *Discipline* to another. But at points of significant change, as for instance in the 1939 and 1968 unions and in 1988, Methodists struggled to reshape the history to warrant the change (Richey 1989).

That orientation to historical self-understanding—a preoccupation derived from Wesley's practice and precept—reflected itself at a variety

of points in the life of Methodism. It both stimulated and derived suste-
nance from the common Pietist passion for recounting individual and
corporate religious experience; it "authorized" the production of endless
histories of the movement, from competent surveys of the whole denomination to quite amateurish local and conference narratives; it expressed itself in myriad studies of Methodist "worthies," the bearers of
the Methodist standard; it found expression in the papers and magazines, particularly the *Christian Advocates,* which reserved disproportionate space for the stories of Methodism; and it led them to require
and feature history, particularly the history of the movement, in the
preparation of Methodist ministers.[3] History served to express and even
to shape Methodist identity and to transmit denominational culture.

This chapter will explore shifts in Methodist identity or culture, or
both, as they are reflected in Methodist histories and proceed then to
reflect about history as bearer and transmitter of denominational identity. The historians treated are Jesse Lee, Nathan Bangs, Abel Stevens,
Matthew Simpson, James M. Buckley, the team of Halford E. Luccock and Paul Hutchinson, William Warren Sweet and Frederick Norwood, each of whom, in some sense, spoke authoritatively for and
about the movement.[4]

Providence

In 1784, the newly organized Methodist Episcopal Church provided itself a constitution or quasi constitution, adapting one elaborated by the British Methodists under John Wesley, a document
known as *The Large Minutes.* The first U.S. *Discipline,* that of 1785,
followed the question-and-answer format of the British *Minutes* and
its sequence of questions (Tigert 1908, 532–602). The 1787 revision
of the first *Discipline* put a new order to the questions and a historical
frame on the constitution. The first asked, "What was the Rise of
Methodism so called in Europe?" the second, "What was the Rise of
Methodism, so called in America?" the third, "What may we reasonably believe to be God's design in raising up the Preachers called
Methodists?" The answers briefly sketched the founding acts and
founding impulses of the movement. The third answer deserves citation; it has been recited down to the present as a statement of
Methodist purpose; it retained the substance of Wesley's answer but
now nuanced to fit the new land. God's design was:

> To reform the Continent, and spread scriptural Holiness over these
> Lands. As a Proof hereof, we have seen in the Course of fifteen Years
> a great and glorious Work of God, from New York through the Jersies,

> Pennsylvania, Delaware, Maryland, Virginia, North and South Carolina, even to Georgia. (*Discipline* 1787:3–4)

These early Methodists had a vivid sense of their country. Even as a small band of itinerants, they had traveled its roads, forded its waters, crossed its mountains, and penetrated its wilderness. This litany of states evoked their direct experience with the outpouring of God's spirit upon its landscape. The first proposition—that Methodism was providentially given and directed—expressed their very being. They found it axiomatic. Methodism was providential. The other propositions they would have found strange and discordant.

Jesse Lee shared the Christmas Conference's vision of Methodism as an impulse of providence. Indeed, we may fittingly view his *Short History* as a fleshed out version of this initial providential reading of the Methodist saga. Jesse Lee missed the 1784 constitutional gathering known as the Christmas Conference because he was some five hundred miles distant when he received the summoning word. He apparently nursed some grudges for being so belatedly informed (Thrift 1823, 67 ff.). He began traveling with Bishop Francis Asbury immediately thereafter, came to exercise considerable influence in the Methodist leadership, blazed the way for Methodism into New England, and served as chaplain to Congress. Lee missed election to the episcopacy by a narrow margin. And, of course, he could serve Methodism in only one place at a time. However, with due allowance for his frailty and finitude, we can say that Lee left his imprint on early Methodism. Sweet termed him "the most popular of all the early Methodist preachers" (Sweet 1953, 176). He both made and wrote Methodist history, as would be the case for Methodist historians throughout the nineteenth century. His *A Short History of the Methodists* (1810) was the first serious effort to sketch the contours of the movement. Lee's construction of the movement did not, however, please all. The General Conference actually rejected the volume; Asbury thought it inadequate on his own role (Bangs 1860, II:322–323; Asbury 1958, II:640–641; Lee 1848: 466). Certainly part of the reason for controversy derived from the very personal vision that Lee provided.

Lee told the Methodist story as he saw it. He had seen enough of the whole that we get from him a remarkably well-rounded account. Subsequent historians have consistently drawn upon the documents he reproduced, the events for which he provides the most complete eyewitness account, the very vividness of his portrayal. The revivals he experienced and led; the conferences he attended and whose legislation he could then report firsthand; the penetration of "enemy" Puritan territory that he led; the general explosion of the movement over the new nation that his extensive travels documented; the advent of the camp meetings which he witnessed—these personal involvements in the development of Methodism gave shape and vigor to his narrative. Doubtless that very personal, idiosyncratic perspective offended his colleagues who could not help but feel that Lee had implicitly claimed for his own what belonged to them all. Yet in another sense, this very personal vision did stand for them, in the way that the historical preface to the *Discipline* stood for them and for their conception of their history, a history of immediate and perceivable instances of God at work. For that is how providence functioned for Lee. He offered no grand theory of providence at work. Nor did he explicitly claim the Methodist connectional system to be providential. Rather, he pointed concretely and specifically to the presence of God among the Methodists. For instance, of a 1788 Baltimore conference Lee reported:

> During the time of the conference, we were highly favoured of the Lord, and souls were awakened and converted. On Sunday, the 14th of September at 3 o'clock in the afternoon, Mr. Asbury preached in Mr. Otterbein's church; and the people were generally solemn and much affected; he then asked another preacher to pray and conclude: and whilst he was praying, an awful power was felt among the people. Some of them cried out aloud. . . . and in a little time there was such a noise among them, that many of the christian people were measurably frightened, and as there was no opportunity for them to escape at the door, many of them went out at the windows, hastening to their homes. The noise had alarmed hundreds of people who were not at the meeting, and they came running to see what was the matter, till the house was crowded, and surrounded with a wondering multitude. In a short time some of the mourners lost the use of their limbs, and lay helpless on the floor, or in the arms of their friends. It was not long before some of them were converted. . . . This day of the Lord's power will never be forgotten by many who were present. (Lee 1810, 139–140)

Lee claimed Methodism to be providential by showing providence at work.

In similar fashion, he showed Methodism's attachment to the United States. He did not wrap the nation around the church. Indeed, along with most early Methodists, Lee followed the pattern of affection-but-alienation that R. Laurence Moore (Moore 1986) shows to be so typically American—a kind of sectarian distancing of self and movement from nation and society at the same time that full loyalty is proclaimed and efforts are even made to convert and transform the society. Lee did make unmistakable his own patriotism and that of Methodism in the United States. He criticized, for instance, the "head preachers. . . all from Europe," some of whom "were imprudent too freely against the proceedings of the Americans" during the Revolution (Lee 1810, 60). He presented the Methodists' own march to independence from Wesley and the British connection as an appropriate development.[5] But Lee did not providentially connect church and nation. Lee thought providence to be rather specifically focused on the work of salvation. Connections of general providence and the fate of nations therein did not interest him.

Providential Design

By 1792, according to Bangs, Methodism had brought "about one-twentieth part of the entire population" under its influence, some 198,000 attenders out of a population of four million. Such growth, "in the short space of thirty-six years," and despite the advantages enjoyed by other denominations, required explanation. Bangs found himself forced "to the conclusion that their prosperity must be attributed to the blessing of God upon their labors." He continued, "We therefore say again, that its forward course can be accounted for only by supposing the sanction of the most high God upon their labors (1860 I: 356–359). At the end of the fourth volume, having covered Methodist church history to 1840, Bangs rendered the same judgment—that the "success and influence of Methodism" had "one true original cause, namely, the divine agency" (IV: 436). Concern with Methodist numerical success led Bangs from the providential charac ter of Methodism toward a second proposition—the providential connection of church and nation.

Like Lee, Bangs was an actor in that which he interpreted. He also made his mark on New England Methodism, particularly as Methodism's foremost spokesperson for Arminianism and against Calvinism. *Nathan Bangs: Apologist for American Methodism* one interpreter called him (Hermann 1973). That he was and more. Bangs labored effectively, not only to speak on Methodism's behalf to "its cultured critics" and the religious establishment but also to remake Methodism so that it might claim its place in the U.S. religious establishment. Bangs played that reshaping role from his office as book agent, effectively the executive secretary and the teaching office of the church. What he wrought might be termed the revolution of the 1820s, the wholesale restructuring of Methodism: creating missionary, Sunday school and tract societies; launching and editing a major weekly, *The Christian Advocate,* and a journal of theological opinion, *The Methodist Magazine;* establishing educational institutions; and founding the course of study, Methodism's four-year national reading course in preparation for ministry (Pilkington 1968, 169–219). Bangs sought to make the church an effective force in national life.

When sketching the hand of providence in this Methodism on which he also had laid a hand, Bangs could not be content with simple and discrete providential instances, though he, like Lee, eagerly pronounced events both large and small to be of divine agency. No, Bangs saw that the divine agency extended also to Methodism as a system and its operation. And Bangs also recognized a providential connection between church and nation. To that end, he chose to begin the saga of Methodism in the United States not with Wesley but with Columbus and proceeded to an examination of "the civil and religious state of the people at the time Methodism was introduced" (I: 11). This was a self-consciously interpretive gesture on the part of a man with quite keen historical skills.[6] Bangs saw "benignant Providence" in the peopling of the land, the development of civil and religious liberties, the respect accorded scripture and the Sabbath, the widespread profession of Christianity, the influence of revivals, the atmosphere of toleration—in short, the creation of a situation "highly favorable" to Methodist "evangelical labors" (I: 22, 26, 30). Methodism's introduction into the land also showed providential design (I:46).

At various points, his providential treatment of the United States was evocative of the Christian republicanism now recognized to be so significant in national and mainstream Protestant life (Noll 1988, 35–43; Shalhope 1982). And yet Bangs did not really offer a providential reading of the nation as such; he did not provide a public theology. Bangs took interest in providence and Methodism, not providence and the United States. Or perhaps we should say, he was interested in the public roles that providence exercised through Methodism. For instance, in measuring the impact of camp meetings and the revivals at the turn of the nineteenth century, Bangs spent some five pages on the "most happy and conservative influence upon our national character," "the conservative influence which vital, experimental, and practical Christianity exerts upon individual character, upon social and civil communities, and of course upon states and empires" (II: 146–148). Though Methodism exercised a politically and socially constructive influence, Bangs insisted that it was purely religious in its intent and operation:

> The influence therefore, which she has exerted upon the civil destinies of the republic, has been altogether of an indirect and collateral character, growing out of that moral and religious stamp with which she strives to mark and distinguish all her children. (II: 150)

Bangs could be quite effusive about the political consequences of such indirection. For instance, he thought the national operation of Methodism functioned to cement the union together and to counter the politically divisive force of state governments.[7] But such notes were quite occasional. Bangs focused upon Methodism. It was the providential character of Methodism, not the providential character of the nation, that interested him. Incidentally, providence worked through Methodism and Methodists for the good of the nation. However, church not state remained providence's aim.

Providential Connection

Bangs had tentatively connected church and nation. Abel Stevens drew the providential connection of church and nation firmly. Firmness was characteristic of Stevens, who held a series of important editorships in the tumultuous middle decades of the nineteenth century: *Zion's Herald,* the New England Methodist paper, then *The National Magazine,* and finally *The Christian Advocate.* Through those immensely influential posts, he spoke a moderating, even conservative word to the church, prizing its unity at the cost, some thought, of its witness.

Stevens entitled the first chapter in his *Compendious History,* "Methodism—Its Special Adaptations to the New World" (1868: 17).[8] The chapter and the volume begins with a striking, but imaginary event of 1757.[9] That year, John Wesley, "inventer" of Methodism, and James Watt, inventor of the steam engine, found themselves at Glasgow University. Stevens imagined a chance meeting of these two in the university quadrangle, the inventors of the two machines for the conquest of the New World. "Watt and Wesley might well then have struck hands and bid each other godspeed at Glasgow in 1757: they were co-workers for the destinies of the new world" (19). Watt had produced the engine for the conquest of the New World physically, Wesley that for the conquest of the New World morally.

> Methodism, with its "lay ministry," and "itinerancy," could alone afford the ministrations of religion to the overflowing populations; it was to lay the moral foundations of many of the great states of the West.
>
> A religious system, energetic, migratory, "itinerant," extempore, like the population itself, must arise; or demoralization, if not barbarism, must overflow the continent. Methodism entered the great arena at the emergent moment. . . . It was to become at last the dominant popular faith of the country, with its standard planted in every city, town, and almost every village of the land.
>
> Methodism thus seems to have been providentially designed more

for the new world than for the old. The coincidence of its history with
that of the United States does indeed seem providential. (18–24)

Between and among these affirmations, Stevens sketched the contours
of the Methodist system, a machine the elements of which seemed
providentially suited to this country's mission. Providence had indeed
blessed the United States with Methodism and Methodism with the
United States. Stevens saw in this new order that vision that Augus-
tine had sought, "the city of God" (176).

Though enunciating the third of the Methodist axioms, Stevens like
his predecessors stopped short of a full-fledged public theology. Indeed, his affirmations about America touched land as much as state,
the New World as much as the new republic. Watt and the steam engine, Wesley and the Methodist engine imaged a providential ordering
of the United States as a whole—land, culture, peoples, society, economy. Providence extended its rule over this country preeminently
through Methodism.

A Conjoint Mission

Matthew Simpson focused Methodist attention more sharply on the
United States and so articulated the fourth Methodist axiom. This was a
fitting service for a man whose life was dedicated to politics, in church
and in state.[10] College professor and president, like Bangs and Stevens
an editor (*Western Christian Advocate*), delegate to General Conferences, then in 1852 a bishop, Simpson employed pen, platform, and
power on behalf of antislavery and union. Confidant to Lincoln, Simpson used his access to Washington inner circles to gain appointments
for Methodists and control over Methodist Episcopal Church, South,
buildings in territory that fell to Union troops. When Lincoln fell, Simpson preached funeral sermons in Washington and at grave-side (Crooks,
1891, 397–403). Simpson's history, unlike that of Stevens (1868), reflected Methodism's Civil War experience, an involvement which had
wedded the Methodist Episcopal Church to the nation.[11]

Simpson's *A Hundred Years of Methodism* appeared in observance
of the U.S. centennial. Appropriately, he began with a survey of national accomplishments, the contributions of the United States to the
world. Then he flashed back to Wesley and British Methodism. It was
U.S. origins, however, not these "foreign" ones that stamped Methodism in this country. "The rise of Methodism," he insisted, "was coeval
with the Revolutionary spirit" (Simpson 1876, 41). Both during the
Revolution and thereafter Methodism suffered because of its British
connection.

> It is somewhat singular that nearly all the troubles and secessions in Methodism have arisen from trying to introduce English ideas and plans into our American Church, or, in other words, from trying to condense our immense continent into the area of a little island. Every agitation has begun by extolling British usages and depreciating American.
>
> In every instance, however, the Church has adhered to American ideas, and has resolutely refused to change her policy at such dictation. (68)

An "American" Methodist church—that was Simpson's topic. It was this dynamic and rapidly growing church, the success story of Methodism in the United States, that Simpson sought to explain. Like his predecessors, Simpson gloried in statistics, in growth.[12] He found "reasons of the remarkable increase of the Methodist Church" in three superior features of its life, "the superiority of its doctrines, the efficiency of its organization, . . . the piety, earnestness, and activity of its ministers and members" (345). Such claims had led his predecessors almost inevitably and immediately to invocation of providence. Simpson made much less of providence than they. When he did speak of it, the nation rather than the church came into focus. Of the war and emancipation, for instance, he said:

> We can now . . . see the guidance of an all-wise Providence, which overruled the counsels of men in the midst of all these commotions. It was the Divine will that slavery should be destroyed. With determined purpose, step by step, the South moved forward in the separation, first, of the Christian Churches, and then in the attempted division of the States, to that fearful war which resulted in the emancipation of the slaves. No instance in history more clearly shows how God has made "the wrath of men to praise him, and the remainder of wrath" he has restrained. (156–157)

Here was Mead's "nation with the soul of a church," (Mead 1975) or perhaps even a church whose soul was the nation. Simpson held all four Methodist propositions. However, the accent fell on the last, the providentially linked mission of church and state. In the spirit of the centennial, Simpson spoke with confidence of this conjoint mission, mindful to be sure of the great cost with which it had been vindicated, but even so, especially so, with a providential, even millennial confidence (209).

Whither Providence?

James M. Buckley struck no such ebullient note. Rather he concluded his assessment and essayed twentieth-century prospects by pondering the question, "Has Methodism lost to a dangerous degree its original vital impulse?" and by invoking John Wesley's worry that "the people called Methodists" might become "a dead sect, having the form of religion without the power." Buckley obviously shared Wesley's worry:

> The founders of Methodism had no enterprises that were not distinctly subordinate to the conversion of men and their spiritual training. Now its enterprises are many and complex, often pervaded by a distinctly secular element, which contends constantly with the spiritual. (Buckley 1900, 685–686)

Jeremiahs in this country have typically prophesied doom to achieve revival and reform (Bercovitch 1978). Buckley was no exception. He called for the renewal of the Methodist spirit and identified the requisite resources (685–686). And yet his rendering of Methodism's history, if carefully read, suggested grounds for pessimism. In Buckley's account, providence had seemingly loosed its grasp on church and on nation.

This judgment about Buckley and providence is extremely ironical, for in some ways Buckley was more self-conscious about providence than his predecessors. He shared that concern with the general editor of the important series in which his volume figured, the American Church History Series.[13] Philip Schaff designed the series to display the professional prowess of The American Society of Church History. For the Methodist volume he chose its preeminent spokesperson. Buckley played a major and a conservative role in its national affairs. He was delegate to General Conferences from 1872 to 1912. He edited the official and national paper of the denomination, *The Christian Advocate,* from 1880 to 1912. On several important matters, most notably women's role in the church, he stood steadfast and effectively against change. The past and history seemed, at times, to be his forte.

At two important places Buckley stopped to consider the relation of the human and the divine. He devoted chapter 8 to the work of the spirit in early Methodists, specifically considering Benjamin Abbott, John Dickins, Caleb B. Pedicord, Thomas Ware, Jesse Lee, and the responses they elicited. Noting that Methodists construed the highly demonstrative behavior evident in conversions and revivals "to be direct results of the power of the Holy Spirit, and manifest proofs of His presence and approval of the work" (217), Buckley inventoried other explanations—naturalistic and particularly psychological explanations—of the phenomena. He conceded that "various factors were involved in producing the effects of Methodist preaching and methods," but that among them "was the might of the Holy Spirit"(220). And the effects when carefully essayed and correlated with scripture, Buckley affirmed, establish "the divine origin of the movement as conclusive as that furnished when holy men of old spake not of themselves, but as they were moved by the Holy Ghost" (220–221). So Buckley wrenched a providential meaning out of Methodism.

Buckley returned to the theme of providence at the end of his narrative, to worry again over Methodism's prospects. For the most part, however, Buckley remained uninterested in the providences underlying Methodist development and content to explain Methodism in naturalistic fashion. Quite a few of the stray exceptions—statements that God's hand can be found in Methodist affairs—occur in passages that he cited (170–171, 173, 176–177, 179, 203, 205, 248). Buckley offered us, then, a curious irony. He insisted vehemently on the importance of providence but proved curiously unwilling or unable to point to its presence and activity. Providence had assumed doctrinal rather than historiographical force for him.

One could hardly assert that his reluctance to advance providential claims for Methodism typified the turn-of-the-century movement. Methodists generally continued the triumphalism so clearly evidenced in Scudder and Simpson.[14] Nor was he typical in his neglect of similar triumphal claims for the nation. Historians after him would entertain the four propositions and search for appropriate meaning thereof. Nevertheless, Buckley had taken Methodism around an important turn. He had effectively given up the affirmation that lent plausibility to the four propositions—that providence could be seen at work in Methodism.

This was a fitting posture to be taken in a volume that would stand cover-to-cover with histories of other American denominations. Buckley may well have felt constrained by the series. He certainly forewarned the reader that he could not, in good conscience, advance · providential claims:

> It is not within the province of the historian of his own communion, and in part of his own time, to pronounce judgment upon the motives of those professing 'like precious faith.' (xviii)

At most, he should aspire to present the developments so fairly that the reader would draw that conclusion (xviii).

The reader intent on drawing the four propositional conclusions would have received help from Buckley only on the first. He did present Methodism as "the lengthened shadow" of Wesley and construe Wesley as "The Man of Providence" (1–2, 40–72). As we have seen, a limited providential meaning for Methodism can be detected. The other claims apparently did not interest him. He chose, in fact, an interesting place to begin the Methodist story, one wholly out of keeping with the other three propositions. He started with Henry VIII and the English Reformation. From such national and denominational humility interesting consequences flowed.

Humpty Dumpty

In spirit and assertions, Luccock and Hutchinson's *The Story of Methodism* resembled Simpson's work, not Buckley's.[15] They chatted with the reader about Methodism; provided upbeat, celebrative, and personal estimates of its power and significance; claimed providential guidance for the movement with a frequency that recalls Lee or Bangs. Yet, their very easiness with the providential claims is striking, perhaps worrisome. Do Buckley's critical premises haunt their breezy confidence? Do their assertions betray superficiality or conviction?[16]

Halford E. Luccock held pastorates, served as editorial secretary of the Board of Foreign Missions (1918–24), and taught in several theological schools, including a long stint as professor of preaching at Yale (1928–53). A prolific writer, from 1924 till his death he contributed to *The Christian Century.* The *Century's* managing editor from 1924 to 1947 and its editor from 1947 to 1956 was Paul Hutchinson. Hutchinson shared Luccock's literary and missionary activities and concerns. He, too, was prolific. Their common journalistic bent is evident in this popular account of Methodism.[17]

Evident also is the premise they shared, namely, that the twentieth would be "The Christian Century." They confidently traced the parallel development of nation and church. One early chapter, entitled "A Tale of Two Villages," examined two English towns "which gave to the English-speaking world the most transforming spiritual forces of the seventeenth and eighteenth centuries" (Luccock and Hutchinson 1926, 28). Scrooby launched the Pilgrims; Epworth was home to Wesley. "From the first, in truth if not in actual chronicle, the Mayflower set sail to plant a new world. From the second, John Wesley went out to save an old one" (34).

Once they had Methodism firmly planted on these shores, they returned to the parallels of church and nation. In "Methodism in the New Republic," for instance, they implicitly compared Asbury and Washington and explicitly compared James O'Kelly and Patrick Henry (213–217). They dwelt on Methodism's popular, even democratic, character and celebrated its pioneer and frontier spirit (217–300). The genius of the movement, in fact, is its spirit of adventure, its willingness to experiment, its pragmatism. They did not invoke Frederick Jackson Turner explicitly but found their own term for the frontier spirit, Methodism's "irregularity" (333–334, 494–495), typified by the camp meeting (264). They found that spirit of adventure also in missions, to which they devoted considerable attention, making their volume in some respects a study of world Methodism. But again and again, they returned to Methodism and the nation. In the late nineteenth century, nation and church were paralleled on seven particulars—the application of polity, spirit, and organization to new conditions; elaboration of national organization; extensive building; the closing of the frontier; an increase in democracy, foreign affairs, and Negro education (440–442). They also paralleled the international perspectives of nation and church in the period after the First World War (486–487). And of course, they took great interest in the causes that riveted the church's attention on the nation—the Civil War, Reconstruction, temperance, the social gospel, and world war.

Such challenges evoked the Methodist spirit of adventure and irregularity. Luccock and Hutchinson end the volume on that positive note, hopeful that Methodism will in the future draw upon that experimental spirit and reach out to the world (494–495). That note concluded a thoughtful discussion of problems—modern developments, post–World War I developments—that tested Methodism. They listed ecumenism, peace, technological-industrial matters, race. They also examined the great Centenary financial campaign that sought to address such challenges by transforming wartime religious mobilization into peacetime enterprise. Methodism initially pegged the campaign at one hundred million dollars. Luccock and Hutchinson entered their skepticism about the campaign, deftly but clearly. Their comments bear citation, for they point to the overreaching that Handy analyzes as constitutive of Protestantism's "second disestablishment" (Handy 1984, 161–164).

> That the Centenary was not all permanent advance will be admitted. There was, it is probable, too much use of war psychology. . . . Moreover, the Centenary did, by certain of its promotional methods, tend to make shoddy thinkers believe that the task of building the kingdom of God is simply a task of perfecting a high-pressure organization of churches and ministers for the raising of certain definitely ascertainable sums of money. In these, and perhaps some other ways, an atmosphere of false excitement and achievement was created, which could not be kept up. Gradually this promotional fever evaporated. With its passing there were left certain problems of adjustment which have perplexed many leaders, and many whom the church had commissioned for work in various difficult fields. The solution of these problems is a matter of time and hard thinking. When the readjustments are completed, the permanent benefit which has grown out of the Centenary will be clear (Luccock and Hutchinson 1926, 487–488).

The hard-thinking that followed—neo-orthodoxy—saw ironies where liberals had claimed providences, perceived an immoral nation where the Centenary had glimpsed the kingdom, recognized cultural en- slavement in visions of a "Christian Century." In Luccock and Hutchinson we find the now liberal Protestant establishment facing the implausibility of its premises. Methodism's four propositions come to rest on "irregularity" not providence, a sandy "human" foun- dation where Methodists had once found rock.

Professional Not Providential Estimates

Luccock and Hutchinson wrote in a historical idiom that Lee and Bangs would have understood. Sweet (1953 [1933]) and Norwood (1974) simply did not.[18] The "second disestablishment" rendered the privileged, providential reading of American history impolitic and im- plausible. So for Methodists, the four propositions no longer guide historical analysis. Or perhaps it would be more accurate to say, those dogmas have now recast themselves as historical generalizations.

Sweet found difficulty in claiming Methodism providential, but in his second chapter, he treated "The Message of Wesley to His Time." That, once "providential," fit of movement and age could be diag- nosed. "Methodism arose out of two great urges: the first was the reli- gious experience of John Wesley; the second was the vast spiritual destitution of eighteenth-century England" (Sweet 1953, 27). So the first proposition found objective form.

The second proposition, the relation of Methodism to U.S. society, consumed Sweet. However, he found the relation to hinge not on providence but on Frederick Jackson Turner's frontier thesis.

> The greatest accomplishment of America has been the conquest of the continent. . . . the most significant single factor in the history of the United States has been the Western movement of population, and the churches which devised the best methods for following the population as it pushed westward were the ones destined to become the great American churches. (143)

A series of chapter titles charted that destiny:

Organizes for a Great Task
Invades New England
Crosses the Alleghenies
The Circuit Rider Keeps Pace with the Westward March
Shares in the Missionary Enterprise
Begins her Educational Task

Conquest defines destiny. Methodism charted its destiny in the nineteenth century through conquest of the frontier (the conquest really of the entire country), the missionary impulse to take the continent.

Stewardship of its missionary calling constituted the reason for Methodism's success, as the largest Protestant denomination. Sweet rendered that third proposition also in objective or human rather than providential terms. Why did Methodism succeed? Sweet insisted that the Methodist Episcopal Church "possessed, or developed, the best technique for following and ministering to a moving and restless population" (143). What were factors in that technique? These included itinerancy, a centralized appointive power, circuits, short appointments, few repreached sermons, "zealous, energetic ministry," lay leadership, Arminian theology, a populist episcopacy, ample religious literature, and an "emphasis upon singing" (143–153).

Sweet's version of the fourth proposition followed readily. Sweet conceived of Methodism as the prototypical church in the United States. He understood Methodism in terms of U.S. society and U.S. society in terms of Methodism.[19]

> As the title of this book implies, the history of American Methodism is here considered as a phase of American history, and it is assumed that it can best be understood in relation to the history of the American people. (8)

So the church found itself caught in society's web, captive to U.S. developments. Wealth was one.

> But such changes as were taking place in American Methodism were inevitable, for the church could not stand apart from the social, educational, and economic changes which were taking place in the nation. In the very nature of the case Methodists were bound to become economically prosperous. (336)

And "the most serious problem faced by American Methodism as a whole at this time was its rapidly increasing wealth" (336).

In this and a variety of ways, Sweet transformed Methodist belief about itself into historical axioms. As such, they could be tested by his graduate students at the University of Chicago. Sweet's intentions were laudable and widely shared by church historians. Church history would be a historical science, a species of history, a respectable university discipline. Sweet wanted U.S. historians as colleagues. As president of the American Society of Church History and mentor to several generations of church historians, Sweet played a major role in secularizing and professionalizing the discipline. He gave such a reading to Methodist history.

Sweet taught at the University of Chicago from 1927 to 1946. For two years thereafter, from 1946 to 1948, he plied his craft at Garrett Theological Seminary. Soon after Sweet's departure, in 1952 to be precise, Frederick Norwood assumed that Garrett position, which he held until his recent retirement. Norwood achieved what Sweet intended, the execution of a Methodist history fully respectful of "secular" historical canons. From its appearance, his *Story of American Methodism* (1974) enjoyed preeminence as the text of choice in the course required of United Methodist seminarians. Had these theologs known about and gone searching for the Methodist propositions, they would have found them, but in such a subtle and historiographically nuanced form as to be scarcely recognizable. Norwood dealt self-consciously and explicitly with these motifs that have been so important to Methodists. He did so in responsible interpretive fashion. A few citations provide some sense of his handling of Methodism's propositions:

[1] Methodism began as a revival, and its history has been marked repeatedly by continuing revivals. From this point of view the denominational story is part of a constant theme in the history of Christianity in all times and places—continuing reformation. Inevitably, it seems, the church must go through such a process, as strong institutions languish and traditions ossify. The history of Methodism consistently demonstrates this theme. (15)

[2] American Methodists, and to a lesser extent United Brethren and Evangelicals, were caught up in the heady surge of the westward movement. A couple of generations of historical scholars have attempted to disparage the hoary Turner thesis on the westward movement as the determinative factor in American history. But all they have been able to accomplish is to qualify it as one factor playing a part with others. For Methodism this surge west determined at least the size and influence of the growing institution, and to some extent its quality and spirit. (16)

[3] [The Wesleyan or Methodist working theology] was so successfully peddled that it became a characteristic mark of American Christians of all kinds. The question remains to be discussed, whether this development was peculiarly Methodist or just plain American. Even Calvinism . . . was deeply affected. . . .

Methodism became in many ways the most American of the churches. Not only in its inception but throughout its development it was most in tune with the American song. (17)

[4] Does this mean that America was Methodized or that Methodism was Americanized? Probably some of both. . . . [Methodism's various developments] all point to a close and continuing love affair, for better or worse, between the Methodist Church and the United States. Who was the dominant partner?

The process of Americanizing and Methodizing brought on a tension which might be judged as the overriding theme of Methodist history in America. (17)

Here Methodism's four propositions found scholarly expression.

Why Methodism?

It would be uncharitable to lay at the feet of Sweet and Norwood a transformation that most church historians, including the present writer, presume and one that the whole denomination effected. The "second disestablishment," in fact, enveloped all mainline denominations. It would be more appropriate to see Sweet and Norwood as mirrors, as their predecessors were mirrors, reflecting the church's self-understanding to church members. We should underscore, however, the importance of this historical reflection, this historical estimate of Methodist identity. As we noted above, Methodists have consistently turned to history when called upon to say who they were, to state purposes, to define themselves. History looms first in the *Discipline.* And these secular versions of the Methodist propositions now render United Methodism's understanding of itself and its belief. In the 1988 *Discipline's* "Historical Statement" (7–15), Methodism's propositions survive, as in Sweet and Norwood, only as historical axioms. Methodists continue to turn to their history for self-understanding. They find a narrative from which providence has departed. In this sense the making of church history into a historical rather than a theological science has interesting consequences for the church. For it means that theological claims that once came readily to Methodist lips now simply are not heard.

"What may we reasonably believe to be God's design in raising up the Preachers called Methodists?" Many now do not find that Wesleyan purpose appropriately rendered by the four propositions and a vision of a Christian America. Certainly those propositions and vision no longer shape Methodist histories or the *Discipline.* That particular constellation is not, however, the only appropriate statement of the Wesleyan purpose. Early Methodists and their first historian, Jesse Lee, claimed providence but did not find it expressed in nationalism or a national ideology. It may be time for Methodists once again to recognize that they may be about reforming the continent and spreading scriptural holiness over these lands without domesticating that purpose into a vision of a Christian United States.

NOTES

1. Methodism's nineteenth-century historians, as we shall see, gave these propositions expressive form. Scudder (1868) gave particularly striking renditions of these four notions. See pp. 270, 363 on (1), p. 521 on (2), p. 524 on (3), and p. 569 on (4).

2. This study works on the propositional level, that is, with what Methodists affirmed about themselves. Those affirmations are derived from Methodist histories. This chapter will endeavor to show how historians initially conceived Methodism's propositions, how they altered those propositions into the above form as nation and church changed, and how they struggled to make sense of the Methodist saga when the propositions no longer made sense. For reasons of control, the study will focus upon the Methodist Episcopal Church, its successor the Methodist Church and its successor the United Methodist Church. For the most part, the generalizations apply, but with important variations, to the experience of the Methodist Protestant Church; the Methodist Episcopal Church, South; the United Brethren in Christ and the Evangelical Association; as well as to members of the Wesleyan family of denominations not contributory to United Methodism.

3. The inclusion of Methodist history within the required reading in the training of Methodist ministers provides part of the rationale for taking history seriously as a statement of Methodist identity. That requirement also serves as an important criterion in this study in determining which histories to take seriously. Beginning in 1816, candidates for the ministry in the Methodist Episcopal Church followed a prescribed "course of study," a reading list initially elaborated and supervised on the regional "annual conference" level and eventually operated as a kind of national college. With the exception of Jesse Lee and James M. Buckley, whose histories claimed preeminence on other grounds, the individuals given attention here figured prominently in the course of study, thus constituting an important formative influence on successive generations of Methodist ministers. In most cases, the individual histories enjoyed a long life on the course. Abel Stevens' *History of the Methodist Episcopal Church* appeared on the course in 1864, 1868, 1880, 1896, 1890 and then again in 1932; his compressed version thereof, *A Compendious History of American Methodism* remained on from 1872 to 1908, with only a curious gap of 1900, when another of his works took its place. The historians and their histories will be treated in chronological order. Each historian provided the major statement about Methodist history in his own day. Lee wrote the first Methodist history and in many ways set the terms

for the genre. Buckley's effort appeared in the prestigious American Society of Church History series (Bowden 1971).

4. For the criteria of selection see the reference to the course of study in the prior note. This argument relies upon L. Dale Patterson's "The Ministerial Mind of American Methodism: The Course of Study for the Ministry of the Methodist Episcopal Church, the Methodist Episcopal Church, South and the Methodist Protestant Church, 1876–1920," (Ph.D. diss., Drew University, 1984), which carefully identifies the literature of the course and the years each item was used. The historians are, as a prior note indicates, representative of the Methodist Episcopal tradition.

5. That saga, and particularly the declaration of independence by a group of the "Southern" preachers through presbyterial ordination (thereby splitting the movement in this country), has been typically written from the Asbury side of the split, a side which sought to remain loyal to Wesley and not separate from him or the Church of England. Here as elsewhere Lee's handling of the story evidences his eagerness to show the American contours of the Methodist story. In so doing, however, he did not formally link church to nation.

6. Bangs prefaced this four-volume statement with a discussion of his sources. Among them, he acknowledged "Bancroft's 'History of the Colonization of the United States'" for his initial discussion. He defended his decision to make "Bishop Asbury the principal hero of the narrative" (I: 6). He also indicated his respect for Lee and dependence upon Lee's *History* (I: 7).

7. In addition to the direct influence which Christian principles were thus brought to exert on the heart and life, the itinerating mode of preaching had a tendency in the natural order of cause and effect, to cement the hearts of our citizens together in one great brotherhood. . . . What more calculated to soften these asperities [state and sectional rivalries], and to allay petty jealousies and animosities, than a Church bound together by one system of doctrine, under the government of the same discipline, accustomed to the same usages, and a ministry possessing a homogeneousness of character, aiming at one and the same end—the salvation of their fellow-men by means of the same gospel, preached and enforced by the same method—and these ministers continually interchanging from north to south, from east to west, everywhere striving to bring all men under the influence of the same 'bond of perfectness'? Did not these things tend to bind the great American family together by producing a sameness of character, feelings, and views? (II: 148–149)

Bangs noted that the church in its General Conference recognized that "a general itinerating superintendency [episcopacy] would "prevent local interests and jealousies from springing up, and tend most effectually to preserve that homogeneousness of character and reciprocity of brotherly feeling by which Methodism had been and should be ever distinguished" (III: 54–55).

This is a point which Donald Mathews has elaborated into a general theory concerning the second Awakening (1969) and C. C. Goen into a theory of the cause of the Civil War (1985).

8. The most frequent reference here will be to the condensed (608 pp.) of Stevens's versions—his *Compendious History*. This appeared on the Course of Study for the quadrenniums of 1872 to 1908, with the sole exception of 1900. That year his *Supplementary History of American Methodism* (New York: Eaton & Mains, 1899), which had just appeared, took its place. The course also featured Stevens's four-volume treatment of American Methodism (1864–67) in 1864, 1868, 1880, 1896, 1900, and again interestingly in 1932. His work covering the whole Wesleyan tradition, *History of the Religious Movement . . . Called Methodism* (1858–61), enjoyed the longest, most sustained tenure on the course, continuously from 1860 to 1928, with the sole exception of 1884. That ninety-two-year reign, 1860 to 1932 (when the work dropped off), attests the great influence enjoyed by Stevens.

9. Stevens's four-volume *History of the Methodist Episcopal Church* (1864–67) began with the same scene but lacks the chapter title. His *Religious Movement* (1858–61) gave only incidental attention to developments in the United States and so did not lend itself to this vignette. Stevens achieved the same point there, the providential fitting of Methodism for the United States, with different staging and assertion (1858–61 II: 434–437).

10. We have noticed above (n. 1), M. L. Scudder's enunciation of these axioms (1868). The viewpoints become a staple of Northern Methodist belief during and after the Civil War. Simpson's volume is the first history featuring such views that figured on the Course of Study. It did not displace Stevens but was put on a different segment of the course, the reading list for local preachers. It first appeared there in 1876 and remained for three more quadrennia (1876, 1880, 1884, 1888).

11. For an even more striking public theology, see Peck (1869: 2, 693, 707).

12. Compare Goss (1866, 159): "The moral influence of Methodism is at least commensurate with its numerical strength. In no department of Christian effort are Methodists behind their sister denominations." Such affirmations abound.

13. The editor was Philip Schaff, who argued strenuously that it was the church historian's office and responsibility to discern the activity of God in human affairs. Schaff was a major, perhaps the

major, figure in the emergence of the discipline of church history (Bowden 1971). The inclusion of Buckley's volume in his series gave it great prominence. It was certainly frequently reprinted or republished, twelve times according to Rowe (1975, II: 209–210). First published in 1896, Buckley's history went through six editions as a part of the ASCH series, the sixth appearing in 1907. Another version was reprinted in a third edition in 1909. The first edition was again reprinted in 1973. It is because of the importance of this series and of Buckley's inclusion in it, that we include Buckley in this study. His work apparently did not appear on the Course of Study.

14. See, for instance, a volume contemporaneous to Buckley's, Henry Wheeler's *One Thousand Questions and Answers Concerning the Methodist Episcopal Church* and especially questions 1 and 66 (1, 16).

15. Luccock and Hutchinson's *Story of Methodism* appeared on the Course of Study from 1932 through 1956. For all of those quadrennia except 1944, it was collateral reading. In 1944, it was required for admission on trial.

16. Illustrative, perhaps, is this statement concerning the crowds who heard Wesley: "Clearly the hand of God was in this, for here were myriads—the word is Wesley's own—of people who never darkened a church door brought to hear a word that was again proving its ancient power" (19). Or again, "Whether he realized it or not, John Wesley returned to his great task in England at the moment when the movement of world forces had marked that 'tight little island' for a spiritual shaking. . . . England was ringed round with revival. It was time something burst loose" (73).

Of the sending of missionaries to the United States: "It was a prophetic moment at which Boardman and Pilmoor sailed" (142). And, "Methodism did not spring to life in America without long years of preparation. There is always a background for spiritual marvels, even when it is least apparent" (172).

Of the events of 1784: "The ordinations of Methodism are entirely outside the mechanical realm. They derive their authority from the fact that their originator, John Wesley, was a man whose ministry was evidently approved of God. And if ever the time comes when the ordaining ministry of Methodism is not thus approved, it will be time to scrap the whole thing, and start again from another life with self-authenticating powers" (158).

A comparison of the shadows of two men on horseback, Napoleon Bonaparte on Europe and Francis Asbury on America: "It is still easy to trace in the affairs of the United States the influence of this single man, Francis Asbury—Methodism's man on horseback. God send us such another" (232)!

17. Their predecessors, even Lee, attempted to be scholarly according to the expectations of the day. Luccock and Hutchinson made no such effort. The volume footnoted only where cited material was protected by copyright. (See, for instance, their references to Ezra Squier Tipple's *Francis Asbury, The Prophet of the Long Road,* 236, 241, 242.) They also offered no bibliography.

18. Sweet's volume appeared on the Course of Study for the quadrennia beginning 1932, 1936, 1940, and 1944, for the first three as a requirement for admission on trial and for the last as collateral reading.

19. Sweet employed this, in a more generalized form, as his organizing principle in *Religion in the Development of American Culture* (1952).

REFERENCES

Asbury, Francis
   1958   *The Journal and Letters of Francis Asbury.* 3 vols. London: Epworth Press; Nashville: Abingdon Press.
Bangs, Nathan
   1837   *An Original Church of Christ.* New York: T. Mason and G. Lane.
   1860   *A History of The Methodist Episcopal Church.* 4 vols., 6th ed. New York: Carlton & Porter; 1st ed. 1838–1841.
Bercovitch, Sacvan
   1978   *The American Jeremiad.* Madison, Wis.: University of Wisconsin Press.
Bowden, Henry W.
   1971   *Church History in the Age of Science: Historiographical Patterns in the United States, 1876–1918.* Chapel Hill, N.C.: University of North Carolina Press.
Buckley, J. M.
   1900   *A History of Methodists in the United States,* 4th ed., American Church History Series. New York: Charles Scribner's Sons. [First published in 1896.]
Crooks, George R.
   1891   *The Life of Bishop Matthew Simpson.* New York: Harper & Brothers.
Discipline
   1787   *A Form of Discipline, for the Ministers, Preachers and Members of the Methodist Episcopal Church in America.* New York: W. Ross.

1988 *The Book of Discipline of the United Methodist Church.* Nashville: United Methodist Publishing House.

Goen, C. C.
1985 *Broken Churches, Broken Nation. Denominational Schisms and the Coming of the American Civil War.* Macon, Ga.: Mercer University Press.

Goss, C. C.
1866 *Statistical History of the First Century of American Methodism.* New York: Carlton & Porter.

Handy, Robert T.
1984 *A Christian America. Protestant Hopes and Historical Realities.* 2nd ed. New York: Oxford University Press.

Harmon, Nolan B.
1974 *The Encyclopedia of World Methodism.* 2 vols. Nashville: The United Methodist Publishing House.

Hermann, Richard E.
1973 "Nathan Bangs: Apologist for American Methodism." Ph.D. diss., Emory University, Atlanta.

Lee, Jesse
1810 *A Short History of the Methodists.* Baltimore: Magill and Clime. Facsimile ed. Rutland, Vt.: Academy Books, 1974.

Lee, Leroy M.
1848 *The Life and Times of The Rev. Jesse Lee.* Charleston, S.C.: John Early for The Methodist Episcopal Church, South.

Luccock, Halford E. and Paul Hutchinson
1926 *The Story of Methodism.* New York: Methodist Book Concern.

Mathews, Donald G.
1969 "The Second Great Awakening as an Organizing Process, 1780–1830." *American Quarterly* 21: 23–43. Also in *Religion in American History,* edited by John M. Mulder and John F. Wilson. Englewood Cliffs, N.J.: Prentice-Hall, 1978.

Mead, Sidney E.
1975 *The Nation with the Soul of a Church.* New York: Harper & Row.

Moore, R. Laurence
1986 *Religious Outsiders and the Making of Americans.* New York: Oxford University Press.

Noll, Mark A.
1988 *One Nation Under God?* San Francisco: Harper & Row.

Norwood, Frederick A.
1974 *The Story of American Methodism.* Nashville: Abingdon Press.

Norwood, Frederick A. (ed.)
   1982   *Sourcebook of American Methodism.* Nashville: Abingdon
          Press.
Peck, Jesse T.
   1869   *The History of The Great Republic, Considered from a
          Christian Standpoint.* New York: Broughton and Wyman.
Pilkington, James Penn
   1968   *The Methodist Publishing House: A History.* Vol. 1: Begin-
          nings to 1870. Nashville: Abingdon Press.
Richey, Russell E.
   1989   "History in the Discipline," *Quarterly Review* 10 (Winter
          1989): 3–20.
Richey, Russell E. and Kenneth E. Rowe
   1985   *Rethinking Methodist History.* Nashville: Kingswood Books.
Rowe, Kenneth E.
   1975   *Methodist Union Catalog: Pre-1976 Imprints.* Multivolume
          series, in process. Metuchen, N.J.: Scarecrow Press.
Scudder, M. L.
   1868   *American Methodism.* Hartford, Conn.: S.S. Scranton & Co.
Shalhope, Robert E.
   1982   "Republicanism and Early American Historiography."
          William and Mary Quarterly 39 (April): 334–356.
Simpson, Matthew
   1876   *A Hundred Years of Methodism.* New York: Nelson &
          Phillips.
Stevens, Abel
   1858–61 *The History of the Religious Movement of the Eighteenth
          Century Called Methodism.* 3 vols. New York: Philips &
          Hunt.
   1864–67 *A History of The Methodist Episcopal Church.* 4 vols.
          New York: Carlton & Porter.
   1868   *A Compendious History of American Methodism.* New
          York: Eaton & Mains, n.d. but 1867/68.
Sweet, William Warren
   1952   *Religion in the Development of American Culture,
          1765–1840.* New York: Charles Scribner's Sons.
   1953   *Methodism in American History.* Rev. ed. New York:
          Abingdon Press. [First published in 1933.]
Thrift, Minton
   1823   *Memoir of the Rev. Jesse Lee. With Extracts from his Jour-
          nals.* New York: published by N. Bangs and T. Mason for
          the Methodist Episcopal Church.

Tigert, Jno. J.
  1908   *A Constitutional History of American Episcopal Method-*
          ism. 3rd ed., rev. Nashville: Publishing House of the
          Methodist Episcopal Church, South.
Wheeler, Henry
  1898   *One Thousand Questions and Answers Concerning the*
          Methodist Episcopal Church. New York: Eaton & Mains.
Wilson, John F.
  1979   *Public Religion in American Culture.* Philadelphia: Temple
          University Press.

14

The Meanings of a Merger: Denominational Identity in the United Church of Christ

William M. Newman

Religious organizational mergers have become a reasonably common event on the U.S. religious scene. Between 1906 and 1969, there were twenty-seven organizational mergers within Protestantism in this country, and since then major unions within Lutheranism and among leading Presbyterian bodies have occurred as well. Of course, "merger" is a somewhat misleading term for describing many of these events. Since many Protestant groups have been created through national, ethnic, racial, and, of course, theological disputes, most twentieth-century mergers between these groups are better understood as reunions. The various chains of events in the formation of the United Methodist Church, the American Baptist Churches, U.S.A., the Presbyterian Church (U.S.A.), and the Evangelical Lutheran Church in America all illustrate the processes of reuniting.

Surely, there are cases where mergers are not reunions. However, most of these bring together what might be called distant family members. For example, when the Evangelical United Brethren (EUB) joined the Methodist Church in 1968, a history of Methodist-type polity and theology among the EUBs facilitated the event. Thus, while their formal names and geographic origins may be different, denominations like these are able to merge under the umbrella of shared theological traditions, polity systems, and historical self-understandings.

The 1957 merger between the Congregational Christian Churches (CC) and the Evangelical and Reformed Church (E&R) did not fit any of these patterns. This was a cross-denominational merger between two sizeable groups having entirely different historical and theological origins. Of course, even reunions require major organizational adjustments, and perhaps some rethinking of identities. But, for reuniting parties, the fundamental elements of identity formation—shared symbols, a shared past, and historic remembrance—are readily at hand. For such groups, the future is shaped not by the recent past, but by an idealized distant past, in which shared points of origin are located. For example, all Lutherans, be they Danish, Hungarian, German, or anything else, are theologically Lutheran, and trace their roots to the ninety-nine theses on the church door at Wittenberg.

What are the resources available for identity formation when a shared historical past is not available, when symbolic elements of traditions differ? This is the dilemma posed by the United Church of Christ (UCC) merger. Yet, this unique feature of the UCC merger creates its heuristic value as a case study. If the elements of symbolic unity may be discerned in this difficult test case, then the mechanisms of identity formation in all religious organizational mergers may be better understood.

To its membership, what does UCC affiliation mean? To answer this question requires embarking upon two excursions, one historical and the other empirical. We will first review briefly the historical identities of the two denominations that became the UCC in 1957. Second, we will examine some data collected recently in a national sample of UCC churches. These data focus directly upon the questions "What does it mean for this church to be part of the UCC?" and "Personally, what does it mean to be part of the UCC?"

Historical Background

New England Congregationalism grew from the English Separatist and Puritan movements that broke from the theological and organizational orthodoxy of the established Anglican Church in the 1600s. Its "gathered church" or "free church" polity arrived in the colonies with the Mayflower in 1620, and its followers rapidly established colleges and seminaries at Yale, Harvard, Dartmouth, Amherst, Oberlin, and Andover. Yet, a national organization only began to emerge in the early 1850s. In the 1870s, this new denominational structure expressed its concern for congregational autonomy by calling itself the Congregational Churches, not the Congregational Church. In spite of frequently being called "New England Congregationalism," this denomination was widely dispersed not only in New England but also in the Ohio valley and the upper midwestern states prior to its merger with the Christian Churches in 1929.

The Christian Church emerged from three diverse religious movements. First, during the late 1700s in North Carolina, a small group called Christians was formed through a schism within Methodism, in which church polity (Bishop's authority) was a key issue. Second, in Vermont in the early 1800s, the First Free Christian Church was shaped through dissent within the Baptist churches. Third, also in the early 1800s, a "Christian" church was formed by the reaction against Calvinist doctrines within Presbyterianism. These three movements became a denomination, the Christian Church, in 1820.

The 1929 merger creating the Congregational Christian Churches united two denominations that had been shaped by reactions against connectional polity systems in several different branches of Anglo-Protestantism. Theological openness and local autonomy were paramount historical themes for both the Congregationalists and the several constituent groups in the Christian Church with which they merged. In contrast, the Evangelical and Reformed Church represented not the religious traditions of the British Isles, but continental Protestantism, not congregational, but presbyterial church polity.

The Reformed Church in the United States was composed of German, Swiss, and Dutch immigrants, who first arrived in the Hudson valley prior to the American Revolution. While Reformed communities developed in Ohio, Maryland, Delaware, and Virginia, the largest settlements would be in Pennsylvania. Following the theologies of Calvin and Zwingli, these churches practiced a highly liturgical or creedal brand of Protestantism. The Reformed Church in the United States developed through a merging of various ethnic Reformed churches (the Reformed Church of Holland, the Reformed German Church, and later, the Magyar Synod). On the eve of its 1934 union with the Evangelical Synod of North America, the Reformed Church in the United States numbered just under 350,000 members, divided into six Synods (Eastern, Potomac, Pittsburgh, Ohio, Midwest, and Northwest).

The Evangelical Synod of North America was the youngest of the four religious communities that would eventually become involved in the UCC merger. Throughout the first half of the nineteenth century, repressive political and economic conditions in the Austrian Empire stimulated massive German immigration to the United States. The German Evangelical Church Society of the West was formed in 1840, and by the 1870s this moderate form of Lutheranism, now calling itself a "Synod," had established seminaries (Eden and Elmhurst) and a college (Elmhurst). By the 1920s the original seven districts had grown to twenty.

The 1934 merger between the Evangelical Synod of North America and the Reformed Church in the United States brought together continental Calvinist and Lutheran bodies into a single communion of just over eight hundred thousand members. Its membership was primarily Germanic, and its geographic center of gravity was in the states of Missouri, Pennsylvania, and Ohio. While this merger amalgamated presbyterial (Evangelical) and modified congregational (Reformed) forms of church polity, it did so in a presbyterial direction, and in the context of a creedal and confessional tradition (the Augsburg Confession and the Heidelberg Catechism).

The seeds of the UCC merger lie in the complex social and religious change patterns that emerged in the United States and elsewhere between the two world wars. By the 1920s, the general secularizing trend in U.S. culture had produced a religious "depression," as indicated by declining memberships and church school enrollment trends as well as financial problems. A flurry of merger proposals (Douglass 1937) were but one component in a series of ecumenical forays that included the creation of the Federal Council of Churches (later to become the National Council of Churches) as well as the "Life and Work" and "Faith and Order" movements. Discussions for the UCC merger began in 1938, and would survive both a World War and a prolonged legal battle in the courts of New York State (*Cadman* v. *Kenyon*, 1950, 1952, 1953). When the merger finally was enacted in 1957, it created a denomination of over two million adherents, situated in more than eight thousand local churches. Its strongest concentrations were in the Midwest, New England, and North Atlantic states, with Alaska the only state lacking UCC churches. The merger had created one of Protestantism's "big seven" ranking national organizations.

Out of Diversity

The story of the UCC has been told often by observers both within (Horton 1962, Douglass 1963, Gustafson 1963, Gunnemann 1977, Bass and Smith 1987) and outside the religious fold (Schmidt 1954, Peabody 1964, MacNair 1965, Newman 1970a, 1970b). All of these writers seem to agree that both the organizational and ideological impediments to this merger were formidable. My own view is close to that of Schroeder (1987), who identifies some half a dozen prominent features that divided the memberships of the two merging denominations. I mention these six factors here because they provide the context of diversity against which a new denominational identity would be forged.

First, the E&Rs consisted of first and second generation, primarily Germanic immigrants. In contrast, the CCs were one of several American denominations viewed as carriers of the culturally dominant WASP tradition. Second, as might be anticipated, the CC membership

ranked higher than the more recently arrived E&Rs on such socioeconomic status factors as educational attainment and income level.
Third, the social ecology of the two communions differed. The 1.4
million CC membership was most concentrated in New England and
the Upper Midwest. The E&Rs, numbering more than eight hundred
thousand claimed the state of Pennsylvania, the St. Louis area, and
parts of the Upper Midwest as home turf. Much of the membership
was dispersed throughout the Midwest, far West, and South. In other
words, the CCs were culturally dominant on much of their turf, while
it was likely that members of many E&R congregations were neither
ethnically nor denominationally the norm for their ecological setting.

A fourth set of differences revolve around theological factors. The
Evangelical and Reformed churches found a common ground in a
highly sacramental, confessional, and liturgical brand of Protestantism.
Historically, New England Congregationalism was identified with a
"gathered" not a liturgical understanding of the religious community.

These differences were, of course, most distinct in the realm of a fifth
factor, church polity. While the Reformed Church had devised a "modified congregational" polity prior to the merger with the Evangelicals,
both of these communions recognized connectional polity systems. Of
course, it was the historical lack of connectional polity in the CC tradition that became the focal issue in the lengthy court battle of *Cadman* v.
Kenyon (1950, 1952, 1953). Dissenting Congregational churches, most
of which would later remain outside the merged denomination, argued
that the congregational polity system provided no organizational mechanism nor theological justification for enacting such a merger.

Finally, Congregationalism was strongly identified with the nineteenth-century social gospel movement. The formation of the Congregational Christian "Council for Social Action" in 1934 reflected a
continuing involvement with social and theological liberalism. This
emphasis was not prominent among the E&R churches.

Given the many social and religious differences between the E&R
and CC constituencies, one reasonably might ask, why merge? Clearly,
when merger was first discussed during the 1930s, there was much in
the social and religious environment that supported the idea. The ecumenical movement, which drew some of its key players from both of
these denominations, surely was an essential ingredient. Between the
1930s and the 1950s, the ecumenical motive within U.S. Protestantism
softened greatly. However, among the national leaders of the E&R and
CC churches, a long history of conflict over this merger had solidified
the resolve on both sides of the issue. The decision in the *Cadman* v.
Kenyon case pointed to closure on an issue in which some church leaders had invested substantial parts of their careers.

As I have indicated more extensively elsewhere (Newman 1970a), the Basis of Union document, and subsequently the Constitution and Bylaws of the United Church of Christ, were designed to facilitate a merger in which little in traditional practice in local churches would change. This strategy of inclusiveness was both the genius and Achilles' heel of the merger. As Fukuyama (1987) has explained in organizational terms, the 1957 merger was only a paper event. It created a new supraorganizational governing entity, but left the day-to-day merging of people and organizations for the postmerger years. Organizationally, the merger only began to occur during the 1960s. Preexisting separate denominational structures were merged through a rather ad hoc, pragmatic, case-by-case process. If this was the genius of the merger in the view of its inventors, it was also the nightmare of the merger for those who lived through the painful tasks of actually reorganizing their church.

However, our concern here is with a slightly different issue. What did this strategy of merging denominations without, at first, changing them in any way, mean for identity formation?

Some Recent Data

Fortunately, some recently gathered information is available with which a preliminary answer to this question may be obtained. Each year the UCC Board for Homeland Ministries Research Office administers a "Soundings" project. Persons from the denomination's directors and corporate members, consisting of parish clergy and laypersons taking an active role in regional and national organizational affairs, serve as conveners of panel groups in local churches. Churches are selected by random sampling techniques in which those churches participating in the prior year's study are deleted from the sampling universe. This results each year in a random, stratified sample. The data examined here are based on 289 group discussions conducted during the 1985 Soundings project, in which group conveners were asked to summarize discussion themes on questionnaire-type worksheets.

Two questions discussed by these panel groups are of special interest here. "What does it mean for this church to be part of the UCC?" and "Personally, what does it mean to be part of the UCC?" Treating these two inquiries as one, the original researchers encountered fifty-four specific response categories to these questions. The researchers also attempted to identify some general categories or "overall impressions" of what membership in the UCC means. I turn first to the materials on overall impressions of UCC identity, which are provided in table 14–1. The table displays the eight general response categories by number of churches and as a percent of the total sample of 289. The percent of formerly CC and E&R churches is shown as well. There are 150 formerly CC and 103 formerly E&R ethnically white churches in the total sample. The remaining churches in the full sample represent other traditions, among them ethnically Asian and African American churches, as well as new congregations or community churches. Perhaps the most striking feature of table 14–1 is the lack of strong agreement among these lay groups about what UCC identity means. A plurality of 29 percent claim that UCC membership has no clear identity or meaning. Nearly equal numbers think the merged denomination has a positive and alternatively a negative image. The lack of an image ("nothing") appears to be more of concern among formerly Congregational Christian (34 percent) than Evangelical and Reformed (22 percent) churches. Accordingly, slightly more of the latter (28 percent) report a "positive" denominational image than do the formerly CC groups (22 percent). The overriding message of this table is that most of the 289 discussion groups did not render a clear, general characterization of what UCC membership means to church members some thirty years after the official merging of the several denominations.

TABLE 14–1*

Overall Impressions of UCC Identity

Response Category	(N)	%	%CC	%ER
Nothing	(66)	29	34	22
Positive	(73)	25	22	28
Image/awareness must be increased	(71)	25	26	24
Negative	(66)	23	22	25
Not informed enough about UCC	(49)	17	18	13
Confused with the Chs.of Christ	(39)	14	10	18
Ambivalent	(26)	9	12	3
UCC is a vague and remote thing	(17)	6	5	5

* Columns add to more than 100 percent of the 289 churches because the response categories were not mutually exclusive.

Given this general pattern, it is perhaps not surprising that when detailed discussions of UCC identity ensued there was an overabundance of specific responses (54 categories), few of which were shared in common by even half of the participating groups. Table 14–2 provides a rank ordering of the seven response categories out of the entire 54 that occurred in a third or more cases. The table shows the percent and number of cases for the entire sample of 289 local churches, as well as for subsamples of formerly Congregational Christian and Evangelical and Reformed churches.

TABLE 14–2

The Meaning of UCC Membership

Response Category	(N)	%	%CC	%ER
Local autonomy	(151)	52	54	51
Freedom of thought	(143)	50	46	52
Tolerance	(134)	46	49	50
Historic identity	(127)	44	44	45
Local church important	(123)	43	40	48
A wider mission	(110)	38	43	35
Networks of Conf. & Asso.	(102)	35	38	30

The four most frequently encountered categories reflect polity and theological issues that have long-standing meaning among these diverse churches and that permeated the years of merger discussion and negotiation. The remaining three categories point toward specifically organizational aspects of religious meaning. Moreover, the rank order of these response categories is exactly the same among formerly CC and E&R churches. That fact alone reflects a certain unanimity within the UCC about how identity issues are perceived and understood in local churches throughout the denomination. However, my own reading of the original questionnaire-type sheets from which these response categories were extracted, and in turn, from which these tables were constructed, indicates some subtle differences between CC and E&R churches within these response categories.

The themes of "local autonomy," "freedom of thought," and "tolerance" are hardly surprising given that the merger united theologically diverse communions, and that assurances were constantly given that merging did not mean change. However, formerly CC groups tended to articulate local autonomy as "self-rule," and, as one participant said, "not beholden to a higher structure." This notion that "we run ourselves" is, of course, a clear reflection of traditional congregational polity. In contrast, formerly E&R participants tended to discuss local autonomy in terms of "freedom to worship as we please" and "being comfortable with the service and worship." It must be remembered that the Evangelical and Reformed Church had a more liturgical style than the larger Congregational Christian denomination with which it merged. Thus, local autonomy, while a common understanding throughout the UCC, clearly has different connotations for the two communions that merged. For E&R members, local autonomy connotes not losing traditional liturgical forms of worship as a result of the merger. For the Congregational Christians it connotes preserving congregational polity.

The categories of freedom of thought and tolerance appear highly uniform throughout the data gathered in these churches. Such notions as "freedom through diversity," "respecting different opinions," and "being open to others" clearly reflect an awareness of the diversity (theological, ethnic, and regional) from which the fabric of the new denomination is knit.

The nub of the identity problem is clearly discernible in the category "historic identity." As might be expected, a majority of the formerly CC groups maintain that being a UCC church means "preserving our Congregational heritage," "honoring Congregational traditions," and that "we are still Congregationalists." Similarly, most E&R discussion groups claim that the UCC means "we are still an E&R church," "we have a strong E&R background here," and "holding to our E&R traditions is not a bad thing." The staying power of older premerger identities was underscored by those instances in which the "Christian Church" and the "German Reformed tradition" were mentioned. However, the fact that parishioners speak of "an E&R tradition" demonstrates the possibility for new identity formation. After all, prior to 1934, the Reformed and Evangelical denominations viewed themselves as quite different, one Lutheran and one Calvinistic, though both strongly Germanic. Obviously, all social differences and similarities are relative. In a smattering of churches, both formerly CC and E&R, people said that "church union is valuable," and that "UCC means a united witness of the four denominations." It is clear that identity change and formation are gradual processes that may be occurring in an uneven way across the UCC.

The last three categories, "local church," "a wider mission" and "networks," point to several different aspects of how people identify religiously in organizational contexts. The theme of religious localism, or the local character of Protestant churches, is a powerful one in these data. "I joined a local church not a denomination," "this local church means more than the UCC," "the local church is the important thing," and "people here think of this as St. [local name], not a UCC church," are typical expressions of this fact. The question of whether this degree of localism would be encountered in other denominations, especially those with connectional polity systems, is an empirically open issue. My own guess is that it varies between types of denominations, but that generally, localism is a very strong element within all American Protestant churches. As such, it is a potential impediment to denominational identification under the conditions of a national merger.

Nonetheless, it is also clear from these group discussions that participation in regional denominational organizations is an important source of the emerging denominational identity within the UCC. The response categories, "a wider mission" and "networks" reflect this. Participants spoke of Conferences and Associations providing "ties to other UCC churches," and "guidance and participation in a wider mission." That these organizational relationships would appear as sixth and seventh on a list of some fifty-four response categories is impressive. It demonstrates the old adage that participation breeds commitment. These data are potentially biased by the fact that the conveners of these panel discussions were clergy and laypersons who, unlike most, have involvements in Conferences and Associations as well as in national agencies of the UCC. Nevertheless, the data show the powerful identity formation potential of effective organizational programs. What these data say is that, for some persons, the UCC is its expression at the Conference and Association levels, and through mission activities beyond the local environment.

Some Conclusions

To gather clues about identity formation in the UCC, the information from group interviews in a stratified random sample of about 5 percent of UCC churches in 1985 has been examined. The findings encountered are both diverse and suggestive.

For the UCC members involved in these discussions, church membership is more local than denominational. Before other things, this is the particular church "I grew up in" or "that my kids were raised in." If people think in denominational terms, these are terms that reflect the somewhat special circumstances of different traditions merged into a new organizational context. Precisely because the UCC merger involved elements of undeniable diversity in theology, liturgy, historic meaning, and even styles of worship, today the emergent identity of the UCC is focused upon local control of such matters, freedom of religious choice, and tolerance for religious differences. Of course, these themes are entirely consistent with broader civic values in the United States. Unity through diversity, and freedom of religious thought and action are traditional American cultural themes. Therefore, it is not difficult to envision their becoming central identity themes in this unique amalgam of American denominations.

However, it must also be realized that religion is a highly salient element in the individual identity kit, and therefore older, established denominational identities are not easily discarded. Today, in the first or second generation of the merged denomination, old labels, among them E&R, Congregational Christian, German Reformed, and Christian Churches, still are meaningful. A diminishing of these denominational labels is contingent upon the succession of generations.

Additionally, middle-level denominational agencies, in this case Conferences and Associations, are meaningful points of contact between local churches and the national denomination. They are to some extent communicators of the meaning of denominational affiliation as well.

What do these data about the UCC suggest about identity formation in merged denominations generally? First, the emerging meaning of the UCC appears to be constructed from rather pragmatic elements. In this sense, if religious organizational mergers can "work," they do so not on the basis of the ideals of those who invent them but on the daily experiences of those who must live with the results of such mergers. While the ecumenical movement was a powerful motivational force for the church leaders who designed the merger, it was not a prominent theme in these group interviews. In fact, only 10 percent of the interviewers encountered "ecumenical" as a response to the question "What does it mean for this church to be part of the UCC?" Second, the formation of denominational identity within the UCC appears to be a gradual process that flows from real-life organizational activities and involvements and that allows placing old religious meanings in the context of practically situated and culturally palatable symbols. Thus, even where elements of theological and organizational homogeneity are present, one should search for the results of these mergers in the long term.

Simply stated, the UCC merger, like most others, is an event manufactured in a top-down manner. National-level denominational leaders orchestrated a new national church organization. Twenty years later, the national leaders and persons in the local pews are still asking, what does this mean? If it means a new religious identity must be articulated—and I think that it does—the new religious identity must encompass the old ones. That is exactly what is happening in the UCC. People do not simply shed one identity for another. Rather, they wrap one in another. Thus, an E&R parishioner says "UCC is our way of being good German Reformed church members." I cannot imagine anyone employed at the national level of the UCC responding that way to the question What does UCC mean?

One implication of this is that organizational mergers may be invented top down, but identities flow from the bottom up. In other words, for most people religious identities are primarily local in nature. To the extent that national denominational labels (UCC) become involved, they are additive not substitutive. A new identity symbol may emerge more readily if the local church, old denomination, and new denomination were all Presbyterian, Lutheran, Baptist, or whatever. Yet, I am convinced that some persons in the new Presbyterian Church (U.S.A.) will say, "Of course, you know we are really Southern Presbyterians," and some in the Evangelical Lutheran Church in America will remind folks that "this parish is really Danish Lutheran." Finally, the UCC merger suggests that with time, the folding of identity labels, one into the other, becomes less cumbersome, easier to manage, a more familiar labeling of reality. Next time I drive past a "First Congregational Church of the United Church of Christ" or a "Saint James Evangelical and Reformed Church of the United Church of Christ," I will understand them as religious communities in the process of becoming.

REFERENCES

Bass, Dorothy C., and Kenneth B. Smith (eds.)
   1987 *The United Church of Christ: Studies in Identity and Polity.* Chicago: Exploration Press.
Cadman v. *Kenyon* (Court Decisions)
   1950 Opinion and Judgment of the Supreme Court of the State of New York for the County of Queens, 197, Misc. 124, 95 N.Y.S., 2nd 133.
   1952 Opinions of the Appellate Division of the Supreme Court, Second Judicial Department, State of New York, 279, App. Div. 1074, 11 N.Y.S. 2nd 808.
   1953 Decision of the Court of Appeals, State of New York, 306 N.Y. 116 NE 2nd 481, 128 N.Y.S. 2nd.
Douglass, H. Paul
   1937 *A Decade of Objective Church Unity, 1926–1936.* New York: Harper & Brothers.
Douglass, Truman
   1963 "From a Member of the United Church of Christ." In *The Challenge to Reunion,* edited by Robert McAfee Brown and David Scott. New York: McGraw-Hill Book Co.
Fukuyama, Yoshio
   1987 "Non-theological Aspects of Church Union: The Institutional Formation of the United Church of Christ." In *The United Church of Christ: Studies in Identity and Polity,* edited by Dorothy C. Bass and Kenneth B.Smith, 35–48. Chicago: Exploration Press.
Gunnemann, Louis H.
   1977 *The Shaping of the United Church of Christ: An Essay in the History of Christianity.* Philadelphia: United Church Press/Pilgrim Press.

Gustafson, James
  1963 "The United Church of Christ in America: Actualizing a Church Union." In *Institutionalism and Church Unity,* edited by Nils Ehrenstrom and Walter G. Muelder. New York: Association Press.
Horton, Douglas
  1962 *The United Church of Christ.* New York: Thomas Nelson & Sons.
MacNair, Wilner E.
  1965 "Meaning and Conflict in the Formation of the United Church of Christ." Ph.D. diss., University of Wisconsin, Madison.
Newman, William M.
  1970a "The United Church of Christ Merger: A Sociological Analysis of Ideas, Organizations, and Social Change." Ph.D. diss., New York: Graduate Faculty of the New School for Social Research.
  1970b "The United Church of Christ Merger: A Case Study in Organizational Structure, Policy, and Ideology." In *Social Problems and Social Policy,* edited by Deborah I. Offenbacher and Constance Poster, 137–145. New York: Appleton-Century-Crofts.
Peabody, Alan B.
  1964 "A Study of the Controversy in Congregationalism over the Merger with the Evangelical and Reformed Church." Ph.D. diss., Syracuse University, Syracuse, N.Y.
Schmidt, Calvin
  1954 "A Study of the Efforts to Unite the Congregational Christian Churches and the Evangelical and Reformed Church." Master's thesis, Princeton Theological Seminary, Princeton, N.J.
Schroeder, W. Widick
  1987 "The United Church of Christ: The Quest for Denominational Identity and the Limits of Pluralism." In *The United Church of Christ: Studies in Identity and Polity,* edited by Dorothy C. Bass and Kenneth B. Smith, 15–33. Chicago: Exploration Press.

15

Presbyterian Culture:
Views from "the Edge"

Louis B. Weeks

Do mainstream Protestant denominations any longer possess and foster particular cultures? Are discernible, distinctive identities present? Do executives in a denomination share common goals, stories, or common values which legitimate their work? Do they possess special sensibilities and worldviews, seek to transmit prized traditions as they endeavor to lead people? How can identities and cultures be understood in this time of complexity and change?

When I conducted the interviews on which this chapter is based, I used the terms "culture" and "identity" interchangeably. I have, however, come to distinguish them. I now use the word "culture" to mean a web of significance spun among interactive people, involving an intricate system of sending and receiving meaning within a human community (Geertz 1973). I use "identity" to mean the explicit recognition of what may be an implicit ethos and a tacit culture, an intentional legitimator of a culture. Though I still find usage overlapping, I can see that people may share a culture and not recognize elements in it; but they will name portions and elements of a common identity.

Obviously congregations, as distinct from denominations, have cultures and distinctive identities, which analysts may observe and describe (Roozen et al. 1984; Hopewell 1987). This is true of Presbyterian congregations. While their culture reflects their denominational heritage, as Roberts and others have shown in this volume, congregational cultures also reflect their particular setting and story—

a persistent localism, as Swatos (1981) put it. Beyond the congregational level, denominations, too, have a shared culture that gives expression to a distinctive identity. At times, denominations have used explicit sanctions such as heresy trials, acts of discipline, and such practices as "shunning" to reinforce orthodoxy and orthopraxy (Richey 1977). But do denominational cultures and identities remain distinctive today in the face of the privatization and new voluntarism that mark U.S. mainline Protestantism (Roof and McKinney 1987; Wuthnow 1988)?

Asked to examine one denomination, the Presbyterian Church (U.S.A.), and to discern responses by denominational executives to these questions, I reviewed the literature on Presbyterianism and listened to a number of leaders to gain insights about this denomination with the expectation that the learnings would be helpful and more widely applicable. I asked twenty-two denominational executives if they believe there is a "Presbyterian culture" and identity that they experience in relation to their work. I also consulted more than fifty others knowledgeable on the topic.

In this chapter, I report first on the background of the Presbyterian Church (U.S.A.), then on Presbyterian leadership and their perceptions about identity, some major subcultures that I discerned, and finally how the leaders understand the transmission of denominational culture within the Presbyterian Church.

Presbyterian Church History

A Presbyterian "denomination" arose with colonial aspirations for independence during the 1700s (Weeks 1988b). With no colonies of their own where Presbyterianism was the established religion, Presbyterians nevertheless exercised disproportionate power in the formation of the United States of America (Hood 1968). When the first Presbyterian General Assembly took place in 1788, a discernible, distinctive culture already existed as an amalgam of several streams of international Reformed Christianity, especially English Puritanism and Scots Confessionalism (Trinterud 1949).

Presbyterian culture centered theologically upon the pertinence of both testaments of scripture for Christian living, literate teaching and preaching in families and congregations, the Westminster Confession, shared leadership among ministers and elders, and strict Sabbath observance. A Presbyterian denomination began in a time of Protestant hegemony, and Presbyterians influenced U.S. culture and politics as did Congregationalists, Methodists, Episcopalians, and Baptists (Leith 1977; Marty 1986). Differences over the education of ministers and varying beliefs on the nature of divine will led to one schism, and the power of the "peculiar institution" of slavery, among other tensions, led to another (Weeks 1983b). All the while various other Protestant denominations arose in the U.S. environment, drawing at least in part upon Presbyterian constituencies. The development of significant regional "dialects" of Presbyterianism took place during the nineteenth and early twentieth century (Thompson 1963), reflecting the impact of localism.

Although Presbyterian cultures varied considerably according to region, class, ethnicity, and location vis-à-vis urban industrial life, a discernible, overarching Presbyterian culture still persisted through the 1920s and 1930s. African American Presbyterians, for example, reared in literate families, attended Presbyterian schools and imbibed the emphases listed above. Others who joined black Presbyterian churches noted the reliance upon scripture, literacy, familial expectations regarding Sabbath, and order in Presbyterian worship and work. Characteristically middle-class, black Presbyterians formed a kind of "elite" among African Americans, somewhat similar to the way that white Presbyterians formed something of an "elite" within the dominant white culture (Wilmore 1983). Equally, other expressions of a central culture remained evident and noteworthy in the denomination (Niebuhr 1929).

As did other mainstream Protestants, Presbyterians formed a comparatively porous culture in the United States from the very beginning. They sought to include others within the hegemony, naturally sharing status with Congregationalists and Episcopalians but also extending some partnership to others—first to Methodists and Baptists, and later to Disciples, Lutherans, and even to Catholics—usually before adherents of those streams of Christian faith returned the sentiments, at least institutionally. Presbyterians typically have been supportive of the social contexts in which they have existed rather than reacting against them, and U.S. Presbyterians followed that pattern. As a possible exception, in what was generally an anti-intellectual society, Presbyterianism offered a "countercultural" alternative (Rudolph 1963; Miller 1985). Typically, however, Presbyterians helped to maintain and strengthen existing social institutions rather than attempting to create alternatives such as parochial schools or other distinctive Presbyterian institutions. This meant their identity remained extremely complex. Rather than protecting or supporting Presbyterian particularity, Presbyterians would identify with the government and support public schools, libraries, and hospitals for all people regardless of denomination. Those in the Presbyterian culture might condescend toward others from positions of power, but they would not usually struggle to preserve a Presbyterian culture that was over against "the world" (Weeks 1983c). Imperialistic? Perhaps. But Presbyterians seldom engaged in narrow sectarianism.

Presbyterians have typically initiated and supported ecumenical endeavors and perceived of the world in ecumenical terms. In this country, Presbyterians participated in comity arrangements with other churches, helped start the Federal and National Councils of Churches, overtured for the beginning of the Consultation on Church Union, and in thousands of grass-roots efforts sought community ministries and pan-Christian work and worship.

The twentieth century has seen denominational merger among the Presbyterians, with the major Presbyterian Church in the U.S.A. (PCUSA) uniting first with the Cumberland Presbyterian Church (1906–1910), then with the United Presbyterian Church in North America (UPCNA) (1956) to form the United Presbyterian Church in the U.S.A. (UPCUSA). After turning down union with the PCUSA and the UPCNA in the 1950s, the Presbyterian Church U.S. offered to unite with the Reformed Church in America which declined, and then united with the UPCUSA in 1983 to form the Presbyterian Church (U.S.A.), referred to hereafter as PC(USA).

Cataclysms of the twentieth century deeply affected Protestant hegemony, and Presbyterians certainly reaped the consequences of the "disestablishment" that mainline Protestants suffered. As the two Presbyterian bodies united in 1983 to form the PC(USA), they had to "celebrate" a decline in membership unparalleled in their history. More seriously, Presbyterians by all accounts have suffered an identity crisis of some sort. Space does not permit a cataloging of symptoms, but a major study reveals startling changes (Coalter, Mulder, Weeks 1990). A complex governing pattern for the new denomination was instituted in 1986.

Against this background, a decision was made in 1987 to move the headquarters of the denomination from its previous centers in New York City and Atlanta to the "heartland" of America. Louisville, Kentucky, was chosen after considerable debate (Weeks 1988a). In the summer of 1988, most offices moved to Louisville, although the pension fund offices remained in Philadelphia, and the Presbyterian Foundation moved to Jeffersonville, Indiana.

Presbyterian Leadership

Deeply impressed with the human propensity to abuse power, and trying to follow both Old and New Testament admonitions in determining governmental structures, Presbyterians have developed a series of representative governing bodies or "church courts" to lead the people. Presbyterians elected lay elders to join ordained ministers in representing them in local church sessions (governing boards) and regional presbyteries. Initially, sessions, and more recently presbyteries, elected representatives to comprise synods (larger regional bodies). Presbyteries also elect representatives to a general assembly, an annual national gathering for the entire denomination's government.

Governing bodies elect moderators who run the meetings and also appoint standing and ad hoc committees, and the General Assembly elects stated clerks, who keep the minutes and assist in court-related responsibilities. In the PC(USA), the General Assembly elects most members of a General Assembly Council that oversees the offices of the denomination.

Certain areas of jurisdiction are prescribed for each court, and certain rulings might be appealed upward. Final authority lies with the General Assembly in most matters. Presbyterians maintain this system, which has evolved from colonial times and is similar in nature to most other connectional, Reformed bodies, through a *Book of Order,* an elaborate set of rules for governance. The system became vastly more complex as Presbyterian denominations in the United States began to employ people for specific tasks during the late nineteenth century. As business, government, education, and other U.S. enterprises developed management systems—tightly structured, hierarchically arranged, and task-oriented—so too did the Presbyterian bodies at all levels (Chandler 1977; Trachtenberg 1982).

The growing corporate structure of the Presbyterian Church brought leadership anomalies similar in nature to those encountered in other free church denominations. As Harrison has shown for American Baptists (1959), much authority and power moved from elected to selected leaders. Governing bodies approved selection of administrators,[1] but committees typically have nominated them. Many other Presbyterian leaders, such as seminary presidents, faculty members, and special envoys and delegates are primarily selected by committees rather than elected by the governing bodies. Since the Presbyterian system outstripped in complexity the governmental apparatus of most other denominations—not to mention the organization of most business, educational, and governmental institutions—the mix of responsibility and authority also became even more complicated for elected and selected leaders as they sought to relate experience elsewhere to their work in the church. Such anomalies paled, however, in the face of initial successes with bureaucratization. Mission activity, both domestic and foreign, educational endeavors, youth ministries, women's and men's organizations, camps and conference efforts, new church development, and new work in social amelioration all flourished during the first two decades of the twentieth century.

In the PCUSA, later in the UPCUSA, strong leaders served as stated clerks and as heads of some portions of the denominational enterprise. In that stream also, but especially in the PCUS, pastors of larger congregations also served as leaders for the denomination, making (or at least strongly influencing) decisions, and providing a personal embodiment of Presbyterian values and webs of meaning. The presence of leaders such as John A. Mackay, John Coventry Smith, and Eugene Carson Blake in the PCUSA and then the UPCUSA, and John Anderson and T. Watson Street in the PCUS, also mitigated the effects of the complicated system. Those interviewed mentioned powerful, earlier leaders among both denominational streams.

Though less evident initially in the PCUS, the more recent emphasis on inclusivity and representation did not initially diminish this strong leadership. Women and members of racial-ethnic minorities within the denomination's leadership also exercised great denominational persuasion in the years following World War II. One director, however, said that as late as 1960 in the PCUS, "If the right twenty white men in the PCUS favored something, it stood a really good chance of taking place."

In an effort to be more sensitive to local initiatives and less "top down" in decision making, the new PC(USA) has adopted a "Structural Design for Mission." Sessions form the center of the structure, with concentric governing bodies surrounding them. That puts General Assembly personnel on the "edge" of the design, supporting other bodies rather than towering above them (hence the subtitle of this chapter: "Views from 'the Edge'"). An elected body of sixty-seven comprises the General Assembly Council (GAC), which oversees the work of the executives, some of whom also sit on the GAC with voice but no vote.[2] Each of the ministry units also has a committee for oversight and decision making, an arrangement that makes for confusion in lines of authority and accountability. Further, the *Book of Order* requires careful attention to the composition of most committees by categories of race, gender, age, and region. Caucuses representing various groups within the PC(USA) also lobby for representation and a share in decision making of some thirty-six hundred committees.

Presbyterians have consistently attended to matters of balance, wanting to share decision making equally between ministers and elders (known historically as "teaching elders" and "ruling elders").

A Presbyterian Culture

When I asked denominational executives whether a Presbyterian culture exists, the resounding response was affirmative. According to almost all, that culture bears at least six attributes. Some named additional characteristics of Presbyterianism as either part of the culture or of the denomination's legitimating identity.

First, almost everyone agreed that Presbyterian culture pays close attention to the "Word," because it values both Christian faith and scripture. Second, it is also "wordy," paying careful honor to education, literate discourse, debate on matters of expression, good grammar, and multiple copies of everything. Third, it values orderly processes in general, the *Book of Order* in particular, and regularly asks about checks and balances on human or church power. Fourth, Presbyterian culture relates faith to life, both personal faith and some sense of corporate faith, and seeks some transformation of society in the name of God. Fifth, it sits uneasily with vast wealth and ostentation. Finally, Presbyterian culture bears elitist tendencies, if not downright participation in gross forms of elitism.

A significant minority of leaders also spoke of Presbyterian inclusivity as a cultural attribute (though only one used the word "pluralism" in this context). Another minority group considered the Reformed view of ministry as central for Presbyterian culture. Finally, one said Presbyterian culture consisted primarily in "mission," and named most of the six characteristics above as secondary ones.

I turn now to further reflection on the six most commonly noted characteristics and report some of the comments from the interviews.

First, consideration of a Presbyterian culture brought to the minds of many executives portions of scripture, autobiographical stories, and explicitly theological matters. For example, Presbyterian emphasis on the incarnation of Jesus Christ, not just on his humanity or his divinity, was cited several times, as was also the classic Reformed tension between the first and second persons of the Trinity with a comparative neglect of the third.

One spoke of Bible stories told by a grandmother as deeply formative (but scarcely distinctive); another said: "You have not asked about a Christian culture, and I think there is one—common assumptions among Christians about God, ourselves, and about life together." One of the minority of those who had joined the Presbyterian Church as an adult said that the church's theological depth attracted him.

Within the Presbyterian culture that almost all of these executives share, Christian symbols and stories bear deep meaning for them, sustaining them in times of crisis. One told of the compassion and understanding she received when subpoenaed in a government action against the sanctuary movement: "In composing my response, I discovered just how Presbyterian I am—depending on the Bible and church teachings." Several spoke of how their involvement in the civil rights movement helped them understand the comfort and courage of reading scripture and of practising Christian solidarity. Others spoke of times of family tragedy and personal grieving (as in Weeks 1983c).

In the new structure for meetings set up by the PC(USA), ministry units, staff meetings, and committees regularly include times for devotion and theological reflection. Worship begins the day at the Presbyterian Center where most executives work. Bibles in several versions, without much dust on them, sit in most offices, along with posters and artwork decidedly Christian in nature, frequently bearing as captions words of scripture.

In one office stands a walnut display case, bearing a part of an animal skeleton. Upon closer inspection one can read the inscription: "In case of Philistines, break glass!" Then one can recognize the donkey jawbone. When I asked that official about the allusion, he replied, "Yes, we probably don't recognize this place is full of Philistines, and sometimes I wonder if I ought not use it on myself." That self-critical, modest anthropology has characterized healthy Reformed Christianity from its inception (as in Leith 1977).

The personal faith and the spiritual vitality of the executives also seemed evident as we talked. I remembered that these leaders chose to remain in the new structure after the "demise of mainline Protestantism" had become a regular news item and after the denomination had chosen to move its headquarters to Louisville. They uprooted themselves and their families, knowing full well the difficulties of denominational leadership, especially in a new structure everyone recognized as complicated and even cumbersome.

Second, if the culture has its core in the Christian faith as Protestants perceive it, Presbyterian executives experience the culture also as "wordy." "Our Presbyterian way involves lots of talking, lots of thinking," one director ventured.

Another director pointed to a practice she observed. If a board or committee member at denomination headquarters speaks in poor grammar, the moderator will frequently repeat the statement in correct phraseology. She also noted that denominational leaders try to proofread their memos; and when errors creep in, others point out with some energy the infelicities and mistakes.

An emphasis on education persists among denominational executives, and they see Presbyterians in particular caring more about such matters. One has received a grant to enable himself and the other directors of ministry units to have study leaves. Several lamented their lack of time for reading and learning as part of current jobs. Most spoke of their own education in the course of the interviews, say of college or seminary influences. Some spoke of education for their children, both in public and in church schools.

Third, and closely related, everyone named Presbyterian polity as part of the culture. Some considered polity of diminished significance in recent years. "Presbyteries and synods don't deserve to be called courts anymore," one leader complained. "They just vote on budget and programs." Others said polity has become increasingly important in the new environment. "We attend to matters of order," one said and told me of seeing the T-shirt with the slogan: "Presbyterians do it decently and in order." "We are the Protestant Pharisees," quipped another.

If the first three characteristics form a cluster, so do the second three. In the fourth place, Presbyterian leaders perceive denominational identity as involving Christians in all of life—vocation, personal ethics, family responsibilities, and the rest. Many mentioned a Presbyterian propensity to seek transformation of society (as in Sussman 1984, 39ff.). "We will never be totally satisfied in a human society," one person asserted. "Prohibition was probably the time we got most out of line with reality in this country," a director explained, "but we all see a corporate dimension to faith and implications for helping people structurally."

Some pointed particularly to the situation of women and African Americans as examples of Presbyterians collaborating to seek social and political amelioration and proximate justice. Others mentioned instances from other nations' cultures in which Presbyterians have interfered in behalf of social transformation. Much of the autobiographical disclosure took place around this topic.

If a Presbyterian culture seeks change in society, it also harbors similar expectations for itself as an expression of the ecumenical church, according to executives in it. The motto of the Presbyterians, *ecclesia reformata, semper reformanda* was cited by several executives in discussing transformation.

Only a minority volunteered the fifth component. But since an early interviewee dwelled upon it, I asked others, who then confirmed its presence in the cluster of identifying characteristics of a Presbyterian culture. Most Presbyterian leaders, elders, and ministers sit uneasily with conspicuous consumption and the parsimonious holding of vast wealth. One director said: "A lot of Presbyterians have a lot of money, but we hold each other to some expectation of sharing wealth and not abusing the privileges it offers. A rich Presbyterian elder knows in most cases when he or she is 'out of bounds,' and a minister who flaunts wealth is scorned." Strangely, only one mentioned the traditional doctrines of stewardship in this connection, although several talked about the "stewardship of power."

Stewardship of money and resources, worldly asceticism (relatively speaking), and other such cultural emphases are difficult to assess because of a sixth point made by many respondents—Presbyterian culture bears some elitism in its baggage. "It is the hind side of our much-talked-about pluralism in the church," one confessed. "Presbyterians white, black, Hispanic, Asian, or whatever, seem to share a sense that just anybody can't be one of us, or rather that it would take a lot of work for some people."

Another director said, apologetically, "Maybe we just have to decide we are who we are, and we need to be the best we can be of what we are, rather than trying to be all things to all people, which we can't do with a straight face anyhow." Two people also named the Episcopalians in this connection as perhaps having an easier time bringing together all kinds of folk with their liturgical emphases. "Our accent on polity, education, and theological rootage makes our way tougher," one concluded on the subject.

Contributing Subcultures

Several important subcultures were identified in the interviews. The first comes by way of the distinctive contributions that each of the two merging denominations brought to the new body. Among those interviewed, no one expressed doubt that distinctive and different denominational cultures had characterized life in the UPCUSA and the PCUS. Almost everyone interviewed had grown up in one or the other. Denominational leaders could point in detail to some of the special characteristics of each group regarding values, responsibilities of leaders, and even the physical arrangements of general assemblies.

Several leaders mentioned the use of formal channels in the UPCUSA and of informal channels in the PCUS for selection of personnel, for regulating issue-oriented groups, for communication between pastors and sessions on the one hand and denominational leaders on the other. One invited a look at the two books of order to see their use. The *Book of Order* in the UPCUSA functioned as a "manual of operations, spelling out things in detail." The *Book of Church Order* in the PCUS remained succinct, perhaps even cryptic, in "giving principles for government." Those books faithfully reflected the differences in culture, she argued, because Presbyterians all value doing everything orderly. "'Orderly' just meant different things."

According to some leaders, the former PCUS worked through informal networks called a "cousin" (or "old boy") system until the merger. However, one person from the PCUS took pains to explain that references to kinship really meant "networks" rather than blood ties. "Everyone at Montreat was a 'cousin.'" [eds. note: see chapter 6 in this volume, on Montreat, by Gwen Kennedy Neville.] "The UPCUSA culture prized fairness more than the PCUS culture did," stated a veteran of both. "They [UPCUSA] sought representation from all regions, genders, races, and sometimes even points of view." The UPCUSA had a wider variety of ethnic minority members than did the PCUS. Because the UPCUSA ordained women to both elder and minister functions from the early 1950s, that denomination drew more easily upon experienced leaders from both sexes.

Also, the leadership of the UPCUSA, particularly the Stated Clerk and some heads of agencies, had entered openly into the civil rights arena in the 1950s, earlier than had leaders in the PCUS. This may have led them to pay greater attention to diverse constituencies. The values gleaned from participation in such events may also have served to enhance prizing "fairness" and representation of diversity in the membership.

While the UPCUSA and the PCUS called upon lay elders as well as ordained ministers for executive leadership, interviewees believed that the UPCUSA seemed to make more of an effort to include both laity and clergy in these top positions. Also, while both denominations were open to recruitment of both professional managers and practicing pastors as leaders, looking to professional managers seemed more characteristic of UPCUSA culture and looking to pastors was more prevalent within the PCUS.

The influence of pastors of some major churches was the essence of the PCUS "ethos," one director explained. "They could serve as pastors of those churches, be heads of agencies, and then perhaps even move to denominational executive positions themselves, as some did. Or maybe they just chaired a standing committee for decades." Such a center for the culture, according to this perspective, was both a "blessing and a curse. Most provided competent leadership and set the tone for those around them, but the pool remained an awfully small one." Another from the PCUS commented that the PCUS honored and respected most those who served in powerful positions while not using the benefits of power personally, and who retired gracefully once they had completed their work.

Seminary connections seem to have meant something in both denominations, and black Presbyterians also mentioned college friendships from Presbyterian schools. "There were six of us from Knoxville College," one executive said, "and we all cared for each other through time." Another pointed to the special place Princeton Seminary had exercised in the earlier PCUSA stream of the denomination's culture. "If you hadn't gone to school there, you surely went for continuing education just to say you knew James McCord (former Princeton Seminary president) or such and such a professor."

A number of leaders saw previously important symbols and institutions in the UPCUSA and the PCUS cultures as having declined in power, even before the merger. The influence of church colleges, conference centers, and other intermediate institutions had waned. Now they questioned whether any gathering places, except perhaps the Presbyterian Women's Triennium held at Purdue University, bear much significance in affirming Presbyterian culture.

The earlier importance and the consequent waning of these identifiable subcultures came up frequently in the interviews. Most denominational leaders perceive that family, congregation, and general Protestant and/or Christian identity have become personally more important for them and, they speculate, for others in recent years. Presbyterian identity *per se* is less important. Several speculated that similar hierarchies of values had existed all along for Presbyterians. Obviously, for most people in the United States, familial culture remains of paramount significance and bears no additional comment. The importance of congregational culture and its relationship to Presbyterian culture does bear consideration. So does the apparent pull between a general Protestant and/or Christian culture and a denominational one.

One synod executive speculated that actually most Presbyterians belong to one of two denominations within the PC(USA)—either a congregational or a connectional church.[3] Members join the congregation, share its life, and worship God within it. Some minority of those also come to join the connectional church, including most pastors and those elders who invest heavily in presbytery, synod, or assembly business. Hence only a minority—but one that includes almost all executives—forms a denominational culture in the first place. Some of those in the denominational culture may even feel alienated from the congregations that initially nurtured them. The rest of the Presbyterian majority remains indifferent, if not actively hostile, toward the connectional competitor.

Finally, the intrinsic ecumenism among Presbyterians, already mentioned, may support another, competing subculture. In the early 1800s many Presbyterians expressed dissatisfaction with the Westminster Standards and formed a "Christian movement" hostile to creeds and confessions, even to the constraints of a denomination. In this latter part of the twentieth century, executives sensed tensions within Presbyterianism in this same area. Some Presbyterians expressed affinities for attending to the future rather than constraining the church on the basis of the past. A few questioned the dominance of Trinitarian imagery in Presbyterian confessions as well as the church's lack of social concern.

The Transmission of Culture

All cultures seem complex and subtle, but any denominational culture in general, or Presbyterian culture in particular, would seem especially so. With its prizing of representation, deliberation, and societal transformation—not to mention the multiple courts and careful balance of powers—Presbyterian culture seemingly would have been in constant jeopardy through the nearly five hundred years of its existence. Rather than dying out, though, it has changed and adapted over time as other durable traditions have done.

Today, however, almost all Presbyterian executives express concern that the denomination's culture will become extinct. Some point to the worldviews of their own children who are "uninterested in the Presbyterian church." One leader said that he attended his first General Assembly at age thirteen and was fascinated. His children care for world issues, but they couldn't care less who gets elected moderator or what the church says about some issue. Other leaders pointed to denominational switching as a special threat to a Presbyterian culture. "How can we expect our church to remain when most new members now come from other denominations?" A few named special interest caucuses within the PC(USA) as "breaking down" a common culture in the interest of single issues.

Executives pointed to various avenues of transmission for a Presbyterian culture—for example, meetings of the General Assembly, the new Presbyterian and Reformed educational ministries curriculum, the denomination's magazine (*The Presbyterian Survey*), the itineration of the moderator of the General Assembly, regional representatives for various denominational programs, and the current emphasis on Reformed evangelism. Some also pointed to the many committees of the Assembly, synods, and presbyteries, to staff members in governing bodies, and to many pastors. But they questioned the effectiveness of these "transmitters" and the others in place currently.

Almost everyone perceived the need for denominational executives themselves to transmit Presbyterian culture, not just for denominational survival but also because each had been nourished in it. "We haven't done a good job of interpreting. That's the 'old saw' everybody uses," one said. "But the truth is we are just starting to get it together ourselves in the new church. I hope we can get out there now."

Conclusions and More Questions

Does a Presbyterian culture exist for the PC(USA)? Yes, according to denominational executives. It may not yet bind as tightly as it did in previous Presbyterian streams which were smaller and more homogeneous, and it may have greater competition than was true previously. But a PC(USA) culture is forming, among the executives and throughout the denomination. It bears much in common with previous Presbyterian cultures, and it may be fed more than previous cultures by interaction with other Reformed bodies and with other portions of the Christian family.

A PC(USA) culture at present remains quite tenuous in nature, but its identifying characteristics include the authority of the Old and New Testaments and the teachings of the Reformed wing of the church. The culture honors education and the "worship of God with the mind," literate discourse, and orderly processes in government, both to check human selfishness and to insure balance in work and worship. The common elements in a PC(USA) culture also include a sense of the relationship of corporate life and piety, a concern for transformation of society in terms of images of the kingdom of God, and a worry about Presbyterian elitism even while participating in it. Doubtless other elements also characterize this PC(USA) culture, ones that subsequent examination may disclose.

Do PC(USA) executives share common values, stories, and goals which legitimate their work? Yes, to a great extent; however, because of the newness of the merged denomination, they have had little experience yet in sharing any stories and values, heroines and heroes, or other "thick descriptions" of their faith. They have had scant time to develop a common culture, one that incorporates vibrant elements of the previous denominational life. Although every single person interviewed expressed the importance of a Presbyterian culture for his or her own formation, many said they were reluctant to dwell upon the topic of a PC(USA) identity. Some harbor the suspicion that others are not concerned with commonalty, especially with perpetuating the heritage of the denomination that feeds them.

Do they possess special sensitivities and worldviews and seek to transmit prized traditions as they endeavor to lead people? Dedicated and mature as most PC(USA) executives are, most do not readily speak of their responsibility to impart to others a "sense of the PC(USA)." It may be modesty that forbids their discussion of a role in transmitting the culture, for most will speak of others among their number who seem to do so. It may also be that the structural design and the complexity in governmental structure inhibit executives who would seek to better foster a new culture for a new church. Many leaders feel they are "on the edge" of the PC(USA) rather than at its heart.

What of the role of moderators, especially the General Assembly moderator? What of the roles of stated clerks? Synod executives?

Executive presbyters? Committees? Pastors? Elders? Teachers? Seminaries? Colleges? Pre-Schools? Church Schools? Denominational curricula? Journals? Other publications? Meetings? Can intentional focus on the culture in these arenas have deleterious as well as salutary effects? What consequences might such focus cause?

Further study of the "two-church hypothesis" (Weeks and Fogleman 1990) is also intriguing. Do members of the "congregational" church who become involved also in the "connectional" church provide a necessary bridge of enculturation and interpretation back and forth between the two "levels" of church? Historically, this seems to have been the case. Is it working today? Could it be that presbyteries, synods, and the General Assembly are providing proportionately fewer opportunities today for this to happen? These questions invite serious study, and the leaders of the Presbyterian Church (U.S.A.) would be well served by broaching such a study.

NOTES

1. Executives, strictly speaking, are also "called," and elected by a governing body. *Book of Order* G-6.0107. By the same token, nominating committees also function in the election of moderators and stated clerks, as well as the General Assembly Council, G-13.0202. But in common reference the distinctions remain.

2. *Book of Order* G-13.0203 provides for a "manual of operations" to be adopted by the General Assembly outlining governance of the administrative staff.

3. This insight came from William Fogleman, of the Synod of the Sun. He points to differences in the nature of membership, leadership, values, and goals of the two. Actually, rather than one congregational denomination, there would be a "denomination" for each congregation. But the simpler image helps in comparing cultures and identities. For further discussion of the "two-church" hypothesis, see Weeks and Fogleman (1990).

REFERENCES

Chandler, Alfred D., Jr.
    1977   *The Visible Hand: The Managerial Revolution in American Business*. Cambridge, Mass.: Harvard University Press.

Coalter, Milton J, John M. Mulder, and Louis B. Weeks
   1990–1992 *The Presbyterian Presence: The Twentieth Century Experience.* A series of seven books gathering results from a major study of the denomination. Louisville, Ky.: Westminster/John Knox Press.
Geertz, Clifford
   1973   *The Interpretation of Cultures.* New York: Basic Books.
Hargrove, Barbara
   1986   *The Emerging New Class: Implications for Church and Society.* New York: Pilgrim Press.
Harrison, Paul
   1959   *Authority and Power in a Free Church Tradition.* Princeton, N.J.: Princeton University Press.
Hood, Fred J.
   1968   "Presbyterianism and the New American Nation (1783–1826)," Ph.D. diss. Princeton University, Princeton, N.J.
Hopewell, James
   1987   *Congregation: Stories and Structures,* edited by Barbara Wheeler. Philadelphia: Fortress Press.
Hunt, George L.
   1965   "Our Calvinist Heritage in Church and State." In *Calvinism and the Political Order,* edited by George L. Hunt. Philadelphia: Westminster Press.
Leith, John
   1977   *An Introduction to the Reformed Tradition: A Way of Being the Christian Community.* Atlanta: John Knox Press.
Luidens, Donald A., and Roger Nemeth
   1987   "'Public' and 'Private' Protestantism Reconsidered: Introducing the 'Loyalists.'" *Journal for the Scientific Study of Religion* 26, no. 4 (December): 450–464.
Marty, Martin E.
   1986   *Protestantism in the United States: Righteous Empire.* New York: Charles Scribner's Sons.
McNeil, John T.
   1954   *The History and Character of Calvinism.* New York: Oxford University Press.
Miller, Page P.
   1985   *A Claim to New Roles.* Metuchen, N.J.: Scarecrow Press.
Niebuhr, H. Richard
   1929   *The Social Sources of Denominationalism.* New York: Henry Holt.
Presbyterian Church (U.S.A.)
   1987–89 *Book of Order.* Louisville, Ky.: Office of the General Assembly.

Richey, Russell (ed.)
 1977 *Denominationalism.* Nashville: Abingdon Press.
Roof, Wade Clark, and William McKinney
 1987 *American Mainline Religion.* New Brunswick, N.J.: Rutgers University Press.
Roozen, David A., William McKinney, and Jackson W. Carroll
 1984 *Varieties of Religious Presence: Mission in Public Life.* New York: Pilgrim Press.
Rudolph, L. C.
 1963 *Hoosier Zion.* New Haven, Conn.: Yale University Press.
Stapert, John
 1988 "Reformed Glue." *Church Herald* 45, no. 2 (January 15): 4, 5.
Sussman, Warren
 1984 *Culture as History: The Transformation of American Society in the Twentieth Century.* New York: Pantheon Books.
Swatos, William H., Jr.
 1981 "Beyond Denominationalism?: Community and Culture in American Religion." *Journal for the Scientific Study of Religion* 20, no. 3: 217–227.
Thompson, Ernest Trice
 1963 *Presbyterians in the South,* vol. 1. Richmond: John Knox Press.
Trachtenberg, Alan
 1982 *The Incorporation of America.* New York: Hill and Wang.
Trinterud, Leonard
 1949 *The Forming of an American Tradition: A Re examination of Colonial Presbyterianism.* Philadelphia: Westminster Press
Weeks, Louis B.
 1983a *Kentucky Presbyterians.* Atlanta: John Knox Press.
 1983b "Faith and Political Action in American Presbyterianism, (1776–1918)." In *Reformed Faith and Politics,* edited by Ronald Stone. Lanham, Md.: University Press of America.
 1983c *To Be a Presbyterian.* Atlanta: John Knox Press.
 1988a "The Presbyterians Chose Louisville: A Case Study in Denominational Relocation." *Urban Resources* 5 (1): Lo 1–Lo 8.
 1988b "Presbyterianism." In *Encyclopedia of the American Religious Experience,* vol. 1, 499–510. New York: Charles Scribners' Sons.
 1992 "The Incorporation of the Presbyterians." In *The Organizational Revolution, Presbyterians and American Denominationalism,* edited by Milton J Coalter, John M. Mulder, and Louis B. Weeks, 37–54. Louisville, Ky.: Westminster/John Knox Press.

Weeks, Louis, and William Fogleman
  1990   "A Two Church Hypothesis." *Presbyterian Outlook* (March
          16):8–10.
Wilmore, Gayraud
  1983   *Black and Presbyterian*. Philadelphia: Black Presbyterians
          United.
Wuthnow, Robert
  1988   *The Restructuring of American Religion*. Princeton, N.J.:
          Princeton University Press.

16

Toward a Post-Denominational World Church

Creighton Lacy

The speaker was president of a major denominational women's society. The time: thirty years ago. The words: "Of course, I am in favor of this church union movement, but I just hate the thought of seven hundred thousand Methodists being wiped out of India." (The Indian Methodists who then related to the U.S. Methodist General Conference have still not united with the churches of south or north India, although their neighbors chose to become a constituent part of the Church of Pakistan.)

Old assumptions and familiar clichés continue to confuse denominational identity in the field of missions. (For the most part, in this chapter, the term "missions" is used to describe the organized outreach of boards and agencies representing various Protestant churches in evangelism and service. The dominant voice herein is of international, overseas programs.) For many decades leaders in the Third World have complained that denominations are a Western luxury which so-called "younger churches" cannot afford. Absurdities abound: the earlier Chinese branch of the Dutch Reformed Church in America, the alleged translation of the Protestant Episcopal Church as the Society of Kicking Overseers.

Geoffrey Wainwright, ecumenical theologian, writes: "Historic, continuing, and perhaps new divisions have had their origins in old Christendom. These divisions have been exported with Christian missions. They need to be overcome, if the obstacles to collaboration and communion are to be removed worldwide" (Wainwright 1989, 2). On the other hand, Sidney Mead seems to suggest that social purposes, of which mission was primary throughout the nineteenth century, create, form, or give identity to denominations themselves. "The tendency of Pietism as a voluntaryism, is to place the central emphasis on the objectives of the group, which is to make the missionary program of a denomination, both home and foreign, definitive for it" (Mead 1977, 83).

Nondenominational Missions

Even in the earliest days of mission history the role of denominations was ambiguous. Writing in 1957 Henry P. VanDusen declared that "just a hundred and fifty years ago you could have travelled this earth from end to end and you would not have discovered one group of any kind, minister, laymen, men or women of different denominations banded together as Christians—not one" (Lee 1960, 76). He had shaved his chronology by at least a decade. The London Missionary Society began in 1795 "with the laudable aim of preaching the eternal Gospel to the heathen without being tied to any particular form of Church order or government" (Neill 1964, 252), though it soon became—like its counterpart, the American Board of Commissioners for Foreign Missions (1810)—a largely Congregationalist agency.

Similarly, the British and Foreign Bible Society was organized in 1804 with a committee made up half of Anglicans and half of Free Churchmen. For the most part these earlier bodies were formed by Christian individuals who were more concerned, as Mead implies, about a common task than church affiliations. The American Bible Society in 1816 claimed participants from at least seven denominations: Presbyterians, Episcopalians, Baptists, Methodists, Congregationalists, Dutch Reformed, and Quakers. The YMCA and YWCA, even the 1872 Sunday School Union, disregarded sectarian attachments. Not until near the end of the century did genuinely interdenominational (as distinct from nondenominational) societies emerge: The Foreign Missions Conference of North America (1893) and the Federal Council of Churches (1908), for example. As Robert Lee sums up: "The early leadership of the ecumenical movement came from outside rather than from within the ranks of official denominational leadership: today the leadership responsibility has been transferred into the hands of denominational officers and official appointees" (Lee 1960, 191–192).

Meanwhile missionaries themselves were beginning to set the predominant pattern, policy, and practice for parent societies and home churches. With few exceptions these did not emphasize denominational identity. Bartholomew Ziegenbalg and Henry Plutschau sailed to India in 1706 as German Lutherans under the Danish Halle Pietist Mission, with later support from the Anglican Society for Promoting Christian Knowledge. William Carey, the "father" of (modern, Protestant, foreign) missions, did not mention his Baptist faith in *An Enquiry into the Obligation of Christians to Use Means for the Conversion of the Heathens*. Early in his career overseas he proposed that a missionary conference should be convened in Cape Town in 1810 (a century before the great Edinburgh assembly) to bring together missionaries of many churches as well as many nations.

Nevertheless, the major exception to this trans-sectarian outlook was the family of Baptist congregations. It has often been debated whether their principal concern was the mode of baptism—immersion versus pouring and sprinkling—or the doctrine of believers' choice rather than the incorporation of infants. When Ann and Adoniram Judson, first U.S. missionaries to go abroad, adopted the Baptist view on their way to India and accepted immersion from Carey's colleague, William Ward, they seemed to endorse both confessional tenets. But their conscientious withdrawal from the American Board of Commissioners for Foreign Missions, which had sent them out, created "an uproar among the Congregationalists" (Tucker 1983, 123). Even in that instance, however, one can detect a conflict of interest, among home supporters at least, between doctrinal and financial, institutional concerns. Similarly the only major sectarian breach in the long history of the American Bible Society centered in the translation of the neutral word "baptism" into descriptive terms implying sprinkling instead of immersion.

Church as Mission

Yet the missionary enterprise expanded in the nineteenth century through both denominational and ecumenical or nondenominational agencies. The Missionary Society of the Methodist Episcopal Church was organized in 1819. The denomination at its quadrennial General Conference just a year later declared: "Methodism itself is a missionary system. Yield the missionary spirit and you yield the very lifeblood of the cause" (Lacy 1948, 21). In 1847 the Presbyterians proclaimed: "The Presbyterian Church [U.S.A.] is a missionary society, the object of which is to aid in the conversion of the world, and every member of this church is a member of the said society and bound to do all in his power for the accomplishment of this object" (Mead 1977, 86–87). These two statements support Mead's contention that denominations grew and flourished and, above all, organized around a central "cause" or "object." They do not imply, however, that such societies took their distinctive characteristics, their "denominational identity," from their mission. Many in the early period, if not today, were convinced that they had a unique, even essential, doctrine and/or polity to share.

Through the nineteenth and early twentieth centuries the principal dynamic for foreign missions came from nondenominational bodies. To the YMCA were added the Student Volunteer Movement and the World Student Christian Federation. The denominational agencies reached out, for consultation at least, to the Home Missions Conference and the Foreign Missions Conference of North America, to the World Missionary Conference at Edinburgh in 1910, and ultimately to the International Missionary Council and the Commission on World Mission and Evangelism of the World Council of Churches.

Who but careful church historians or denominational savants can cite the denominational identity of the outstanding missionary pioneers: Robert Morrison, Lottie (Charlotte) Moon, David Livingstone, Ida Scudder, Hudson Taylor, Mary Slessor, Albert Schweitzer, Clara Swain, John R. Mott, Frank Laubach, Timothy Richard, Isabella Thoburn, Samuel Zwemer, and the rest? Each possessed strong "denominational identity," even denominational pride, but that was not paramount in their mission; it was often known only by their colleagues. Counterbalancing his own thesis, Mead comments:

> Just as voluntaryism and sense of mission forms the center of a denomination's self-conscious life, so they provide the basis for the interdenominational or supra-denominational consciousness and cooperation which has been such an outstanding aspect of the American religious life. (Mead 1977, 84)

Sources for Denominationalism

Do modern missionary programs enhance denominational pride or sense of identity? Are local church members interested in adding more Presbyterians or Moravians or Lutherans in far-away places? Occasionally, but not often! The denominational emphasis and information reaching the pew comes not from grass-roots members or even from pastors, and only reluctantly from missionary representatives; it comes principally from the bureaucracy.*

Said one church member, himself a former denominational mission executive: "'Mission' and 'unity' are not high priorities in my local

---

* To supplement this study, two questionnaires were circulated, one to missionaries and one to local church members or pastors. The eighty-two replies came from members of eight denominations in eighteen states and represented missionary service in twenty-one different countries. Personal quotations and illustrations in the following pages come from those questionnaires.

church—[there is] a deep-seated pattern of both suspicion and hostility towards both." Said another: "Missionary emphasis is very poor denominational-wide . . . because of the lack of a worldwide viewpoint." Where does the responsibility lie? Where should it lie? Ought the priority in a local church to be "denominational-wide" or a "worldwide viewpoint"? On the survey reported here, three questions were asked concerning the importance of denominational identity and the necessity of increasing denominational church membership through missions. Fewer than half of the individuals responding claimed to hold such priorities themselves. But two-thirds adjudged denominational considerations as "important" or "very important" for local church members and for denominational officials.

Some pastors and some church members defended—or explained—their denominational emphasis. Obviously one major reason for denominational organization and denominational appeals is to provide on-going financial backing for mission projects. "I would like to see us minimize denominational identity while maximizing denominational support," stated one university professor, "a two-fold objective which unfortunately seems an impossible dream." A pastor's wife commented: "Ideally it would seem more efficient to have missionary work ecumenical, yet then there would probably be fewer involved. Perhaps some diversity, with networking and coalitions, is best."

Occasionally other factors surfaced. One minister remarked that so many members in his church come from other denominational backgrounds, with little denominational loyalty or familiarity, that "we do a lot of education about our denomination's mission projects because of the lack of background. However," she added, "no one feels strongly that our own denomination is the only one to give to." Similarly a former missionary observed that the older members in her congregation are "localized, independent, and don't mind isolation, (whereas) new members are not outward-looking as a rule."

Frequently the pressure to emphasize "our own" program comes from the church hierarchy. One young minister, employed in a community service agency rather than a parish, has experienced "negative comments from administration if one ventures too far from conference-first activities. The clergy seem afraid to branch beyond their own pulpits." In short, the missionary enterprise, along with other aspects of church life treated in this volume, raises the broader question of whether denominationalism is not, in the last analysis, a support for vested institutional interests rather than a vital contemporary theological issue.

Missionary Perspectives

Viewed from "the front lines," from the distant outposts of evangelism, there appears to be even less justification for denominational divisions. To be sure, most missionaries recognize the practical imperatives of financial support and institutional loyalty. Some admitted that they were more familiar with their own denominational work, that ecumenical activities in their areas were extremely limited, that they were writing letters for local churches or articles for denominational journals. "Traditional mission interpretation has programmed [people] in the direction of [church growth, institutional expansion, denominational trends]," said one.

Others were more explicit. "We were expected to raise money and enhance support." "I try to help people understand what our Board is doing around the world and to help them know how their money is being used." "I try to help them know specifics about our mission program, since many church people give money to causes pushed by TV ads, where a large percent goes to administrative costs." "I was responsible for obtaining the financial support required for any and all projects with which I was working. You stress what you need." "Our mailing lists included mostly [our own denomination], for whom we own a special responsibility in spiritual growth." (Perhaps only a theology professor would have emphasized the spiritual growth of the church "back home" without mentioning specifically the financial cultivation.)

Even these concerns were often broadened and clarified in replies to the questionnaire. "We understand," wrote one missionary who has spent his life in narrow denominational fields, "that [our] church is just the arena where we live out our Christianity and do our part for the 'cause of Christ' and the universal church." "We use denominations as our place to take hold and gear into the larger issues," said another. "We assumed that this denominational interest was not exclusive. 'Success' was in the context of nondenominational objectives," asserted a third. A college teacher who had served previously as a missionary declared: "The universality of the gospel (God's redeeming love for all) and the unity of the body of Christ should always be exalted before later historical, denominational developments or traditions." "The Wesleyan heritage provides dynamic direction for Methodists," acknowledged a former missionary and personnel secretary, "but always in the context of a larger understanding of gospel and church." And a couple working with refugees and orphans rather than in direct evangelism replied simply: "The denomination is not important, just Jesus."

Ecumenical Concerns

In these questionnaires it is apparent that the overwhelming proportion of missionaries view the task in transdenominational terms. From the beginning of modern Protestant missions many organizations have stressed their nondenominational character: the American Bible Society, the YMCA, the Wycliffe Bible Translators, the Africa Inland Mission, and many more. What is noteworthy, however, is that these agencies which specifically seek to transcend sectarian identity range from liberal conciliar families to conservative, even fundamentalist, bodies. Methodist Bishop James K. Mathews wrote of his father-in-law, the noted world evangelist E. Stanley Jones that "he found the Christian movement scattering its energies about marginal issues of doctrine and denominations and left it centered on Jesus Christ as the one and central issue" (United Methodist Board of Global Ministries 1988, 87).

Today most exclusiveness, most discrimination in recruitment policy or operating practice, seems to arise from biblical or theological emphases rather than denominational identity. Wrote one young conservative evangelical, dedicated to an independent, individual faith mission: "I have consciously avoided using denominational language at all times. The challenge of evangelism in the Islamic world is so great that we must emphasize a united Christian witness and cooperate as much as possible."

Sidney Mead makes much of "the persistent American view that an ecumenical movement must begin with working together rather than with agreement on fundamental theological propositions, on 'life and work' rather than on 'faith and order'" (Richey 1977, 85). For the most part questionnaires returned by missionaries revealed cordial personal relations across denominational lines. Responses ranged from grateful paeans of appreciation for individual friendships and outstanding service to "admiration for their dedication, joy in their competence." "Denomination was irrelevant," insisted one former mission executive.

That is not to say that all is peace and harmony. At least a quarter of those replying to an inquiry about personal relations with Christians of other denominations acknowledged some divisiveness. Yet without exception this division was based on perceptions regarding styles of worship or biblical interpretation—and the spirit in which these differences were held—not along denominational lines. "If they are open to cooperation . . . friendly, except fundamentalists. . . . We keep clear of fundies. . . . Excellent with like-minded, cordial but cautious with . . . strong fundamentalists." "There are some whose themes and tones would make me uncomfortable, but with most I could live and work gladly." One couple went so far as to say, "We are invited but do not enjoy participating in prayer meetings with people from very fundamental groups." Another, more flexible, remarked, "They were more conservative than I was/am. There was no conflict but also no common view." Obviously such comments come from mainline Protestants, but they might also arise within the same denominational structure.

In some instances these theological—or temperamental— differences may have contributed to ecumenical growth. "I found that people of fundamentalist groups tended to become more tolerant of differences," said one member of the United Church of Japan. A woman who once taught in an interdenominational Protestant seminary and a Roman Catholic high school in Africa concluded: "I feel we have separated more on 'liberal-conservative' lines than denominational since I have re-entered U.S.A."

Church Developments Abroad

Certainly missionaries have been influenced, more profoundly and directly than members of local churches, by significant developments in former mission areas, the so-called foreign field. Even in the nineteenth century some comity agreements for friendly, voluntary division of geographical territory were at least partially effective for a while: in China, India, and the Philippines, for example. With the exception of the United Church of Canada (1927) and more recently the Uniting Church of Australia (1977), all major interconfessional church unions began in one-time mission fields: the Church of Christ in China (1927), the Church of South India (1947), the Kyodan in Japan (1941 or 1947), the Church of Pakistan (1969), and others. Said one former missionary to India: "Had denominational pride been stronger, the effort toward Christian unity might not have met with the same degree of success." (For some, like the Methodist woman quoted in the opening paragraph, such a statement could be read as critical of declining loyalties in the home church, or laxness on the part of missionaries. To that Lutheran professor of theology, however, the pluralistic climate of India, as well as the ecumenical history of the church there, is a blessing, not a regret.)

As the world has become increasingly interdependent, as independence has swept away colonialism in most of the globe, so autonomy and national identity—not denominational identity—have become paramount goals for emergent Christian communities. The most conspicuous of these developments has been the formation of a "post-denominational" church in China, where both doctrinal and polity decisions are made at the local (that is, community or congregational) level, in what seems to have been the pattern of the early church. Voices of concern over divided Christendom have been raised for at least a century. As long ago as 1895 a missionary to China, C. F. Reid, wrote in distress about the "divided condition" of Methodist societies at work in that country:

> Here we are, seven children of Wesley, without even so much as a common name to indicate we are kin to each other. These seven Methodisms bear names so unlike that no Chinese would ever suspect that they are more to each other than they are to either Baptist or Presbyterian. Not one in fifty of our native members has any idea of the relationship. (Lacy 1948, 187)

Olin Stockwell, who later spent more than two years in a Chinese prison, declared in 1944:

> The cry for church unity is coming from many quarters, and most of all from our Chinese friends. . . . We came to China nearly a hundred years ago, each denomination bringing the flower pot that it loved best. But through these hundred years that little flower of faith has been watered by Chinese rains and warmed by a Chinese sun and its roots have grown strong and deep, so much so that many think it has outgrown its original pot. Many feel that it is time to take these flowers out of their original containers and plant them together in a Chinese garden. Each flower will still retain its beauty and its particular grace, but they will be growing in Chinese soil, unhampered by foreign pots. The objection to denominations is not only that they divide the church, but that the divisions have been imported, having no reality in Chinese life and experience. (quoted in United Methodist Board 1978, 150)

Few people realized then how soon and how successfully the Chinese church would declare itself as "post-denominational."

Bishop K. H. Ting has been for the past two decades the principal spokesman for the church in China, chairman of the Three-Self Patriotic Reform movement, and more recently of the China Christian Council and the Nanjing Theological Seminary. In "A Call for Clarity" he explained these developments. When he moved to Nanjing in the early 1950s, there were "still many denominations separated by deep divisions":

> The members of one denomination in particular would not even pray with the rest of us. Now the brothers and sisters of this group are not only willing to pray with us, but even to share the sacraments together. . . . We are no longer separated by denominational walls. (*China Notes,* IX: 1,147)

As in the Church of South India, which has made a conscious and deliberate effort to preserve doctrinal and liturgical elements from participating communions, Chinese Christians insist that they can share and broaden the traditions they have inherited from their missionary origins. Wrote Chen Zemin, vice-principal of Nanjing Theological Seminary:

> We realize and respect the characteristics and particular contributions of various denominations that have evolved in the historical development since the Reformation. We have also learned the lesson of harmful dissensions and disruptive effects of denominationalism. We try to conserve the valuable heritages without being tied to the denominational structures. . . . We . . . believe that unity with variety, not uniformity, will more manifest the abundant grace of God. (*China Notes,* XXIV, 1, 321)

This local autonomy, even eclecticism, has opened the way for a wide choice of sacramental forms: modes of baptism or styles of communion. It has led to the establishment of a dozen regional seminaries, and to variations in local self-government. The only ecclesiastical task carried out thus far on a nationwide basis is the production of Christian literature: Bibles, hymnals, and educational materials. Most challenging to denominational identity, however, "the Christians at Shanghai" in the summer of 1988 elected two new bishops, whose functions are strictly pastoral and spiritual, not administrative. The two men chosen, both of them ministers in local congregations, were respectively a "former (Southern) Methodist" and a "former Episcopalian." It remains to be seen whether other regions will follow the lead of this major city, and whether future bishops may be elected from "former" Congregationalists or Presbyterians or Seventh Day Adventists or Little Flock. The vice-chairman of the China Christian Council told this writer in 1989 that most of the resistance to such amalgamation, most of the pressure to preserve denominational identity, has active encouragement from denominational agencies and officials in the West, not from within China.

Widespread Agreement

What is noteworthy for this study, however, is the widespread approval from Christians in other parts of the world as well as from former missionaries to China. "I'd like to see it everywhere," declared one. "Denomination is history in China," said another, "a condition in which I fervently rejoice." "We have a lot to learn from what is happening there," added a third.

For the majority of missionary respondents, the reasons for minimizing denominational identity lie not so much in practical, institutional considerations as in a broader understanding of faith and mission. "Christian activities were never denominational," wrote a former missionary in Pakistan. "Denominational differences are administrational more than doctrinal; where they are doctrinal, they are divisive and often misunderstood." From Brazil, a writer serving an autonomous church comments, "Denominations are confusing to people here." "In the missionary field," wrote a teacher from Japan, "denominational differences are more of an obstacle than a help, as they are confusing to new Christians." From an agricultural specialist in Pakistan: "My call was in Christian service to all." Similar sentiments were numerous: "Basically I consider that the work of mission is 'Christian' rather than 'Lutheran.'" "The cause of Christ is our mission, and not just to make Methodists."

"In Christ We Are All ONE!"

The question for this study, perhaps insoluble, is whether such ecumenical commitment, a desire to downplay denominational identity, arises from one's particular background and experience, or whether it is a deliberate effort to expand horizons in local congregations. "The denomination seems less and less important," wrote one couple from Korea, "to church members who are vitally interested in missions. They are interested in how Jesus can change lives." "I think they are interested in concrete persons or situations—lives changed, people fed and built up, nationals taking responsibility, villages developed," said a former missionary to China. A layman who has participated in mission work in Ghana, Sierra Leone, Liberia, India, and Pakistan believes many people at home "are interested in church growth, but in the spread of Christianity, not specific denominations."

Gradually this lesson is being learned. "I can't remember ever being asked anywhere, 'How many [of our denomination]?'" declared a teacher in Korea. "Many American Christians are interested in seeing that there are converts to the Christian faith as a result of Christian missions. In that sense they are interested in church growth. I don't think they are much concerned about the growth of their denomination as such." One explanation offered is that so many local congregations are now made up of people from other traditions that they do not become firmly committed to a sectarian theology or a single missionary agency.

A significant number of respondents disagreed, however, often blaming the denominational hierarchy or local pastors for what one called myopia. A question on this survey asked whether "supporters of missions in the local church are primarily interested in such matters as church growth, institutional expansion, denominational trends." "Yes, for the years I was working," wrote one retired missionary, "probably less now." "In my local church," admitted a former missionary now retired, "there isn't much interest in church growth but a lot in denominational trends." "Some in our local churches are still mainly denominationally conscious and do not affirm ecumenical ventures." "Most of my contacts have been with persons who have a view of missions as 'conversion of the heathen.' It has been difficult to discuss other faith communities and partner churches." "Yes," said a missionary still serving in Brazil:

> I think most North American [*sic*] Methodists want to know about what Methodists are doing, . . . and many only want to hear about what North American Methodist missionaries are doing, not yet realizing that the Third World churches have developed their own leadership and that the missionary is just a very small part of what is happening in the church in these countries.

Often the responsibility has been laid directly on pastoral leadership—or the absence of knowledge and concern. "I think they are primarily interested in these [institutional] dimensions," declared a former missionary in China and Brazil, "because they have been the principal context of most missionary education for 75 years." Added a college teacher in another church: "I haven't seen any effective 'mission' education in recent years to link our denomination and the people to specific or general interests in missions." More significantly, he added: "Local church members are not being well served by the present generation of ministerial leadership." A representative of still a third denomination concurred: "Over the years we have visited many churches. In most the information about and interest in mission is at a low ebb. The most likely cause is the leadership or lack thereof." "Some are [concerned with denominational issues], some aren't," wrote a missionary from India, "pastors maybe more so than laity." A retired missionary from Pakistan put the focus even more sharply: "A great deal depends on the pastor to promote mission. Therefore the seminaries need to put more into this area in the pastoral training."

Understandably, concern for denominational identity—and support—seems to increase as one moves up in the hierarchy. One missionary attributed his withdrawal from the mission field in part to "lack of support (for ecumenical projects) from our bishop (and) the Board staff."

Some early missionaries apparently taught the denominational lesson too well, at least institutionally if not theologically. Wrote one respondent: "Here in Korea the denomination is very important to the nationals and a lot of emphasis is placed on it; most missionaries [both Catholic and Protestant] do not feel it is that important." And from Pakistan: "From my experience the feeling of denominational loyalty is much stronger among the clergy of the overseas churches than among missionaries."

In one incident rare in mission annals the Methodist work in southern Fukien, China, was transferred in 1934 to Presbyterians. Discussions had been underway since 1901 (based on factors such as dialect, geographic isolation, economic relations, and lack of contact with larger Methodist bodies). The major opposition, however, came not from missionaries but from Chinese Methodists, who preferred to retain their name and organization, as well as their episcopal supervision and appointive system (Lacy 1948, 70 et passim). For a decade (1911–1920) the two largest Christian printing establishments in China, the Presbyterian Mission Press and the Methodist Publishing House, negotiated for a merger, but for unspecified reasons "the final step was never taken" (Lacy 1948, 189).

"An Essential Outlook"

What conclusions, if any, can be drawn from such "hit-or-miss" inquiry, from considerable assorted reading, and from lifelong observation within the missionary movement? Without a doubt the world church, in a time of increasing internationalization, is leading local congregations to greater awareness, more intelligent understanding, and broader support of ecumenicity rather than denominationalism. One of the wisest, most experienced church executives declared in his questionnaire: "I think foreign missions/missionaries have generally been the ecumenical leading edge." This is not a new insight. Robert E. Speer served from 1891 to 1937 as chief administrator in the Board of Foreign Missions of the Presbyterian Church in the U.S.A. "For Speer," it has been said, "missions and ecumenism were ultimately inseparable." In fact, at the organization of the Federal Council of Churches in 1908 he "claimed that an ecumenical outlook was absolutely essential in foreign missions, and that churches in the mission field were far ahead of churches in America when it came to effective cooperation" (Patterson 1980, 25).

To be sure, Speer's biographer admits that "his approach emphasized a pragmatic interdenominational cooperation rather than an institutional union of diverse church bodies" (Patterson 1980, 26). There are many "ecumenists" today as well as eighty years ago who would defend "denominational identity" on the ground of historical and theological tradition as well as practical effectiveness. There is no doubt that organizational structures are necessary for financial support as well as administrative order. Others would argue that divergent confessional emphases must be preserved, that one must be conscious and proud of one's own heritage before one can share it creatively with others. These issues are dealt with in various ways elsewhere in this volume.

Certainly many missionaries share such views. "I hesitate to make denominations distinct from 'the cause of Christ,'" wrote one former missionary to China. "My loyalty is not contra any others." Others frankly recognized the necessity for denominational backing, financial and spiritual. A teacher in a united national church acknowledged: "I am aware of the weakness of interdenominational work since there are always budget problems in trying to get money [for ecumenical projects, including cooperative agencies in this country]. . . . I know that local pastors have to put their denominational quotas first." "Missionaries are loyal to the extent that their salary support comes from a particular organization," added a lay agricultural expert from Pakistan. "You must be loyal to those who make it possible for you to serve. One can be very critical and yet loyal."

On the whole, however, it appears that missionaries and mission board executives are less concerned with "denominational identity" than are other segments of the American church. In *The Social Sources of Church Unity,* Robert Lee lists four major trends which he believes may counter the negative traits mentioned in Richard Niebuhr's *The Social Sources of Denominationalism.* These four factors are organic mergers, the conciliar movement, local community churches, and comity (Lee 1960, 82). A number of illustrations in this chapter suggest that all of these trends either originated in or have been more fully implemented on the "mission field" rather than in home churches. The formation of united churches in many countries overseas, the development of interdenominational institutions especially at college and seminary levels, the recognition that indeed denominations do on the whole represent doctrinal and historical divisions in the West which have little meaning or significance for the Third World—all these factors tend to subordinate sectarian considerations.

Underlying all these elements is the growing conviction that the good news of Jesus Christ, if it is to be convincing in a pluralistic, multireligious world, must emphasize one Lord, one faith, one baptism, one God and Father of all.

One layman who has been long engaged in ecumenical programs of medical administration wrote:

> We are where we are as Christians, not as U.C.C., Methodists, etc. We work for national churches which are usually products of mergers of several historic mission groups. Most of us are in work (e.g. health

care) that lends itself to nondenominational cooperation. This certainly includes Catholics.

A couple in India serving in a "mainline" church went still further: "We have felt that denominational chauvinism should be challenged, as part of the universal mission of the church in the world." Another questionnaire concluded: "Frankly, I can't get very excited over the importance of your subject." Perhaps this was his way of saying, for most missionaries, that "denominational identity" is, or should be, "irrelevant."

Whatever the practices of baptism or episcopacy, whatever the emphases of personal conversion or social transformation, whatever the labels of liberal or conservative, missionaries on the whole appear to be more conscious than "home folks" of these words: "I have other sheep that do not belong to this fold. I must bring them also, and they will listen to my voice. So there will be one flock, one shepherd" (John 10:16). Or they recall Christ's exhortation for unity: "I ask not only on behalf of these [nations or denominations], but also on behalf of those who will believe in me through their word, that they may all be one . . . that the world may believe that you have sent me" (John 17:20–21). Or they note the Great Commission is to make disciples of the Lord: "You will receive power . . . and you will be *my* witnesses" (Acts 1:8, emphasis added), not witnesses of denominational culture or identity.

REFERENCES

China Notes
 n.d. New York: National Council of Churches of Christ in the U.S.A.
DuBose, Francis M. (ed.)
 1979 *Classics of Christian Missions.* Nashville: Broadman Press.
Lacy, Walter N.
 1948 *A Hundred Years of China Methodism.* Nashville: Abingdon Press.
Latourette, Kenneth Scott
 1941–1945 *A History of the Expansion of Christianity*, vols. 4-7. New York: Harper & Brothers.
Lee, Robert
 1960 *The Social Sources of Church Unity.* New York: Abingdon Press.
Mead, Sidney E.
 1977 "Denominationalism: the Shape of Protestantism in America."

In *Denominationalism,* edited by Russell E. Richey. Nashville: Abingdon Press.

Niebuhr, H. Richard

1929   *The Social Sources of Denominationalism.* New York: Henry Holt.

Neill, Stephen

1964   *A History of Christian Missions.* Baltimore: Penguin Books.

Patterson, James Alan

1980   "Robert E. Speer and the Crisis of the American Protestant Missionary Movement, 1920–37." Ph.D. diss. Princeton University, Princeton, N.J.

Richey, Russell E. (ed.)

1977   *Denominationalism.* Nashville: Abingdon Press.

Tucker, Ruth A.

1983   *From Jerusalem to Irian Jaya.* Grand Rapids: Academie.

United Methodist Board of Global Ministries

1988   *Missionaries of the United Methodist Church through the Camera's Eye.* New York: General Board of Global Ministry.

Wainwright, Geoffrey

1989   "Duke and the World Church." *News and Notes* [newsletter for alumni and friends of Duke University] 4, no. 2 (1989).

Epilogue:
Beyond Establishment,
but in Which Direction?

What have we learned from these forays into denominational culture and identity, their transmission and transformation? In this epilogue, we attempt to draw out some of these learnings, putting them forward as a partial contribution to the "critical ecclesiology of denominations" for which Gilpin calls in his chapter on theological schools. Such a critical ecclesiology—with emphasis on "critical"—is sorely needed. While this task is well beyond the scope of this epilogue, our authors have provided a number of pointers and building blocks for this effort. They also have offered some helpful clues for those entrusted with the leadership of the churches. We hasten to add that our conclusions are those we as editors have drawn from our reflections on denominations generally and especially on the essays of this volume. They may not in all cases reflect the opinions of our authors.

Responses to Disestablishment

In the Introduction, we acknowledged that mainline Protestantism has moved "beyond establishment" in the sense of an unofficial hegemony that mainline Protestants exercised culturally and socially in nineteenth- and early twentieth-century America. The combined impact of pluralism and privatization in matters of religion and culture has eroded much of this hegemony. This erosion, together with the serious hemorrhaging at the level of membership, has left mainline

Protestants with a severe crisis of identity and purpose. Luiden's essay on the Reformed Church in America indicates the severity of the problem for that denomination, and it is indicative of the experience of others as well.

Responses to the "disestablishment" of mainline churches have varied. One response, represented among our authors especially by Lacy, has been to welcome the trend on theological grounds. Denominations exemplify the brokenness of the body of Christ. They not only contribute to divisiveness and narrow parochialism, they dishonor Christ's body by the classism, racism, ethnocentrism, and nationalism to which they have often given expression. These failures, as we have noted, have been most forcefully exposed in H. Richard Niebuhr's classic work, *The Social Sources of Denominationalism*. Whatever positive purposes they may have served in the past or continue to serve at present (for example, administrative coordination and funding for mission efforts), denominations and their cultures not only reflect sinful divisiveness but also hinder the efforts of the church to give expression to its mission of reconciliation.

While they may or may not share Lacy's theological critique of denominations, others among our authors believe that traditional denominations and their distinctive cultures are basically irrelevant in a post-establishment period, especially in some of the settings in which the church finds itself. Whether it is on the mission field of Third World societies (Lacy), on the mission field of secular university campuses where denominations have established campus ministries (Stokes), on campuses of church-related or former church-related colleges (Bass), or among African American Christians (Jones), traditional mainline denominational cultures and structures have little currency. While supporting the mission work of one's denomination may promote denominational loyalty at home, Lacy and those whom he surveyed make clear that the culture- and time-bound aspects of denominational traditions have little currency in non-Western societies, except perhaps as a means of supporting vested interests. Things are not very different in the academic milieu of the secular university with its norms of scientific rationality and of resistance to "sectarianism" of any sort. The real issue for campus ministry, as Stokes notes, is fostering a *Christian* identity among students and faculty. "Remedial religion," not "remedial denominationalism," is the challenge. The norms of the modern secular university have also long since undercut most claims and efforts of denominationally sponsored colleges and universities to be transmitters of their denomination's culture. Rather than keeping students within the denomination's fold, at their best Christian colleges seek to preserve a broad tradition of liberal learning and value-centered inquiry, consonant with a Christian orientation. Likewise, Jones argues that African American culture is much more central in shaping the religious life of black Christians than the cultures of the predominantly white denominations to which many blacks belong, or out of which some of the historic black denominations arose. In short, a second response to disestablishment is the recognition that in many settings denominations and their particular cultures are increasingly irrelevant and out of touch with the realities they confront.

Yet a third response (though not by our authors) has been attempts to "circle the wagons" in what we referred to as a kind of neo-denominationalism. As we indicated in the Introduction, by "neo-denominationalism" we mean a turn to a heightened denominational emphasis, usually manifested in inward-focused strategies of self-preservation that promise to stem membership declines and institutional drift. There is little pretense of being a religious establishment; rather, survival takes center stage.

We do not deny that some neo-denominationalist strategies may have positive consequences—for example, renewed attention to denominational heritage. As we will emphasize below, it is important to reappropriate critically one's denominational roots, whether this is the Reformed tradition or the Lutheran, Anglican, or Wesleyan heritage. Discovering how these traditions can continue to shape and inform church life as *living* legacies, open to revision from a critical perspective, can contribute to revitalization. Holper's discussion of recent efforts to rethink ordination in his chapter on Presbyterian ordination practices provides an example of such a critical approach to denominational identity. It takes seriously both the broader ecumenical tradition of which the Reformed tradition is a part and the vital issues in contemporary culture. Thus it is not simply an effort to repristinate a past ecclesiology but to keep it a living tradition. We would remind readers, however, that Luiden's chapter on the Reformed Church in America suggests that recovery of one's heritage is not, by itself, a panacea. Neither are other, more questionable manifestations of neo-denominationalism. These include what Martin Marty (1990, 2) refers to as "denominational rescue programs," turned out by denominational headquarters and imposed on local congregations from the top down.

Frequently, too, neo-denominationalism shows itself in heightened and uncritical emphasis on denominational distinctiveness at the expense of ecumenism and cooperative efforts. As Gilpin notes, the shared moral vision for public life in the United States that propelled and sustained cooperative efforts among mainline denominations has become subordinate to denominational particularity. Support for ecumenical organizations—local, national, or global—is diminished. This includes not only councils of churches but also ecumenical ventures in campus ministry, as Stokes has noted in her chapter. Similarly, as Gilpin observes, recent pressures on candidates for ordained ministry to attend seminaries of their own denomination are manifestations of neo-denominationalism.

Here then are three kinds of responses to disestablishment. Except for the neo-denominational response, from which we dissent, we recognize the validity of the first two. Denominations deserve criticism for their contributions to parochialism and divisiveness by which they have fragmented the body of Christ. Likewise, denominational expressions of the church are appropriately viewed as irrelevant in some settings in which the church seeks to minister.

Yet denominations persist. Despite their disestablishment and their declining roles, they have not gone the way of the horse and buggy or the Edsel. But are they soon to do so as survivals of a past that is no more? Or do denominations have a more enduring role in the religious ecology of a post-establishment society?

A Continuing Role for Denominations?

In reflecting on the character and role of denominations generally and especially on the essays of this volume, we believe the answer is at least a tentative yes. We recognize that our view is a contrarian one, in partial disagreement with those, like Robert Wuthnow (1988), who argue that we are seeing the end of denominations as American religion is restructured. (Our position is also contrary to that of some of the contributors to this volume.) As social and cultural forms, denominations continue to be one way, among others, of embodying religion and meeting religious needs in a highly pluralistic society. By and large, for most people in this country they are the primary vehicles of religious belonging and meaning, and they appear to have considerable staying power—even in an era beyond establishment.

One reason for their staying power and their continuing role is suggested by Martin Marty's phrase that we cited in the Introduction. He described denominations as "betwixt and between" institutions, referring especially to their "caughtness" between the type of society which earlier brought them into being and the pluralist and privatist society of the late twentieth century. But we see them as "betwixt and between" in another, more positive way. In spite of the difficulties they face and failures they have experienced, denominations—especially those we call mainline—also stand "betwixt and between" other forms of contemporary religious expression.

They are an alternative to a more universal, church-type religious organization such as is often found in Europe. Whether Protestant or Catholic, these organizations are established religions in the full sense of the word and purport to embody the official religious expression for an entire society. As we have noted, mainline Protestantism, taken as a whole, came close to realizing an unofficial churchly hegemony in the nineteenth- and early-twentieth-century United States before radical pluralism and other changes made it an impossible dream. Like churchly religion, however, mainline Protestants continue to have a clear concern for public life, a characteristic that we view quite positively. While there is no likelihood for church-type forms of religion to exist in contemporary U.S. society, the same is not true for sect-type and mystical religious expressions. In *Megatrends Two Thousand,* John Naisbett and Patricia Auburdene (1990) predict an intensifying clash in the twenty-first century between evangelicals and New Agers—representatives respectively of Troeltsch's sectarian and mystical types of religious organization. Denominations stand between these two forms and provide an alternative for those who are attracted neither to the authoritarianism of sect-type religious groups or the highly individualistic, self-as-God, mystical expressions.

With their quasi-gemeinschaft, communal quality, especially at the local level, denominations offer a way of involvement in the Christian faith that is neither authoritarian nor privatistic. While each denomination "denominates" a particular expression of the faith, as several of our authors have demonstrated, none claims to have the whole truth. In David Martin's words, "The denomination . . . claims that while there are doubtless many keys to many mansions it is at least in possession of one of them, and that anyone who thinks he has the sole means to open the heavenly door is plainly mistaken" (Martin 1962, 5). In this sense, denominations prevent a kind of "Maoism" in religion, either churchly or sectarian, in which a single model is imposed on everyone. Yet, by providing corporate, communal expressions of religion—"coherent traditions of piety" as Gilpin called them—in the midst of radical pluralism, denominations also are an alternative to the extreme individualism of the mystical type represented today by New Age spiritualities.

To say this is not to deny Niebuhr's critique of the "social sources" of denominations. The communal memories and traditions of piety and practice which denominations preserve are partial and incomplete, and they reflect the social location and experiences of those who shaped them originally as well as of their current participants. They are admixtures of Christian truth and social factors and experiences which cannot be neatly separated into the "religious" and the "social." This is both their bane and their genius. Commingling of the religious and social has, to be sure, fostered divisiveness and led to many gross distortions of the gospel in classist, racist, sexist, and nationalistic expressions. Holper's chapter notes ways in which some of these distortions have affected ordination practices. But, on the positive side, this religious and social mix has also made denominations vehicles for shaping individual and group identities and countering individualism and isolation.

Chapters by Neville, Roberts, and Olson are helpful in making this point with reference to Protestantism. As Neville notes, at the heart of Protestantism is an emphasis on the individual person's unquestioned worth before God. This new status frees the person from traditional, ascriptive ties to a particular place or community. One is free to move out from these ties to fulfill his or her individual calling—a point which Max Weber made much of in his various analyses of the development of the West. At the same time, however, Neville argues that the imperative to move outward requires periodic returns to sacred places and meanings, for renewing communal bonds in such settings as family reunions, homecomings, and denominational assemblies such as Montreat. The covenantal structure of most Protestant worship that Roberts highlights also plays out the theme of individual responsibility within a covenantal relationship with God and the neighbor. Regular worship is a way of renewing that relationship. The friendship networks that congregations foster are subcultures (within congregational and denominational cultures) that also provide regular occasions in which mobile individuals gather to experience community centered in shared convictions, as Olson's chapter illustrates. Thus various expressions of denominational life provide occasions for experiencing community as counterpoint to the individualism and atomization (partly the fruit of Protestantism) that characterize American culture. While the forms by which this happens may be similar across denominations, each denomination's culture—its distinctive "dialect" and "markers"— gives a different nuance to the experience of belonging and meaning. In reflecting on the significance of denominations, both in the past and present, William Swatos makes a similar point:

> Denominations fit people into the local community while providing reference to a larger society. They provide *place* in the socio-cultural milieu, in such a way that the transient and the eternal are harmonized into a meaningful whole in the consciousness of the participant. . . . To align with one denomination or another in a community gave one a heritage—practically a family—whose boundaries transcended time and place. (Swatos 1981, 223)

The black church experience described by Lawrence Jones is a particularly apt example of the power of religio-communal organizations and culture in overcoming isolation and providing African Americans with a place to stand and a frame of reference for interpreting their life experiences.

Viewing denominations in this more positive light involves an "about face" from perspectives on diversity and denominationalism that were strong among mainline Protestants earlier in this century and which many (including some of our authors) continue to hold. Gilpin outlined these perspectives as he examined changing attitudes toward denominations by theological educators. Earlier, diversity implied conflict, and competition and was viewed negatively—often for good reason. The hoped for unity often implied that those "others" should become like "us"—the minority like the majority—if they wanted to belong in U.S. society, much as earlier hopes for racial integration were often built on the premise that blacks would adopt white culture. Today, however, we have been forced to come to terms with differences and have come to appreciate their positive as well as divisive aspects. The terms we use to describe our present reality, "pluralism" and "multiculturalism," reflect a move away from viewing differences as only divisive and sinful. They imply a respect for diversity, dialogue across cultures, and an appreciation of the richness of human experience that racial, ethnic, gender, generational, regional, and religious differences bring. Denominational pluralism can reflect this more positive appreciation of differences and offer a context for dialogue that is not possible for sectarianism. At the same time, it provides a counter to the excesses of privatism and isolation found within many individualistic spiritualities. Insofar as denominations do not absolutize their traditions and practices, they provide alternative places and occasions in which individuals experience belonging and meaning in a multicultural, diverse society. As "communities of memory" they preserve and transmit particular, if partial, understandings of God's dealings with humankind, and particular, if partial, traditions of piety and moral perspectives as guides for practice. Thus understood, the cultures that denominations transmit, the transformations they undergo as they seek to understand God's ways in changing circumstances, and the means by which transmission and transformation occur take on new significance.

Differences and Similarities in Mainline Cultures

Several of the authors have helped us to appreciate some of the particular "dialects of meaning" and "traditions of piety" that mark off denominational boundaries. The church school that the Moores studied, for example, is effective in transmitting values that are central to the United Church of Christ culture, even when members—expressing core UCC values of tolerance and inclusiveness—downplay the importance of their denominational identity. Newman's reanalysis of data from the national sample of UCC congregations discovered remarkably similar themes; though not surprisingly, there were variations that reflect the different streams that flowed together at the formation of the denomination through merger. Keith Roberts's and Linda Clark's chapters also focus on congregations. Roberts heightens our sensitivity to ways that rituals, symbols, sensory experiences, space, and norms about such matters communicate and sacralize meanings that continue to reflect denominational traditions. Clark's chapter shows how a transdenominational heritage—expressed, for example, in hymns such as "Amazing Grace"—is nuanced and particularized as it is refracted through different denominational cultures. Methodists and Episcopalians both love the hymn, but they use and understand it somewhat differently, in keeping with their particular cultures. Her analysis also reveals that the hymn, despite its broad appeal, has a better "fit" with some denominational cultures than others. Neville helpfully contrasts the cultural themes of major mainline Protestant denominations in the South—Presbyterian, Methodist, and Baptist—and shows how each denomination's summer assemblies are one of several places for intense cultural transmission, as themes of the denomination's culture are enacted in sacred space and time. Likewise, Richey and Weeks call attention to several dimensions of the cultures of Methodists and Presbyterians respectively that continue to provide markers for those denominations.

Many of the authors also pointed to cultural themes that mainline Protestants hold in common—admittedly sometimes more as ideals than as practiced realities: a refusal to absolutize one's tradition but to understand it as always in need of reform and revision; emphasis on free, critical inquiry; willingness to confront new ideas and bring one's tradition into dialogue with the new; tolerance and respect for diversity (at least up to a point); a commitment to cooperative efforts with other church bodies; a sense of responsibility for society, expressed both in acts of charity and in efforts at social reform. In the Introduction, we noted that mainline Protestants confronted modernity more so than other Western religious traditions. These themes and others common to mainline Protestants[1] reflect that encounter. We can observe the themes in operation in the Sunday school described by the Moores as well as in the responses of the Presbyterian denominational leaders whom Weeks interviewed. They permeate the women's organizations, which, as Zikmund notes, have long held together denominational loyalty and ecumenical commitment. Also, as our authors have noted, denominations fostered higher educational institutions, seminaries, and campus ministries, not simply in an effort to hold on to their students but also out of a conviction that liberal learning and values were part of what is required to exercise responsible Christian custodianship of the culture. Custodianship of the culture is also expressed in Methodist historians' efforts to interpret the providential character of their denomination's contribution to the moral good of the nation. Even as they promoted Methodist distinctives (and sometimes nationalistic ideologies) in their histories, they gave expression to values shared by other mainline Protestant bodies. In sum, it is possible to identify transdenominational themes characteristic of mainline Protestants. While they are nuanced differently by the cultures of particular denominations, they nevertheless form a core of shared emphases that have made possible various cooperative efforts—local, regional, and national. These shared emphases have historically been distinguishing marks of denominations that we call mainline. The denominations form, in Marty's phrase, a "communion of communions," each of which lives its life partly in response to its separate tradition and partly to the calls for a common Christian vocation (Marty 1981, 3).

For the reasons we have noted, we believe these cultures—both those aspects which are denominationally particular and those which are shared—enable individuals to locate themselves religiously in a diverse, multicultural society. Through the values and perspectives they promote, they provide ways of understanding life and models for action in the daily lives of their adherents. As Roof and McKinney concluded in their study of American mainline religion, "Even among [members] whose churchgoing is low and whose group attachments are weak, the traditions persist and sustain their own particular constellations of moral and cultural views" (1987, 220).

Weak Plausibility Structures

As we express this relatively positive word about the continuing significance of denominations as communities of memory with traditions of piety and practice, we also know that mainline Protestant denominations are in serious trouble. Here we are not speaking only of membership declines. Many aspects of the cultures of particular denominations are out of touch with the changed realities that the church confronts in the late-twentieth-century United States. Many of the plausibility structures on which the churches have relied to transmit and sustain cultures are no longer effective. We have known for some time that mainline Protestantism cannot count on the broader U.S.

culture as a plausibility structure for sustaining and transmitting its culture in the way that it did earlier in this and previous centuries. The small-town experiences that made a Protestant culture massively real and believable to the two editors of this volume may still exist in some areas of the nation, but such changes as mass communication, ease of travel, high rates of mobility, and large-scale immigration have made it highly unlikely. We have also seen, from several of the chapters, that many of the other plausibility structures on which we have counted are no longer effective. Most denominational colleges have never functioned especially well in this regard, as Bass points out in her chapter, and we have noted the plight of denominational campus ministries. Similarly, Gilpin has chronicled the relative absence of denominational emphases in theological seminaries, whether denominationally sponsored or not. Ordination practices—earlier emphasizing distinctive elements of denominational heritage—have also been profoundly affected by trends in the broader culture. As Holper has shown, professionalization, bureaucratization, and specialization are among the forces that have reduced denominational distinctiveness and emphasis on communal traditions in ministry practices in favor of what we might somewhat crudely call "ministry by interchangeable parts."

What happens when we move to the local level, where we suspect that religious and denominational identities have the greatest likelihood of being shaped? Olson's research among conservative Protestants shows that congregations, and especially the friendship networks they spawn, are potent plausibility structures for transmitting and sustaining distinctive beliefs and providing experiences of belonging. Alas, the same does not appear to be true among mainline Protestants—or so he speculates. Mainline Protestant culture, with its commitment to pluralism, its emphasis on inclusiveness and diversity, and its refusal to absolutize its perspective as key emphases, works against strong religious identity. These emphases neither promote the sense of "over-againstness" that conservative Protestant themes foster, nor do they encourage dense fellowship ties. And this is one of the factors that, for mainline Protestants, weakens the power of subcultures such as congregations and friendship networks to foster identification with the denomination and its particular culture. It is difficult for a sieve to hold water!

In general, our experience leads us to agree with Olson's somewhat bleak assessment of weak, mainline plausibility structures at the local level. Before accepting it wholly, however, we point again to the Moore's chapter on the UCC church school. We will grant that this church school is stronger and more vital than most with which we are acquainted, but it suggests an interesting and somewhat paradoxical counter-perspective on mainline plausibility structures. While identification with the denomination is played down in the congregation, church school participants are nevertheless strongly committed to the core themes of both their denomination and mainline Protestant culture generally. This congregation with its educational program is effective in transmitting a culture emphasizing inclusiveness, tolerance of diversity, freedom, ecumenism, and intellectual searching—all grounded in core beliefs about God and Jesus and reflecting a United Church of Christ as well as a mainline Protestant culture. Yet, the very profile that these beliefs form works against a strong emphasis on denominational loyalty and identification—in this sense agreeing with Olson's conclusion. Nonetheless, our guess is that, when members of this congregation relocate geographically, they are more likely to search out a similar congregation—either UCC or one of another mainline denomination—than to join a congregation with a less open, less inclusive stance. That may not reflect denominational loyalty, but it would suggest a rather strong identification with the themes of their denomination's culture and central elements of mainline Protestantism. We are again reminded of the "betwixt and between" character of mainline Protestants: between the strong and often intolerant stance of the sect and the radical individualism of the mystical alternative.

Other chapters—for example, Zikmund's discussion of women's organizations and Neville's discussion of summer assemblies such as Montreat—also provide at least partial exceptions to our overall conclusion about weak plausibility structures in mainline Protestantism. Both types of organizations continue to be relatively strong. As Zikmund notes, however, women's organizations are in considerable flux as the changing role and status of women in the broader society calls them to redefine their purpose.

Possibilities for Cultural Renewal

All of this is not to suggest that cultural transmission is impossible for mainline Protestants or that it is impossible to develop strong plausibility structures by which the culture is transmitted and transformed. It does suggest, however, much more attention to these matters on the part of denominational leaders, locally and nationally. To this end, we consider several strategies based on what we have learned.

First, denominational leaders, locally and nationally, must give greater attention to their denomination's distinctive culture and its relation to a broader Protestant and Christian culture. In suggesting this, we do not wish to be misunderstood. We are not promoting neo-denominationalism, nor do we believe that emphasizing a denomination's distinctive culture, including its traditions, is likely to have a major effect on denominational decline. As we have noted, Luidens's analysis of the experience of the Reformed Church in America in trying to promote its distinctive identity is a case in point. We believe, however, that knowing one's particular tradition, asking what it has meant in the past and reflecting on its continuing significance for the church's present *praxis,* is critical to congregational and denominational life and to the lives of church members. As we have emphasized, denominations are communities of memory, bearers of particular understandings of God's activity and purposes and of particular patterns of piety and practice. Without such memories—especially memories kept vital through critical reflection—denominations and their members risk becoming rudderless. In his book, *After Virtue,* Alasdair MacIntyre (1981, 201) comments: "I can only answer the question 'What am I to do?' if I can answer the prior question 'Of what stories do I find myself a part.'" He continues: "Deprive children of stories and you leave them unscripted, anxious stutterers in their actions as in their words." That, we believe, is equally true for denominations and their congregations. Mainline Protestant traditions, with their emphasis on openness and inclusiveness, may not promote cohesiveness to the same degree as their conservative counterparts, but they offer rich and distinctive theological and moral visions, language and other symbols for constructing religious and moral discourse appropriate for those who are satisfied with neither fundamentalist absolutes nor New Age individualism. Presbyterians appear to have recognized the importance of such memories and visions as they have constructed their new statement on ordination.

Second, if there is a consistent message that comes through a number of the chapters, it is the importance of *local* expressions of a denomination's culture and plausibility structures at the *local,* grassroots level. Denominational identities are forged from the ground up, as Newman's study of the United Church of Christ shows. People do not join denominations; they join congregations and through them become members of denominations. It is at the congregational level that the primary encounters with the denomination's culture occur. It is in congregations and other local expressions of denominations that members encounter their denomination's distinctive memories and patterns of piety and practice, expressed through the congregation's own more local worldview and ethos. In congregations, members engage in rituals, experience the symbols of the tradition, and sing the hymns that carry a denomination's particular rendering of the faith. The congregation's teaching ministry is also an important bearer of tradition. Through it, participants encounter other dimensions of both

Christian and denominational culture and reflect on their relation to present piety and practice. And it is in fellowship occasions and friendship networks, at the local level, that bonds are cemented and meanings transmitted. William Swatos (1981, 266) sums up the importance of these and other local expressions of a denomination's culture:

> The churches experiencing growth are those giving people a sense of place—individual meaning and purpose in a physical and spiritual community. These groups also give the appearance—even if the leadership has, in fact, moved in from elsewhere—of having grown from the locality of interest rather than being superimposed upon it.

If, then, denominational identity is to be strengthened and reshaped, it will begin at the local level. Luidens's account of efforts by Reformed Church in America leaders to renew the denomination using "top-down" strategies makes this point with some force.

In spite of emphasizing the local, we do not deny the need for other forms of denominational and ecumenical efforts and organizations for at least two reasons: First, many areas of the church's mission are simply beyond the capacity of local congregations or other local expressions of the church to address. Citywide councils of churches are better positioned structurally to address citywide issues than any particular local congregation. Similarly regional, national, and international expressions of the church are better positioned structurally to address regional, national, and international issues. These broader-than-local needs were, in fact, what gave birth to voluntary, cooperative efforts in the first place—for example, "freedman's bureaus" following the Civil War, the American Board of Commissioners for Foreign Missions, the Women's Christian Temperance Union, the Sunday school movement, and so forth. Many of these movements, which were nondenominational in origin, evolved into denominational bureaucracies[2] that continue to provide resources to local communities and address issues beyond the capacity of local congregations.

Second, and especially germane to the focus of this book, national and international expressions of the church, whether denominational or ecumenical, are important antidotes to the parochial tendencies that local expressions of the church encourage in the absence of broader perspectives. As we think about our own identification with denominational and ecumenical culture and transcendence of narrow parochialism, we recognize that this identification has developed through involvement in translocal expressions of the church—youth camps, conferences, assemblies, and other expressions. Zikmund's chapter makes this point effectively as she shows how women's organizations have countered parochial tendencies by helping women to encounter global and ecumenical concerns within a local, denominational context. Many of the independent megachurches, so successful in attracting adherents, offer tempting models for mainline Protestant leaders. However, operating only at the local level cuts them off from the richness of broader denominational and ecumenical resources.

A third strategy flows from the first two: In attending to their tradition, especially at the local level, leaders of denominations and congregations should be highly intentional in using all the resources available to them for transmitting and transforming their denomination's culture. All that the church does, every symbol, every ritual act, every social interaction is important, for good or for ill, in transmitting a denomination's culture. If we might be forgiven for taking liberties with Paul's metaphor of "treasure in earthen vessels," we would emphasize that our denominational (and ecumenical) heritage is a treasure in earthen vessels. This is to say that there are no disembodied meanings. No tradition can exist for long that is not embodied in symbols, rites, organizational expressions, and so forth. If our denominational identities are weak—as a number of our authors make clear—perhaps a part of the reason is that we have paid insufficient attention to the earthen vessels of their embodiment. We have, perhaps, taken them for granted or ignored the educative, or more accurately, the enculturating power of all aspects of congregational and denominational gatherings. Rituals, hymns, physical symbols and space, fellowship hours, homecomings, family gatherings, friendship networks, retreats all have enculturating power. Methodists sing their culture in the hymns of Charles Wesley; Episcopalians enact theirs in the rites of the *Book of Common Prayer.* Those in the congregational tradition rehearse their covenantal heritage in annual meetings—the ecclesiastical version of the New England town meeting—and in the plain architecture of the "meeting room." And, as Gwen Kennedy Neville has shown, Presbyterians gathered at an assembly such as Montreat enact their denomination's Reformed tradition in a variety of nonverbal as well as verbal ways. Being intentional about such occasions and resources—these earthen vessels in which meanings are embodied—is an important means of keeping one's traditions vital and connected to the experiences of those who participate in them.

The importance of keeping traditions connected to the experiences of participants brings us to a fourth strategy for cultural renewal. Among the most powerful plausibility structures are those that exhibit "elective affinity"—to use Max Weber's helpful concept—between participants' life experiences and social worlds and the meanings and the particular dialects and markers of a denomination's culture.

From the very earliest times, church leaders have consciously or unconsciously used stories, symbols, and rites that connected with the life experiences of those they attempted to reach. Wherever the church has taken root, it has done so by making such connections.[3]

Perhaps the clearest example of this elective affinity in the chapters of this book is found in Lawrence Jones's analysis of African American churches. While they have inherited cultural traditions from historically white denominations, most African American churches—regardless of denomination—have selected out of the Judeo-Christian heritage those symbols and stories that have special resonance with blacks' historic experiences of slavery and freedom. Symbols and stories of exodus and deliverance, cross and resurrection provide a powerful interpretative framework for dealing with those past and present experiences of oppression. Similarly, Barbara Brown Zikmund's story of women's organizations attests to the important role that these organizations have played in providing symbols and settings that connected with the life experiences of women and gave them a place to belong and to exercise leadership in a male-dominated society. As women's roles have changed under the impact of the feminist movement, these organizations have had to adapt or face decline or extinction. Those organizations most likely to succeed in continuing to connect women with the denomination's culture are those that are best able to adapt their symbols and styles to the changing circumstances and issues that women face today. And, as they do so, the denominational cultures themselves will undergo transformation, as Fred Hulper has illustrated with reference to ordination practices.

One of the secrets of success of today's megachurches—despite their lack in some cases of rootage in a heritage—is their capacity to create niches or subgroups within the large congregations that address the needs of particular groups—young singles, single parents, recently divorced persons, charismatics, social activists, and so forth. Obviously this risks pandering to consumer-oriented religiosity and fostering homogeneous enclaves at the expense of a community that transcends barriers. Nonetheless, the strategy recognizes the bonds that exist between particular symbols of the tradition and the experiences, needs, and interests of particular groups of people.

This brings us to a final point: the crucial need for "testing the spirits" of our traditions and cultures, their transformations and adaptations, in terms of their faithfulness to the gospel and the broader ecumenical vision of Christian life. As we pass on the tradition, as we seek to adapt it to meet the changing world in which we live and to relate it to the life experiences of constituents, we must avoid distortions and idolatry—baptizing partial expressions of the faith by treating them as absolutes. We must also prevent pandering to religious consumerism as seen by providing, in Reginald Bibbey's apt phrase, "religion a la carte."

Undertaking this evaluative task is not easy. It is not only a matter of assessing the continuing relevance of some aspect of a denomination's heritage. It also involves asking whether that heritage, as well as efforts to adapt it to meet changing circumstances, are faithful to the broader Christian heritage. The metaphor of a hologram as contrasted with a photograph is a useful one to describe what we might hope for in such an assessment. Cut a photograph into pieces and we get partial views of the whole image. Cut a hologram into pieces, and each part contains an image of the whole, intact. The parts are not identical; each represents the whole from a particular point of view; and none is as vibrant and intense as the whole.[4] Obviously if denominational traditions and cultures showed exact, intact representations of the whole, there would be little need for undifferentiated traditions and cultures. Nonetheless, if we think of them, like the hologram, as means of particularizing the central convictions of the faith which most Christians hold in common so that they incarnate the gospel appropriately in different times, places, and circumstances, then the hologram image is a helpful reminder of what is at stake when we "test the spirits."[5] What is obviously flawed about this metaphor is that participants in denominations have too often ignored the critical, partial perspective suggested by the metaphor and claimed to have the whole truth. Neo-denominationalism is, perhaps, the latest version of this malady.

The metaphor is a useful one, however, in suggesting the possible new directions. If we accept that mainline Protestantism has indeed moved "beyond establishment," if we give up neo-denominational efforts to turn back the clock, then we may be less tempted simply to adapt to or compromise with the surrounding culture. We may, as we "test the spirits," discover we have a new freedom to shape the church's existence by visions drawn from our particular denominational heritage that embody the more universal ecumenical tradition in which we all share.

In undertaking to draw together this collection of essays and reflect on their significance, we have opted for a vision of the church's future that sees denominations as playing a continuing and important role. Both the contributors and editors have tried to avoid a narrow denominational focus or what we have criticized as neo-denominationalism. At the same time, however, we note once again that several of the chapter authors, especially Creighton Lacy, have strongly questioned a denominational future for the church. Lacy's critique is made on both practical grounds—denominations make no sense from the perspective of non-Western cultures—and on theological grounds—they are affronts and barriers to the unity we have in Christ.

We acknowledge the seriousness of this critique and the challenge it presents. We too share Lacy's vision of Christian unity. But we also believe, for reasons we have tried to make clear, that denominations have a continuing role to play in embodying particular expressions of the broader Christian vision in ways that enable people to locate themselves and order their lives by it while honoring their diverse experiences and cultures. Denominations need not violate the unity we have in Christ, but rather can be one way of making possible its concrete embodiment—pieces of a hologram instead of a photograph. To that end, how denominations transmit and transform their particular visions and values is of considerable consequence for the future of the church.

NOTES

1. Edward Farley (1990, 137) has called attention to a somewhat similar list of themes which characterize the Presbyterian church's struggle between what he calls "critical modernism" and its opponents. While Farley interprets the themes through Presbyterian experience, he implies that most are shared in one way or another by all mainline Protestants.

2. Craig Dykstra and James Hudnut-Beumler (1992) have traced the evolution of Protestant denominational organization through three stages, paralleling broader organizational developments in the civil society. The three stages are: "constitutional confederacy," "corporation," and "regulatory agency." The emergence of the voluntary societies that evolved into denominational bureaucracies resulted during what Dykstra and Hudnut-Beumler refer to as the "corporation" stage.

3. Recent biblical scholarship (for example, Meeks 1983) has called attention to the power of the apostle Paul's interpretation and practice of such rites as baptism in addressing the social situation of many of the new converts to Christianity. While the converts were a disparate group—for example, people of means (especially wealthy women), artisans, tradesmen, masters and slaves—what they held in common were discrepant statuses, statuses that were partly valued, partly devalued in the social world of the first century. Paul's interpretation and practice of baptism provided powerful, mostly nonverbal symbols of participation in a new reality that redefined the converts' statuses and gave them a new sense of personhood in fellowship with

Christ and with each other. The new community into which they were inducted and their fellowship together in love feasts and the Eucharist further socialized them into the church's culture and sustained its plausibility.

4. Peter Senge (1990, 212) has used this useful image in another context. We find it helpful in thinking about denominations and the broader Christian vision.

5. For an extremely thoughtful and helpful treatment of these issues, see Robert Schreiter's book, *Constructing Local Theologies* (1985). While Schreiter's examples of "local theologies" focus primarily on theological interpretations that have developed among various groups in Third World societies as they have tried to give expression to the gospel in ways appropriate to their settings, denominational traditions, and their continuing transformations may also helpfully be thought of as a type of "local theology." Particularly helpful is Schreiter's effort to state criteria for assessing the faithfulness of local theologies to a core Christian identity. For his discussion of these criteria, see pp. 117ff.

REFERENCES

Dykstra, Craig, and James Hudnut-Beumler
    1992   "The National Organizational Structures of Protestant Denominations: An Invitation to Conversation." In *The Organizational Revolution: Presbyterians and American Denominationalism,* edited by Milton J Coalter, John M. Mulder, and Louis B. Weeks, 307–331. Louisville, Ky.: Westminster/John Knox Press.
Farley, Edward
    1990   "The Prebyterian Heritage as Modernism: Reaffirming a Forgotten Past in Hard Times." In *The Presbyterian Predicament: Six Perspectives,* edited by Milton J Coalter, John M. Mulder, and Louis B. Weeks. Louisville, Ky.: Westminster/John Knox Press.
MacIntyre, Alasdair
    1981   *After Virtue.* Notre Dame, Ind.: University of Notre Dame Press.
Martin, David A.
    1962   "The Denomination." *British Journal of Sociology* 13: 1–14.

Marty, Martin E.
  1981   *The Public Church.* New York: Crossroads.
  1990   *Context* 22 (November 15).
Meeks, Wayne A.
  1983   *The First Urban Christians: The Social World of the Apostle Paul.* New Haven, Conn.: Yale University Press.
Naisbitt, John, and Patricia Auburdene
  1990   *Megatrends Two Thousand.* New York: William Morrow & Co.
Roof, Wade Clark, and William McKinney
  1987   *American Mainline Religion: Its Changing Shape and Future.* New Brunswick, N.J.: Rutgers University Press.
Schreiter, Robert J.
  1985   *Constructing Local Theologies.* Maryknoll, N.Y.: Orbis Books.
Senge, Peter M.
  1990   *The Fifth Discipline.* New York: Doubleday Currency Books.
Swatos, William
  1981   "Beyond Denominationalism?: Community and Culture in American Religion." *Journal for the Scientific Study of Religion* 20 (September): 217–227.
Wuthnow, Robert
  1988   *The Restructuring of American Religion.* Princeton, N.J.: Princeton University Press.